Studies in Legal History

Published in association with the American Society for Legal History

Americanization of the Common Law

The Impact of Legal Change on
Massachusetts Society, 1760-1830

William E. Nelson

Harvard University Press
Cambridge, Massachusetts
and
London, England

Library of Congress Catalog Card Number 74-21231
ISBN 0-674-02970-4 (cloth)
ISBN 0-674-02972-0 (paper)
Printed in the United States of America

To Elaine

Preface

When I began my research for this book several years ago, I hypothesized that the American Revolution was an event of such transcendant importance that it must have affected the course of American law. To test my hypothesis I decided to study the legal system of one American state, Massachusetts, for the fifteen-year period before the coming of independence and then for the half-century after independence to observe both the short-run and the long-run impact of the Revolution. My research disclosed that the law of Massachusetts did change substantially in the seventy years between 1760 and 1830 in a variety of ways. The various changes in the law, I became convinced, also reflected more basic changes in American thought and society over the same seventy-year period. Although the evidence was not always as clear or overwhelming as I might have liked, I tried to interpret the historical data before me so as to portray my sense of the social and intellectual change that must have accompanied postrevolutionary legal change.

Even for those who disagree with my interpretation, I hope that this book can serve an independent function of making available to legal and historical scholars the vast quantity of source material heretofore buried in courthouse files and archives throughout the Commonwealth of Massachusetts. In my research for this study I sought to read not only all published statutory and judicial material for Massachusetts between 1760 and 1830 but also all available manuscript material, including unpublished judicial opinions, lawyers' notes, and, most commonly, records of pleadings, judgments, and other papers incorporated into official court files. Much of the manuscript material, especially that contained in the court files, is extremely repetitive and is of little interest to the legal historian. Some of the material, however, is not repetitive. I have tried to cite all the nonrepetitive material either in the text or in the notes and to construct an index that will guide a reader to his topic of interest. I hope that these efforts will enable future students of particular subjects in the legal history of Massachusetts to pinpoint precise sources without having to undertake the same systematic search of all the sources that I did.

In the course of several years of work I inevitably accumulated innumerable debts. My first debt is to the clerks of court and their staffs in the thirteen county seats to which I traveled; their unfailing assistance and courtesy greatly expedited my research and made stays in their towns far more enjoyable than they would otherwise have been. I owe a particular debt to the staff of the clerk of the Supreme Judicial Court in Boston for educating me in the use of the records and assisting me in obtaining my own microfilm copy. I owe similar debts to the staffs of the Essex Institute, the Harvard Law School Library, the Massachusetts Historical Society, and Pilgrim Hall, especially to John Cushing, Lawrence Geller, Peter Gomes, Edith Henderson, and Dorothy Potter.

I am especially grateful for financial assistance from the American Bar Foundation and the Charles Warren Fund of the Harvard Law School to aid in my research and a grant by the William Nelson Cromwell Foundation to subsidize publication of this volume. I am indebted to the James Duncan Phillips Library of the Essex Institute in Salem for permission to quote from the Memorandum Book of Theophilus Parsons and from the Sargeant Papers; to the Harvard Law School Library for permission to quote from William Cushing's Reports, from Samuel Howe's Lectures, and from Parsons's Precedents; to the Massachusetts Historical Society for permission to quote from the Cushing Papers, from Francis Dana's Minute Books, from Robert Treat Paine's Minutes of Trials and Law Cases, from the Paine Papers, from the Sullivan Papers, and from Edmund Trowbridge's Legal Papers, and to Harvard University Press and the Massachusetts Historical Society to quote from the *Legal Papers of John Adams*. Chapter 2 was previously published in the *American Journal of Legal History*, XVIII (1974), 1-32, while an earlier version of Chapter 5 appeared in the *University of Pennsylvania Law Review*, CXXII (1973), 97-136. Both chapters are published by permission. Occasional portions of other chapters have appeared in the *New York University Law Review*, XLII (1967), 450-482; the *University of Pennsylvania Law Review*, CXX (1972), 1166-1185; and the *Yale Law Journal*, LXXVIII (1969), 500-515; and are also published here by permission.

Although I accept full responsibility for my conclusions, many people have worked on the manuscript and made substantial contributions to it. Alan Bulliner and Donald Klawiter each worked for several months doing research while I was writing the final draft; Donald Lewis edited the draft for publication; and Winifred Cole typed an almost error-free final manuscript. Many colleagues read the manuscript, either in whole or in part, at various stages in my work and gave me valuable criticisms and suggestions, among them Bernard Bailyn, Jerome Cohen, Lawrence Friedman, Stephen Goldstein, Frank Goodman, George Haskins, Morton Horwitz, Stanley Katz, and Noyes Leech. Bruce Ackerman read and discussed every chapter with me at length and continually encouraged me to understand the historical task as the articulation of social theory as well as the narration of recorded facts.

My greatest debt of gratitude is to my wife, Elaine, who worked with me at courthouses, proofread innumerable drafts, listened to my ideas, and otherwise turned an often tedious task of research and writing into fun.

William E. Nelson

Philadelphia
September 1974

Contents

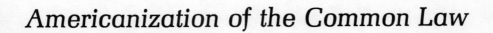

Americanization of the Common Law

1. Law in a Changing Social Order

The era of the American Revolution appears on the surface, at least, to have marked the beginning of a fundamental transformation in the structure of American society. Before the Revolution, which occurred little more than a century and a half after their initial settlement, the thirteen North American colonies of Great Britain were in many ways still in their infancy. In 1760 the colonies had a total population of some one and one-half million and an area of settlement that rarely extended as far as two hundred miles inland. The coming of independence, however, marked the commencement of a social, economic, and intellectual revolution that set the United States on a course of transcontinental nationhood—a course that became visible during the lives of revolutionary leaders such as John Adams, Thomas Jefferson, James Madison, and John Marshall. By the time these leaders died in the late 1820s and the 1830s, the United States had become a nation of some thirteen million people laying claim to lands stretching from the Atlantic to the Pacific and with settlements extending from the Atlantic to the west bank of the Mississippi. In the half century after the attainment of independence, in short, the outlines of modern America emerged.

The economy of the colonies in the 1760s was overwhelmingly agricultural. There were no true cities and few large towns: Philadelphia had a population in 1760 of 23,000, followed by New York with 18,000 and Boston with 16,000. No other town had as many as 10,000 people. By 1830 New York had a population of 200,000; Philadelphia, 175,000; and Boston, 60,000; while other cities, such as Baltimore (80,000) and New Orleans (45,000), had grown up in places that had been mere hamlets, forts, or trading posts in 1760. Many of the cities of 1830 were surrounded by burgeoning industrial regions: eastern Massachusetts, for example, had become a center of cloth manufacture; eastern Pennsylvania, of iron manufacture.

Economic growth was facilitated by improvements in the transportation network. In 1760 intercolonial travel was exceedingly difficult,
and some colonies had as much contact and commerce with Great
Britain as they had with each other. The sea and its estuaries were
virtually the only arteries for colonial commerce. By 1830, on the other
hand, the Erie Canal had been opened, the Mississippi and the Ohio had
become major commercial arteries, and a national network of roads and
turnpikes had been constructed. Moreover, 1830 saw the construction
of the nation's first railroad.

These changes in the country's economic life were paralleled by
equally striking changes in its political life. The most important change
was the development of national unity. Whereas colonials had rejected
the plan of union drawn up at Albany in 1754, by the 1830s national
unity had become a vital symbol for many Americans who, like Daniel
Webster, fervently believed that "Liberty *and* Union, now and for ever,
[were] one and inseparable."[1] With national unity came nationaliza-
tion of political strife. Politics in the mid-eighteenth century had
consisted largely of struggles between locally prominent families for
control of their local or provincial governments; by 1832 the first
national political conventions had been held and the modern party
system had been born.

Numerous changes also occurred in American intellectual life. Whereas Americans of the 1760s had depended on British imports for much
of their reading matter, Americans of the 1830s had begun to develop a
poetry and literature of their own, and national periodicals were
disseminating that literature as well as news. Education was also
becoming standardized with the publication of Noah Webster's school
readers, and in the North free public elementary education was
becoming widespread. Even higher education had made impressive
gains: whereas there had been a mere six colleges in the colonies in
1760, over seventy had been founded by 1820.[2] Perhaps the most
significant development was the emergence of the modern American
religious pattern; the established churches that had existed in nine of
the American colonies in the 1760s had all been disestablished by the
1830s, and diversity of religious belief had become an accepted feature
of American life.

Law both contributed to and was affected by the social, economic,
political, and intellectual changes that attended the birth of modern
America. In the process the law made vast strides. By 1760 not a single
American lawbook had been printed; by 1830 nearly every state was
publishing its judicial reports, and the first legal periodical[3] and
several significant legal treatises had appeared. Law had become
America's leading profession and an important mechanism for ordering
its continuing development.

Few attempts have been made to trace the emergence of modern American law from its colonial antecedents during the half century following the American Revolution. The present monograph makes a limited attempt to do so by studying in depth the legal development during the period from 1760 to 1830 of one state—Massachusetts. I chose Massachusetts because it was always an important state and yet remained small enough to permit exhaustive examination of the vast quantity of source material, including legislation, judgment rolls, judicial opinions, published writings, and office papers that have been preserved from the period. Since this study is one of a single state whose development was in many ways unique, broad conclusions about the legal history of the entire United States are, of course, unwarranted. Nonetheless, the work of other scholars suggests that the trend of legal development in Massachusetts was sufficiently similar to that of other states that conclusions drawn from Massachusetts evidence can provide working hypotheses for studying how the legal system of prerevolutionary America was transformed into the legal system of today.

It is difficult to comprehend how greatly the legal system of prevolutionary Massachusetts differed from that of modern America. The most important difference was that Massachusetts juries during the fifteen years preceding the War of Independence possessed far greater power than juries do now. Like those in twentieth-century America, they had substantial power to resolve factual issues in the cases they heard. But whereas modern juries must follow the law as stated to them by the court, juries in prerevolutionary Massachusetts could ignore judges' instructions on the law and decide the law by themselves in both civil and criminal cases.[4] The evidence of juries' power over the law is quite strong. First, we have statements by contemporary commentators like John Adams attesting to their power. Second, we know that all cases were tried before panels of at least three judges, who on some occasions delivered conflicting instructions and on other occasions gave no instructions at all. Third, we know that even when the judges were in agreement on their view of the law, counsel was free to argue law to the jury; hence in nearly every case juries received at least two conflicting interpretations of the law. Finally, we know that once a jury had incorporated its own view of the law into its verdict, judges had no power to set that verdict aside even if the jury had failed to follow their instructions.

The fact that juries rather than judges regularly decided the law applicable to litigated cases tells us much about prerevolutionary law and society. It demonstrates first that the law applied in the towns of Massachusetts on a day-to-day basis was not the product of the will of some distant sovereign; on the contrary, jury verdicts given without benefit of binding and unambiguous judicial instructions must have reflected jurors' experience either with the common law as it had been customarily applied in their towns or with other customs that their towns observed as law. The power of juries over the law also tells us that the legal system did not serve as an instrument for the majoritarian resolution of group conflict and the enforcement of the will of the most powerful group. Prerevolutionary society was not, as American society is today, divided into organized interest groups seeking to gain control of the institutions of government and then enact and enforce laws in their own interest. A society so divided cannot exist, I believe, when juries have power to accept or reject whatever law they wish. The divisions in society at large will be reflected in juries that are randomly selected. Those juries will frequently be unable to reach unanimous verdicts, and over time uncertainty and inconsistency will appear in verdicts reached by different juries. In a legal system in which juries have the power to find the law, whatever disputes arise cannot be resolved by mere majoritarian fiat but must be resolved by a process of consensus building that produces legal rules acceptable to a broad base of society as a whole.

The rules of substantive law in prerevolutionary Massachusetts sustained the building of consensus. Consensus was promoted by the fact that nearly all members of society shared common ethical values and imposed those values on the occasional individual who refused to abide by them voluntarily.[5] Although this ethical unity was weakened in the prerevolutionary period by an increasing religious diversity growing out of the Great Awakening and by increasing disharmony and litigiousness among townspeople, the legal system still supported the idea that a religious establishment should declare and promulgate moral standards for the community at large and the idea that the courts of law were appropriate instruments for punishing those who violated the standards. The best illustrations of both the promulgation and the enforcement of moral standards are the innumerable criminal prosecutions brought against people who failed to attend church on Sunday or otherwise defiled the Sabbath.[6]

Ethical unity was furthered by the existence of legal rules that insured economic and social stability.[7] Economic stability meant, in essence, that the distribution of wealth would not change substantially or rapidly over time, while social stability meant that individuals would have well-defined places in their community and well-defined relationships with the community's other inhabitants. Of course, cracks began to appear in this stability as the eighteenth century progressed, perhaps because stability was no longer as highly valued as it had been in the seventeenth-century Bay Colony. Stability was threatened, for example, by increasing numbers of paupers and landless younger sons who found themselves without an economically productive place in their ancestral towns and accordingly had to migrate and seek to earn a living elsewhere;[8] when they arrived in a new town, they had neither a place in its economy nor any well-defined relationships with its townspeople. Stability was also threatened by growing opportunities to participate in commerce and in various sorts of speculation, particularly land speculation. Nonetheless, the rules of law, which had been formulated at an earlier time and to which prerevolutionary society adhered perhaps only out of an unthinking respect for the past, still promoted economic and social stability in important ways.

For example, although men could enter into certain sorts of speculative contracts if they were willing to fulfill the necessary formalities, the law impeded such contracts by making the formalities, such as registering contracts with magistrates, inconvenient and expensive. Similarly, the rules of property insured that men to whom resources initially had been distributed would often retain monopolistic control over those resources. The law of this period, in sum, unthinkingly promoted an economy that encouraged people not to increase their wealth through either speculation or competition but to accept the niche in society in which they happened to find themselves. Although the precise function of prerevolutionary property and contract law is unclear, it may be that the economic stability it furthered minimized competition and hence animosity among individuals within local communities and thereby made it easier for communities to remain united on fundamental ethical values, which in turn furthered the building of that consensus without which the legal system could not have functioned.

The War of Independence ushered in the beginning of a new legal and social order of Massachusetts. Although little legal change occurred during the war itself, the attempts of the revolutionary generation to explain and justify the war and its political results set loose new intellectual and social currents which ultimately transformed the legal and social structure of the new state.

The first breach in the old order occurred in the 1780s, when agrarian debtors, mostly in western Massachusetts, began organizing politically to complain that existing judicial procedures prejudiced their defense in suits begun by creditors to collect debts. Their argument was that access to justice was one of the rights of man for which the War of Independence had been fought and that the structure of the legal system and the legal profession precluded them from effective access to the courts in debt collection suits. But when they organized to petition the legislature they were met by a counterorganization of lawyers and creditors. During the next decade, for the first time in Massachusetts history, the politics of the state was dominated over an extended period by interest groups that were divided over a fundamental socioeconomic issue.[9]

Thereafter similar divisions continued to occur. By 1810 the state was split politically over another central social question: whether to retain its religious establishment. Of course, the fact of this division seriously impaired the state's ancient ethical unity. More important, though, was the outcome of the religious controversy—the effective disestablishment of the church. Together with decisions made some two decades earlier to cease prosecuting people for conduct such as defiling the Sabbath, which was regarded by society merely as immoral rather than truly criminal, disestablishment marked the final end of the era in which men thought it proper for government and related institutions to impose a common set of ethical values on individuals in the community who did not voluntarily share them.[10]

While the ethical unity inherited from the colonial period was being destroyed, the legal system continued to adhere to various rules of property and contract that had promoted economic and social stabiltiy in the past. It quickly became apparent, however, that with the decline of colonial ethical standards, rules that had once had a stabilizing effect would now have precisely the opposite effect.

The inversion in the impact of the rules of property and contract occurred because of ambiguity in the central doctrine of Massachusetts law throughout the period—the concept of private property, which can either promote or impair stability. In the colonial period, ethical standards, especially concepts of fair exchange associated with the law of contract, had insured that individuals would use their property consistently with the ethical sense of the community and with the preservation of the community's economic and social stability. In the nineteenth century, however, the demise of the old ethical standards left the owner of property free to use it as he wished. As a result, some owners began to argue in contract cases that they should be free to exchange their property for other property even though the exchange was not fair or equal; when their arguments began to meet with success, they became able to improve their position in the community at the expense of others, thereby upsetting the community's ancient order and hierarchy. Whereas the prerevolutionary law of contract had sought to protect people from losing their property in unfair exchanges, postrevolutionary contract law did not recognize the concept of fair exchange but was premised instead on the notion that a person could use his property as he pleased, even if he gambled it away foolishly and lost his wealth and status in the community as a result or used it unscrupulously to gain wealth and status.

A parallel development occurred in the law of corporations. Most corporations before the Revolution were subordinate governmental agencies, such as parishes, towns, and common fields. They had been created in order to enable individuals to pool their wealth for community purposes. In the first decade of the nineteenth century, however, new forms of corporation such as the manufacturing corporation arose. The appearance of these new corporations forced courts to reconsider the issue whether the state could compel individuals to contribute resources to corporations, and the courts, seeking to protect private property rights, drew distinctions between two sorts of corporation—the municipal or governmental corporation, which could tax individuals, and the private corporation, which could not compel individuals either to become members or to contribute their property for corporate use. With this line of decisions a new economic institution, the business corporation, was born; this new form of corporation was free from the restraints imposed by the ancient requirement that a corporation serve community rather than private ends. The rapid maturation of this new institution, of course, soon provided men with a mechanism for amassing wealth and power that would totally destroy the old economic order.[11]

While the end of ethical unity and social and economic stability in Massachusetts necessarily meant that society could not retain the same form it had taken in the prerevolutionary period, the demise of the prerevolutionary social system did not automatically give birth to the materialistic and competitive society that characterized nineteenth-century America. Nineteenth-century society was the product instead of a final force that emerged during the revolutionary period—a desire for economic growth. Particularly after 1790 the Massachusetts economy grew and changed so rapidly that by 1830 what had been an essentially agrarian subsistence economy, in which commercial activity was confined to a few coastal ports, was transformed into an industrializing, market economy of statewide dimension.

The transformation of the economy produced much legal change, the most important element of which was the emergence of legal doctrines that recognized the materialism of the age and legitimated the idea of competition. Consider, for example, the law of property. In the prerevolutionary period the law treated numerous economic resources, such as water flowing in streams, as the property of the first person to appropriate the resource to his own use; by virtue of his property right, the initial user was thereby able to exclude latecomers from competing for the resource. In the early nineteenth century the inherited rules of property began to impede the economic activity of men who were seeking to exploit a resource such as water with new technology and thereby promote the Commonwealth's economic growth. Eighteenth-century Massachusetts law, for example, would have given a farmer who was using water to irrigate his land a property right to that water, with the result that if a mill operator sought to use the same water to turn a mill wheel, the farmer would have had a right to deny him its use. In the first third of the nineteenth century, rules of this sort seriously

impaired the development of the Massachusetts economy by entrepreneurs such as millers who wished to use new sophisticated technology. The result was that the courts, sympathizing with the entrepreneurs, overturned many rules conferring property rights on initial
resource users and instead legitimated a competitive ethic that favored
more efficient over less efficient users without regard to their priority
in time.[12]

The needs of business entrepreneurs also changed the legal system by
depriving juries in civil cases of their right to decide the law. As I
suggested earlier, a jury system in which juries have power to find law
can function only in a society with substantial ethical unity and
economic and social stability. As unity and stability broke down near
the turn of the century, the jury system began to function less
efficiently and with less certainty and predictability. Certainty and
predictability, however, were the very qualities that business entrepreneurs needed most in order to rationally allocate resources for
economic growth, and they accordingly began to complain about the
jury system's inefficiencies. As a result juries lost their power to find
law. By 1830 law was stated to juries by the court, and their verdicts
were set aside if they failed to follow the court's instructions. Although
judges themselves made much law, they looked whenever possible to
the legislature as the ultimate lawmaker, and interest groups freely
competed to gain control of the legislature so that law would be framed
in their own interest. By 1830, in short, Massachusetts had become a
society in which individuals freely competed with each other for
control of economic resources and groups competed with each other
for control of political power.[13] American law and society had thus
begun to assume their modern form.

Before turning, however, to a detailed analysis of these legal changes
in postrevolutionary Massachusetts and of the forces producing the
changes, we must consider the question whether Massachusetts law
changed merely because the state's lawmakers were following English
law. That is, we must explore briefly the extent to which Americans
after the Revolution received English law. In Massachusetts, reception
was authorized by a clause in the Constitution of 1780 providing for
the continuing effectiveness of all laws that had theretofore "been
adopted, used, and approved" in the Commonwealth.[14] Although
that clause did not talk specifically of receiving English law, the
Massachusetts courts, unable to determine precisely which laws were in
effect in 1780, construed the clause as authorizing reception of the
entire common law and statute law of England in effect at the time of
the Revolution, "except such parts as were judged inapplicable" to the
Commonwealth's "new state and condition."[15]

The courts of Massachusetts often turned to ancient English precedents to resolve pending cases, as in *Draper* v. *Jackson*,[16] where the

issue was whether a note and mortgage made payable to a husband and wife became an asset of the wife or of the husband's executor upon the husband's death. Relying on cases reported only in English abridgments[17] and on two more recent English cases,[18] the Supreme Judicial Court held the note and mortgage to be the property of the wife. *Draper* fit conveniently into the theory of the reception clause justifying adoption of ancient English law, but on occasion Massachusetts judges went beyond the theory and followed even postrevolutionary English precedents. It was particularly appropriate in commercial cases to "adopt the principles of the English courts," since it was "very desirable that, in maritime law, there should be a uniformity among all great commercial nations."[19] Even when there was no commercial need for uniformity, however, the courts sometimes followed contemporary English decisions: *Melvin* v. *Whiting*,[20] for example, followed the trend of English authorities in reducing from sixty to forty years the period for which an incorporeal interest had to be held in order to transform it into a prescriptive easement.[21]

But the Massachusetts courts did not always follow English law. Sometimes the rejection of English law was explicit, as in *Conner* v. *Shepherd*,[22] where the issue was whether a widow was entitled to dower in uncultivated land of which her husband had been seised in fee during their marriage. After noting that the widow was entitled to dower according to common law, the Supreme Judicial Court observed that uncultivated lands in England typically were held as appendages to improved and cultivated estates; in Massachusetts, on the contrary, "many large tracts of uncultivated territory [were] owned by individuals, who ha[d] no intention of reducing them to a state of improvement, but consider[ed] them rather as subjects of speculation," to be sold as they increased "in value with the population and improvement of the country." The court observed that to permit assignment of dower in uncultivated lands would create "an impediment to their transfer" and would thereby discourage people from speculating in them. Moreover, it found that if dower were assigned widows would be unable to use the land, since to clear it would constitute waste; the court thought it "not an extravagant supposition, that lands actually in a state of nature may, in a country fast increasing in population, be more valuable than the same land would be with that sort of cultivation, which a tenant for life would be likely to bestow upon it. . . ."[23] The court thus held the English common law rule inapplicable to the state and condition of land in Massachusetts and denied the widow her common law dower.[24]

More frequently the courts purported to follow English law when in fact they did not. In *Vandine, Petitioner*,[25] the issue was whether a bylaw of the city of Boston prohibiting the collection of refuse without a license was binding on a person who was not a Boston resident. The court analyzed a number of English precedents which, it concluded, distinguished between municipal and business corporations: bylaws of municipal corporations were found binding on nonresidents, whereas bylaws of business corporations were thought to be binding only on agents and shareholders. In fact the English cases drew a very different distinction, between bylaws made pursuant to an ancient custom or an act of Parliament, which were binding,[26] and other bylaws, which were not binding.[27]

The Supreme Judicial Court similarly misread English law in *Thurston* v. *Hancock*.[28] *Thurston* was a suit by an owner of a house that had been undermined when his neighbor made an excavation four feet away from the wall of the house. The plaintiff relied on a series of English cases that had granted relief to owners of houses undermined as a result of digging on neighborhood land, rendered uninhabitable by noxious smells from a neighboring pig sty, or made inaccessible by a change in the grade of a highway.[29] The Massachusetts court, however, ignored all but one of the English cases cited by the plaintiff, arguing erroneously that English law gave relief only to plaintiffs who possessed prescriptive easements; in the one case discussed by the court,[30] it found the report "very short and unsatisfactory" and hence unworthy of credit.[31] It accordingly held for the defendant.

Examination of individual decisions thus discloses that Massachusetts courts at times received and followed English law and at other times did not. The same is true if one compares English and Massachusetts law more broadly. Throughout the period from 1760 to 1830, it appears that the law of contract and the law of negligence developed along parallel lines in England and Massachusetts.[32] On the other hand, the Massachusetts law of civil[33] and criminal procedure,[34] its substantive law of crime,[35] and its law of debtor and creditor[36] were consistently different from the corresponding law of England, while its rules regulating an owner's use of his property initially paralleled English rules[37] but then, in the nineteenth century, became substantially different.[38]

In short, one cannot explain developments in Massachusetts law, either in individual cases or in broad areas, as a consequence of adherence to English law. Massachusetts judges often did follow English law, probably for a variety of reasons, such as the convenience of citing precedent to dispose of the many cases in which they lacked time to consider fully the merits of competing policies. But they did not follow English law when it was inconsistent with the needs and conditions of their new state. Thus the legal and social development of Massachusetts often diverged from that of England—which suggests that by the last third of the eighteenth century each society was pursuing its own independent course even on those occasions when the two courses seemed superficially to be parallel.

The Prerevolutionary
Legal System, 1760-1775

2. The Legal Restraint of Power

One of the most intense concerns of Americans in the prerevolutionary period was to render individuals secure in their lives, liberties, and properties from abuses of governmental power.[1] Men sought to prevent extension of "the Power of Officers beyond all Bounds" out of fear that if official power went uncurbed "no Man ... [would be] safe" and it would be "in the Power of every Officer to distress his Neighbors."[2] In Massachusetts, at least, colonials succeeded in restraining governmental power to an extraordinary degree.

To the modern mind, the most powerful institution in prerevolutionary Massachusetts ought to have been the General Court, the province's legislature, which was authorized to dispose of the province's lands, levy taxes, and enact laws. But its powers were not as extensive in practice as they were in theory. In the 1760s the General Court had already disposed of the bulk of the unsettled land and at that time needed to raise little money by taxation since the provincial government provided few public services.[3] Some colonials even had doubts about the power of the General Court to enact laws,[4] arguing that legislation "contrary to eternal truth, equity, and justice" would be void, since "the supreme power in a state ... [was] *jus dicere* only ... [,while] *jus dare*, strickly speaking, belong[ed] only to GOD."[5] Arguments against legislative power, however, were ambiguous ones, contending on the one hand that "something must exist in a free state, which no part of it can be authorised to alter or destroy,"[6] but simultaneously recognizing that legislatures possessed broad power to alter the common law. The difficulty lay in articulating the limits that "eternal truth, equity, and justice" placed on legislative power—a difficulty that was not resolved in the prerevolutionary period; all that Americans of that era could do was to persist in their vague belief that somehow law was to some extent fundamental and immutable and hence incapable of legislative alteration.

The legislative product of the General Court reflected the ambiguities in prerevolutionary thinking. Consider, for example, the work of the legislature elected in 1761, as typical a year as any. The great bulk of the General Court's acts in that year were essentially administrative, involving questions of raising and appropriating money,[7] organizing and granting jurisdiction to local units of government,[8] and responding to specific local needs.[9] The Court also acted on a number of occasions in a quasi-judicial capacity when it granted new trials to litigants in pending actions.[10] In that year it passed only three acts that were arguably legislative in the sense that they changed law or made new law—an act making robbery a capital offense,[11] an act prohibiting the arrest of royal soldiers and sailors for debt,[12] and an act incorporating the Society for the Propagation of Christian Knowledge.[13] The first two acts, in particular, indicate that the General Court did have authority to alter rules of law; however, it was an authority that was only sparingly exercised.

The executive branch of the provincial government, consisting of the governor, lieutenant governor, secretary, treasurer, and some lesser officials, was even weaker than the General Court. Its weakness is shown most clearly in an analysis of the governor's powers. Apart from his negative power to veto acts of the General Court and spending of the province's money and his administrative power to appoint many lesser officials, the governor had only one power of any substance: with the consent of the Council he could call on military force to execute the laws.[14]

The structure of local government was in many ways analogous to that of the provincial government. The dominant institution was the town meeting. Although the meeting had legislative power to enact bylaws on such subjects as fire prevention, rubbish and garbage disposal, and minimum maintenance standards for private and town property, in practice towns enacted bylaws infrequently.[15] In large measure, meetings were concerned with administrative matters such as taxation, election of officials, appointment of teachers and ministers, repair of highways, regulation of the poor and insane, control and distribution of town land, and supervision of the meetinghouse.[16] The selectmen, who were the principal officers of the town, discharged day-to-day executive functions, subject, however, to the approval of the meeting.[17]

The final component in the prerevolutionary governmental apparatus was the courts. The courts were the principal link between the provincial government in Boston and the local communities. Colonial government, unlike our own, did not consist of a vast bureaucracy with clear chains of command reaching upward to central political authorities. Instead there were a number of courts, whose judges and subordinate officers were appointed and in part enforced law enacted by political authorities but met in various localities under scrutiny of the community as a whole and responded to community needs and community interests.

At the base of the judicial hierarchy were the one-man courts of the justices of the peace.[18] Appointed on a county-by-county basis, these justices had exclusive jurisdiction over civil suits where the amount in controversy was under forty shillings and title to land was not in question.[19] The individual justices also had criminal jurisdiction over petty offenses such as profanity, defamation, and minor trespasses, for which they could impose fines of up to twenty shillings and sentence convicted prisoners to the stocks, the whipping post, or prison for a maximum of twenty-four hours. In civil cases appeals lay to the Inferior Court of Common Pleas;[20] in criminal cases to the Court of General Sessions of the Peace;[21] on appeal, the parties received a trial de novo.

Each county had its own Court of General Sessions, composed of all the justices of the peace for the county. It met quarterly and had jurisdiction to try all misdemeanors committed within the county. It also possessed broad supervisory powers over town governments and over the local economy. Sessions courts approved the establishment and alteration of roads and bridges;[22] appointed holders of ferry licenses, liquor licenses, and licenses to sell coffee, tea, and china; approved town bylaws, provided that they were not on subjects regulated by the provincial legislature;[23] supervised town administration of the poor law;[24] punished vagabonds;[25] levied county taxes;[26] approved county accounts and expenditures; regulated the county prisons;[27] and performed a number of other miscellaneous functions.[28] Sessions was, in effect, the county government; the only significant regulatory power it lacked was that of control over public health procedures, especially over the licensing of smallpox innoculation hospitals and the imposition of quarantines for smallpox.[29] Courts of Sessions even had quasi-legislative power: they made rules about the payment of costs in proceedings brought before them,[30] about procedures for rehearings of their determinations,[31] and about the access of grand juries to depositions taken before justices of the peace in preliminary examinations;[32] in one instance a court even adopted a regulation to prevent stench from mussels on a beach.[33] Appeal lay from sessions to the Superior Court.

Every county also had its own Inferior Court of Common Pleas, which had original jurisdiction over all civil suits except those in which the crown was plaintiff or in which a justice of the peace had original jurisdiction. Each inferior court, which sat quarterly, consisted of four judges, any three of whom constituted a quorum, and had its own bar and its own rules of practice. Appeal again lay to the Superior Court.[34]

The province's highest court was the Superior Court of Judicature, Assize, and General Jail Delivery, a single court with five justices, any three of whom made up a quorum. It, too, had its own bar, which was not organized on a county-by-county basis, although many lawyers practiced before it only in their home counties. By statute, the Superior Court exercised common law jurisdiction as full and ample as that of the King's Bench. Most of the Superior Court's jurisdiction, though, was appellate, with original jurisdiction generally being limited to pleas of the crown and civil suits in which the crown was plaintiff. Under its appellate jurisdiction, an appellant usually received a trial *de novo* before all the justices of the court,[35] but those trials were rarely the second full-scale trial in a case. For litigants usually appealed to the Superior Court not after trial in the County Court of Common Pleas had been completed, but after Common Pleas had rendered judgment on a sham pleading point—a point that was raised specifically to avoid a full-scale trial in the lower court followed by another in the Superior Court. Thus the full-scale trial in the Superior Court was usually the first such trial; after that trial, however, the losing party was entitled, provided he had not previously lost a full trial below, to bring an action of review, which afforded an opportunity for a second trial in the Superior Court—a total of three opportunities for a full-scale trial. The province charter also permitted an appeal to the Privy Council in personal actions where the amount in controversy exceeded three hundred pounds, but the Superior Court, asserting that it alone, "by the Clauses in our Charter relative to this Matter, . . . [was] to judge of the Limitations of Appeals,"[36] frequently denied appeals.[37] Although a party who had been denied an appeal could obtain leave for one directly from the Privy Council,[38] that remedy was of little avail, for the Massachusetts court did not recognize the legitimacy of appeals so taken and in such cases would generally either refuse to assist the appellant in putting evidence in writing for transmission to the council or decline to order execution of the council's final judgment.[39] Thus almost all cases begun in Massachusetts remained there for final judgment.

As the above survey of their jurisdiction shows, the courts had vast coercive power of a criminal, administrative, and civil nature. That power was of particular importance to political authorities for a number of reasons. In the absence of a bureaucracy, those authorities often possessed little coercive power of their own and therefore often had to turn to the courts. Thus, when an individual elected to town office refused to serve, the town itself could not coerce him but had to petition the court of sessions to impose a fine.[40] Similarly, a man who sought to pursue a trade in a town without the town's permission could only be punished by a court.[41] Courts, in short, were the only agency that had jurisdiction to fine or otherwise punish and hence ultimately coerce people who broke the law.

Moreover, even when political authorities sought to exercise the few powers that they alone possessed, they found themselves subject to judicial supervision. For example, courts often listened to complaints of illegal taxation. As long as the necessary procedural preconditions had been satisfied,[42] the courts would grant a tax abatement to a petitioner who demonstrated that he had been assessed more than a person in his town in similar circumstances[43] or that some other person in his town was not being asked to pay taxes at all.[44] Someone who was being taxed on his poll or property by two towns[45] or by a municipality of which he was not a resident[46] or for municipal services he was unable to use[47] could also have his taxes abated, as could a petitioner who showed that town officials had used illegal procedures in collecting a tax.[48] Similarly, Anglicans, Baptists, and Quakers who had procured from their ministers certificates of their membership in a dissenting church could obtain abatement of taxes collected for the use of the Congregational establishment;[49] a minister of one of those sects could also sue to recover all such taxes that had been collected from his parishioners.[50]

More importantly, officials were subject to common law actions for damages whenever in the exercise of their duties they committed a wrong.[51] Such actions were frequently brought, for instance, against sheriffs for their own misconduct or that of their deputies, for whom they were liable. Most such suits alleged some misfeasance or neglect in performing a duty relating to civil litigation, such as failing to serve a writ of attachment, failing to take bail of a defendant, failing to keep attached goods in possession pending trial, or failing to levy execution or to levy it properly.[52] Suits could be brought against constables for similar misfeasance or neglect, as well as against jailers who permitted prisoners to escape.[53] All officials were also subject to damage actions for improper arrests[54] and for wrongful invasions of a subject's property; in one case a plaintiff successfully brought suit against a local official who had seized the plaintiff's vacant house for use as a smallpox hospital without first obtaining a warrant to do so,[55] while in another a man sued a royal customs official who had seized his ship and its cargo for failure to pay duties.[56] A fundamental rule was that an arrest, a search, or a seizure of goods following a search was an actionable wrong unless made pursuant to a lawful warrant;[57] "Probable Cause [was] no Excuse to a[n] ... officer making a Seizure,"[58] search, or arrest, "for it would be extremely bad to leave it to the discretion of the Court officer to assume w[ha]t[ever] power to search w[ha]t[ever] house he thinks fit."[59]

A final check on' government officials for misconduct in office, similar to their liability in damages, was their liability for monetary penalties imposed on them by statute. Such penalties were recoverable in actions of debt and case brought by private individuals who, in return for their efforts, received a portion—usually one-half—of the penalty recovered, while the remaining portion went to some public agency. Suits for statutory penalties lay against innumerable officials and other holders of governmental privileges, among them moderators of town meetings who permitted unqualified persons to vote,[60] mill owners who obstructed the passage of fish upstream,[61] and men who held office without taking the requisite oath.[62] There was, in short, little that one acting on behalf of government could do without rendering himself liable to legal action in the event that he wronged another.[63]

Given the vast powers of the courts, it is not surprising that men kept close watch over them. Colonials perceived that "an impartial administration of justice" was of great "moment to the people," since it was "the courts of judicature ... which procure[d] safety to ... [their] property and protection to ... [their] persons."[64] All realized that their "rights and properties ... [were] utterly insecure ... when the laws of the land, those impregnable bulwarks of ... safety, ... [were] either ... suspended or not executed."[65] Even Chief Justice Hutchinson agreed that those who "execut[d] the Law ... [ought] not to enquire into ... [its] Reason and Policy" but ought merely "to enquire what is Law, and see that the Laws are inforced,"[66] for to permit courts to determine policy would introduce "a Union of Legislative and Executive Power"—"the worst Sort of Tyranny...."[67] Colonial Americans, in sum, wanted to be ruled by fixed laws, not by judges with vast discretionary powers that could be used by potentially arbitrary rulers.

To bind judges to the rule of law and thereby render the lives, liberties, and properties of individuals secure, the legal system sought to deprive judges of all discretion in administering their vast powers and of effective ability to bring those powers to bear on individuals. It accomplished that end through two bodies of legal doctrine—the doctrine of precedent and the rules governing the relationship of judge and jury.

Men as politically antagonistic as Thomas Hutchinson and John Adams viewed the doctrine of precedent, which required judges to decide cases in the same way that other judges had decided them in the

past, as a means of limiting judicial discretion and thereby insuring
judicial adherence to the rule of law. Both men thought it vital that
"the Laws of every State ought always to be fixed, [and] certain"[68]
and that "every possible Case . . . [be] settled in a Precedent, leav[ing]
nothing, or but little to the arbitrary Will or uninformed Reason of
Prince or Judge."[69]

Americans of the prerevolutionary period expected their judges to be
automatons who mechanically applied immutable rules of law to the
facts of each case. Their expectation had a solid foundation in the
realities of the Massachusetts legal system, for law changed only slowly
and imperceptibly in the mid-eighteenth century. Men who were
practicing law in the 1760s, unlike lawyers of today, did not witness
the courts handing down decisions that frequently modified—either
explicitly or implicitly—existing law or otherwise made new law.
Statutes altering substantive law were, as we have seen, equally rare.
Nor could mid-eighteenth-century lawyers remember a period when law
had changed rapidly as a result of statute or judicial decision; the last
such period in Massachusetts had been at the beginning of the
eighteenth century,[70] but the records remaining from that period
were rarely consulted in the 1760s and did not, in any event, disclose
the full extent of the earlier change. Instead, lawyers had for a half
century watched inactive legislatures and judges who adhered to
precedent with a simple-minded rigor and consistency. The mere
citation of precedent, in short, seemed to solve virtually every legal
problem.

The success of precedent lay in the fact that the problems to whose
solution it was put were simple, elementary ones. The jury charge is a
typical example of such a problem; even today, the compilation of jury
instructions raises fewer difficult legal questions than most other law
tasks, for instructions usually state obvious and basic rules and leave to
the jury the subtle and difficult job of applying those rules to a novel
and unique set of facts in a manner that will do justice in the case at
hand and adjust the law to emerging social needs. The charge given in
one of the Boston massacre trials by Judge Edmund Trowbridge,
regarded by his contemporaries as the most learned and able member of
the Superior Court bench, is illustrative; apart from a discussion of the
evidence, it consisted of statements of basic, black-letter rules of
law—statements that were mere paraphrases of the British authorities
from which Trowbridge had extracted them.[71] John Adams's summation in the same case, where he was permitted to argue the law to
the jury, was similar: he cited, with one exception, only British cases
and texts, usually paraphrasing or even quoting them verbatim.[72]
Other judges and lawyers made similar presentations of law to
juries;[73] indeed, in the fifteen years before the Revolution, con-

temporaries identified only one case before a jury in which "the Authorities produced ... [did not] seem to come up to the present Question."[74]

The courts were also called upon to apply rigid rules of precedent in numerous instances in which defendants sought to have writs abated for technical insufficiencies such as a plaintiff's improper choice of writ, insufficient service of process, improper joinder of parties, or misidentification of a party.[75] Courts could and readily did apply precedent in deciding these technical pleas. Again, the application of precedent did not prevent the courts from doing justice and adjusting the law to emerging social needs, since pleas in abatement attacked only the technical sufficiency of writs and, if granted, did not bar renewal of a suit;[76] hence abatement of a writ had no ultimate impact on the merits of litigation.[77] Equally important were the ready availability and clarity of most of the precedents needed to resolve the simple, recurring issues that arose with such pleas.

Because, as we shall see next, juries determined both the law and the facts in most colonial cases, and because pleas in abatement on technical grounds accounted for roughly 90 percent of all dispositions in contested cases other than those in which jury verdicts were rendered, courts rarely faced law tasks more difficult than drawing up jury instructions or deciding pleas in abatement. When they did, judges and lawyers could, on occasion, respond with some sophistication: on such matters as pretrial motions and motions for judgment after special verdicts, for example, counsel might consider how, as a general matter, "Acts are to be construed"[78] or the weight to be accorded to the "great Principles" of the law in a particular case.[79] They might also draw analogies to prior decisions "within the same Reason,"[80] distinguish their opponents' citations,[81] or point out the undesirable results that would flow from a decision contrary to the one for which they were arguing.[82] Arguments of this sort were rare, however, except in cases on politically sensitive matters such as slavery,[83] religion,[84] impressment of seamen,[85] or the propriety of the Superior Court's issuing writs of assistance.[86] In nearly all cases, the mere citation of what had been done in the past by either the Massachusetts or the English courts was the most effective argument available to counsel,[87] with Massachusetts precedents apparently carrying somewhat more weight than English ones.[88] For when "Usage had been uninterrupted, and the Construction of the Law thereby established," the courts "would make no Innovation"[89] but would follow the old rule even when "abstracted from the Custom" there existed "no Reason why it should" be followed.[90]

Like the doctrine of precedent, the jury was viewed as a means of controlling judges' discretion and restraining their possible arbitrary tendencies. Few in Massachusetts would have disagreed with the sentiments of the Middlesex County Convention when in 1774 it observed that "no state can long exist free and happy . . . when trials by juries . . . are destroyed or weakened. . . ."[91] For, as John Adams explained, the jury system introduced into the "executive branch . . . a mixture of popular power"; as a result, "the subject . . . [was] guarded in the execution of the laws,"[92] and "no Man . . . [could] be condemned of Life, or Limb, or Property or Reputation, without the Concurrence of the Voice of the People."[93] Jurors did indeed represent the voice of the people, for they were closely tied to local communities. Jury panels were selected by the clerk of court's sending to each town in the county a writ of venire facias directing the town to select by lot a specified number of inhabitants for jury duty. A total of twenty-four to thirty men were summoned for each Superior Court panel; that panel was then divided into two juries of twelve, which between them heard all the civil cases in a given term. The panel was then reassembled for criminal cases; in selecting a jury from it, the accused was allowed a specified number of peremptory challenges, depending on the charge, plus an unlimited number of challenges for cause. In the unlikely event that he exhausted the panel, the sheriff summoned additional veniremen from among bystanders. Jury selection in lower courts was similar, except that one panel was returned for both the Common Pleas and the General Sessions courts.[94]

Litigants had a right to trial by jury in all cases before the Superior and Common Pleas courts and in criminal cases and cases involving the laying out of highways before the courts of sessions.[95] The right to trial by jury in such cases was never questioned during the prerevolutionary period, and few such cases went to trial without a jury. In most of those that did, the parties had agreed on the facts and desired the court's ruling on a point of law; on one other occasion a defendant had pleaded usury, and trial of that issue was to the court on the oaths of the parties.[96]

The vital fact about the jury system, however, was not that juries tried nearly every case but that they had vast power to find both the law and the facts in those cases. Although there were several devices at common law in England for controlling jury findings of law and fact, few of those devices were used in Massachusetts. The ones that were used, moreover, were more restrictive of the fact-finding than of the law-finding powers of the jury.

Under the common law writ system, which was given wide application in prerevolutionary Massachusetts, pleading can serve the function of not only giving parties notice of each others' claims but also framing a single, simple factual question for the jury, to which the jury can return an answer of yes or no that will completely dispose of the case.

The key to such a system is widespread use of special pleading and adherence to the rule that in giving evidence of the facts of their case parties "must abide by their Allegations."[97] When this is done, no legal issues can come before the jury, for all questions of law are removed from the case by the court's prior determination of the legal sufficiency of proffered pleas. Moreover, the jury is not confused by extraneous facts, since the court excludes from evidence all facts that do not tend to prove or disprove the single issue of fact raised by the pleadings.[98] For if parties "might be allowed to give Evidence of Facts that did not appear in the . . . [pleadings], it would be unne[ce]ssary to have any . . . [pleadings] at all. . . ."[99]

The effect of special pleading can be seen in a typical action of debt on a penal bond with a conditional defeasance. When the defendant pleaded his performance of the condition, the plaintiff could interpose a demurrer to his plea—a demurrer that would require the court to decide whether performance was a good defense. On the other hand, the plaintiff could deny the defendant's performance; then only the factual issue of the defendant's performance or nonperformance would remain in the case. Evidence on such matters as the execution of the bond, fraud, or usury could not come before the jury, since such evidence could not assist the jury in rendering a yes or no answer to the question whether the defendant had performed the act constituting the condition. Moreover, the jury might not even know the legal consequences of its answer; if, for example, it answered affirmatively the question whether John Doe had completed construction of a house for Richard Roe in 1763, it might not know whether its answer rendered Roe liable to Doe for the price of the house or Doe liable to Roe for failure to complete the house on time. Special pleading thus had the capacity of limiting the jury only to finding facts and depriving it of all discretion in applying law to the facts.[100]

If a defendant wished merely to deny the allegations advanced in the plaintiff's writ, he would plead what was known as the general issue in lieu of a special plea. The general issue was so called because it imported an absolute and general denial of each and every allegation in the plaintiff's declaration; all those allegations were put in issue before the jury. A plea of the general issue did not frame a single, precise factual question for the jury. There were two reasons for this. The first was that a typical plaintiff's declaration alleged several facts, all of which were put in issue by a general denial. The second was that the courts did not, as they did in the case of a special plea, restrict parties to proof only of facts tending to establish their allegations. The test of admissibility of facts under the general issue was not relevancy thereto but whether, as a matter of law, the proposed evidence ought to constitute a good defense to the plaintiff's action. Thus a defendant might be permitted to present to the jury not only evidence relating to facts raised by the plaintiff, such as evidence of performance in an action of assumpsit,[101] but evidence of other facts as well. The courts ruled, for example, that a defendant in an action on a contract could introduce evidence of an arbitrator's report,[102] while in an action of assault he could introduce evidence tending to show justification of the blow.[103] The effect of both rulings was to permit a defendant to put in evidence under the general issue facts that could also have been pleaded specially. Although it is impossible to determine precisely when a defendant could so prove special facts under the general issue,[104] it is clear that the determination was not made as a matter of relevancy to the plaintiff's allegations but on the basis of other considerations. Thus a defendant's offer of proof of title was rejected in an action of trover for cutting trees not because the defendant's title to the trees was irrelevant but because title to land could be tried only in the county in which the land was located.[105] The consequence of permitting proof of special facts under the general issue is also clear: instead of being confronted with a single issue on which they heard only directly relevant evidence, juries heard evidence on several issues, among which legal relationships were unclear and subject to determination during the course of the jury's deliberations. Jurors thus had to find not only facts but also the legal consequences of facts; that is, in the absence of other restrictions they possessed power to decide the law as well as the facts.

Juries were frequently put in a position to exercise such power, for parties usually preferred to try cases under the general issue rather than under a special plea. Special pleading beyond the initial plea by the defendant and replication by the plaintiff was rare.[106] The reasons for its rarity are unclear. It could be that colonial lawyers lacked sufficient knowledge of the rules of special pleading and therefore refrained from using it, but this is unlikely in view of the broad knowledge of other technicalities of the common law that they commanded. A second possibility is that the facts of colonial cases were rarely complex enough to warrant special pleading, but this too is unlikely, since there were some complex cases, as well as many simple ones, in which at least one of the parties might have benefited from interposing a special plea.[107] A third possibility, which will be explored below, is that judges and lawyers preferred to have juries rather than judges decide the law as well as the facts of their cases; whatever the cause may have been, this was the consequence of their infrequent use of special pleading. In short, although it had the potential of reducing jurors' discretion, special pleading did not realize that potential in prerevolutionary Massachusetts. Other rules and practices, however, had some of that effect.

In addition to the rules of evidence discussed above, which excluded proof of facts deemed irrelevant to the issues, Massachusetts common law during this period had several other rules that excluded evidence deemed unreliable. One basis of these rules was a mistrust of juries. "Courts ... [were] not tied up to ... strict Rule[s] in Admission of Evidence" when they were trying a case themselves, but "when ... [cases were] to go to Juries"[108] it was necessary to be more careful, for "Nothing should go to a Jury which would only tend to deceive and inveigle them...."[109] Hence the courts formulated exclusionary rules to bar certain sorts of potentially unreliable evidence, despite arguments that it was "abridging the Privileges of the Subject, [for the court] to settle a Point which wholly lies with the Jury to determine."[110]

The exclusionary rule most frequently invoked was that which rendered "Persons interested in the Matter in Question" incompetent as witnesses. The theory for exclusion was that "from the nature of human Passions and Actions, there ... [was] more Reason to distrust such a biased Testimony than to believe it."[111] The law "adapt[ed] ... itself to the human species, with all their feelings, passions and infirmities" and did not "go upon the absurd supposition, that men are stocks and stones; or that in the fervour of the blood, a man can act with the deliberation and judgment of a philosopher."[112] Thus, in order to "prevent" witnesses "from sliding into Perjury,"[113] testimony of interested witnesses was excluded. Much technical law became encrusted on that basic rule. Members of a corporation, for example, even if they themselves were not parties, were not permitted to testify in a suit involving the corporation since they would be liable for costs if the suit were lost.[114] Similarly, an administrator could not testify unless the estate he was administering was insolvent and he accordingly could expect no commission out of the assets he collected.[115] In fact no one could be a witness in an action if a party, in the event he lost the case, had a right to look to the proffered witness for recourse.[116] As the cited cases indicate, the rule contemplated the exclusion of testimony of witnesses who would be directly and immediately subject to a legally enforceable gain or liability as a result of the outcome of the case. The rule was extended further to exclude testimony of witnesses who had no such direct interest. Thus in *Rex* v. *Jackson*, a criminal prosecution for assault, it was doubted whether either the complainant or the defendant's wife could testify, even though neither had a direct pecuniary interest in the prosecution's outcome.[117] And in *Bartlett* v. *White* the Superior Court extended the rule even further, holding that Baptists other than the plaintiff, a Baptist who had sued to recover damages for an allegedly unlawful collection of a religious tax, could not testify.[118] For, as Chief

Justice Hutchinson had observed in another case, testimony ought not be allowed "where the Interest was ever so small";[119] in the *Bartlett* case the proffered witness did have some interest in the outcome, in the sense that the case created a precedent even though it did not adjudicate the rights of Baptists who were not parties to the action.

A rule analogous to the one rendering interested witnesses incompetent was one that excluded the testimony of people convicted of serious crimes. The theory was that "when the Crime is so great and of such a *Nature* . . . as it is to be supposed that the Person guilty has lost all Sense of Truth, and would not hesitate at violating his Oath, in such case . . . [the convict's testimony ought] not to be admitted. . . ." On the other hand, "if the Crime . . . [were] not of such a Nature as the least to invalidate the Credit of the Witness's *Oath*," as would be true in the case of a conviction for libel or for petit larceny, then the witness's testimony ought to be admitted.[120]

The final rule seeking to keep unreliable evidence away from the jury was the hearsay rule. Although lawyers honored rules against the admission of hearsay more in the breach than in the observance,[121] they were cognizant of the rules. Two reasons were given for excluding hearsay. First, such testimony was not based on the witness's first-hand knowledge but on his mere "credulity"; second, it was not a statement made under oath.[122] The latter reason was somewhat similar to the reason given for rendering interested persons and criminals incompetent. The "passions" of an interested person would, it was feared, cause him to forget his oath and "slid[e] . . . into Perjury," while a criminal "would not hesitate at violating his Oath"; in the case of hearsay, one of the dangers was the complete lack of an oath. The oath—and the moral and religious sanction that it implied—was seen as the best way of insuring that witnesses would tell the truth. The immense weight that colonials attached to oaths can also be seen from the instructions given to jurors to direct their evaluation of testimony. Prerevolutionary jurors were not told, as jurors are today, to weigh the credibility of witnesses and to consider the inherent probability or improbability of their testimony. Instead they were directed, in effect, to presume that all witnesses who had sworn an oath had told the truth. Therefore they were instructed to reconcile all inconsistencies in the testimony;[123] it was, for example, a standard rule that the testimony of a witness who said that he had observed an event outweighed the testimony of several who said they had not observed it, "because the Affirmative may swear true, and the Negative also."[124] The law was also wary of drawing presumptions and inferences from testimony,[125] for presumptions and inferences lacked the sanctification of an oath.

The colonial approach to evidentiary questions rested in large part, then, on a conception of truth that we do not share. The conception—

that truth would emerge not from a weighing of credibilities and probabilities but from the sanctity of an oath—looked backward to earlier times, in which God-fearing men had attached enormous importance to a solemn oath. To the extent that such notions persisted, they reduced somewhat the power of juries to determine facts both by keeping evidence from them and by reducing their freedom in weighing the evidence that they heard.

A third technique for controlling juries is for courts to instruct them on the law and, as we have seen above, on how to sift and weigh evidence. In colonial Massachusetts, however, instructions were scarcely an effective means of jury control. First, it appears that in many civil cases no instructions were given at all[126] and that even in those cases where the jury was charged the charges were often brief and compressed. Detailed charges were often unnecessary, for courts could and did assume that jurors were "good judges of the common law of the land."[127] "The general Rules of Law and common Regulations of Society, under which ordinary Transactions arrange[d] themselves, . . . [were] well enough known to ordinary Jurors,"[128] and therefore they were directed that, as to most matters, they "need[ed] no Explanation [since] your Good Sence & understanding will Direct ye as to them."[129] A further reason for the ineffectiveness of instructions was that they were often contradictory. One potential source of contradiction was counsel, who on summation could argue the law as well as the facts,[130] at least as long as he did not clearly misinform the jury.[131] Most confusing of all was the court's seriatim charge: each judge sitting on the court that tried a case gave his own interpretation of the law—an interpretation that could and sometimes did differ from those of his brethren.[132] Since all cases were tried before at least three judges in addition to counsel, jurors were often left with final power to determine which judge's interpretation of the law was correct.

Even if instructions had provided a useful mode of communicating rules of law, juries could not have been compelled to adhere to them. For once jurors have received evidence on several factual issues in a case, the only way to compel them to decide in accordance with the court's view of the law is for the court to set aside a verdict as contrary to its instructions. In prerevolutionary Massachusetts there were three sorts of motion that litigants could make in order to request a court to set aside a jury's verdict—a motion in arrest of judgment, a motion for a mistrial, and a motion for a new trial. All three, however, were unsatisfactory to insure that juries adhered to judicial instructions on the law.

The motion in arrest of judgment was generally not used to control juries but rather to attack judgments founded on defective pleadings.

Motions in arrest were granted in criminal cases, for example, if an indictment failed to allege all the relevant elements of the crime of which the defendant stood convicted,[133] if an indictment was brought against a person incapable of committing the crime,[134] or if an indictment was otherwise uncertain or insufficient,[135] and served a similar function in civil cases.[136] Motions in arrest could be used to control juries only when a jury returned a verdict on an issue that had not been framed by the pleadings.[137]

Motions for a mistrial, a second sort of postverdict motion, were used to set aside verdicts rendered by jurors who had followed improper procedures. Mistrials were ordered and verdicts set aside in civil cases if they had been rendered by eleven instead of twelve jurors,[138] if a party had not had an opportunity to present his entire case to the jury,[139] if the jury had received evidence other than that given in open court,[140] if jurors had not agreed on a verdict but, in spite of their disagreement, had rendered one for a defendant under the erroneous impression that if they failed to return a verdict the defendant would still be entitled to costs,[141] or if a party had tampered with the jury.[142] In criminal cases, on the other hand, mistrials were granted only in misdemeanor cases;[143] in felony cases the court lacked power to set aside a verdict with procedural defects similar to the ones which would require that a verdict in a civil case be set aside.[144]

A third postverdict motion was the motion for a new trial on the ground that the verdict was against law or evidence. Logically, such verdicts were of three types—verdicts against the law, verdicts against the evidence (that is, verdicts with no support whatever in the evidence), and verdicts against the weight of the evidence (that is, verdicts in favor of the party with the weaker evidence in cases where the evidence was conflicting). As the Superior Court noted, it was "rare" that it would grant a motion for a new trial.[145] It never granted such a motion on the ground that a verdict was either against all evidence or against the weight of the evidence, although Chief Justice Hutchinson observed in dictum that such a motion would be appropriate in the former case.[146] Moreover, it was clear that a motion for a new trial would not be granted on the ground that a verdict was against the law solely because the jury had disregarded the court's instructions; in two politically notorious cases that were tried in the early 1760s, crown officials against whom jury verdicts had been returned unanimously assumed this rule to be true.[147] The court did on one occasion set aside a verdict on the grounds that it was against the law and damages were excessive,[148] but the flaw in that verdict was not that the jury had disregarded its instructions. The flaw was in the original pleadings: the plaintiff's writ had contained a general allegation that he had suffered thirty pounds damage, but at the same time it had set forth specific items of damage totaling only sixteen pounds. When the jury returned a verdict for thirty pounds, the court granted the motion to set aside the verdict—a motion, however, that resembled a motion in arrest of judgment rather than the typical motion for a new trial.

As one looks generally over the various rules regulating the division between the functions of judge and jury, it becomes clear that although the jury's power to find facts was limited by rules excluding relevant evidence and keeping the jury from weighing probability and credibility, its power to find law was virtually unlimited. The frequent use of the general issue, which left to the jury the ultimate determination of the legal consequences of the facts of a case; the practice of counsel and judges giving the jury conflicting instructions on the law, which permitted the jury to select the rules for determining the legal consequences of facts; and the infrequency with which jury verdicts were set aside after trial tended to give the jury wide power to find the law. Special pleading and careful restriction of evidence admitted under special pleas were the only techniques available for restricting the jury's power to find law, and those techniques were only occasionally used. The power of the jury over the legal aspects of a case was therefore great indeed. With regard to decisions about the law, the "Jury ha[d] a right to do as they please[d],"[149] and "no verdicts . . . [were] thrown out."[150] In the words of John Adams, "a general Verdict, given *under the Direction of the Court* in Point of Law, . . . assuredly determine[d] . . . the Law." Even when a jury acted contrary to the direction of the court, Adams argued that its verdict determined the law, for it was "not only . . . [every juror's] right but his Duty in that Case to find the Verdict according to his own best Understanding, Judgment and Conscience, tho in Direct opposition to the Direction of the Court."[151]

Lawyers thus believed that juries should have the power to find law, apparently so that they could serve when needed as a restraint on judicial power. The law-finding power of juries had a number of consequences, however, that appear to have been unanticipated. One set of consequences arose out of the fact that law found by juries to fit the circumstances of individual cases has great potential for flexibility, for records of jury determinations of points of law are seldom preserved, and hence those determinations do not become precedents with a binding effect on future juries. In each case, a jury is free, if justice requires, to reach the same result reached by other juries in analogous cases in the past; if, on the other hand, justice requires departure from past verdicts, the jury is free so to depart. Moreover, no record is kept of such departures, and therefore legal change and development are imperceptible; men have the valuable illusion of legal stability. Explicit rules of law, such as the rules of pleading considered above, remain unchanged, while substantive law is still extremely flexible in its ability to adapt itself to social needs in individual cases. The broad power of juries to find law thus gave the legal system real flexibility while simultaneously giving the illusion of stability—two values that are important in doing justice in individual cases and in convincing litigants that justice has been done them.

The law-finding power of juries also made possible adherence to the doctrine that judges—the agents of a potentially arbitrary executive—ought to follow precedent and so not alter the rules of law. For, as we have seen, the vast power of juries in general left judges with only a few rather simple law tasks, such as instructing juries and deciding pleading motions, which could be mechanically performed by looking to precedent.

Most important, perhaps, the law-finding power of juries meant that the representatives of local communities assembled as jurors generally had effective power to control the content of the province's substantive law. Because of the power of juries, the legal system could not serve as an instrument for the enforcement of coherent social policies formulated by political authorities, either legislative or executive, whether in Boston or in local communities, when those policies were unacceptable to the men who happened to be serving on a particular jury. The ultimate power of juries thus raises the question whether the judgments rendered in the courts on a day-to-day basis were a reflection more of law set out in statute books and in English judicial precedents or of the custom of local communities.

Many lawyers relied openly on "the custom of the town"[152] as authority for their position, often with success. When James Otis, for example, urged that a case be decided in accordance with what "ha[d] ever been the Custom," the court agreed;[153] on the other hand, when another lawyer "prayed that Custom might not bar him" from relief, the court unanimously rejected his prayer.[154] Sometimes "the Custom of the Town" was given effect because "the Parties are to be supposed to intend according to the Custom";[155] that is, custom was applied because the parties had agreed that it should govern their transactions. In at least two cases, however, lawyers urged the application of custom not because of the agreement of the parties but because of its own intrinsic force or merit. Thus in *Baker* v. *Mattocks* Otis argued that, custom having been settled, " 'tis of great Importance that the Principles should be kept to."[156] His argument, as one judge understood it, was that rejection of long-accepted custom "would be attended with great Difficulty at this Day. . . ."[157] In *Doane* v. *Gage*, the custom of whalers was put forward as the rule for determining title to a whale on the ground that "the Customs of Whaling are certain Regulations dictated by observation, Experience, . . . [and] Common Sense among Whalemen" and that the particular custom involved "seem[ed] to be a wise, prudent, and equitable one."[158] Custom, in sum, was applied as law when its rules were sound, when men intended it to be applied, and when failure to apply it might lead to social or economic chaos.

It would be wrong, however, to conclude that community custom was the sole source of prerevolutionary law. In most reported cases, lawyers called the attention of jurors not to rules laid down by custom but to rules of common law. Lawyers informed juries that their pleas were "founded on the Law," that the jury "must determine by Law," and that a particular verdict was required by "the Law of the Land. . . ."[159] The usual function of custom was only to fill in interstices in statute or common law. As one lawyer explained, reliance on "the Custom of the Town" would be "an Argument of some Weight" when there was "no Law," but when "the Law is express," no "pretended Custom" could "controul it."[160] It was doubted whether custom could "prevail against plain Law";[161] that is, if custom were inconsistent with the law or "placed in Opposition to Law"[162] it was generally assumed that law rather than custom should prevail. There is not enough evidence to know whether juries typically followed local custom or common law when they were in conflict, and hence it is impossible to state with certainty whether the law of Massachusetts was ultimately grounded in custom or in common law. The unceasing efforts of counsel to find the rules of common law and to argue those rules to juries suggests, however, that juries were swayed by those rules, that they generally decided cases in accordance with them, and hence that the common law of England rather than local custom was the usual basis of the law. But the fact remains that in every case they decided juries possessed the power to reject the common law and that juries as well as judges and even legislators did on occasion permit local custom to prevail over clear common law.[163] In short, the communities of prerevolutionary Massachusetts freely received the common law of England as the basis of their jurisprudence but simultaneously reserved the unfettered right to reject whatever parts of that law were inconsistent with their own views of justice and morality or with their own needs and circumstances.

The power of juries over the substance of the law, the restraints that the doctrine of precedent imposed on judges in their performance of their few law tasks, the lack of coercive power on the part of officials, and their liability to damage judgments at the hands of juries rendered formal institutions relatively weak. Officials were, in essence, incapable of exercising their coercive powers without the consent of the local communities they "governed." The question remains why a legal system that was structured to render officials so weak was acceptable to the dominant groups in society.

Part of the answer has already been suggested. Security of life, liberty, and property was a preeminent value, and governmental institutions with unfettered coercive power would have posed an unending threat to that security. If the power of judges and other officials had been unrestrained and arbitrarily exercised, "rights and properties ... [would have been] utterly insecure," "no Man ... [would have been] safe," and it would have been "in the Power of every Officer to distress his Neighbors."[164] Royalist and Anglican officials, in particular, would have posed a serious threat to the Puritan-oriented majority of the hinterland. The antiauthoritarian response of the province's legal system, which made it impossible for officials to act without the approval of local communities, apparently insured that officials would act only against people who violated community norms of morality and justice, while people who followed those norms would be safe and their rights and properties secure. For the Puritans, who dominated nearly every town in eighteenth-century Massachusetts, that response was ideal.

A more difficult question to answer is why officials tolerated restraints that prevented them from effectively governing the province. Why, in particular, did the judges tolerate a legal system that left them much weaker than the judges of England, who had broad power to shape law by virtue of the fact that special pleas were often interposed[165] and that they could grant new trials when juries failed to follow their instructions?[166] Consider, for example, the case of *Erving* v. *Cradock*,[167] in which a Massachusetts shipowner brought a writ of trespass against a royal revenue officer who had seized his vessel and obtained its condemnation in admiralty on a charge of smuggling. All five judges of the Superior Court were convinced that the admiralty decree was *res judicata* and a bar to the common law trespass suit, and they so instructed the jury. Yet when the jury ignored their instructions, returned a verdict for the shipowner, and, as a practical matter, thereby reversed the admiralty decree, the judges did not set the verdict aside and grant a new trial, although they fully realized that such verdicts nullified the Navigation Acts. Even more surprising is the fact that counsel for the revenue officer pleaded the general issue, thus committing the res judicata question to the jury rather than pleading the admiralty decree specially and leaving its legal effect to the determination of the court. Why should the crown, through its counsel and its judges, have abdicated to the jury responsibility for deciding whether the Navigation Acts could be enforced in Massachusetts?

In part the answer lies in the Bay Colony's early history. The first settlers were averse to complex rules of pleading,[168] and it seems likely that special pleading was not practiced in the colony's nascent years. The early settlers also refused to compel jurors to return verdicts against their consciences and so gave judges no power to set aside jury verdicts with which they disagreed.[169] Finally, there was much dispute in the early years of the colony over the question whether magistrates should have discretion to decide cases other than in accordance with known rules of law, and the question was resolved in favor of placing limits on magisterial discretion.[170] In sum, the early settlers had begun to formulate the matrix of a legal system that left few law tasks to judges and that, like the later doctrine of precedent, required them to perform those tasks in accordance with known rules.

The judges of the eighteenth century thus inherited a legal system that gave them little law-making power. But why did they retain the restraints they inherited on their power while altering many other elements of the legal system during the seventeenth and eighteenth centuries? Why did they adhere to precisely those traditions that made centralized government so difficult and hence were most inimical to the interests of their master, the crown?

In large part, the answer is that judges lacked the power to do otherwise. The crown was their master only in theory. Although the judges of the common law courts were appointed by the governor with the consent of the council and their commissions ran only during pleasure, no judge was removed from office by the governor and council during the period from 1760 to 1774—which suggests that judges were subjected to little direct interference from the executive.[171] This was important, for to have judges "dependent on the Crown" would, men thought, result in "natural evil consequences . . . obvious and truly alarming,"[172] for it would subvert "a free administration of justice. . . ."[173] "It was taken as a maxim by all . . . that it was the function of the judges 'to settle the contests between prerogative and liberty' . . . and that in order for them to perform this duty properly they must be 'perfectly free from the influence of either.' "[174] Once appointed, judges appear, in fact, to have been reasonably free from the influence of the prerogative, but their freedom from the lower house of the legislature, collectively the representative of the towns, was much more in doubt. Their salaries were under legislative control, and when it appeared likely in the 1770s that the crown would undertake to pay those salaries, the legislature threatened to impeach judges who accepted such payments.[175]

The susceptibility of judges to local pressures was heightened by the fact that judges were drawn not from the lower reaches of the English bureaucracy, as were many royal officials in the colonies;[176] rather they were men of local prominence. The key to becoming a judge was not that one was a lawyer, for nearly all Massachusetts judges were not, but that one was a man of substance who commanded the respect of his community. This is suggested by a survey of the backgrounds of the eleven men who served as justices of the Superior Court between 1760 and 1774. Nine of them had never practiced law, although three of the nine had studied for the bar. All nine, however, had either been born into prominent families or become men of substance who were repeatedly chosen by their townsmen for public service. Stephen Sewall, for example, who was chief justice in 1760, was a nephew of a former chief justice and was a tutor at Harvard College for thirteen years before his initial appointment to the bench. His successor, Thomas Hutchinson, the son of a former councillor, was a wealthy Boston merchant who had represented Boston in the General Court for several years, during four of which he had served as Speaker of the House, and who had later become a member of the council. After serving for many years as lieutenant governor, he was appointed to the governorship in 1771. He was succeeded on the court by Benjamin Lynde, the son of a former chief justice and nephew of an inferior court judge, who had been trained in law but had never practiced and who had served four years in the House of Representatives and a total of twenty-nine years on the council. The last chief justice of the colonial period, Peter Oliver, who assumed that position in 1772, was a country gentleman without legal training who had twice been elected to the House and had served for eight years on the council. The five other nonlawyers on the court were John Cushing, the son of a Superior Court justice, who had served in both houses of the legislature; Chambers Russell, a scion of a leading Charlestown family, who also had served in both houses of the legislature; Foster Hutchinson, the brother of Thomas Hutchinson; Nathaniel Ropes, who had served in both houses of the legislature; and William Brown, a member of a prominent Salem family, who had legal training but no practice and who had served in the House of Representatives and commanded the Essex County militia. The only lawyers on the court were William Cushing, the son of one justice and grandson of another, and Edmund Trowbridge, who had risen from humble origins to become the most respected member of the bar in prerevolutionary Massachusetts.[177] Lower court judges had similar backgrounds.[178]

Men who had obtained power in part because they possessed the trust and confidence of their fellow subjects would not lightly undermine their power base by violating that trust. Although they were appointed by the crown, judges usually sought to retain the confidence and respect of their townsmen and hence would be unlikely to reject legal traditions, such as those concerning the power of juries, that were

widely esteemed in their community. The pull of the community can
best be seen perhaps in the fact that when the seven members of the
Superior Court who were living in 1776 were confronted with a choice
of loyalty to the crown or loyalty to their community, nearly one-half
chose their community; only four went to England, two of whom were
Governor Hutchinson and his brother Foster, while three remained in
Massachusetts and retained the respect and patronage of their country-
men.

Even if judges had been inclined to ignore precedent and to overrule
jury decisions on questions of law, it is doubtful whether they could
have enforced their judgments. The crucial fact about government in
prerevolutionary Massachusetts was that subordinate officials like
sheriffs, deputy sheriffs, and constables—the men with legal responsibility for enforcing judgments—could do so only when local communities
were willing to permit judgments to be enforced. The difficulty was not
merely that subordinate officials were liable to suits for damages, for
that liability could have been judicially limited. A greater difficulty lay
in the Anglo-American tradition of government—a tradition with roots
in the Middle Ages and still very much alive in the eighteenth-century
English world. In that tradition, government did not have vast bureau-
cratic armies of officials to enforce its laws, but instead relied on its
subjects to aid the few officials who did exist in their task of law
enforcement.[179]

The ultimate difficulty, as will appear, was that these officials simply
lacked effective power to coerce men to obey the law. Many incidents
attest to the impotence of officialdom. In 1747, for example, when a
naval officer sent an impressment party ashore at Boston to seize men
for the royal navy—a most unpopular act in Massachusetts—the local
populace assembled a mob that took control of the town until the men
who had been impressed were released.[180] A royal customs official
encountered similar difficulties some two decades later in Taunton,
near the Rhode Island border, when he attempted to seize a vessel
engaged in smuggling. Before he could physically bring the vessel to the
nearest vice-admiralty court for condemnation, a mob took control of
the ship and carried away its illicit cargo, which apparently was
returned to its original owner. When the customs collector returned to
search for the cargo several days later with a party of some seventy
royal marines and sailors, he was met by the local sheriff, who
thereupon served a warrant for the collector's arrest to answer to a
3,000-pound action for trespass for seizing the vessel. Aware that his
"handfull of men . . . would be nothing against a whole Country," the
collector was forced to submit.[181]

Provincial officials had no more actual coercive power than royal
ones. When, for example, the sheriff of Suffolk County in 1765

arrested a known leader of the Stamp Act riots, he was threatened by
the townspeople that if the leader were not released a new mob would
attack the customs house and no one in town would defend it; the
sheriff complied with the town's demand.[182] Likewise, when a
parson who led a dissenting religious sect in an inland community was
threatened with coercion by a committee of the General Court, a body
far more powerful than any individual sheriff, deputy sheriff, or
constable, he responded:

> Let them come into my field, I will breake theare Heads; when it
> was answered to Him that the General Cort's Committey might
> Command Assistance, and he would not be abel to do it, and His
> reply was this: I do not fear it, I can have anofe to assist me in
> that afare; Let them Come in to my field if they Dare, I will split
> theaire braines out.[183]

The parson's resolve fortunately was never tested, as all parties to the
dispute preferred a compromise to mindless violence, which would have
given victory to no one.

The ultimate reason, then, that judges and indeed officialdom as a
whole accepted the restraints on their powers was that violence in
eighteenth-century Massachusetts simply could not bring victory over
recalcitrant individuals who had supporters in their town. The basic
problem was that if an official failed by himself to coerce a recalcitrant
person he could not call for the aid of a substantial body of force other
than his fellow townsmen, organized as the militia; if the townsmen
were on the side of the recalcitrant person, they would not, of course,
aid the official. Until the late 1760s officials did not have large numbers
of professional armed forces to whom they could turn for help, and
even thereafter the British army proved to be a rather ineffective law
enforcement agency, as its one foray into the hinterland on April 19,
1775, attests. In sum, the only way for officials to ensure enforcement
of the law was to obtain community support for the law, and the best
way to obtain that support was to permit local communities to
determine the substance of the law through legal institutions such as
the jury.

3. The Law of a "Civil and Christian State"

Having observed that the legal system of prerevolutionary Massachusetts delegated effective law-making power to local communities, we must inquire into how the communities used that power. What was the state of the substantive law that governed daily life? What values did that law protect, and what groups, if any, did it favor?

Of course, the very fact that every local community had nearly plenary power to formulate its own rules of living meant that the province lacked a substantive law in the sense of a body of rules formulated and enforced by a sovereign authority as a means to the attainment of forward-looking policy goals. Nonetheless, courts and juries did decide cases. Lawyers, moreover, perceived that a consistent body of legal principles governed those decisions, and, as we have seen, juries probably did follow the principles most of the time, even though they always had the power to reject them. Thus, although the courts ordinarily did not consciously legislate rules of law to promote specific policy goals or to benefit identifiable interest groups, juries were constantly deciding cases and thereby giving effect to inarticulate community values. To the extent that jury verdicts followed a consistent pattern, they benefited some sorts of men more than others.

One set of values enforced in prerevolutionary communities was ultimately of a religious and moral nature. The most cursory survey of the available source material indicates that the law of the 1760s as it was enforced by juries required of men an uncompromising adherence to truth and an austere mode of life that left no room for sensuous pleasure. The legal system looked askance at those who sought gratification in sexual activity, who thrilled at "Singing Fidling & Dauncing,"[1] or who found relaxation in a leisurely Sabbath stroll. It also displayed an anxious concern that excessive consumption of liquor would lead to "debauchery"[2] and a reproachful dislike of those who "Lived in more of Splendor"[3] than their place in life justified. It showed equal scorn for men who through want of probity or common honesty misled their peers. In sum, the communities of Massachusetts aspired to be "Civil and Christian State[s]" and not "a Savage & Barba[ric] People, Lead by their Lusts, [and] Gove[rned] by their Passions. . . ."[4]

The source of most of these stringent standards lay in the Puritan beginnings of New England.[5] Although Puritanism had lost much of its forcefulness by the 1760s, juries of the period, perhaps only as a matter of reflex, continued to give effect to puritanical traditions.

The continuing vitality of lingering puritanical standards is seen most clearly in the law of crime. Like the criminal law of nearly every society, that of colonial Massachusetts sought to give protection against forcible seizure of goods and violence to the person. Out of a total of 2,784 criminal prosecutions between 1760 and 1774,[6] 355 prosecutions—some 13 percent of the total—were for offenses against property, including such crimes as robbery, burglary, breaking and entering, larceny, receiving stolen goods,[7] and counterfeiting. Even more numerous were prosecutions for crimes of violence, in which such offenses as homicide, assault, trespass, and disturbing the peace are included. Crimes of violence accounted for 15 percent of all prosecutions—419 in all. People could also obtain protection against threats of violence in quasi-criminal proceedings, in which peace bonds were required of defendants against whom petitioners "on Oath swore that . . . [they were] in Danger of . . . Life & Limbs"[8] or some other great bodily harm.[9]

Nonetheless, the criminal law was concerned primarily with protecting community religious and moral values. As in earlier Puritan Massachusetts, the primary objective of criminal law in the prerevolutionary period was to give legal effect to the community's sense of sin and to punish those who breached the community's taboos. The majority of all criminal prosecutions fell within Blackstone's category of "Offenses against God and Religion."[10] Of the 2,784 prosecutions in the Superior and General Sessions courts between 1760 and 1774,[11] 1,074 or 38 percent of all prosecutions, were for sexual crimes, including adultery,[12] cohabitation,[13] indecent exposure,[14] lewdness,[15] and prostitution.[16] The great bulk of sexual offenses—over 95 percent of them—were for fornication.[17] With one exception, when a black man was brought into court on suspicion of having committed fornication with a white woman,[18] only mothers of illegitimate children were brought into court; one might accordingly think that fornication was punished less because it offended God than because it burdened towns with the support of those children.[19] The many paternity suits brought as an incident of fornication prosecutions were indeed largely concerned with protecting

towns, as is indicated by the requirement that the father of an
illegitimate child give a bond to save harmless the town in which the
child was born[20] and by the rule that a paternity suit would be
dismissed if the father had already given security to the town[21] or
had assumed the duty of supporting the child by marrying its
mother.[22] But though concern for the economic security of the
towns cannot be denied, the fact is that prosecutions were brought
against mothers even when they had married their partners and when
no economic interests were therefore at stake;[23] moreover, the same
penalties were imposed in those prosecutions as in cases where economic interests may have played a part.[24] That fornication when
committed by a woman who did not marry happened to burden her
town does not detract from the fact that fornication remained an
offense against God for which she, like the woman who did later marry,
deserved punishment.

Also within the category of offenses against God and religion were
prosecutions for violation of the Sabbath, such as missing church and
traveling or working on Sunday,[25] for blasphemy,[26] and for
profanity.[27] Most profanity prosecutions occurred before individual
justices of the peace;[28] other religious offenses, however, were tried
at General Sessions. In all, some 359 religious offenses were tried in the
Superior and General Sessions courts—some 13 percent of all cases tried
there—which together with the prosecutions for sexual offenses totaled
1,433 cases, or 51 percent of all prosecutions.

There remain 577 prosecutions brought for a wide variety of other
offenses. Among the most common were prosecutions for killing the
king's deer, for violation of the liquor licensing laws, for failure on the
part of a town to repair roads or bridges or to maintain schools, and for
various sorts of frauds and market violations, such as peddling,[29]
selling deleterious foods,[30] using false weights,[31] and pursuing a
trade without approval by the town selectmen.[32] Also prosecuted
were such crimes as drunkenness,[33] keeping "a Disorderly House"
and "Entertaining youth both males and females to Hold frolicks in his
House,"[34] "Permit[ting] Singing Fidling & Dauncing" in a tavern,[35] opening a school without the approval of the local clergyman,[36] "equivocating in his Evidence" in a criminal case,[37] and
refusing without good cause to serve as a town official when
elected.[38] Most interesting of all are the various prosecutions for
verbal crimes. Women, for example, were prosecuted as common
scolds;[39] people could be prosecuted for contempt for sending an
insulting letter to a court,[40] for calling grand jurors "a pack of stupid
fools . . . [who] know Nothing about their business,"[41] or for saying
of a justice of the peace that he was "no more fit for a Justice than the
Devil . . . [and was] a Justice of a Tird"—expressions that the justice
thought "to be Violations of those Rules of Decency and good Manners

that every one ought to observe towards each and every of his Majesty's Justices of the peace . . . [and which] tend[ed] to bring the said Office and Authority in general into Contempt. . . ."[42] Finally, although there were no prosecutions for seditious libel in the fifteen years before the Revolution, there were a number for lesser forms of libel—for saying of a preacher that he "preach[ed] false doctrine"[43] or of a fellow subject that he was "a Devillish Lyar,"[44] "a Drunken Rascal,"[45] or "a damn'd theifish bitch by God. . . ."[46] Such defamation was an essentially different sort of crime from seditious libel, for a conviction could be had only upon proof that the defendant had acted with a malicious intent to deceive[47] and that his words were in fact false.[48] The essence of the crime was that the defendant had spread a falsehood; indeed, in some cases the crime for which the defendant was prosecuted was called not defamation or libel but "falsely and maliciously . . . spreading a Lye. . . ."[49]

The nature of many of these miscellaneous offenses suggests that the law's concern with preventing sin did not end with the suppression of fornication and the punishment of breaches of the Sabbath. The law was also concerned with fraud, with general indecency and immorality, and with lying—all of which were matters with religious connotations. In fact, all crime was looked upon as synonymous with sin. Thus grand jurors were urged by a judge to present wrongdoers so "that they may Receive the Just Demerit of their Crimes [and so that] all vice prophaness & Imorality may be Suppressed & man-kind Reformed and Brought to act with a Due Regard to God. . . ."[50] Several years later the same judge, disturbed that despite efforts made by the government to create "a Civil and Christian State," the people "remain[ed] a Savage & Barba[ric] People, Lead by their Lusts, Gove[rned] by their Passions . . . ," charged another grand jury to make "Inquiry into all Capital Offenses . . . , More Especially as to ye Sin of Murder."[51] Even theft could be looked on not merely as an offense against property but, like fornication and murder, as a sin against God, which government was obliged to suppress; one lawyer, for instance, spoke of clients who had been indicted for "the ignominious narrow-Soul'd Crime of Sheep-Stealing. . . ."[52]

Related to men's view of crime was their view of the criminal. The typical criminal was not, as he is today, an outcast from society, but only an ordinary member who had sinned. Like sin, crime could strike in any man's family or among any man's neighbors. As Sir Michael Foster, with whose work Massachusetts lawyers of 1760 were especially familiar, observed:

For no Rank, no Elevation in Life, and let me add, no Conduct how circumspect soever, ought to tempt a reasonable Man to conclude that these Inquiries [into criminal law] do not, nor possibly can, concern Him. A Moment's cool Reflection on the utter Instability of Human Affairs, and the numberless unforeseen Events which a Day may bring forth, will be sufficient to guard any Man conscious of his own Infirmities against a Delusion of this Kind.[53]

Blackstone concurred,[54] and his contemporaries in Massachusetts, aware of no contrary authority and constantly reminded by their clergymen of the omnipresence of sin,[55] probably would have too.

The court records of the 1760s and 1770s indicate that all elements of society, from farmers and laborers to gentlemen, committed crimes.[56] Moreover, a convicted criminal was not placed in a prison and segregated from the rest of society; between 1760 and 1774 there were few instances of a person being imprisoned for more than one year.[57] The usual penalties—which did not sever a criminal's ties with society—were fines and mild corporal punishments that left no permanent mark. Nor did the only punishment that was commonly of a long duration—the sale into servitude of a convicted thief unable to pay treble damages—result in the thief's segregation from society; rather, its probable effect was to integrate him more fully into society by reorienting him toward normal social contacts.

In short, the criminal law was not used to segregate and punish a distinct, identifiable, and downtrodden criminal class. On the contrary, the criminal law served the function of enforcing puritanical religious and moral standards that continued to linger in the province as a whole and of reintegrating those who had violated the standards into the existing community structure.

Much of the law of civil wrongs[58] was likewise concerned with religious and moral values. For example, in civil defamation, as in criminal defamation, the essential element of the offense was that the defendant had spoken "false scandalous & lying words,"[59] for which a plaintiff could bring suit even in the absence of actual damages, at least in cases involving slander per se.[60] Usually the "lying words" for which suits were brought were lewd, ludicrous, or both; the triviality of defamation suits is one of the best indicators of the litigious nature of the period. Ministers, for example, brought suits when accused of being "as drunk as the Devil last night"[61] or of being "a liar and a Robber . . . [who] preach[ed] no Gospel Truths."[62] Similarly, a man who "g[o]t his living by Trade" could bring an action of "slander of Trade,"[63] as could a manufacturer of a boat when a defendant said that the boat "was only fit to drown people."[64] Still another man sued a woman who had accusèd him of offering her money in one hand while he "pulled out his Secret parts & held them naked in his other hand. . . ."[65]

Two other causes of action whose essence was recovery of damages for a lie were malicious prosecution and fraud. The central thrust of the action for malicious prosecution, like the action for defamation, was that the defendant had *"falsely and maliciously laid a charge"* to the plaintiff.[66] In malicious prosecution, however, a plaintiff could recover a judgment not only against a person who spoke injurious words and commenced a prosecution but against the officer who arrested him as well.[67] Likewise, in suits for fraud the thrust of the plaintiff's claim was that the defendant had knowingly made a false affirmation at the time of a sale.[68] Fraud suits were brought for such matters as selling land[69] and slaves[70] to which the seller knew he lacked title, knowingly selling adulterated goods,[71] and making false affirmations during a sale as to the character of a slave.[72]

The final area of law in which religious and moral values appear to have had substantial impact was the law of debtor and creditor. One example of that impact was the law's prohibition of usury,[73] which, as one debtor argued, had originated in the rule of "the law of Moses [that] Interest for money lent to any of the Nation of the Jews is not allowable."[74] Religious and moral values were even more important in another way. The central fact about debtor-creditor law—a fact which, as we shall see, those values will help explain—is that creditors had extensive common law remedies to collect debts and that whenever common law remedies were insufficient or in doubt statutes were enacted to provide even better remedies.

A judgment creditor, for example, could at his option levy execution on an unpaid judgment in one of three ways. First, by virtue of a 1713 statute that had reversed the seventeenth-century Massachusetts rule, a judgment creditor could arrest the body of his debtor and keep him imprisoned until the judgment was paid—a useful technique for forcing a debtor to discharge assets that he had secreted away or for securing payment of a judgment by a sympathetic friend of an impecunious debtor. Second, a creditor could have his debtor's goods and lands appraised at their fair and just value and could then seize property so appraised to the amount of his debt. This option was useful if a creditor wished to obtain specific property in satisfaction of his debt; if, on the other hand, his object was to obtain full payment, he would not want to take property at an appraised value which, especially in periods of economic recession, would likely be higher than its market value.[75] For this reason the creditor was given a third option—to have his debtor's goods and chattels sold at auction and to obtain his satisfaction out of the proceeds of the sale.[76] When in 1768 a dissenting opinion by Judge Trowbridge raised doubt as to the availability of this third option,[77] its availability was made clear by legislation.[78]

A creditor had to exercise his option and attempt to levy execution

within a year and a day of the rendition of judgment[79] but had an
indefinite time in which to complete collection. After the end of the
year he could bring a writ of scire facias to revive the judgment;[80]
writs of debt and scire facias were also available to make a judgment
effective and thus make execution possible in a county other than the
one in which judgment had originally been rendered.[81] In short, a
creditor could proceed against his debtor's person or property, which
he could either seize or sell, in any Massachusetts county for an
indefinite period after the rendition of judgment.[82] The only
limitation was that a creditor could not seize necessary wearing apparel
or household goods.[83] Even after a debtor had died, his goods and,
by still another statute that had reversed the common law rule, his land
would be distributed through the court of probate and hence would be
subject to claims of his creditors before they passed to his heirs.[84]

A mortgagee similarly possessed broad rights against his mortgagor.
Not only did he have the right to foreclose on the mortgaged premises,
but in addition he could bring suit on the underlying debt even after
foreclosure and obtain execution to the extent necessary to make him
whole.[85] This was true even if the mortgaged premises at the time of
foreclosure had been of sufficient value to make the mortgagee whole
and had declined in value while the mortgagee was in possession, at
least as long as the decline was due to circumstances beyond his
control.[86] The doctrine that a mortgagee had to elect to proceed
either against his mortgagor personally or against the mortgaged
premises was not followed in prerevolutionary Massachusetts; he could
proceed against both.

Creditors had broad remedies not only against their immediate
debtors but against others as well. A judgment creditor could, for
example, levy execution on property of his debtor's wife, even if she
had acquired the property before her marriage;[87] against the executor of his debtor to the extent of estate goods in the executor's
hands,[88] even if the estate was insolvent;[89] against a bail who
failed to produce the debtor in satisfaction of the judgment, at least to
the amount of the bail bond;[90] against the comaker of a promissory
note who was a mere surety, even though no proof was offered of the
creditor's inability to recover from the principal;[91] and against
anyone who assisted a debtor in avoiding imprisonment for debt.[92]
Finally, by virtue of a statute enacted in 1759,[93] creditors obtained
a remedy not available through common law against goods and chattels
that a debtor who had absconded or was otherwise absent from
Massachusetts had left in the hands of a third person, who was deemed
a trustee. Recovery against the trustee was, of course, limited to the
amount of the goods that the absconding debtor had left in his

hands;[94] moreover, the trustee could interpose whatever defenses the debtor himself may have possessed.[95]

Even the law of negotiable bills and notes was in large part structured to protect those who had advanced credit and received negotiable paper in return. The most important fact in furthering their security was that the concept of negotiability extended to transactions involving parties other than merchants. Thus the courts rejected one plea that a suit on a bill of exchange should be dismissed since the plaintiff had "not declared and averred that the . . . [drawer of the bill] was a Man useing Merchandize and Commerce."[96] Although it apparently was still necessary in the 1760s to allege fictionally that such bills were drawn "according to the custom of merchants,"[97] all agreed that an instrument executed by a nonmerchant was negotiable if it contained words of negotiability customarily used by merchants, such as "or order," in an appropriate place.[98]

Extension of the concept of negotiability to transactions involving nonmerchants gave creditors remedies they would not otherwise have had. Endorsees, for example, were allowed to sue distant endorsers on the warranties implied in their endorsements despite the absence of privity of contract,[99] and endorsees were similarly permitted to sue makers of negotiable notes and acceptors of bills of exchange on their obligation to pay not only in the absence of privity[100] but even in the absence of notice of the endorsement.[101] The liability of endorsers, makers, and acceptors in these cases meant that the holder of a negotiable instrument could look to several parties for payment. The holder of a nonnegotiable note, on the other hand, could sue only the maker in the absence of formal contracts making other parties liable as sureties. The concept of negotiability also cut off potential defenses of parties liable on an instrument, thereby giving further security to the credit holder. A holder, for example, did not have to plead and prove the consideration for which the instrument was given;[102] a promissory note was enforceable, even as between its two original parties, although no consideration had been given in return for it.[103] The only defense that remained available to a maker of an instrument was payment: the Superior Court twice ruled that an endorsee of a note who had taken after payment to the endorser but without notice thereof could not obtain a second recovery against the maker, apparently on the theory that an endorser could not pass to his endorsee greater property in a note than he himself had had at the time of the endorsement.[104]

Debtors in general were almost powerless. Although the General Court passed two insolvency acts under which debtors who delivered up all their goods could have obtained discharges,[105] both were disallowed by the Privy Council,[106] and the benefits of the acts were extended only to debtors who had taken advantage of them during the period between their enactment and their disallowance.[107] In the absence of effective insolvency legislation, all a debtor could do was to hinder or delay his creditor by making a fraudulent conveyance—a technique that offered little hope of long-term success[108]—or by appealing from a judgment of a Common Pleas court—a technique that was often used to gain several months' respite until the judgment was affirmed by the Superior Court.[109] The only permanent impediment that a creditor might face in executing his judgment on a given piece of property would be competition from another creditor seeking recovery out of the same property;[110] indeed, the General Court had adopted the two disallowed insolvency statutes largely because "great inequality and injustice ha[d] been occasioned to . . . creditors, and law-suits ha[d] been greatly multiplied" as a result of such competition.[111] But that competition, no matter how harmful to creditors, did little to mitigate the rigors of the law on debtors.

The troublesome question is why Massachusetts law gave such extensive remedies to creditors. The answer is not simply that Massachusetts followed the common law, for, as we have seen, the General Court on a number of occasions improved on the common law position of creditors. Nor does the answer seem to be that creditors constituted a powerful, identifiable interest group that controlled the legislature and the judiciary and hence dominated the legal system. If creditors had controlled the General Court, it seems unlikely that insolvency legislation advocated by creditors to provide for more equitable distribution of debtors' property would also have provided discharges for debtors; on the contrary, the provision for discharges looks like a concession to debtors for the purpose of procuring their support. Moreover, the allocation of the vast majority of the seats in the General Court to small agrarian towns,[112] nearly all of whose inhabitants were debtors, renders inconceivable the hypothesis that creditors controlled the Court. If any interest group controlled the legislature, it must have been debtors,[113] although the substance of debtor-creditor law renders that hypothesis quite inconceivable as well.

Indeed, any hypothesis suggesting that debtor-creditor law was a political issue in prerevolutionary Massachusetts or that its substance was a product of the power of one interest group will likely prove fruitless. Although individual debtors who were subjected to the rigors of the law must sometimes have felt oppressed, it does not appear that debtors organized themselves politically, as they would after the Revolution, to seek redress or to obtain modification of the law. Moreover, even if debtors had been organized, it is doubtful that they could have controlled the substance of the law. We must recall that the legal system of the province was structured so as to delegate effective law-making power to local communities, thereby requiring all law to have widespread support among all interest groups if it was to be consistently applied. The structure of power in this period accordingly points to shared values and ideas as the basis of the law.

There is some evidence that debtor-creditor law was, at least in part, a product of a shared moral or religious belief that debtors ought to make full repayment of all they had received. In the view of one student of law near the time of the Revolution, debtor-creditor law simply would not hold a man "excusable[,] if by Mismanagement he ... [was] unable to discharge his debts. ..."[114] It may indeed have been thought immoral to excuse such men, for, as Cotton Mather had explained earlier in the century, the "grand Cause of Peoples running into *Debt*" was that they could "not bear the Humiliations of a *Low and a Mean Condition* in the World," especially when they had "sometimes Lived in more of Splendor. ..."[115] Much credit in eighteenth-century Massachusetts must, in fact, have been extended to facilitate the purchase of consumer luxuries; Mather's statement suggests that men who purchased and then proved unable to pay for those luxuries were deemed unworthy of the law's aid.

Such an ethical explanation of debtor-creditor law gains plausibility from its consistency with the broader puritanical antipathy toward enjoyment of earthly pleasures which still permeated eighteenth-century criminal law. Some readers will nonetheless have difficulty with the explanation. The source of their difficulty lies in the fact that money lending in prerevolutionary Massachusetts must have facilitated not only consumer purchasing but also the aggregation of capital for purposes of economic growth. A body of debtor-creditor law that spurned purchasers of consumer luxuries hence must also have shown no mercy toward risk-bearing entrepreneurs who found themselves unable to pay debts as a result of unexpected fluctuations in the marketplace. Such harshness to entrepreneurs may seem incongruous, as it would indeed be in twentieth-century America. But in eighteenth-century Massachusetts, as the next chapter will urge, it was not.

4. Rules of Unity and Stability

In analyzing the bodies of law that effectively empowered the communities of Massachusetts to manage their own affairs and to compel their inhabitants to abide by communal ethical values, the rules determining the distribution of wealth among individuals—a matter of fundamental importance in any legal system—have scarcely been touched on. The chief impact of those rules in the prerevolutionary period, when ethical unity and social and economic stability were gradually declining, was to safeguard the unity and stability that remained. To the extent that the legal system was capable of affecting social reality, it insured that the distribution of wealth did not change substantially or rapidly over time and that men had well-defined places in their community and well-defined relationships with the community's other men. Incentives for individuals to compete with each other for control of economic resources were eliminated, and one cause of social instability was thereby reduced.

Although a stable distribution of wealth and status can exist in the absence of hierarchy, the social order in prerevolutionary Massachusetts was hierarchical.[1] By the eighteenth century Western society had been structured hierarchically for centuries, and there was no reason to think that its structure would change. Colonials simply assumed that some men were subordinate to others, that "some degree of respect" was "always due from inferiors to superiors,"[2] and that "euerye man subordinate . . . [was] ready to yield a willing submission wthowt contempt or repyning" to his social superiors.[3] Some feared that if the hierarchical order were upset, "the bands of society would be dissolved, the harmony of the world confounded, and the order of nature subverted."[4]

Perhaps the legal system continued to safeguard social stability because stability had been highly valued in the seventeenth-century Puritan Bay Colony, when many of the legal rules to be discussed in this chapter were formulated. However, stability remained important to prerevolutionary communities for other reasons as well. First, the political theory of the age assumed that there was a close link between liberty and economic stability. The assumption rested on a Harringtonian belief—a belief permeating Anglo-American thought in the eighteenth century—that political power ultimately rested on ownership of land. As one contemporary English writer, portions of whose work were reprinted in Massachusetts, argued, government must "depend . . . upon its natural bottom of property."[5] Only when a man's private property was firmly protected by laws did he have the independence requisite for participation in the politics of a free state. Another English writer developed this theme when he urged voters to elect men with landed estates to parliament, since only "Gentlemen of . . . *Estates* . . . [would be] secure . . . against [the] Temptation" of accepting bribes in return for their support of ministerial policies.[6] Similarly, men could be trusted as voters only if they possessed secure property in sufficient amounts to counteract any temptation to sell their votes at the polls. In short, a central assumption of eighteenth-century political theory was that unless the distribution of wealth was safeguarded from fluctuation and manipulation the crown and its rich sycophants would use their wealth to bribe others to give them power and would then manipulate both government and law to further increase their wealth and power. By stabilizing the distribution of wealth, the law would deprive the avaricious of the opportunity to use power to obtain more wealth and thus deprive evil men of the incentive to obtain power. If property rights were stable, it was thought, liberty would be safe.

The rules of law promoting economic and hence social stability also served as a precondition, of which contemporaries seemed unaware, to community morality and religiosity. It seems likely that a legal system that encourages people to increase their stock of material possessions will create a speculative and competitive atmosphere in which economic success becomes more vital to the competitors than the pursuit of religious and moral values. Since prerevolutionary communities did not have such a legal system but instead had one that impeded opportunities for economic change and discouraged competition among men who tried to take advantage of the opportunities that nonetheless arose, those communities were probably better able to pursue noneconomic ends.

The pursuit of those ends and the hindering of competition, finally, helped to facilitate the governance of the province. Since prerevolutionary Massachusetts could not be governed by means of coercion, rules could be made into effective law only when they were a product of compromise among all groups in a community. Again, it seems likely that men who are competing to control valuable economic resources or attempting to profit at each other's expense in exchange transactions will develop personal enmities that will make compromise and accommodation more difficult. In Massachusetts, however, men who were striving together toward ethical ends were probably able to compromise political disputes and thereby participate in government by consensus of the prerevolutionary province.

The legal system helped to maintain the social order and promote community unity by several means. One was to guarantee a minimal subsistence income to all. In part, that guarantee was given substance by distributional rules such as the seventeenth-century legislation that had abolished inheritance by primogeniture in Massachusetts in cases of land held in fee simple,[7] although not in cases of land held in fee tail.[8] Thereafter, in the absence of a will all children, brothers and sisters alike, shared equally in their father's fee simple inheritance, subject only to the eldest brother's receiving a double portion. Since a parent by will could still give all his land to one child, the consequences of partible inheritance cannot be known with certainty in the absence of a detailed study of colonial wills. Nonetheless we can speculate that partibility resulted in a wider distribution of land—the chief source of wealth—and hence greater economic security among younger children. Similarly, the province's adherence to the common law rules of dower[9] must have increased the economic security of widows, many of whom might otherwise have experienced difficulty in supporting themselves. The law even gave servants and slaves, the lowest people in the social hierarchy, some certainty of future income by virtue of their right to seek judicial relief if their master "abuse[d]" them[10] or failed to provide them with "Suitable Meat Drink Lodging and Apparrel."[11]

These distributional rules were bolstered by the poor law.[12] The Massachusetts poor law in large measure paralleled the English law, which was enacted when the Elizabethan poor turned to beggary and thievery as a means of support.[13] The various Massachusetts rules guaranteeing to men who might otherwise have been poor either income or resources capable of generating income must have prevented similar social chaos, although there is no evidence that the prerevolutionary generation was conscious of the function that such guarantees served.

Far more important to the maintenance of the social and economic order were the rules concerning the ownership and use of land and other forms of wealth. At the root of the law of land was the common law concept of seisin. The significance of seisin was that it gave legal protection to existing patterns of resource allocation. The basic rule of land law was that "Prior Poss[essio]n" would be deemed "a good Title ag[ains]t him who hath no Title."[14] By so protecting a person who either was in actual possession of land or was otherwise taking profits from it, the law promoted stability by giving men the assurance that they could continue to use in the future the land they were using in the present. Stability was such an important value that the courts would sometimes enforce a title resting solely on possession even as against the holder of a superior title by grant. For example, the courts protected the rights of occupants who were in open possession of land and claimed it as their own against subsequent bona fide purchasers.[15] Such protection was granted to the extent of the occupant's claim[16] whether he was in actual or merely constructive possession[17] of the entire lot claimed, but not if the occupant had not held the land under claim of right[18] or if his possession had been merely transitory.[19]

Seisin also protected other rights analogous or incidental to rights in land. Protection was extended, for example, to church pews—considered a form of realty.[20] A landowner was also permitted to maintain suit against a neighbor who interfered with his accustomed use and enjoyment of his land.[21] Among the customary rights protected were easements by prescription—usually easements of way appurtenant to land,[22] but also on one occasion an easement to make customary use of servient land so as to enhance enjoyment of the dominant land.[23] Customary rights to take timber from common lands were also protected,[24] as was the ancient "usage and custom immemorial" of the shoresmen of Plymouth to market all fish brought into Plymouth harbor on vessels in which they had a joint interest.[25] Of the various customary rights to which legal protection was extended, rights in water were the most important and economically valuable, however. Here too prior possession was the key fact. In the many cases involving disputes between owners of milldams on the same stream who were competing with each other for limited supplies of water to run their mills, the basic rule was the rule of prior appropriation or some variant thereof: the first person to erect a dam and a mill on a stream could make whatever use he wished of the water and bring suit against anyone who interfered with that use.[26] Subsequent users were limited by the patterns of resource allocation that were already in existence at the time they began their use.[27]

Suits for flooding as a result of the construction of milldams and millponds also appear to have resulted in protection of prior use and occupation. In every case brought for flooding during the prerevolutionary period, plaintiffs alleged title in themselves[28] or their predecessors in interest[29] prior to the building of the dam that caused the flooding. Moreover, a key element in proving damages was to establish that the plaintiff had been taking profits from the land prior to the flooding;[30] if the plaintiff or someone claiming under

him had not previously been on the land, he could not have been taking
profits, no damage could have resulted from the flooding, and hence
there could be no lawsuit.[31]

Protection of prior or customary rights did not occur only in cases
involving use of land. Similar protection against newcomers was
accorded to holders of licenses to engage in quasi-public occupations,
such as running a ferry, thereby assuring, to the extent the law could,
the stability of market as well as of land allocations. In one case, for
instance, the court recognized that since the operator of a ferry was by
ancient grant "the owner of all ferry rights" in the vicinity of his ferry,
a license could not be granted to a prospective competitor unless there
was enough business for two ferries;[32] likewise a licensee "seized
in . . . [his] demesne as of fee" of a ferry was permitted to maintain an
action against a competitor for damages for loss of business and
consequent injury to his property.[33] Ferries also looked like a form
of property in that a son had a presumptive right to succeed to his
father's license upon his father's death or retirement.[34]

Liquor licenses may similarly have been regarded as a form of
property or quasi property. Sons, for instance, regularly succeeded to
their fathers' licenses upon the fathers' deaths,[35] and licenses were
bought and sold along with the inns and shops to which they were
appurtenant.[36] Concepts of descent and conveyance of property
thus appear to have been recognized. That a liquor license was regarded
as something akin to property is also suggested by the fact that people
desiring licenses could bring petitions in General Sessions to compel
their issuance;[37] as long as the petitioner was a man of "sober life
and conversation" and there was a need for an inn or retail shop where
he proposed to maintain one,[38] his petition for a license had to be
granted. The emphasis in the ferry and the liquor license cases differed,
however. While rights akin to property rights were protected in both,
protection was granted in the liquor cases only against the public and
not against a competitor entering business after the initial license in the
neighborhood had been granted. Indeed, a newcomer seems to have had
as much right to his license as an existing retailer or innkeeper. The
ferryman, on the other hand, was protected against both the public and
his competitors.

The law also regarded many laborers as a form of property. Many
cases confirm the widely known fact that slaves were regarded as
"Property."[39] In one case a plaintiff sued in covenant for breach of a
warranty that no one but the seller had any property interest in the
slave;[40] in another case the court held that title to the child of a
female slave born while the slave was leased by her owner to another
rested with the lessor rather than with the lessee;[41] while in a third
slaves were held to be heritable.[42] Indeed, slaves could not even

lawfully marry.[43] What is less well known is that indentured servants, apprentices, and even children were similarly regarded: one jury verdict, for instance, gave to the "owner" and "proprietor" of an indentured servant "recompence" for the servant's enlistment in the royal forces during the French and Indian War.[44] The underlying concept in the case appears to have been one of just compensation for private property taken for public use, for, as one commentator noted, servants "were a part of property as firmly secured by the laws of . . . [the] country as any you enjoy, as much your right as the ox you have paid for or the inheritance you have purchased."[45] That apprentices were similarly thought of is indicated by the fact that the deed or indenture creating an apprentice was, unlike a modern labor contract, incapable of subsequent mutual modification by the original parties to it,[46] for the indenture was not a contract but rather a conveyance made by parents or guardians of their property in a child.[47] Perhaps the strongest indication of the fact that children, apprentices, and indentured servants were all, like slaves, regarded as a form of property comes from the fact that their owners could sue for their wages if they hired them out and maintain trespass and trover for loss of their labor if someone took and carried them away[48] or otherwise induced them to leave.[49] The key point about these cases is that the pleadings, issues, and substantive law applied were identical whether the person for whose loss the plaintiff sought recovery was a slave, a child, an indentured servant, or an apprentice; all were equally regarded as a form of property. As property, they were all securely under the legal control of their master, who, during the prescribed term of employment, could prevent them from working for others and could obtain a court order[50] or impose reasonable corporal chastisement to compel them to work for him. The supply of labor, in short, was rendered as stable as the law could make it.

One might think that the rules conferring extensive powers on the first users of economic resources had the effect of creating a society in which those individuals, by virtue of their independence and security, would be able to pursue their own ends, choose their own values, and live in a culture of nonconformists. This seems unlikely, however. Rights in property were not granted for the benefit of the individual; on the contrary, property rights received legal protection only to the extent that a person used his property consistently with the community's interests.

Communities intruded on the property of individuals in many ways. Perhaps the most significant encroachments on landed property had to do with the building of roads—a landowner always held his land subject to the public's right to construct a road across it if public necessity and convenience required.[51] Although the committees of General Sessions that established roads were directed to do so "with ... least Prejudice to Private Property,"[52] many roads did seriously inconvenience property owners,[53] especially by cutting farms in half and thus requiring owners to build fences on both sides of a road to prevent their animals from escaping into the road.[54] One who had title to the land on which a road was built would, of course, receive damages for his resulting costs and inconveniences.[55]

The building of a road, however, was the only restriction on the use of private property that resulted in compensation in the form of damages. Many other restrictions imposed on land for the public benefit were uncompensated. Urban landowners, for instance, were subject to a number of restrictions: in Boston they were required to use their property in accordance with the town's zoning regulations,[56] while in other towns they were required, in order to prevent fires, to have chimneys periodically swept[57] and inspected.[58] Similarly, owners of dams had to maintain sluiceways so that fish could pass upstream[59]—unless the sessions court found that the stream contained so few fish that the sluiceway would be of slight public utility.[60] A similar balancing of private right and public need is apparent in ferry cases, with the courts of sessions regulating both ferry rates[61] and ferry safety[62] and service,[63] even to the extent of requiring a ferryman to be polite to his passengers[64] and to secure the court's permission before he could discontinue his service for lack of passengers.[65] And, as already noted, owners of slaves, servants, and apprentices were required to provide them with "Suitable Meat Drink Lodging and Apparrel"[66] so that they did not become a public charge.[67]

Finally, holders of liquor licenses were required to maintain their establishments so as not to impair public morals. A liquor license would be denied if the public had no need for a new inn or shop and an additional one would lead to "debauchery"[68] or if the petitioner was morally unqualified[69] or not sufficiently known in the locality that was being asked to judge his qualifications.[70] Licensees could expect not to have their licenses renewed if on days of public fast and thanksgiving they served persons other than necessary travelers[71] or if, in violation of the rules of Harvard College, they extended credit to minors who were students at the College.[72]

In short, people could not use their property in a manner that was inconsistent with the community's ethical standards or its economic needs. This suggests strongly that private property served community needs first and individual convenience second, and it thus becomes necessary to understand precisely which community needs the law of property served.

As towns were being settled in the seventeenth century and, in parts of the province, in the eighteenth, the rules insuring stability of resource allocation served one important economic end. One of a new town's most pressing economic needs was a transportation and manufacturing infrastructure—it had to have roads, bridges, and ferries to link it to other towns and to establishments like sawmills and gristmills to turn raw materials into the basic necessities of life. The need, it should be noted, was not for a developed transportation and industrial structure that would provide goods and services most efficiently and cheaply to a community capable of generating a substantial demand for them; it was for an economic infrastructure that because of paucity of demand might be unprofitable during the town's early years. Every town, for example, needed a gristmill because conditions of transportation, even after the first roads had been constructed, usually made it infeasible to transport grain to a neighboring town. Since communities did not want to construct mills as public enterprises, it became necessary to induce private capital to build the mills despite the likelihood that, at least for a time, they would be unprofitable. The primary inducement was the grant of a practical monopoly: by assuring the miller that no one could challenge or interfere with his appropriation of the town's best watersite, the law virtually assured him that in most towns no one could become as effective a competitor without paying him for the privilege of doing so.

By the 1760s, however, the rules permanently allocating control over scarce resources to the first user appear to have impeded economic growth and efficiency in the province as a whole. By that time many towns may well have generated enough business for two mills, and if the law had entitled a new miller to equal use of the best watersite with the old miller many towns may well have had more than one effective miller. The law required, however, that a newcomer negotiate directly with the existing user. Since the existing user often had monopolistic control of a resource that was essential to participation in the market, he would demand a price reflecting his anticipated monopoly profits; since the competitor had no expectation of earning similar profits, he would be unwilling to pay such a high price and hence would not enter the market. As a result, customers were probably paying more in one form or another to have their corn ground by a monopolist than they would have paid in a free market.

But there were probably compensations of a subtle, psychological sort for having one miller in a town—which at this stage of research can only be suggested without being demonstrated. As we have seen, competition often produces tension and animosity among the competitors; absence of competition removes one important source of tension, and it is not improbable that the noncompetitive communities of prerevolutionary Massachusetts were, on balance, less tense and more harmonious than competitive communities would have been. They may also have been more religious. One supposed advantage of competition is that it induces competitors to strive for business efficiency and material gain above all else; some men, at least, when striving single-mindedly for material gain are likely to find their religious endeavors diminished.

The law of property, in sum, reveals much about the traditions of the communities of prerevolutionary Massachusetts. While the law sought to create an infrastructure that would provide for basic economic needs, it was not very concerned with economic efficiency. The ultimate aspirations of the legal system were ethical rather than economic: it encouraged men to live in harmony rather than affluence and to pursue spiritual rather than material ends. While the increasingly materialistic realities of life in America may often have undermined the law's aspirations, property law in the 1760s still promoted ethical living in preference to the unrestrained pursuit of wealth.

The chief effect of the law of contract, like that of the law of property, was to promote social stability and ethical unity. Before it is possible to understand why it had that effect, however, it is essential to understand some of the highly technical rules governing the litigation of matters of contractual exchange.

The common law as it was applied in prerevolutionary Massachusetts did not know of any coherent, substantive law of contract. Instead, litigation concerning contractual exchange could arise under several different writs, each with its own substantive law. The principal writ used to litigate matters of exchange was assumpsit. It came in several varieties. One of them was indebitatus assumpsit, which lay whenever a plaintiff conferred a benefit of fixed value on a defendant or on a third party in the defendant's behalf[73] or when the parties had entered into a relationship giving rise to a duty or obligation on the part of the defendant to pay a fixed sum.[74] Although in order to bring indebitatus assumpsit a plaintiff had to plead that the defendant, being indebted to him, had promised to pay that debt,[75] the allegation of a promise was but a fictional plea designed only to make a suit in assumpsit possible and thereby to give the plaintiff the benefit of the procedural advantages[76] that assumpsit, a variety of the writ of case, had over other writs.[77]

If a plaintiff could not frame his cause of action as one for a fixed or certain amount, he could not recover in indebitatus assumpsit[78] but had to sue in either quantum meruit or quantum velebant. Quantum meruit lay to recover whatever sum a plaintiff reasonably deserved for labor or services rendered to a defendant in the absence of any customary rate of wage or agreement as to compensation.[79] Quantum valebant lay on behalf of sellers seeking to recover the reasonable value of goods sold in the absence of a customary price or an agreement as to price.[80] The important point about indebitatus assumpsit, quantum meruit, and quantum valebant is that recovery was allowed in the absence of any agreement; the defendant was held liable because he had put himself into the position of a recipient of goods or services for which he ought, in good conscience, to pay. As Judge Trowbridge observed in *Palfrey* v. *Palfrey*,[81] the implied contracts on which quantum meruit and quantum valebant lay were formed not by any agreement, but "are such as reason & justice dictate; Therefore if one is under obligation from the ties of natural justice to pay another money and neglects to do it—the law gives the sufferer an action upon the case, in the nature of a bill in equity to recover it; And that mere justice & equity is sufficient foundation for this kind of equitable action." In short, a person who merely entered into the status of recipient of goods or services put himself upon the community's sense of justice as to the price he should pay.

While indebitatus assumpsit, quantum meruit, and quantum valebant rested on concepts not of agreement but of justice and equity, the final form of assumpsit, special assumpsit,[82] did rest on notions of promise and agreement. In pleas of special assumpsit, a plaintiff was required to allege and prove five facts—a promise by the defendant,[83] a promise by the plaintiff or some other consideration for the defendant's promise given in return,[84] that the defendant's performance was due and owing at the time of suit,[85] a request for[86] and willingness to accept[87] that performance, and finally the defendant's breach or nonperformance.[88] The key allegation that gave special assumpsit its unique characteristics was the second—that the defendant's promise had become binding by virtue of the consideration given for it.

As they were used in prerevolutionary Massachusetts, the various writs of assumpsit gave effect to dominant ethical values by impeding transactions of a speculative nature and exchanges in which a person with superior skill or market knowledge through some form of overreaching took more than the value of the goods or services with which he parted. "For men to *Over-reach* others, because they find them *Ignorant*, or scrue grievously upon them, only because they are Poor and Low, and in great *Necessities*" was thought to be "*an Abomination*" scarcely distinguishable from thievery.[89] Speculative contracts, particularly wagers, were also deemed unethical and were treated as illegal, partly because they provided opportunities for some sharp individuals to take "unlawful advantage" of others and partly because it seemed wrong for a man "to gain a living" without producing a tangible good or service in return.[90]

By impeding speculation and overreaching the various writs of assumpsit also helped to preserve the unity and stability of society. A society in which speculative transactions are commonplace is almost invariably an unstable one, as winners gain sudden wealth and losers find themselves in sudden poverty; men's relationships with each other in such a society change so drastically over a short period that no man can be certain of his place. Similarly, a society in which overreaching is commonplace is rarely a close-knit one, for when the victims learn that they have been cheated they are likely to develop animosities that will impair the society's harmony.

The law of the period not only treated as illegal and hence refused to enforce gambling or wagering contracts, the most extreme form of speculative contract; more important, it made it difficult to enforce purely executory contracts—contracts, that is, for some sort of future exchange, in which neither party has begun performance of his part of the bargain. At least in the context of a market in which prices fluctuate and goods can be purchased from alternative sources, executory contracts are not merely a means to insure future availability of goods or services, which will always be available from a number of alternative sources, although perhaps at higher prices; executory contracts are attempts to secure future performance at a price determined in the present. Since they involve a wager by all parties as to the future value of the performances promised by other parties, they often seem speculative, although they may merely be attempts by the parties to insure against extreme fluctuations in the marketplace.

Clearly indebitatus assumpsit, quantum meruit, and quantum valebant could not be used to enforce executory contracts, since those writs required a plaintiff to allege some performance on his part for which he was seeking recovery of a fixed or reasonable price. In theory, however, executory contracts could be enforced in special assumpsit, since "in Case of mutual Promises . . . the Plaintiff . . . [was] not obliged to aver Performance on his Part."[91] But in fact special assumpsit was rarely used to enforce such contracts. An important exception to the rule that a plaintiff in special assumpsit did not have to allege performance occurred when "the Contract be, that one shall do an Act, and for the doing thereof, the other shall pay &c."; then "the Performance of the Act . . . [was] a Condition precedent to the Payment . . . and must be averred in an Action for the money."[92] For instance, before he could maintain assumpsit for his agreed salary, a minister had to plead his own past performance of clerical duties for which he had not been paid,[93] while a seller of goods had to plead his delivery of the goods before he could sue for their price.[94] Conditions precedent could also arise from the express terms of a contract.[95]

Throughout the prerevolutionary period, with two exceptions, plaintiffs suing in special assumpsit always pleaded performance of their promises. Ministers, for example, pleaded their performance of ministerial services,[96] while men who had contracted to do other work or labor pleaded performance of their work.[97] Sellers and lessors of goods pleaded that they had delivered the goods.[98] Conversely, in suits for a seller's failure to deliver or perform, purchasers of goods or services pleaded payment or some other performance on their part.[99] Likewise, in cases involving agreements to settle litigation or to submit disputes to arbitration, plaintiffs always pleaded that they had foreborn prosecution of their suits[100] or had submitted their claims to the arbitrators who had rendered their award,[101] while in suits on promissory notes and bills of exchange plaintiffs pleaded that the instruments on which they were suing had been made in return for "value received."[102] Finally, in a case in which three brothers had agreed to contribute to the support of their impoverished father, the plaintiff alleged performance of his part of the bargain and pleaded that his brothers had not performed theirs.[103]

The two sorts of suits in which plaintiffs did not allege performance on their part and yet were able to obtain legal relief were suits for breach of promise to marry and suits by employers for breach of employees' promises to work. In the former a plaintiff did not allege mere disappointment at not being married. The essence of the cause of action, always brought by a woman, was that the plaintiff had lost other opportunities to marry, either because she had had sexual intercourse with the defendant[104] or because she had turned down another offer of marriage while waiting for the defendant to perform his promise.[105] A plaintiff in a suit for breach of promise to marry, in short, was not alleging breach of a mere executory contract but was in essence claiming that she had suffered detriment from her justifiable reliance on the defendant's promise.

Closest to true executory contracts were the cases in which an employer sued an employee who quit in the middle of his term.[106] The employer alleged no performance on his part; his agreement was to pay wages only at the end of the employee's term. Nor did he allege any specific loss or detriment resulting from reliance on the employee's promise to work—he merely alleged generally that he suffered "great Loss Disappointment and Trouble...."[107] These few cases of executory contracts were, however, unique in that they concerned employer-employee relations, a subject on which the law, in order to render the labor supply secure, granted special privileges to employers.[108]

As a general rule, then, executory contracts were not enforced even in special assumpsit unless the plaintiff pleaded performance of his part of the bargain. The significance of requiring a plaintiff to allege performance of conditions precedent was that this requirement transformed the nature of a promissor's obligation; it meant that he was held liable not because he had agreed to be liable but because he had received a benefit from the promissee for which he ought in conscience to pay. While enforcement of conditions precedent would not have this transforming effect in the nineteenth and twentieth centuries, when courts would decide whether to enforce them by looking to the terms of the parties' agreement, the prerevolutionary courts did not take such an approach. Instead, they determined whether to enforce conditions precedent by looking to the relationship that the parties had assumed; thus, all ministers and sellers of goods had to plead their performance of their part of a bargain before bringing suit. The inflexibility was made necessary by lawyers' reliance on precedent, as reflected in their form books. Theophilus Parsons's book of precedents, for example, contained two forms of action for ministers' suits for salary, in both of which the plaintiff had to plead his performance of past ministerial services; there is no suggestion that this plea was capable of variation.[109] If lawyers adhered to their forms—and there is no reason to think they did not—then the rule concerning the effect of conditions had to be the same in all ministers' suits. Variations to conform to the facts and intent of the parties in each case would be difficult, and usually a promissee in special assumpsit could recover damages only because he was in a special relationship to a promissor to whom he had rendered a benefit—a benefit for which the promissor ought in conscience to pay. The requirement that a plaintiff in special assumpsit allege performance made suits in special assumpsit in effect the equivalent of suits in other forms of assumpsit, in which a plaintiff recovered only for benefit conferred.

But how much would a plaintiff recover? Would he be secure in his ability to recover the true value of his performance, or would an able or knowledgeable adversary be permitted to take advantage of him? In quantum meruit and quantum valebant, of course, the plaintiff would recover only the reasonable value of his performance. The same was true in indebitatus assumpsit. In indebitatus, liability did not depend on the fictional promise of the defendant. In suits in indebitatus against executors and administrators, the central allegation was that the defendant "undertook the Administration . . . and thereby became obliged to pay the Legacy aforesaid to the Plaintiff . . . ";[110] in common sale of goods cases, where "the delivery . . . [was] sufficient to prove [the] Sale,"[111] liability was created by the delivery and receipt of goods, not by the promise to pay. In a similar case, where a town advanced money "for the necessary Support of the Defendant's Wife and Children"[112] in his absence, the defendant became liable to the town merely by virtue of the town's advancement of the funds, even though he had not requested that it support his family and had never promised to pay for that support. In other cases the vital allegation was that the defendant "according to the Custom of Merchants became obliged to pay the Plaintiff his Damage. . . ."[113]

That liability in indebitatus assumpsit resulted from the underlying indebtedness rather than the subsequent promise was significant because it meant that the parties to an exchange could not control the scope of their liability. Instead, the scope was determined at least in part by custom. This was true, for example, in the whaling industry, where men became indebted "agreeable to the long established custom in the whale fishery,"[114] and in marine insurance cases, where the courts would determine whether a deviation, which had the effect of canceling the policy, had occurred by looking "to ye usage" and that "a Voyage performed in the usual manner doth not affect ye Insurance. . . ."[115] In landlord-tenant cases the tenant was liable to pay all real estate taxes when it was customary in the town in which the land was located for tenants to do so.[116] Similarly, the issue whether a workman had breached his warranty of workmanlike performance[117] depended on whether "there was as good care taken as good workmen [customarily] take."[118] Most important, price as well as other contractual terms could be fixed by custom: "[A] person purchasing Goods without any special Promise . . . [was] supposed to promise the Payment of the Customary Price."[119] It was assumed by courts, lawyers, and clients alike that fixed prices existed for "Goods sold by a Shopkeeper,"[120] "for Work done by Tradesmen, . . . for a Yard of Cloth, or a Day's Work by a Carpenter."[121] One finds other cases where parties contracted with reference to "the rate" at which one of them "Usually Sold" goods "to his Customers"[122] and where an owner of logs agreed to give a "reasonable Reward" to the owner of a mill, "viz. one half of the boards produced out of the Logs sawed. . . ."[123] In short, the prices of many goods and services were fixed by custom, and when any price was fixed it could be recovered in a suit in indebitatus assumpsit.

In special assumpsit, on the other hand, prices were not fixed, and it appears that parties were able to control the terms of their contracts provided that the terms they agreed on were not contrary to some clear rule of law or inconsistent with the allegations that would be required in a writ if a plaintiff had to bring suit to enforce the contract. In special assumpsit a person assumed liability because he promised to do so, and hence he could control many of the terms of his liability by altering the scope of his promise. He was barred only from making a contract that required one of the parties either to violate some legal prohibition, such as the prohibition of business on the Sabbath,[124] or to fail to perform some legal duty, such as the duty of a sheriff to arrest an indigent on whom he served a writ of capias[125] or the duty of a seller of goods to deliver them before maintaining an action for their price.[126]

Normally one had the option of assuming either customary or promissory liability. If a recipient of goods or services made no special promise to pay, he became liable in indebitatus assumpsit, quantum meruit, or quantum valebant for their customary or reasonable value, but if he made a special promise, he became liable in special assumpsit to the extent of the promise. At least when the promise was in writing,[127] the seller of the goods or services was barred by the promise from suing in indebitatus assumpsit for customary value,[128] while the buyer was bound by his promise and hence barred from claiming in defense "that ye Consideration which he rec'd . . . was not of half ye Value" of his promise[129] or otherwise represented only a partial consideration.[130] In particular, it seems clear from the form books from which lawyers copied their writs that parties could bargain about price, since the forms for special assumpsit usually left the price term blank and hence subject to variation to accommodate the particular bargains of the parties.[131]

But although the law permitted one to assume promissory rather than customary liability, it did not encourage it. While it may have been possible as a matter of legal theory to defend against a duty to pay customary price by pleading an inconsistent oral agreement,[132] the law of evidence made such a defense impractical because it barred parties to an oral contract from testifying to its contents.[133] It was advisable to put a special promise in writing to insure its enforcement. The writing requirement probably deterred overreaching at the expense of the weak and unskillful; an even greater deterrent was the apparent practice of filing written contracts with justices of the peace.[134] In short, the legal system protected a person's economic security by providing that before he could make a bad bargain he had to give the bargain sufficient thought to commit it to writing and had to present it to a public official, who could advise him of its unwisdom. Indeed, it may even be that before someone could be bound by a special promise to pay a price other than a customary price, his promise had to be approved by a public officer; there is one case where a court held an action on a promissory note barred by the fact that the note had not been "approbated" by a justice of the peace.[135]

Of course assumpsit was not the only writ available to litigate matters of exchange.[136] Individuals could bind themselves to perform purely executory promises for which they received nothing in return[137] if they made their promises in written instruments under seal and delivered the sealed instruments in the presence of witnesses[138] to the recipient of the promise. Two writs were available to enforce sealed promises. The first was the writ of covenant, in which the essential element of the cause of action was a writing under seal delivered by the promissor to the promissee in accordance with the parties' intent.[139] Usually such covenants were executed to create or transfer some interest in land, such as a leasehold[140] or a fee simple.[141] The second writ was debt, which could also be brought on a bond or other sealed instrument containing the agreement of the parties.[142] The plaintiff, as in covenant, had to allege the due execution and delivery of the bond,[143] which was the essence of his cause of action, and, in addition, had to make one further allegation—that the bond or sealed instrument on which he was bringing suit and the damages he was seeking were for a sum certain.[144] The difference between debt and covenant was that in covenant a plaintiff brought suit for unliquidated damages, whereas in debt the suit was for a specified sum of money fixed by the sealed instrument.[145] Of course, the parties to a contract rarely knew at the time they made it what the precise extent of damages would be upon some subsequent breach, but this difficulty could be circumvented by use of the medieval penal bond with a conditional defeasance.[146] A penal bond consisted of the bond itself, promising to pay a specified sum of money on a specified date, and a condition promising performance of some other promise prior to that date and providing that the promise in the bond would be void if the promise in the condition were so performed. Since the condition could contain any promise, the penal bond with conditional defeasance was a highly flexible commercial instrument that was used to enforce promises to pay rent,[147] to indemnify the promissee,[148] and to insure submission to arbitration.[149] By suing in debt a plaintiff took the issue of damages away from the jury, since the jury had to give damages in the amount of the penal sum provided in the bond. However, if those damages were in excess of a plaintiff's "just debt and damages," a defendant could petition the court to exercise chancery powers conferred by statute and to reduce the damages to a just amount, namely, the value of the performance promised in the condition to the bond.[150]

The total picture of the law of exchange that emerges, then, is one of a substratum of doctrine insuring that exchanges of goods and services would normally occur at the rates that were customary or otherwise reasonable at the time of the exchange. This substratum made no provision for exchanges at other than customary rates or rates adjudged reasonable by the community, nor did it permit people to enter into enforceable agreements to exchange goods in the future. In short, it did not allow people to increase their wealth by making speculative or otherwise one-sided exchange bargains. It sought rather to promote stability by insuring that a person who gave up wealth in one form would receive equivalent wealth in return.

Atop the substratum, however, were other layers of law that expressed the legal system's concern that people should perform promises seriously undertaken and that thereby afforded them some flexibility to modify customary and community norms of exchange. For example, so long as a person had received some performance of value and had promised in writing to pay a particular price for it, he would be held to his promise without regard to the precise value of whatever he had received. Indeed, if someone put a promise under seal his promise would be enforced even if he had received nothing in return. Executory promises and bargains as to price, although apparently not common, were thus made possible. However, even in permitting enforcement of such promises and bargains, which created opportunities for unequal exchanges, the legal system did not lose its concern for economic stability, for it required that the parties go through certain formalities, which offered someone who was in danger of being overreached time to reflect and obtain the advice of others.

To the extent that it impeded change in the allocation of wealth, the law of contract may also have furthered ethical unity. A person who loses money in speculative transactions or in transactions entered into with imperfect knowledge often feels cheated. Sensing that the person who gained at his expense did so by failing to disclose relevant information, he may tend to feel an animosity that may long linger, only to arise under circumstances disruptive of community unity. By impeding speculative bargains and bargains whose terms did not reflect community norms of fair exchange, prerevolutionary law reduced the likelihood of such animosity and may thus have promoted social unity. By further allowing bargains in which there were opportunities for overreaching to be made only in the presence of others and under circumstances that promoted careful deliberation, contract law may similarly have reduced the likelihood of social rancor.

But prerevolutionary contract law probably furthered ethical unity and stability in the allocation of wealth and status at the expense of economic efficiency. Although careful empirical research would be necessary to confirm any correlation, it seems likely that the people who gain most in freely negotiated contracts are those with the greatest entrepreneurial skills, while those who lose most are those with the fewest skills. Two important entrepreneurial skills are an ability to predict future market trends and a knowledge of current market values; a man with these skills is better able than a man without the skills to make investments at a lower cost that are likely to satisfy future market requirements. To the extent that a legal system seeks to maximize economic growth and development, it should allocate resources to people who possess such skills. The legal system of prerevolutionary Massachusetts probably retarded economic growth by impeding the efforts of such men to acquire additional resources.

Thus identical tensions between economic and noneconomic values can be observed in the law of contract, the law of property, and the law of debtor and creditor. In the law of property, the rules permanently allocating resources to the first user promoted stability and unity but also nourished monopolies, which in turn retarded economic growth and efficient resource allocation. In the law of debtor and creditor, the rules giving extensive remedies to creditors and thereby furthering community ethical notions necessarily imposed heavy burdens on risk-bearing entrepreneurs who proved unable to earn anticipated profits with borrowed capital; indeed, the prospect of those heavy burdens may sometimes have deterred entrepreneurs from borrowing capital and undertaking risky ventures. In the law of contract, the same rules of law that promoted unity and stability may also have impeded the transfer of resources to knowledgeable entrepreneurs, thereby again retarding economic growth.

The law of pre-Revolutionary Massachusetts, in sum, created a society in which, by virtue of the poor law and distributional rules such as the intestacy laws, all men were assured of the bare necessities of life and in which, under standard property and contract doctrine, every man was secure in the enjoyment of those necessities and luxuries to which he had become accustomed. The law did little to encourage men to increase their wealth, however, particularly if they sought to do so by borrowing, or to stimulate the economic development of the province as a whole. Rather, through the criminal law, the law of civil wrongs, and the law of debtor and creditor, the legal system—perhaps only by way of reflexive adherence to traditional ethical standards—encouraged people who were increasingly interested in pursuing earthly wealth and pleasures to pursue other worldly values in their stead.

The Postrevolutionary Legal System, 1780-1830

The legal system of prerevolutionary Massachusetts, in which disputes were resolved by appealing to widely shared ethical values that were in turn protected by the rules of law itself, seemed eminently satisfactory to all elements of prerevolutionary society—except perhaps the immediate representatives of the crown, who found that the system frustrated their exercise of power.[1] There is no evidence that any of the men who led Massachusetts into the War of Independence or any of those who followed acted for the purpose of bringing about fundamental changes in the rules and institutions of which the legal system was comprised. As a result, the war years themselves saw few changes in the law, and even fewer of them proved permanent. To those who lived through the Revolution, the most important legal event was the closing of the royal courts in the summer and fall of 1774,[2] but that event had no lasting significance, for by 1777 identical state courts had reopened in all but two counties, and in those counties they reopened in 1780 and 1783.[3] The other important legal development of the war years was the enactment of regulatory legislation essential for fighting the war,[4] but this too generally ceased to remain in effect once the war had ended. The legal system that emerged from the war was, in short, virtually identical to the old colonial legal system. But thereafter change was dramatic.

"There is nothing more common," wrote a South Carolinian in the 1780s, "than to confound the terms of the American Revolution with those of the late American war. The American war is over, but this is far from being the case with the American Revolution. On the contrary, nothing but the first act of that great drama is closed."[5] Historians of American law must similarly distinguish between the War of Independence and the American revolution, the long-term movement that began as men sought to justify the war and master its consequences. For while eight years of war left virtually no permanent imprint on the legal system of Massachusetts, the effects of the revolution were overwhelming.

The American revolution set loose new economic, social, and intellectual forces. Most Americans looked on the revolution "as the greatest blessing which Providence ever bestowed upon them"—as "the best means of rendering America happy, free, and great. . . ."[6] They "rejoice[d] in the amelioration of their forms of government. . . "[7] and sought "to establish a system of laws . . . dictated by the genuine principles of Republicanism."[8] No one disputed that the substance of American law should be "characteristic of the spirit and principles of our independence."[9] But they did have differences over the precise meaning of republicanism and independence. For some, as we shall see, the coming of independence and the creation of a republican government meant little more than that change would occur in what we would today call constitutional law; these men wanted no change either in the rules of private law or in the structure of society. For others, however, the attainment of liberty—the central principle of republicanism and independence—required not only constitutional change but changes in the very fabric of society and in the rules of law as well.

As these different understandings about the proper direction of law emerged, innumerable changes in legal institutions, procedures, and substance occurred. We shall see that in the struggle between those who desired change and those who opposed it the ethical unity of Massachusetts was breached. Ironically, the efforts of social conservatives to preserve the state's economic and social stability in the absence of true ethical unity resulted in the creation of legal doctrines that undermined stability even further by enhancing the freedom of individuals. In short, we shall see that the forces of change set loose by the revolution completely destroyed the old social structure, which the War of Independence had been waged to preserve.

5. The Reform of Common Law Pleading

The first breach after the Revolution in the stability and ethical unity of Massachusetts occurred in the mid-1780s, when substantial segments of the population in western agrarian strongholds organized to reform legal institutions and procedures that they found oppressive and unduly expensive. Although the Constitution of 1780 had enjoined that "every subject . . . ought to obtain right and justice freely,"[1] the costs of litigation were such that many agrarian debtors felt that right and justice were unobtainable. To them "judicial proceeding[s]" appeared so "intricate" that their usual outcome was only "to throw an honest man out of three quarters of his property" if he put his case to law.[2] Agrarian leaders were determined "to vindicate the rights of the poor against the aggressions of power and violence"—a determination that even the judges of the Supreme Judicial Court later found "sound" and worthy of being "cherished."[3]

The reform movement was in part directed against the legal profession. The less thoughtful reformers argued that the legal system's expense resulted from a conspiracy among lawyers "to perplex and embarrass every judicial proceeding . . . [and] to delay every process. . . ."[4] Their remedy was to abolish lawyers and have every litigant plead his own cause.[5] Some concessions were made to this antiprofessionalism during the 1780s: litigants were granted permission by statute to plead their own cause, they were forbidden to employ more than two attorneys simultaneously in any one case,[6] and they were permitted to employ as attorneys persons not admitted to the bar.[7] But then the bar regrouped and fought vigorously and successfully to resist any further concessions and to erode those already granted. Over the course of the next decade, the judiciary, under pressure from the bar, emasculated the reform legislation with the result that professional lawyers regained their monopoly and wealthy clients were free to retain as many lawyers as they wished.[8] At the same time, steps were being taken by statute[9] and by court rule[10] to insure the existence of a well-educated and highly organized legal profession, which soon attained a dominance of practice that the profession had never possessed in the colonial period. The clearest indication of that dominance is perhaps the fact that whereas only two of the eleven judges who had served on the Superior Court from 1760 to 1774 had been lawyers,[11] the profession claimed the allegiance of all but two of the twenty-six men who in the half century after independence served on the Supreme Judicial Court,[12] the new name given to the old Superior Court. The antiprofessional movement of the 1780s, in short, was simply overwhelmed by a professional counter-movement.

A second factor that the agrarian reformers thought contributed to the oppressiveness and undue expense of the legal system was the state's antiquated judicial machinery. They all agreed that "the existence of the Courts of Common Pleas, and the Court of General Sessions, in their present mode of administration, ha[d] given general disgust to the good people of this country . . . , [were] an amazing expence to the subject, and . . . without the least conceivable advantage."[13] They accordingly suggested that the sessions courts be abolished, their criminal business transferred to Common Pleas, and their administrative business given to town selectmen. To lower costs in Common Pleas suits, they sought both an enlargement of the jurisdiction of individual justices of the peace and the passage of a confession act. Appearance before a single justice meant lower fees, while a confession act permitted a debtor to appear before a single justice, acknowledge his debt, and promise payment at a future time, when the creditor could obtain execution without having to bring an expensive suit.[14] Other reformers, observing that "not one cause in ten" begun in Common Pleas "finally issued there" and that "the time and expense usually attending a suit in the Common Pleas . . . [was] only preparatory to a trial" in the Supreme Judicial Court, proposed to have the functions of the Common Pleas courts taken over by the Supreme Court.[15]

Some minor jurisdictional reforms were accomplished during the 1780s, the most important of which were a 1783 act giving jurisdiction to justices of the peace in all actions where title to land was not involved and where the amount in controversy did not exceed four pounds,[16] a 1786 act providing new procedures for the submission of controversies to referees,[17] and a series of temporary acts giving justices of the peace jurisdiction over personal actions even when the amount in controversy did exceed four pounds.[18] Fundamental jurisdictional reforms met with opposition, however, and were not achieved for another twenty years, when the ancient judicial structure collapsed of its own accord under the weight of an ever increasing case load.

A third way the reformers sought to make justice freely and equally accessible was by simplifying the rules of procedure. They contended that "the state of pleading in this Commonwealth [had become such] that an honest man . . . [could] not obtain" right and justice "without being obliged to employ a lawyer, at a great expence. . . ."[19] "Artful men in England," they explained, "ha[d] so entangled the mode of managing a cause with the nice distinction of special pleas (and . . . [the courts in Massachusetts had] unfortunately adopted the pernicious practice) that in short justice . . . [could] scarcely be obtained unless it [was] dearly purchased."[20] "[I]nstead of obtaining justice 'freely,' 'completely,' and 'promptly,' " many litigants saw their "causes . . . carried through every tedious labyrinth"[21] and juries "hindered from coming to a speedy decision of a cause, by the labouring pleadings" of the common law.[22]

The reformers sought to abandon technical and outmoded pleading forms and to have judgments rendered "according to the merits of the case. . . ."[23] "[P]leas," it was urged, should "be simple, and the clerk [should be] authorized to write them in short form for each of the parties."[24] There was no "occasion or need . . . of all the parade of written pleas, replications, rejoinders, &c. &c. in common trials at law," since all that a court needed to know was "the fact, the law, and the equity of the case";[25] then the issue of causes would not "depend upon adroitness of advocates . . . [but] upon their intrinsic justice."[26] Specifically, the legislature was urged to enact a statute "for pleading the general issue in all cases, and admitting special matter to be given in evidence" under it, as a "means of opening more fully the merits of the cause, and being free from the necessity of making formal pleas. . . ."[27]

The methods by which the reformers waged their fight for legal change shattered the ethical unity of Massachusetts. In general they did not attempt to promote their program by demonstrating its consistency with values and aspirations shared by all groups in the state. Moreover, in their attack on the legal profession, the reformers showed an utter lack of respect for the vital economic interests of their opponents. No attempt was made to build a consensus in support of their proposals—on the contrary, the proponents of reform organized a propaganda campaign, sought to gain control of a majority of the state legislature, and ultimately—in Shay's Rebellion—carried their movement to the battlefield. They sought, in short, to mobilize power rather than persuade. The ensuing struggle within the state and the local communities represented a new style of politics, radically at odds with inherited notions of social stability and ethical unity.

A second and, over the long run, probably more important impact on the legal system occurred when the seemingly least important of the reformers' demands—the abolition of common law pleading—was met. The abolition did not occur instantaneously through legislative action; the common law system was gradually transformed by the work of the courts over a period of more than a half century. The process of transformation was tedious, dull, and for most laymen probably incomprehensible, significant primarily to lawyers who were seeking to understand the mechanics of the litigation process—the heart of any early nineteenth-century law practice. Nonetheless, the end of common law pleading did have some broader social significance, and after the process of abolition has been examined in detail that significance will be outlined.

Although the system of common law pleading was not the principal cause of the high cost of litigation, it was a factor.[28] The rules of pleading in use at the time of the Revolution were outmoded and unduly technical. Although they may at one time have served a rational function, rules dealing with matters such as the forms of action, service of process, joinder and identification of parties, and other procedural niceties had ceased to do so by the second half of the eighteenth century. They did introduce complexity, technicality, and, by producing needless dismissals and reinstitutions of suits, expense into the litigation process.[29]

Except in actions to try title to land, the common law forms of action were in full vigor in the prerevolutionary period. All of the actions customarily in use in England, such as trespass, trover, case, debt, covenant, assumpsit, and replevin, were also in use in Massachusetts, and one even finds obscure actions such as recout in occasional use.[30] Under the common law system a plaintiff was required to name the form of action under which he was bringing his suit. If he did "not name . . . his plea,"[31] "give . . . any name to this his Action,"[32] or "declare . . . in an action of Debt or Trespass on the Case, or in any other Action or Plea known in the Register or in the Law,"[33] his writ would be abated. Writs were also abated when a plaintiff brought the wrong cause of action—trespass, for example, instead of case for obstructing the flow of water to a milldam;[34] case instead of debt on a bond;[35] debt instead of trespass for a statutory penalty for cutting the plaintiff's trees;[36] debet and detinet, a variety of debt, instead of detinet only on an administrator's bond.[37]

Each form of action, moreover, had its own form of general denial, so called because it imported an absolute and complete denial by a defendant of each and every allegation in a plaintiff's declaration. For example, in trespass either vi et armis or on the case the appropriate form of general denial was not guilty; in debt, owes nothing; in debt on a bond, it is not the defendant's deed; in assumpsit, never promised. If the defendant pleaded the wrong general issue, as not guilty to a plea of assumpsit or owes nothing to a plea of trespass, or if he pleaded a sham issue, such as that he had no money, that he was a Son of Liberty and therefore ought not to be sued,[38] or, as John Adams colorfully pleaded in two cases, "Law is perfect reason without passion"[39] and "the Law of nature is common to brutes & men,"[40] then judgment would be given on demurrer for the plaintiff. Of course, lawyers had little difficulty in pleading the correct general issue: the relevant rules of law were clear and simple. However, in the Court of Common Pleas they often pleaded the wrong general issue in order to secure a judgment from which they could appeal to the Superior Court without having to go through the mechanism of a full trial.[41]

If a defendant did not wish to plead the general issue, he could plead specially. Although special pleading was used only rarely before the War of Independence, it became more frequent thereafter.[42] Special pleas could be of a great variety, depending on the circumstances of a defendant's case. A defendant might plead an accord and satisfaction, arbitration, conditions performed,[43] infancy, or some other fact that precluded the plaintiff from maintaining his action.[44] He could also put in a plea in justification, as in actions of assault and battery, self-defense, or defense of freehold;[45] in trespass, that the defendant did the act complained of by virtue of some office that warranted him to do it; or, in an action of slander, that the plaintiff really was as bad a man as the defendant said he was. Finally, a defendant might plead the statute of limitations or some other statutory defense.[46]

The response to a special plea by a defendant was a replication by the plaintiff, traversing or confessing and avoiding the special plea. That could be followed by a rejoinder by the defendant, followed in turn by a surrejoinder, a rebutter, and a surrebutter.[47] A number of technical rules made special pleading a supremely refined and difficult art. First, a plea was required to be single—that is, it could contain only one factual allegation; moreover, a party could set forth only one plea, unless he obtained the court's permission to plead double. Second, a party's plea had to answer his opponent's allegations in every material point. A plea also had to be direct, positive, and nonargumentative, certain as to time, place, and persons, capable of trial, and properly averred in the common form—"and this he is ready to verify."[48] A final rule was that the defendant could not put in a special plea that amounted merely to a denial of all or part of the plaintiff's charge but had to advance some new fact not mentioned in the declaration. In a writ of assumpsit, for example, where a plaintiff alleged nonpayment or nonperformance by the defendant as one of several essential parts of his cause of action, the defendant could not in turn plead payment or performance,[49] for that plea merely denied an element in the plaintiff's claim and advanced no new fact. The defendant could, however, plead payment by some specified means[50] or some specific mode of performance of his contract,[51] for such a plea would add new facts and not merely negate facts already pleaded by the plaintiff.

It was only in cases involving title to land that the rules of common law pleading had been somewhat modified by the time of the Revolution. Although court records contain occasional references even to such obscure writs as novel disseisin,[52] the ancient English actions such as entry, ejectment, formedon, and others had in general been embraced in colonial Massachusetts within a single generic form of action variously called a plea of ejectment, a plea of entry, or, more simply and more frequently, a plea of land, which avoided ancient technicalities and led to a trial like that in any other civil suit.[53] In a plea of land, a plaintiff was required to allege the nature of the estate of which either he or the person through whom he claimed had been seised[54] within thirty years prior to the commencement of his suit.[55] The proper general denial was that the defendant was not guilty or that he did not disseise the plaintiff; if a defendant entered an erroneous plea such as that he never promised, judgment would be entered for the plaintiff. A defendant also had the option of pleading specially.

In addition to the generic plea of land, the only other writ in frequent use in litigating title to real property was the writ of trespass quare clausum fregit.[56] As in the plea of land, a plaintiff in trespass had to allege that the land in question was "the plaintiff's close,"[57] an allegation superficially resembling the allegation of seisin in a plea of land. However, the allegation that the land was the plaintiff's close, unlike the allegation of seisin, did not, on a defensive plea of the general issue, put seisin in issue: that is, if a defendant pleaded the general issue of not guilty, a judgment on a writ of trespass would not determine seisin of the land and would not be res judicata in a subsequent suit between the same parties for that land. A defendant could, however, put seisin in issue, if he wished, by pleading in lieu of the general issue that the land was "his own proper soil and freehold"; a judgment on that plea would have an effect similar to the effect of a judgment on the generic plea of land—it would determine who was seised of the land,[58] although a plaintiff in trespass could recover only damages for interference with his seisin and not, as in a plea of land, the land itself.[59]

After a plaintiff had selected the correct writ, he was required to have it served on the defendant. Service in a civil action could be accomplished at the plaintiff's option by a summons or by a capias or, under special circumstances, by other means ordered by the court.[60] When a summons was used, a proper officer was simply commanded to summon the defendant, if found within his precinct, to appear at a specified term of the Court of Common Pleas for the appropriate county.[61] In the case of a capias, the officer was directed to attach the goods or estate of the defendant or for want thereof to take his body, if found in his precinct.[62]

Three basic rules regulated the service of process, both summons and capias: process was required to be served by an officer,[63] the writ had to be served by the particular officer to whom it was directed,[64] and service on a defendant had to be accomplished at least fourteen days before the court sat[65] and had to notify the defendant of the time at which the court would meet.[66]

A plaintiff also had to be certain that all parties who ought to be joined in litigation were joined and that parties who ought not to be joined were not. Rules on this subject were quite technical.[67] Joint obligors and joint promissors, for example, both had to be joined in a suit on their promise, and process had to be served on both of them.[68] Joint promissees also had to be joined, although a husband was not required to join his wife if a promise had been made jointly to her,[69] for a wife was "neither privy to the Contract nor the Person to whom the Money is to be paid."[70] A wife, on the other hand, did have to join her husband,[71] even if she was a white woman and he was a black slave.[72] Tenants in common were also required to join in land pleas and in personal actions such as trespass, assumpsit, and nuisance.[73] Joint bailors, on the other hand, did not have to sue their bailee together,[74] and agents were not required to be joined in suits against their principals.[75] A plaintiff also had to be certain to bring any executor or administrator before the court in cases of claims for or against a decedent;[76] such claims lapsed if they were not brought during the period of probate administration.[77]

The most technical of all the pleading rules was one requiring parties to litigation to be precisely identified. Pursuant to this requirement, civil and criminal actions were dismissed when there was no person by the exact name and description given the named defendant.[78] Civil and criminal actions were similarly dismissed for failing to state the full name of a party to the writ[79] or for misspelling or otherwise misstating a party's name[80] —either his Christian name[81] or his surname.[82] There was an even greater need for certainty in naming parties in suits involving corporate litigants, and here too writs were abated for misnomers.[83]

In addition to making a plaintiff give all parties their proper names, the law required him to state correctly without any misspelling the town and county in which all parties resided.[84] The requirement that a writ state the residence of the parties served not only to identify them but also to insure that service of process was made on a defendant at his proper residence.[85] Moreover, since venue in transitory actions depended on at least one of the parties being a resident of the county in which the suit was brought, the rule also served to insure proper venue.[86]

In order to provide further identification of the parties, the plaintiff also had to state correctly the addition, that is, the occupation or social rank, of both plaintiff[87] and defendant.[88] Failure to do so was ground for abatement of a writ and, in criminal cases, for dismissal of an indictment.[89] More suits were abated or dismissed for improper additions than on any other ground, and much elaborate learning proliferated on the subject of additions: one finds the bench and bar of the Superior Court debating, for instance, whether the description of blacksmith should include a nailer[90] and whether a militia captain was a gentleman by way of commission, reputation, or courtesy.[91] In one case a writ was even abated because the plaintiff's testator had been given an improper addition.[92]

As noted earlier, many pleading rules were carried to such extremes that they ceased to serve any rational function. For example, a frequently invoked rule provided that a defendant could obtain abatement of a writ if he had the same name as his father and was not called junior, as long as both father and son were of the same town.[93] Likewise, a defendant who was mistakenly called junior could obtain abatement.[94] It seems absurd that cases should be decided on the basis of whether the plaintiff had or had not named the defendant junior in his writ, yet many cases were so decided. Moreover, colonial law could be even more absurd. Consider *Munson* v. *Clark*, a paternity suit.[95] The rule in paternity was that a mother could not obtain support for her illegitimate child unless she had accused the defendant of being its father during the time of her "travail."[96] In *Munson* the mother had accused the defendant of being the father, but since she had failed to call him junior during the course of her accusation the court dismissed her suit. *Munson*, of course, is an extreme case, but it is illustrative by virtue of its very extremity.

A plaintiff finally had to surmount several other procedural obstacles. One was the requirement that his writ be endorsed either by himself or by his attorney;[97] the endorser was liable for costs in the event that the plaintiff lost his action.[98] Another requirement was that the writ bear the teste of the appropriate court official—in the case of Common Pleas, the first justice.[99] A writ would also be abated if another writ was already pending on the same cause of action,[100] while a suit by an administrator would be abated if he failed to produce his letters of administration.[101] A plaintiff was also required to allege damages[102] and moreover to make the allegation in proper form.[103] Finally, he had to avoid the pitfall of a variance—that is, an inconsistency in his allegations, either between two different places in his writ[104] or between a writ and a subsidiary instrument, such as a bond,[105] an account,[106] or a will.[107]

Even before Shays's Rebellion, in which high litigation costs, high taxes, and lack of currency were the chief complaints,[108] the courts and the legal profession had begun to take hesitant steps toward reform. The process of reform was a gradual and ambiguous one, and the reasons for reform are often unclear. Reform occurred piecemeal, as individual lawyers, either lacking precise knowledge of common law pleading rules or seeking some strategic advantage in litigation at hand, entered pleas that were not in proper form. Although opposing counsel sometimes waived the informality, the want of form was often called to the court's attention. The courts, sensing the validity of reformers' complaints about the undue expense of technical pleading rules and seeing that reduced adherence to form threatened no tangible interest of the law or the legal profession,[109] often decided to permit counsel either to ignore or to amend the informality. As various decisions of this sort cumulated over time, the ancient system of common law pleading was destroyed, and new rules of pleading emerged in its place. But while destruction of the old technical pleading system was at least in part a response to awareness of its deficiencies, there is no evidence that men consciously perceived the contours of the new system until, after it had largely come into existence, they began to articulate the reality that confronted them.

The first step toward a modern system of pleading was taken quite early, in September 1776, when the Superior Court adopted a rule providing that prior to joinder in demurrer, any plaintiff could "have leave to amend his Writ and declaration upon his paying the Deft. his costs" to the date of the amendment or "agreeing to a Continuance at the Defts. Election."[110] This new rule was not given immediate effect in some of the lower courts, which continued to dismiss cases on technical grounds[111] until the legislature provided in 1784 that judicial proceedings should not "be abated, arrested, quashed or reversed for any kind of circumstantial errors or mistakes . . . nor through defect or want of form only" and explicitly confirmed the power of the courts "on motion . . . [to] order amendments."[112] The rule and the statute even then had no effect on the question of misjoinder of parties,[113] which was deemed "an exception to the merits," at least in contract actions,[114] but on other technical questions of pleading its effects were transforming. By the mid-1780s it was clear that misnomers[115] and errors in additions[116] were freely amendable;[117] indeed, there is no record of any suit being dismissed after 1784 for a misnomer or an improper addition.[118] Other technical errors, such as a mistake in a party's residence,[119] a failure on the part of an infant to bring his suit by a prochein ami,[120] a failure to have a writ properly attested,[121] an error in the ad damnum of a writ,[122] and an error in the plaintiff's statement of his claim[123] could also be cured by amendment. Plaintiffs were even permitted to add new counts to their writs if those counts were consistent with and for the same cause of action as the original counts,[124] although such amendments would not be permitted if they added a new cause of action to the plaintiff's writ[125] or otherwise affected a defendant's substantive rights.[126] Amendments were permitted after as well as before verdicts[127] and on other documents, such as bills of particulars,[128] as well as on original writs. Sheriffs' returns of the mode of service of process and improper directions in writs concerning such service were also amendable,[129] with the result that technical lapses in the service of process were ignored[130] as long as actual service had been properly made.[131] Courts were slowly coming to the view that the only material issue was whether the defendant had had actual "personal notice and information of the service. . . ."[132]

One sees in the law of venue a parallel lessening of concern for form and a growing recognition that technical objections were of no significance as long as the forum was a fair and convenient one. The courts rejected arguments, for instance, that a corporation could have no residence for purposes of venue and hence could be sued only in the county of which the plaintiff was a resident,[133] that a sheriff could be sued only in the county of which he was sheriff,[134] and that when an act committed in one county resulted in an injury in another the plaintiff could bring suit only in the county of the act.[135] As Chief Justice Parsons noted, venue was "considered [only] as a necessary part of technical form, but not as a substantial part of the writ,"[136] and, as the Supreme Judicial Court had noted elsewhere, it accorded little weight to "an objection . . . which was merely captious and dilatory in its nature, not at all affecting the merits of the action. . . ."[137] "[C]ourts in all countries," said the judges, "looked with disfavor upon . . . objections, which, through adherence to form, would obstruct the course of justice. . . ."[138]

By the early nineteenth century, then, the emerging concern in pleading was with substance, not with form. This concern was of great significance, for it compelled the bench and bar to think about law in substantive categories, such as "tort" and "contract,"[139] rather than in the old procedural categories of trespass, assumpsit, and the like.

Once men began to think in the new categories, the ancient system

of common law writs began to collapse. Although defendants throughout the half century after the Revolution could procure the dismissal of
writs that failed to indicate the "kind of Plea or Action . . . brot by the
Plft. . . . ,"[140] that joined two forms of action,[141] or that sought
recovery in the wrong form of action[142] or were otherwise "informal"[143] or insufficient,[144] many plaintiffs nonetheless recovered judgments on writs containing such defects when their opponents
either failed to object to their writ or raised their objection unseason-
ably.[145] There were, for example, many actions where plaintiffs
were victorious which were given no name—one was labeled merely "a
plea of Grievous complaint";[146] another, a "Plea of the for the
Recovery" of certain nails;[147] a third, "a Plea for not performing his
[the defendant's] promise";[148] while others merely stated the facts
on which the plaintiffs relied.[149] There were also cases where
plaintiffs gave their writs the substantive name of their cause of action
rather than their proper formal name—pleas, for instance, of "Trover &
conversion,"[150]   of   "Assault   &   Battery,"[151]   of   "Defamation,"[152] and of "posession."[153] In other cases, plaintiffs either
brought the wrong writ—covenant and debt on an unsealed agreement,[154] case on a sealed agreement,[155] case for dower,[156] or
case for a trespass committed with force and arms[157]—or joined two
forms of action in a single writ[158] and nonetheless were able to
recover judgment, as technical rules concerning the propriety and form
of writs were "gradually relaxed"[159] and ignored.

It is impossible to attribute all these departures from proper form
solely to carelessness on the part of court clerks, attorneys, and parties
not represented by attorneys;[160] many of the departures appear to
have been conscious attempts on the part of skilled attorneys to compel
the courts to focus on the substantive rather than the procedural
aspects of their cases, perhaps in order to obtain some tactical
advantage.[161] A clear illustration of such an attempt is *Taylor* v.
Eustis,[162] a contract action where the plaintiff pleaded the existence
of a sealed promise by the defendant for which he, the plaintiff, had
given consideration. The plaintiff's successful attempt to sue in case
rather than in debt appears to have been a deliberate attempt to
subsume sealed as well as unsealed promises under a single substantive
rubric of contract for which a plaintiff could have an election of a
remedy either in debt, where the court might determine the amount of
damages,[163] or in assumpsit, where damages would be fixed by the
jury.[164] This particular attempt would fail in the 1810s[165]
despite the fact that it had considerable support,[166] but in many
other instances the Supreme Judicial Court did cease to analyze claims
in procedural terms and instead began to recognize that plaintiffs had
substantive rights for the enforcement of which they could elect one of

several writs. In suits for statutory penalties, for instance, where the statute did not prescribe the remedy, a plaintiff could bring trespass,[167] debt,[168] or case.[169] Similarly, a plaintiff could maintain trespass, trover, or assumpsit against a trespasser who cut down and sold his trees;[170] trespass or case for damages from a runaway horse frightened by the discharge of a gun;[171] indebitatus assumpsit or account against a bailiff;[172] debt or case for misbehavior by a public officer;[173] and, during much of the early nineteenth century, trespass or case against a sheriff for a trespass committed by his deputy.[174]

The Supreme Judicial Court's preference for substance over form was explicitly enunciated in *Cole* v. *Fisher*,[175] where it held "a contest about the form of action . . . [to] be of little avail to the defendant" and left "the case to the jury, to settle it as a question of fact, upon the principles . . . [therein] stated."[176] Similarly, it refused in another case "to disturb . . . [a] verdict upon a question of form only" when "upon the whole justice ha[d] been done between the parties. . . ."[177] The primary concern of the court had become the existence or nonexistence of a substantive right in the plaintiff; if he had such a right or had suffered an "injur[y] . . . or wrong . . . in his person, property, or character," the Massachusetts constitution provided that he "ought to find a certain remedy, by having recourse to the laws. . . ."[178] Thus if a plaintiff had a right but could not obtain a writ conforming to the usual forms, it was nonetheless "the . . . constant practice of the Court to grant him a writ, by which he [might] obtain his remedy"[179] or to permit him to plead without writ.[180]

Substance also triumphed over form in the emergence of new rules of defensive pleading. In prerevolutionary law, it will be recalled, each writ had had its own proper general issue; if a defendant pleaded the wrong general issue, his plea was held insufficient and was rejected. By the 1790s, however, the sufficiency of a defendant's plea was coming increasingly to depend on the substantive nature of the suit brought against him rather than on the form of action that the plaintiff had used. The propriety of a defensive plea, as one lower court explained, was no longer measured by technical rules but "in the common scales of Justice by the weights of Law. . . ."[181] Thus, if a plaintiff had a cause of action for which he could bring one of several forms of action, it became the rule that the defendant could plead the general issue appropriate to any of those forms. Suits for statutory penalties are illustrative: such suits could be brought in debt, case, or trespass. Before the Revolution a defendant was required to plead that he was not indebted, if the plaintiff chose to bring his writ in debt; or not guilty, if the plaintiff chose either case or trespass; but in the late 1780s it became the practice for defendants to plead not guilty to writs of debt[182] as well as to writs of case and trespass, although it remained true that not indebted was the more proper plea.[183] Likewise, by the 1790s pleas of not guilty had become acceptable in response to writs of case[184] and debt[185] brought against executors for legacies, whereas in the prerevolutionary period the plea of never promised had been the only proper response to a writ of case, and the plea of not indebted the proper response to a writ of debt;[186] not indebted also became available to executors sued in case.[187] Similarly, in replevin it became permissible in the 1790s to plead—in addition to the pleas appropriate to replevin—that one was not guilty.[188] The significance of these new rules lies in their apparent recognition that the commission of statutory wrongs, the failures of executors to pay legacies, and the wrongful taking of chattels constituted some generic form of wrong—a tort—for which a plaintiff could bring a variety of different writs to obtain damages or some other form of restitution and concerning which a defendant ought to have an election, similar to that which the plaintiff possessed, either to plead generically that he was not guilty of the tort or to plead in the form appropriate to the plaintiff's particular action.[189]

One finds a similarly emerging substantive concept of contract by looking at the changing rules of defensive pleadings in writs of debt, covenant, and assumpsit. In prerevolutionary law, each had had its own proper general issue, but by the 1790s strict pleading rules had disappeared. Thus it became possible to put in the assumpsit plea of never promised to writs of covenant[190] and debt,[191] and the debt plea of not indebted to a writ of assumpsit.[192] In one writ of assumpsit a jury even returned a hybrid verdict that the defendant both was indebted and had promised,[193] while in one writ of covenant the court upheld a plea that the defendant never covenanted[194]—an adaptation to the writ of covenant of the assumpsit plea of never promised. In these cases, in short, the ancient categories of debt, covenant, and assumpsit were blurred, and a new category of contract, under which lawyers were seeking to subsume the entire law of obligation, was emerging.[195]

One way in which lawyers sought to treat all cases of obligation as part of a new category of contract was by transposing the doctrine of consideration into two sorts of action where proof thereof had not previously been required—suits on negotiable and on sealed instruments. As a result, by the beginning of the nineteenth century the maker of a promissory note, in a suit by the original promissee, could introduce in his defense evidence not only of an illegal consideration[196] or a failure of consideration[197] but even of a want of consideration in the original transaction, which would render the note "void as a *nudum pactum*...."[198] These cases led, in turn, to a reversal of the colonial rule[199] that a plaintiff in a suit on a note did not have to plead and prove consideration; an 1827 case held that he did.[200] For a brief time near the turn of the century the courts even held that a defense "that there was no Cons[ideration] for the Note" could "be gone into" in a suit by an endorsee against a maker,[201] although ultimately they rejected such a rule in response to the needs of the commercial community, which used negotiable securities as "a substitute for money" and "a circulating medium."[202] By 1830 the courts had arrived at the modern view that a maker cannot go into the defense of consideration in a suit by the endorsee unless the endorsee obtained the note after maturity or otherwise did not fulfill the requirements of being a holder in due course.[203]

Similar efforts were made by defendants in suits on sealed instruments to go into questions of consideration. One lower court in 1800, for example, held a bond under seal void because it had been given for an illegal consideration,[204] while several years earlier Theophilus Parsons, who later became chief justice of Massachusetts, had argued that a "coven[an]t . . . [was] void for want of Cons[ideration]."[205] There were at least two categories of cases in which the courts accepted his argument and permitted defendants to impeach a sealed instrument for want of consideration—cases of covenants not to engage in competition with the plaintiff's business[206] and cases in which a receipt of consideration was not averred in the deed sued on by the plaintiff.[207] Moreover, as late as the 1820s the Supreme Judicial Court was "not prepared to say" whether "a failure of consideration . . . [would] avoid a deed."[208] But by 1810, after a decade of confusion, it had become clear that except in the special categories noted above, a total want, as distinguished from a failure of consideration, would not avoid a deed; in the words of the court, a "covenant . . . , although voluntary and gratuitous on the part of [its makers, would] . . . yet [be] binding on them. . . ."[209]

Even in reaching this result, however, the courts came to analyze sealed contracts under the broader, more general rubric of contract. The rule at which they arrived in covenant cases, for instance, was not that consideration was not a requisite of sealed as well as unsealed contracts but that proof of consideration was not needed in the former case because "a bond, from the solemnity of its execution, import[ed] a consideration. . . ."[210] One accordingly could not impeach the bond for a want of consideration, although one could "avoid the bond, by shewing that it was obtained by fraud or duress, or that the consideration . . . [was] illegal or against the policy of the law."[211] Perhaps one could also show that the consideration had failed.[212] Moreover, although the courts refused to permit a defense of want of consideration in suits on sealed instruments, they did treat sealed contracts like other contracts in several other ways. One way was to apply the same measure of damages in covenant as in assumpsit;[213] another was to hold that a contract under seal, like any other contract, could be discharged by a new parole agreement[214] for which a consideration deemed by the parties to be full and adequate had been given.[215]

The breakdown of the old formulary categories and the emergence of new substantive ones can also be seen by studying defensive pleas in cases that fell on the borderline between the newly emerging categories of tort and contract. By the 1790s, for example, in suits against sheriffs for their own or their deputies' misfeasance,[216] in suits against bailees for negligent treatment of or failure to return the plaintiff's goods,[217] and in suits for fraud or breach of warranty,[218] a defendant had the option of pleading either not guilty or never promised; that is, a defendant could treat an action either as one in tort or as one in contract whenever the nature of the suit was unclear. Similarly, if a writ such as assumpsit, to which never promised was the proper general issue, was brought on a cause of action such as breach of promise to marry, to which the tort issue of not guilty was the proper response, the tort issue had to be pleaded.[219] Courts, in short, no longer thought in terms of specific pleas as answers to specific writs—rather in terms of the underlying nature of the cause of action—and required defendants to plead in answer to it.[220]

Emerging concepts of tort and contract also caused the development of other pleading rules, such as the rule that counts in tort and contract could not be joined;[221] that joint victims of a single act of misfeasance could not join their claims in tort, although joint promissees could join claims in contract;[222] and that joint tortfeasors could plead separately in defense, while joint promissors could not.[223]

These concepts were not, of course, entirely new; prerevolutionary records contain occasional references to them.[224] What was new was the emphasis on substance over form and the rejection of British forms—that is, the writ system—as an intellectually acceptable mode of thinking about law. Once the old formulary categories had been rejected, new categories were needed, and Massachusetts lawyers turned to substantive categories, to which they adapted the ancient forms of action and their ancient defenses. That adaptation was, however, but a single step along the path from common law pleading to the modern Massachusetts variant of code pleading.

The next step, which occurred during the first two decades of the nineteenth century, was the development of a unitary defensive plea under which a defendant could introduce whatever facts constituted a defense on the merits to the plaintiff's cause of action against him. Part of this development was the recognition that the particular varieties of the general issue appropriate to particular actions were a mere matter of form and that a plea of the wrong general issue was, as a general rule, immaterial. Thus in the courts of Common Pleas, where litigation as to the propriety of a particular general issue was usually solely a matter of which party would be appellant and which party respondent in proceedings in the Supreme Judicial Court, judges began around 1800 to regard pleas of the general issue as purely fictitious and to determine on a basis not disclosed in the records[225] which party would have to take the appeal. This development can be seen first in the courts' upholding of unusual pleas—pleas, for example, of never promised to a writ of trover for conversion[226] or to a writ of debt for a statutory penalty,[227] of not the defendant's act and deed to a writ of ejectment in which the plaintiff claimed under a deed,[228] of never accepted to a writ of case against an alleged acceptor of a bill of exchange,[229] and of he is not answerable to a writ of case against a sheriff who wrongfully released property taken on an attachment;[230] then in the inconsistency with which courts dealt with pleas of never promised[231] and not guilty[232] made in response to writs of assumpsit; and finally in the ultimate result achieved in the 1810s, when the litigants could simply agree without a plea on the part of the defendant to appeal the case to the Supreme Judicial Court.[233]

Incorrect pleas of the general issue also came to be treated as harmless formal errors even when they formed the basis of a jury verdict. It appears, for example, that as early as the 1780s a plea of an incorrect general issue would be cured by the jury's return of a verdict on the proper issue;[234] the basic rule was that defects of form caused by a failure to adhere to "the strict rules of pleading" could be objected to only on demurrer and that an "objection . . . [after a verdict came] too late."[235] Later, in the early years of the nineteenth century, the courts also arrived at a rule that an informal verdict rendered on proper pleadings would not be permitted to affect the outcome of the litigation. When "the only error or mistake arose from a mere slip in drawing up the verdict," that slip "clearly . . . ought not to be allowed to vacate the judgment."[236] Even when both the pleadings and the verdict were technically informal, a court might render judgment on the verdict,[237] particularly if the losing party had been at fault in causing the informality;[238] the procedure in such a case was for the court to read the verdict to the jury in proper form and, if the jurors unanimously agreed to that verdict, the court would then "authorize it to be recorded."[239] The court would not render judgment, however, if the pleadings were so defective that the court was at a loss as to what judgment to render.[240]

The general issue was not the only defensive plea to undergo

modification around the turn of the century; the rules for special
pleading were also modified. First, a series of statutes in the last two
decades of the eighteenth century gave liberty to plead the general issue
and to put special matter in evidence thereunder to specified categories
of defendants—defendants in all actions before justices of the peace
except suits involving title to land;[241] executors, administrators, and
guardians;[242] and justices of the peace, sheriffs, and other local
officials.[243] These statutes sought to assist these defendants in
avoiding the vagaries of special pleading.[244] Judicially created rules
offered similar assistance to other defendants. One rule permitted a
defendant on a plea of the general issue to reserve with the plaintiff's
consent the right to put special matters in evidence.[245] A second
practice—pleading double—let a defendant join a special plea to a plea
of the general issue,[246] even if the two pleas were inconsistent;[247]
since the general issue would always be a sufficient defense, a defendant, by joining a special plea to it, obtained the benefits of the
special plea without undergoing the risk of being thrown out of court as
a result of a formal, technical error in it. Although theoretically a
matter of discretion, "leave to plead double . . . [was] granted almost
as a matter of course, & without much consideration. . . ."[248]
Moreover, in cases where a special plea was joined to the general issue,
juries usually returned and the courts then rendered judgment on a
verdict that decided only the general issue;[249] the courts reasoned
that the jury could not have decided the general issue without
implicitly deciding the special issue as well.[250] In short, special pleas
were completely ignored, except to give defendants who joined a
special to their general plea the right to put special matter in evidence
under the general issue; that is, special pleading was virtually abolished.
Old rules of special pleading survived only when defendants pleaded
specially without simultaneously pleading the general issue.[251]

During the first third of the nineteenth century, then, the rules of
pleading were dramatically transformed. In cases where the common
law system proved constraining, litigants were able to bend the system
to fit the needs of their case. If a plaintiff had a just claim or a
defendant a just defense, technical rules of pleading no longer could be
interposed to prevent adjudication on the merits. Pleadings no longer
had to follow the ancient forms; the only requirement of a pleading was
that it give "notice to the opposing party, of matters intended to be
given in evidence by either party to a suit, as shall be necessary to
prevent surprise, and to afford opportunity for preparation for
trial,"[252] for a party could "not be supposed to come prepared to
defend against any cause of action [or defense], of which he ha[d] no
notice in the declaration" or in the plea in response to it.[253]

The courts had thus traveled most of the distance toward a system of notice pleading by 1830, and the legislature soon intervened and completed the task by statutes enacted in 1836 and 1851. The 1851 act, which was the result of study by a commission of eminent lawyers appointed within a year of the enactment of the Field Code in New York,[254] was the Massachusetts alternative to a code.[255] Like the Field Code, the 1851 act formally abolished the individual common law writs in personal actions, but it did not substitute a single, unitary cause of action for them. Instead it created generic pleas of contract, tort, and replevin for litigating personal actions[256] that took their place alongside the ancient generic plea of land used in real actions. Meanwhile, the 1836 act, passed during the course of study of the state's law by another eminent commission,[257] had confirmed the earlier judicial abolition of special pleading and further provided that "all matters of law or of fact in defense of . . . [an] action . . . [could] be given in evidence under the general issue. . . ."[258]

Long before this legislation, though, the abolition of common law pleading had begun to have consequences that were often unforeseen and that required compensatory modification of other rules of law. One advantage of common law pleading is that in addition to giving parties notice of the essence of each others' claims it narrows the issues that can arise upon trial by requiring the parties to select before trial, at least in part, the legal theory they plan to pursue. Particularly if the parties have engaged in special pleading, the issues on which litigation will turn are precisely identified before trial begins. With the abolition of common law pleading, issues were no longer formulated and defined before trial but during the very course of trial, as the parties offered evidence and made legal contentions on the basis of that evidence. "Causes of great importance" were, as one commentator noted, "often . . . tried by a Jury merely upon the general issue, when the facts . . . [were] complicated & intricate, the evidence of great length & variety & some times contradictory, & where questions of great nicety & difficulty . . . [were] involved in the discussion."[259]

Two problems arose. One was determining the res judicata effect of prior judgments where facts had been put in issue by means other than pleadings and hence were not of record.[260] The other was that preparation for trial became more difficult and hazardous; as one defendant argued, the complaint to which he had to respond was "so general, that it . . . [was] impossible [that] any man . . . [could] prepare to defend himself in the same. . . ."[261] Whereas litigants at common law had often had to prepare evidence only on a small number of precisely defined issues, a litigant under the new pleading system had to prepare to meet many potential issues, only some of which would arise. Moreover, he faced the danger that issues he had never anticipated might be brought up and that he might "be surprised by a piece of evidence which at another time he could have explained or answered. . . ."[262]

In order to insure that parties would "not [be so] surprised by new matter,"[263] new procedural rules had to be formulated. Thus the courts developed prohibitions against the admission of evidence to which there was an objection of surprise[264] and provisions, even after a verdict had been returned, for "a new trial, in case either party be unfairly surprized by the other."[265] The hazards of preparing for trial without being able to anticipate with certainty the issues that would arise also compelled the courts to develop rules authorizing the granting after verdict of a new trial on the grounds of newly discovered evidence[266] that was material to the issue,[267] that was not merely cumulative,[268] and that had not remained undiscovered through fault of the movant.[269] Newly discovered evidence became, in fact, "the most common cause for granting new trials. . . ."[270] As a general matter, new trials were granted whenever a party had not had adequate opportunity to present his claim.[271]

The unforeseen consequences of the abolition of common law pleading indicate most clearly what was at stake in the nineteenth-century struggle over pleading reform and why that reform could not take place overnight, as the reformers of the 1780s had demanded. Although common law pleading was antiquated, unduly technical, and expensive, and hence in need of reform, it nonetheless provided a working system for the trial of cases. More important, it provided lawyers with a conceptual framework for analyzing an otherwise amorphous body of legal rules. Thus, although lawyers recognized at an early date that the rules of pleading were in need of reform and began to take cautious steps in that direction, full reform could not occur until new substantive categories for analyzing the law and new procedures for insuring the fair dispensation of justice were developed.[272]

The emergence of substantive categories did far more than merely facilitate the abolition of common law pleading; it transformed the very meaning of law. In the prerevolutionary period, law had been seen merely as a series of writs and procedures manipulated by trained professionals in order to focus questions for resolution by juries in accordance with anticompetitive and other ethical values shared by the community at large. The abolition of common law pleading forced men to abandon such a view of law, while the emergence of a substantive conception forced them to see law as a set of formal standards dictating particular results in particular cases. The new substantive conception thereby forced lawyers arguing in favor of opposite results to a new articulation of the basis of their differences: they could no longer argue about how certain procedures should be manipulated or even about whether those procedures should exist but were forced to debate the question of what values ought to control the disposition of a case. In doing so they made plain the existence of differences over fundamental social values.

To the extent that society became aware of those differences, the old ethical unity of Massachusetts was undermined, for different values came to be cherished by different groups of men.

6. Law as the Guardian of Liberty

One value that naturally emerged from a revolution fought in liberty's defense was a heightened concern for liberty's preservation. Having "long struggled, at the expence of much treasure and blood, to obtain liberty for . . . [themselves and their] posterity,"[1] Americans of the revolutionary generation saw liberty as the very "object" of law[2] and were prepared to struggle against any doctrine that "manifestly tend[ed] to destroy the Liberties of the People,"[3] lest law become "an instrument of oppression."[4] Many believed that the Revolution had been uniquely "important to the liberties of America"[5] because "the idea of liberty . . . [had] been held up in so dazzling colours"[6] that Americans would be led to create "a broad Basis of Civil and religious Liberty . . . [that] no length of Time . . . [would] corrupt. . . ."[7] America would become a "Land of Such . . . Liberty as never before ha[d] been experienced"[8] and "an asylum for the oppressed and persecuted of every country," whose "example and success . . . [would] encourage the friends and rouse a spirit of liberty through other nations. . . ."[9]

Similar rhetoric quickly surfaced in the courts. Judges were urged to determine "point[s] of liberty & justice"[10] in accordance with "common Rights and the Law of the Land"[11] and to act "with that anxious regard for personal liberty and to prevent vexatious oppression, which all governments ought to feel. . . ."[12] Throughout the late eighteenth and early nineteenth centuries lawyers continued to urge judges to reject rules of law that "however expedient under a government of prerogative . . . [were] not suited to the spirit of our free institutions. . . ."[13]

Such reasoning produced challenges to a wide variety of traditional legal restraints. Thus one man charged with being a vagabond thought it appropriate to urge in his defense that America was "a free country,"[14] while another, who had been subjected to a form of preventive detention for uttering threats, argued that he had been placed in a "situation, in which no subject of a free government ought, or can, legally be placed, and which is equally forbidden by principles of humanity, as of justice."[15] The contagion of liberty even led to claims of license for immorality, when one frequenter of "the Hill" in Boston "pretended he had a right to visit all Whore-houses. . . ."[16]

Although these challenges met with no success, others were successful. Postrevolutionary libertarianism was, indeed, a potent force for legal change—perhaps the most potent one in the closing decades of the eighteenth century. Liberty had many different meanings, however, just as it does today, and as a result libertarianism affected the legal system in a variety of ways.

On the one hand, the preservation of liberty meant the preservation of institutions and procedures that empowered the governed rather than the governors to determine the law's substance. A key difference in the eyes of contemporaries between American government and monarchic or aristocratic governments was that America had a "government of the people"[17] "founded on principles not known to the laws of any other country."[18] By the end of the eighteenth century Americans had come to the view that ultimately "sovereignty . . . remains in the people,"[19] that all government is but "the *trustee* . . . of the people and *accountable* to them . . . ,"[20] and that officials of government are the "servants" and "mere tools" rather than the rulers of the people.[21]

Shared ideas about the sovereignty of the people and the accountability of government to the people resulted at an early date in a new understanding of the role of legislation in the legal system. This new understanding was part of a broader change in men's conception of a "constitution." Whereas a constitution had been seen in the colonial period as a body of vague and unidentifiable precedents and principles of common law origin that imposed ambiguous restrictions on the power of men to make or change law, after independence it came to be seen as a written charter by which the people delegated powers to various institutions of government and imposed limitations on the exercise of those powers. It became clear that the legislature possessed "full power and authority . . . to make, ordain, and establish, all manner of . . . laws, statutes, and ordinances . . . as they shall judge to be for the good and welfare of this Commonwealth," provided that "the same be not repugnant or contrary to this Constitution. . . ."[22] A constitution, that is, sorted out powers and defined jurisdictions. Certain powers were reserved to the people and thus became a matter of constitutional law, which, it was thought, the people alone had jurisdiction to change.[23] Other powers, including the power to modify or even entirely to repeal the common law, now fell explicitly within the jurisdiction of the legislature.

The shift in the understanding of legislative power can be seen vividly in statutory preambles. Virtually every colonial statute had contained a preamble that explained the necessity of legislating and, if the legislation in question produced any significant change in substantive law, sought to justify that change by demonstrating that the new statute was not really a change at all but a mere extension of doctrine consistent with the law's fundamental principles. This practice continued into the revolutionary period: of sixty-five acts adopted by the last two legislatures sitting prior to the adoption of the Constitution of 1780, only two did not contain preambles. Moreover, the preambles of the only two statutes that altered common law rights sought to explain that the alterations were not actually alterations. The preamble to a 1780 act depriving people of common law causes of action for damages inflicted by committees of correspondence prior to independence explained that damage suits had been "commenced . . . by evil and disaffected persons" and were, in effect, "manifestly calculated and designed for the destruction of the just rights and liberties of the people of the said province . . . "[24]—rights and liberties that the 1780 legislation was merely trying to protect. The preamble of the other act, a 1779 statute confiscating the estates of absentee Loyalists, likewise explained that the legislature was not depriving subjects of sacred common law property rights but was simply enforcing the social contract, which the Loyalists had breached by depriving the "government . . . [of] the personal services of all its members . . . in times of an impending or actual invasion," as a result of which each absentee "justly incurr[ed] the forfeiture of all his property, rights and liberties, holden under and derived from" the social contract.[25] The legislature of Massachusetts—unlike its counterpart in New York, which was already functioning under a constitution—was not yet prepared to alter common law property rights on the basis of "the sovereignty of the people of th[e] . . . State in respect to all property within the same."[26]

But it became willing to do so upon the adoption in 1780 of a state constitution. As the decade progressed, preambles became increasingly infrequent: in 1782, 23 percent of all legislation was passed without them; during the next five years, 31 percent; during 1788-1789, 49 percent. Legislation was coming to rest solely on a "be it enacted" clause—a naked assertion of sovereign legislative power. Moreover, many acts, including those lacking preambles, effected important changes in substantive legal rights; among those statutes were an "act prescribing the Manner of devising Lands,"[27] an "act directing the Descent of intestate Estates,"[28] an "act . . . for abolishing the Principle of Survivorship in joint Tenancy,"[29] an "act for preventing common Nuisances,"[30] and an "act . . . suspending . . . the Collection of private Debts. . . ."[31] But the clearest illustration that legislation was coming to rest on the arbitrary power of a majoritarian legislature rather than on its conformity with past law and principle was the ease with which statutes altering common law rights were enacted and repealed in the 1780s in response to changing election results. One need only look at the act of 1782 that deprived judgment creditors of their common law right to obtain satisfaction out of the proceeds of their debtors' goods sold at auction[32] and then at the act of 1784 that restored the right.[33] A final indication of the recognition of the legislature's sovereign power to change the law was the appointment in 1780 of a special committee of judges and lawyers to draft law reform bills for legislative enactment.[34]

New ideas about the relationship between government and the governed also produced changes in the rules of law concerning the rights and liabilities of various public officials. The perception that officials were agents of the people rather than of some distant, arbitrary governor raised doubts about the continuing validity of colonial rules holding officials strictly accountable for their infringements on liberty and for other wrongs. For the public now had an interest in "lightening the burdens of an office"[35] that common citizens might be called upon to fill and that all citizens had an interest in seeing filled by honest and competent men.[36] Moreover, the agents of the people scarcely seemed to pose the threat to liberty that the agents of the crown had earlier.

Such thinking led to a number of legal changes that reduced the liability of officials in common law actions for damages. The first change was made by a 1793 statute that gave sheriffs, their deputies, and town and other local officials the privilege of giving special matter in evidence under the general issue[37]—a privilege granted by the legislature "to relieve [officials] from the trouble and danger of special pleading. . . ."[38] Another statute three decades later, whose purpose again was "to lighten . . . the burdens of . . . office . . . [and] protect assessors in executing the requirements of their towns and parishes,"[39] immunized local tax assessors from suit for all good faith errors made in the execution of their duty.[40] A third statute protected moderators of town meetings from suits by residents claiming unlawful deprivation of their right to vote; it permitted moderators to rely on the tax lists drawn up by the tax assessors unless the resident claiming the right to vote had made objection to a list at the time of its publication.[41] Officers carrying out judicial warrants received similar protection as a result of the judiciary's development of the rule that the due issuance of a warrant was an absolute defense to an officer who was being sued for an unlawful search or arrest.[42] The courts likewise aided agents making contracts on behalf of the government by holding them not personally liable on the contracts.[43] Even legislators received judicial aid from the courts' broad construction of the legislative privilege from civil arrest.[44] Even with the benefit of special privileges, however, suits against officials remained common, particularly against sheriffs[45] and constables[46] but also against tax officials,[47] surveyors of highways,[48] jailers,[49] and even justices of the peace.[50]

Far more important changes in the law relating to officialdom occurred when the courts sought to insure the responsiveness of officials to the will of the people by safeguarding the integrity of the constitutional processes by which men obtained office. Courts held, for example, that if the executive made an unlawful appointment it was "the duty of the judiciary to pronounce such . . . appointment null and void."[51] More often, though, the courts were concerned with the preservation of the electoral process. Thus they decided cases concerning property qualifications[52] and residence requirements for voting,[53] alleged election frauds,[54] and other alleged voting irregularities.[55]

But the most important requisite for a political system in which "chief magistrates and Senators &c. . . . [were] annually eligible by the people" was that "their characters and conduct . . . be known to their constituents" so that those constituents could make intelligent choices in casting their ballots.[56] Unfortunately, the common law of defamation, both civil and criminal, placed political communication under close and confining restraint. If a newspaper printed an unfavorable political commentary about an official running for reelection, its publisher was liable in damages to the official unless he could prove that every statement in the commentary, including every statement of opinion, was factually true. He was also liable to prosecution for criminal or seditious libel, on the theory that such libel eroded public support of the government; not even truth was a defense, since the truth of a libel merely increased the erosion of public support.[57]

For several decades the courts struggled with the common law of defamation in an effort to modify it to fit the needs of the state's new republican system of government. Their difficulty resulted chiefly from their inability to overcome the assumption that the punishment of "dangerous or offensive writings . . . [was] necessary for the preservation of peace and good order, of government and religion, the only solid foundations of civil liberty."[58] The publication of a malicious libel was, according to the Supreme Judicial Court, "an offence . . . which must be adhered to so long as the restraint of all tendencies to the breach of the publick peace, and to private animosity and revenge is salutary to the commonwealth."[59] The court also argued that able and honest men were needed to serve in public office and that "no man of character would be willing to accept an office, if, in consequence, he ceased to be protected by the law from the calumnies of his fellow-citizens. . . ."[60] This last consideration was especially persuasive to judges who for most of the half century after the War of Independence placed such a high value on integrity of reputation that in suits involving nonpolitical defamation they consistently bent the rules of law in favor of plaintiffs whose reputations had allegedly been impaired.[61]

Considerations of this sort caused the courts to reject arguments such as one made in 1799 that "sedition may be committed in a Monarchy but not in a Republic" since "their Govt. is overthrown by it, [but] here is only a change of Men."[62] Judges in Massachusetts were unwilling to abandon the concepts of seditious libel and of noncriminal defamation, although they were willing to modify those concepts. One line of modification was suggested in 1801 by James Sullivan, then attorney general and later governor of the Commonwealth, in *A Dissertation upon the Constitutional Freedom of the Press in the United States of America*.[63] Recognizing the need for popular scrutiny of the behavior of public officials,[64] Sullivan sought to distinguish between publications concerning measures of government, which ought to be privileged and hence not indictable,[65] and libels made "with an intent to subvert the government . . . [or] to bring it into hatred or contempt," which "ought to be punished."[66] Sullivan proposed to create a narrow category of privilege for libels whose purpose was to inform voters about the policies and programs of candidates for office. A number of cases decided about the time Sullivan was writing adopted such an approach. In 1798 and again in 1804 courts held in civil actions brought to recover damages that letters sent to superiors of public officials in order to inform them of the misconduct and oppression of their subordinates were privileged,[67] while in 1802 the Supreme Judicial Court held in another civil suit that a libel published to prevent the plaintiff's election and to procure the election of another was similarly privileged.[68] Subsequently, however, the privilege granted in these cases was held to be a qualified one which would be forfeited if the defendant had acted with malice.[69]

The Supreme Judicial Court adopted a similar approach in criminal cases in the 1808 case of *Commonwealth* v. *Clap*,[70] where Chief Justice Parsons held that libels constituted "offenses against the state" because "their direct tendency [was] to a breach of the publick peace . . ." but then held that a "defendant . . . [could] repel the charge, by proving that the publication was for a justifiable purpose. . . ." "Upon this principle," according to Parsons, a man could "apply by complaint to the legislature to remove an unworthy officer. . . ."[71] Moreover, when a man "consent[ed] to be a candidate for a public office conferred by the election of the people, he must be considered as putting his character in issue. . . ." Thus "publications of the truth of this subject, with the honest intention of informing the people, . . . [were] not a libel."[72] Since Parsons further held that "every man holding a publick elective office . . . [fell] within this principle," on the presumption that he would seek reelection, the privilege created by the *Clap* case appeared to be a rather broad one. The defendant Clap, however, was himself sentenced to two months' imprisonment, since his libel had been published "maliciously and with intent to defame . . . ," and malice overcame the qualified privilege that the law conferred.[73]

Subsequent cases did not always adhere closely to the rules of privilege laid down in these early cases. Thus the Supreme Judicial Court in a civil action in 1812 rejected a defense that "the defendant, as a voter in . . . [a town] meeting, had a legal right to scrutinize into, and to animadvert upon, the . . . conduct" of the town clerk.[74] By the 1820s the courts were quick to find malice on the part of defendants who had defamed officials,[75] even if a defendant believed that what he had said was true,[76] and, as a result, the qualified privilege of inquiring into the conduct of public officials remained quite limited in both civil and criminal cases for another century.[77]

Ultimately, a more successful approach to change—the one followed by the federal Congress in the Sedition Act of 1798 and by most other states—was to make truth a defense in all defamation cases.[78] During the colonial period in Massachusetts, as we have seen, truth had been recognized as a defense in all cases, civil and criminal,[79] except perhaps in seditious libel cases. Evidence of truth had also been admitted in two seditious libel prosecutions in 1797 and 1803.[80] But in *Commonwealth* v. *Clap* in 1808,[81] Chief Justice Parsons definitively held that truth alone was not a defense in a criminal prosecution—a position reaffirmed in *Commonwealth* v. *Blanding*[82] two decades later upon the fear of the judges that "a further relaxation . . . [in the law of libel could] scarcely take place without involving the community, families and individuals, in those contentions and acrimonious conflicts which will render the social state little, if at all, better than savage."[83] The legislature, on the other hand, had no such fear and in 1827 provided by statute that truth, which had remained a defense in civil defamation cases,[84] should similarly be a defense in criminal cases.[85] This act had the practical effect of abolishing the law of criminal libel.[86] With its abolition, the power of officials to act without public scrutiny was limited, and their accountability to the public increased.

While new attitudes were developing during the 1780s about the law-making power of the legislature and the legal position of official-dom, older attitudes toward the role of judges and juries remained prevalent. Thus the prerevolutionary objective that judges be made independent of the executive received constitutional sanction in the provision that judges be appointed to serve during good behavior.[87] Given the fact that judges were appointed rather than elected, it seemed clear that they ought not to have power to make law; hence, as had been true before the Revolution, legal innovation on the part of the judiciary continued to be frowned upon. Courts, men continued to assume, were to be agencies of permanence and stability—an assumption that could "be inferred with certainty from the general nature of the judicial power...."[88] Contemporary commentators agreed almost unanimously[89] that it was "the duty of judges to conserve the law, not to change it...."[90] Judges were "no more than the mouth that pronounces the words of law, mere passive beings"[91] sworn to decide cases "according to the known laws and customs of the land; not delegated to pronounce a new law, but to maintain and expound the old one."[92] As one Massachusetts commentator observed, "the Judges of this State have not the 'power of bending the laws to their pleasure.' "[93] "[N]o axiom . . . [was thought] more dangerous than that the spirit of the law ought to be considered, and not the letter; if this . . . [were] adopted, the same laws that condemn today, will acquit tomorrow, according to the different opinions which different Judges may form of its spirit."[94] Moreover, if judges were to "put such a construction on matters as they think most agreeable to the spirit and reason of the law . . . , they [would] assume what is in fact the prerogative of the legislature"[95] and become "paramount in fact to the Legislature, which never was intended and can never be proper."[96] Courts thus could have no "power to repeal, to amend, to alter . . . or to make new laws . . . ";[97] 'a knowledge of mankind, and of Legislative affairs . . . [could not] be presumed to belong in a higher . . . degree to the Judges than to [legislators]."[98] The special skill of judges lay rather in their knowledge of the "strict rules and precedents, which serve to define and point out their duty in every particular case that comes before them...."[99] Thus courts ought to "take the law as it is, and by all due and proper means execute it, without any pretense to judge of its right or wrong."[100]

Prerevolutionary ideas about the importance of the jury system to liberty also remained dominant. For Americans after the Revolution, as well as before, the right to trial by jury was probably the most valued of all civil rights; as one historian has noted,[101] it was the only right universally secured by the first American state constitutions. In fact, the Massachusetts constitution, after making provision for trial by jury in both civil and criminal cases, further provided that "this method of procedure shall be held sacred...."[102] And when the federal Constitution failed some seven years later to provide for "trial[s by jury] as free and impartial as the lot of humanity will admit of,"[103] its failure provoked a storm of criticism in the Massachusetts ratifying convention.[104] To Americans of the revolutionary generation, in short, "the right . . . of a free subject . . . of an opportunity of being acquitted . . . by a verdict of his peers, & of vindicating his innocency & establishing his good fame in the face of the Country" was a vital one.[105]

To secure that right, the legislatures of the revolutionary period introduced trial by jury into several sorts of cases in which trial had formerly been to the court. The most significant of the changes was the introduction of jury trial into admiralty courts,[106] which, had they continued to sit without juries, "would have met . . . [with] universal disapprobation. . . ."[107] Jury trials were also introduced into paternity litigation.[108] Finally, the legislature's high regard for the jury led it to require a jury verdict in cases brought to confiscate lands held by Tory refugees, even when those refugees defaulted by nonappearance.[109] Retrenchment, however, also occurred as a result of legislation that increased the jurisdiction of justices of the peace[110] and thereby deprived litigants in cases transferred to the justices of their former right to a jury.[111]

Except for the changes in the law of criminal libel, postrevolutionary developments in Massachusetts law relating to the functioning of governmental institutions did not produce social or political divisions in the final quarter of the eighteenth century. The aim of the War of Independence had been to preserve and strengthen popular control of those institutions, and there was little objection to rules of law that were designed to do so. Legal change, essentially on an institutional level, was not productive of any substantial social change in postrevolutionary Massachusetts.

For the postrevolutionary generation, liberty also meant that government ought not to be able to punish an individual for a crime except after a proceeding in which the accused had been given the same procedural opportunities to prove his innocence as the state had been given to prove his guilt. This notion of liberty as procedural fairness again was one shared by society at large. Although the notion necessitated reform of much of the law of criminal procedure, that reform proceeded without apparent political division or social controversy. It seemed clear to all that rules that had been "established in arbitrary times" and were "expedient under a government of prerogative, . . . [were] not suited to the spirit of our free institutions."[112]

Concern for "the legal rights of the subject"[113] manifested itself most clearly during the first decade after the Revolution in the inclusion of provisions in both state and federal constitutions safeguard-

ing the procedural privileges of criminal defendants.[114] Thereafter
the courts continued "to guard against oppression and unnecessary
vexation,"[115] particularly as they came to see that defendants in
criminal cases were engaged in an unequal struggle with government. As
the most perceptive American student of criminal law in the early
nineteenth century explained, "a criminal in his trial—squalid in his
appearance, his body debilitated by confinement, his mind weakened
by misery or conscious guilt, abandoned by all the world, . . . stands
alone, to contend with the fearful odds that are arrayed against
him."[116] Even if he had counsel assigned him, "this counsel . . . [was] generally the youngest counsellor at the bar, who . . .
[was] thus made to enter the lists with one of the highest abilities and
standing, with a reputation so well established as to have made him the
choice of government as the depository of its interests."[117] Against
such odds, this inexperienced counsel was made to defend "the life of a
fellow being . . . , [which was] more important than any question
concerning property."[118] Few men doubted that "the rights of the
citizens of the *United States* . . . [would have to be placed] upon a
firmer and more substantial basis" than this.[119]

One way in which the courts advanced individual rights "in the
administration of criminal law" was to "require . . . of the public
prosecutors the most scrupulous exactness, believing it to be the right,
even of the guilty, to be tried according to known and practiced rules;
and that it were a less evil for a criminal to escape, than that the
barriers established for the security of innocence should be overthrown."[120] Indictments, unlike civil pleadings, were accordingly
held insufficient when they contained formal or technical defects.[121] The courts realized that such "strict adherence to technical
forms . . . [could] be inconvenient in particular cases; . . . [could] appear at times to be beneath the dignity of the law,"[122] and could
even "savour a little of nicety,"[123] but they were nevertheless
convinced that "unless known rules . . . [were] observed, there . . .
[would] soon be no certainty in indictments."[124] "[T]o relax the
rules of pleading heretofore established" would only lead to new rules,
and "it would not afterwards be found more easy to comply with
them. . . ."[125]

Of greater importance was the construction that the courts placed on
the procedural protections accorded by the Massachusetts constitution,
such as the provisions regulating arrests, searches, and seizures. The
constitution provided that every subject ought "to be secure from all
unreasonable searches, and seizures of his person . . . and all his possessions" and more specifically that arrests could be made only under
sworn warrants or in accordance with the law of the land.[126]
Pursuant to these provisions, the courts carefully restricted the power

of justices of the peace to authorize arrests and to commit people to prison,[127] particularly when the arrest was being made to benefit a particular person rather than to preserve the public peace.[128] The courts also refused to permit people who had been acquitted to be arrested and imprisoned after trial, on motion of the attorney general, on a new charge.[129] Peace bonds, however, could be required even after an acquittal, upon a complainant's oath that a defendant was endangering him.[130] In addition, individuals "whom it was dangerous to the safety of the people to permit to go at large" could be imprisoned pursuant to statute.[131]

The courts reached more consistently libertarian results in cases dealing with searches and seizures. Their aim in such cases was "to preserve the repose and tranquillity of families within the dwelling-house . . . ,"[132] which could "not be lawfully forced unless for purposes especially provided for by law."[133] Thus, by the early nineteenth century, general warrants of the type common before the Revolution had been proscribed "because of the danger and inconvenience of leaving it to the discretion of a common officer to arrest such persons, and search such houses as he thinks fit."[134] A search warrant could only be granted upon an oath stating that a crime had been committed, and, in theft cases, that the party complaining thereof had probable cause to suspect that stolen property was in a particular place. The reasons for the suspicion also had to be stated, and any warrant issued had to enumerate the specific places to be searched and goods to be seized.[135] As was the rule in the case of an officer making an unlawful arrest, "an officer [attempting to seize goods] without a precept . . . [was] no officer" in the eyes of the law, and the victim of the seizure was entitled to use reasonable force to defend his property; whatever hardship such a rule placed on officers was said by the court to be "a hardship resulting from the voluntary assumption of a hazardous office. . . ."[136]

Other constitutional provisions also came before the courts in criminal cases. It was held, for example, that confessions of the accused were to be rejected in criminal prosecutions[137] "if procured by any threat of harm, or promise of favour or benefit."[138] Another case that came before the Supreme Judicial Court construed the constitutional provision against ex post facto laws.[139]

Adherence to and development of common law rules and ancient provincial customs also provided important procedural protections to persons accused of crime. One ancient colonial practice that the courts continued to follow was the assignment of counsel in capital cases.[140] An important common law rule was one prohibiting a defendant from being placed twice in jeopardy for the same offense.[141] Massachusetts courts also adhered to the doctrine that a receiver of stolen goods or other accessory to a crime could not be put to trial until his principal had been convicted[142] and to the common law presumption that when "the liberty of the subject is concerned, . . . [a] statute ought to receive a construction favorable to the prisoner."[143] While continuing to permit indictments for common law crimes,[144] the courts also continued to follow the common law rule prohibiting the judicial creation of new common law offenses.[145] On the other hand, the Supreme Judicial Court refused to apply the common law rule prohibiting new trials in favor of defendants in capital cases, noting that "however expedient under a government of prerogative, [the rule was] . . . not suited to the spirit of our free institutions. . . ."[146]

A number of judicial practices first adopted during the postrevolutionary period also showed special regard for the procedural rights of persons accused of crime. When, for instance, a defendant charged with a capital offense sought to plead guilty, his plea would not be accepted and he would be informed that he did not have to plead but could "put the government to proof of" its charges. A renewed plea of guilty would then be accepted only after the accused had been "allow[ed] . . . a reasonable time to consider what had been said to him" and after an examination had been conducted "under oath . . . as to the *sanity* of the prisoner; and whether there had not been tampering with him. . . ."[147] The courts were equally protective of defendants who showed signs of mental derangement; they would not be put to trial if a jury found they were incompetent to stand trial.[148] Another important development occurred in *Commonwealth* v. *Andrews,*[149] where the court announced a doctrine of waiver strikingly similar to the modern doctrine.[150] The case involved the question whether a defendant charged with receiving stolen property, who had a right not to be tried until the thief was convicted, had waived that right by submitting to trial. The court held that "in criminal cases, an express relinquishment of a right should appear, before the party can be deprived of it. Here is no such relinquishment, but merely a silent submission, which probably arose from ignorance at the time that such right existed."[151] And, in a final reform, the practice of having justices of the peace interrogate defendants on their preliminary hearing was ended. The practice had been prevalent before the Revolution and had continued during the years immediately following.[152] But in the 1790s signs of its impending demise appeared. Although one defendant confessed to the details of his offense before a justice as late as 1793,[153] three other abstracts of preliminary hearings in the 1790s indicate that the only question asked a defendant was whether he was guilty or not guilty of the crime charged.[154] In 1797 printed forms came into use for recording preliminary hearings, and the forms left

space for an answer by an accused to only one question—whether he
was guilty or not guilty[155]—indicating that the standard practice was
for justices to ask only this question. In the early nineteenth century it
was even doubted whether this question was permissible.[156] In
short, for several decades after the War of Independence the judges of
Massachusetts, in their effort to promote liberty, decided nearly every
question of criminal procedure that came before them in a manner
favorable to defendants accused of crime.

Liberty acquired yet a third meaning in the postrevolutionary
era—one that was essentially egalitarian. As the Declaration of Independence itself had recognized, all men were created free. Many felt
that a society that permitted some men to manipulate the rules of law
to keep others subordinate could not fairly be called a free one. Hence
it was frequently argued that "when the liberty of one man . . . [was]
attacked," that attack was "tantamount to an attack on the liberties of
all. . . ."[157] For those who accepted the argument, it followed that
the legal system, as it related to groups such as slaves, women, and
religious dissenters, would have to be modified so that all people would
enjoy equal rights before the law.

The earliest manifestation in Massachusetts of this libertarian impulse
was the abolition of slavery. Immediately after independence, men
began to argue that "the law of God . . . [was] against slavery"[158]
and that it ill became men who had "long struggled . . . to obtain
liberty . . . to enslave others who ha[d] an equal right to liberty. . . ."[159] Men saw the "absurdity" and incompatibility of slavery
and liberty and hoped that "the situation of America" would become
such "that the slave-holder could not be found in the land."[160]

Slaveholders were accordingly advised that they had "no right to
keep . . . [their slaves], but had better set . . . [them] at liberty . . . ,"[161] and a number of young lawyers, including such future
leaders of the profession as Theophilus Parsons and Perez Morton,
began to take practical steps to make that advice a reality.[162] They
met with almost instantaneous success. As early as 1777 Parsons won a
case in which the Essex County Court of Common Pleas held, as a
matter of law, that a man could not be restrained of his liberty on the
ground of his being a Negro slave[163]—a decision that the same court
reiterated one year later.[164] The Supreme Judicial Court apparently
accepted these decisions as binding, for in 1780 it directed a plaintiff
who had brought suit against a defendant for allegedly inducing his
slave to run away to amend his writ so as to claim that the runaway was
not a "molatto man servant" but an apprentice;[165] the amendment
appears to have been a prerequisite to getting the case before the jury,
where the plaintiff then won a verdict. Moreover, the court held some

years later that a black man who had been purchased as a slave in 1779 had not in the eyes of the law ever been such, for "at that time all Negroes were considered in fact as Free: although they had been imported from Africa & Sold here as Slaves."[166] The Supreme Judicial Court also took that view on two occasions in the early 1780s. The first was in 1781 in the case of *Caldwell* v. *Jennison*,[167] where a jury, following arguments on the validity of slavery as a matter of law, found that the particular slave who had brought a suit for his freedom was a freeman. Whatever doubts may have remained as a consequence of the form of this decision were completely removed two years later, when in *Commonwealth* v. *Jennison*, a criminal prosecution for enslaving a Negro, the Supreme Judicial Court charged a jury that

> whatever usages formerly prevailed or slid in upon us by the example of others, on this subject they can no longer exist. Sentiments more favourable to the natural rights of mankind, and to that innate desire of liberty, which heaven, without regard to complexion or shape, has planted in the human breast—have prevailed since the glorious struggle for our rights began. And these sentiments led the framers of our Constitution of Government—by which the people of this Commonwealth have solemnly bound themselves to each other—to declare—*that all men are born free and equal*; and that *every subject is entitled to liberty*, and to have it guarded by the laws as well as his life and property. In short, without resorting to implication in construing the Constitution, slavery is as effectively abolished as it can be by the granting of rights and privileges wholly incompatible and repugnant to its existence.
>
> The Court are therefore fully of opinion that perpetual servitude can no longer be tolerated in our government. . . .[168]

Despite the clarity of these decisions and the clarity with which courts in the next two decades construed them, they did not have the effect of immediately abolishing all slavery in Massachusetts. Throughout the late 1770s and the early 1780s individual slaves still were compelled to bring lawsuits in order to assert their freedom,[169] and in one suit a jury even returned a verdict for the master.[170] As late as 1784 a prosecution for maltreatment of a slave can be found,[171] while in 1786 the owner of a "Negro Man Servant" sued a person to whom he had leased the man in order to recover wages due under the lease.[172] Moreover, there is no way of knowing how many blacks remained enslaved even after that date because they lacked either the means or the inclination to bring suit for their freedom. Thus, as has often been the case with race relations in American history, compliance with the law did not occur nearly as rapidly as the law itself changed.

Women composed another group that sought to benefit from the contagion of liberty. Even before independence from England had been declared, John Adams had received a letter from his wife urging that

> in the new code of laws which I suppose it will be necessary for you to make, I desire you would remember the ladies, and be more generous to them than your ancestors. Do not put such unlimited power into the hands of husbands. Remember, all men would be tyrants if they could. If particular care and attention are not paid to the ladies, we are determined to foment a rebellion, and will not hold ourselves bound to obey any laws in which we have no voice or representation.[173]

During the next five decades women often resorted to the courts in an attempt to secure equal rights under the law, but, at least in Massachusetts, they met with mixed success.

The basic rule of law that women were trying to alter was one that gave a married woman no legal personality separate and apart from her husband. Thus she was incapable of entering into contracts,[174] of managing or disposing of her own property,[175] or of suing and being sued.[176] "Upon the strict principles of law, a *femme-covert* . . . [was] not a member . . . [and had] no *political* relation to the *state*. . . ."[177] Married women were even deemed incapable of committing crimes, at least when they were in the presence of their husbands, since a wife was presumed to be under her husband's command, and "if he commanded it, she was bound to obey him, by a law paramount to all other laws—the law of God."[178] A woman was not even permitted to administer her late husband's estate if, during the course of the administration, she remarried.[179]

Judicial positions slowly began to change only in the 1820s, as the position of women in society changed. The Supreme Judicial Court observed in dictum, for example, that "femmes covert . . . may be answerable for" crimes.[180] More important, as the breakup of marriages became more common and more women came to live and to maintain businesses apart from their husbands, courts modified the rules of law relating to the right of such women to manage their affairs independently. In the eighteenth century and the first decade of the nineteenth, a woman who acted as sole,[181] who had entered into an agreement to run a business separately,[182] or whose husband "had been absent six or seven years" and probably "would [never] . . . return,"[183] had nonetheless been denied all legal rights, as had been women living with their husbands.[184] In the 1820s, however, the courts held that a woman who had been legally separated from her husband[185] or a woman whose husband had deserted her and resided in a foreign country or another state, where he could not be compelled to support her,[186] could manage and convey her own property, sue and be sued, and enter into contracts. Even women who were not separated from their husbands but who conducted separate businesses with which their husbands were not associated were permitted to exercise such rights as against the outside world,[187] although their husbands retained power to reduce their wives' separate property to possession at any time.[188] Still, in 1830 the progress that women had made toward liberation remained slight.

A third group that had had an inferior status at the outset of the Revolution consisted of the members of dissenting religious sects. For them the Revolution appeared to present the perfect opportunity to tear down the Congregational religious establishment and to achieve a separation of church and state. For few men in postrevolutionary Massachusetts doubted that "every person ha[d] an unalienable right to act in all religious affairs according to the full persuasion of his own mind, where others are not injured thereby";[189] indeed, the constitution itself provided that "every denomination of christians . . . [should] be equally under the protection of the law" and that "no subordination of any one sect or denomination to another . . . [should] ever be established by law."[190] Few men, in short, were prepared to defend the old colonial denominational establishment or "to deny . . . liberty of conscience."[191]

But many still believed that "the importance of religion to civil society and government [was] great indeed. . . ." Religion, they thought, kept "alive the best sense of moral obligation, a matter of . . . extensive utility, especially in respect to an oath, which . . . [was] one of the principal instruments of government" and which lay at the heart of the legal system's fact-finding process. It was feared that if "the restraints of religion [were] once broken down, as they infallibly would be, by leaving the subject of public worship to the humors of the multitude, . . . we might well defy all human wisdom and power, to support and preserve order and government in the State."[192] As the Constitution of 1780 itself observed, "the good order and preservation of civil government, essentially depend[ed] upon piety, religion and morality," which could "not be generally diffused through a community, but by the institution of the public worship of GOD. . . ."[193] No one, in short, thought that God needed the aid of the communities of Massachusetts, but many feared that orderly and coherent communities committed to the pursuit of ethical ends could not exist without the support of God.

The framers of the Constitution of 1780 sought to invoke God's aid by creating a nondenominational Protestant religious establishment.[194] For some three decades, the courts effectively carried out the framers' program. In deciding church-state questions, the courts refused "to assume the character of theologians"[195] or to enter into "questions of dogmatical theology," since they would "be at a loss to find legal principles on which to decide them."[196] Moreover, "religious opinions ... [did] not concern the public interest. ..."[197] That courts assumed a nondenominational, secular approach to matters of religion can be seen from their characterization of the "Office ... [of minister as being] as much a civil as an ecclesiastical one"[198] and from their refusal "to admit ... [the existence of significant] distinction[s] among the different denominations of religious societies in this state";[199] "men of liberal minds," according to Chief Justice Parsons, could "with a good conscience attend indifferently the public worship of different denominations. ..."[200] As a result of the 1780 constitution, then, religion had ceased in the eyes of the law to be a spiritual matter; "the people of *Massachusetts* ... [had] adopted and patronized a religion ... [only] to promote and secure the happiness of the citizens" and to "supply the defects in civil government. ..."[201]

Legal theory favoring a nondenominational establishment did not, however, square with social fact. When the courts during the 1780s worked out the precise legal nature of the new establishment, which rested on the constitutional injunction that the legislature "require, the several towns, parishes, precincts, and other bodies-politic, or religious societies, to make suitable provision ... for the institution of the public worship of GOD ... in all cases where such provision shall not be made voluntarily,"[202] it soon appeared that the new establishment would remain a predominantly Congregational one. The basic reason for this was that the legislature, following the adoption of the constitution, did nothing to modify the territorial parish system of the colonial period, by which nearly everyone in the Commonwealth was assigned to membership in whatever parish he happened to inhabit. Since nearly every parish in the postrevolutionary period continued to support a Congregational church, the onus of dissent remained upon non-Congregationalists. The only question was how burdensome that onus would be—a question that could be broken down into two legal issues concerning the power of parishes to levy taxes in order to support religious worship. The first issue was whether parishes could collect taxes from all of their inhabitants, including dissenters. The second issue concerned the uses to which parishes could put the taxes they had collected.

The first issue was presented to the courts in 1782 in the case of *Bolkcom* v. *Wilkerson*,[203] which was brought by the Baptists in order to test the continued constitutionality of a Congregational establishment. The case had arisen when the plaintiff Bolkcom, a Baptist, refused to pay taxes levied by the Congregational parish in which he resided and instead submitted to arrest; his suit was for damages for the arrest. Bolkcom contended that the new religious establishment was unconstitutional because it violated the constitution's provision against the subordination of one sect to another—a contention that indeed made much sense. Although Bolkcom's parish was willing not to tax him if he would obtain a certificate of the sort that colonial dissenters had been required to obtain, Bolkcom argued that the certificate system constituted subordination, since it placed on Baptists a burden that Congregationalists did not have to bear; the only way Baptists could avoid being specially burdened was by being granted a right simply not to pay religious taxes. Congregationalists argued in response that if men could decline to pay taxes on grounds of conscience, large numbers who were not true dissenters would feign conscience and pay no taxes, following which even a nondenominational establishment would collapse.

The Court of Common Pleas of Bristol County agreed with Bolkcom, and for two years its decision stood as the law of Massachusetts.[204] But when the same issue was presented to the Supreme Judicial Court in another case in 1784,[205] that court reached the opposite result, holding that certificates were necessary in order to obtain tax exemption and further that certificates were invalid unless they were procured from an incorporated religious society. The latter part of the decision was particularly damaging to the Baptists, for Baptist and most other dissenting congregations had never obtained legislative incorporation. The decision therefore meant that a denominational religious establishment, from which tax exemption was unobtainable, would continue in fact, though not perhaps in theory, to exist in Massachusetts.[206]

The extent to which dissenters would be subordinated to Congregationalists remained unsettled, however, for the uses to which parish moneys could be put had not yet been decided by the courts. There were several subissues here. One was whether an individual parish could establish a church of a denomination other than Congregational if it wished to do so. Courts said that parishes could,[207] but until the Unitarian schism in the 1810s the only non-Congregational parishes whose existence was recognized by the courts were those that had never been Congregational entities.[208] In fact, the courts placed significant obstacles in the path of Congregational parishes that might otherwise have sought to alter their denominational allegiance. Thus, in a case begun before the Revolution but decided in 1778, the Superior Court held for the first time in Massachusetts history that once he had been settled by a parish a minister possessed "an estate for life . . . determinable [only] upon misbehaviour or incapacity which renders the person unfit for the Office."[209] The court reasoned that "if the clergy have no fixt continuance or estate in their offices it will be the greatest

discouragement to men of learning and worth settling in the minis-
try . . . ";[210] moreover, the minister's duty "of inveighing against
vice . . . would not be done if he were liable to be deprived of his office
at the whim of a majority of a parish."[211] The significance of this
decision lay in the fact that the power of a parish to terminate a
minister's life estate for "misbehavior or incapacity" was a narrowly
limited one. In order for a parish to act ex parte the misbehavior had to
be "of the grosser sort; such as habitual intemperance, lying, unchaste
or immodest behaviour, &c."[212] In the event of lesser forms of
misbehavior or incapacity such as a disagreement between parish and
minister "in their religious sentiments and opinions," a minister could
only be dismissed upon "the advice of an ecclesiastical council" held in
accordance with "the ancient and immemorial usage of Congregational
churches. . . ."[213] Adherence to this ancient institutional arrangement for resolving doctrinal disputes meant that the Congregational
church, by deciding disputes in favor of Congregational ministers and
parishes and against dissenting ministers and parishes, could insure that
parishes did not lapse from their Congregational allegiance. Such a lapse
was possible only if both minister and parish agreed on it or, as
occurred during the Unitarian schism, when a sufficient number of
neighboring clergymen were willing to assent to it. The other obstacle
to denominational change was the rule that parish inhabitants who had
elected to obtain tax exemption certificates ceased thereafter to be
voting members of the parish.[214] As a result, when the time came to
select a new minister to replace one who had died or resigned,
Congregationalists had more power in the parish than their percentage
of the total population justified, since dissenters were not permitted to
vote.[215]

Once it was clear that dissenters would be required to pay taxes
raised by parishes and that those parishes would remain under Congregational control, only one possibility of relief remained. During the
colonial period, as we have seen, dissenting ministers could recover
taxes collected by parishes from members of their congregations,[216]
and the Constitution of 1780 appeared to sanction that practice by
explicitly providing that all sums collected from any taxpayer "shall, if
he require it, be uniformly applied to the support of the public teacher
or teachers of his own religious sect or denomination. . . ."[217] There
was some doubt, however, whether a dissenting congregation had to be
incorporated in order for its minister to bring suit to recover taxes paid
by its members. When this question was first presented to a three-judge
panel of the Supreme Judicial Court in the 1785 case of *Murray* v. *First
Parish in Gloucester*,[218] the panel instructed the jury that incorporation was required—a result that would have forced dissenters either to
obtain legislative incorporation or to pay taxes for the support of the

established church. However, when the case came before the full court in the next year on a writ of review, the court reversed itself and Chief Justice Cushing instructed the jury that if incorporation were required "the general benefits of religious equality and freedom would be precarious instead of being absolutely granted," contrary to the objects of the constitution, which were "to secure to every subject toleration in matters of religion; to prevent any subordination among the different sects of protestants; and any unequal burthens in consequence of a difference in religious professions or sentiments."[219] The only requirement that the courts imposed on dissenting ministers was that they be associated with a particular congregation in a single town; itinerants who preached before two or more congregations on alternate Sundays could not recover taxes.[220] But a religious teacher could recover taxes even if he was not an ordained minister[221] and even if the parishioner for whose taxes he was suing had joined his congregation for convenience rather than out of religious conviction.[222] Dissenting clergymen who had the care of a single congregation even received the same tax exemption that ministers of the established church enjoyed.[223] Dissenters who were duly organized in congregations and who supported a full-time minister were thus placed nearly on a par with Congregationalists. Although dissenters were required to pay taxes, their taxes, like the taxes of Congregationalists, were used only to support their own sect. Congregationalists nevertheless retained some superiority by virtue of their control of parish institutions and hence of the mechanisms for levying and collecting taxes.

The compromise settlement worked out in the courts in the 1780s endured for over two decades, until Chief Justice Parsons, who had been counsel for the Congregational parish in the *Murray* case, held for the court in the 1810 case of *Barnes* v. *First Parish in Falmouth* [224] that a minister could not recover taxes paid by members of his congregation unless the congregation was an incorporated one, thereby overruling *Murray* sub silentio and in effect fully reestablishing Congregationalism. But rather than strengthening the establishment the *Barnes* decision provoked its downfall, for it aroused dissenters as never before and, following victory in the 1811 elections, enabled them to obtain legislative action.[225]

Although the religious establishment officially lingered on until 1833, the Religious Freedom Act of 1811[226] in effect destroyed it. The act, in which the legislature sought to clarify the provisions of the constitution, on which the courts had been basing their decisions since the 1780s, overruled nearly all of those decisions and constituted a complete victory for the dissenters—which was confirmed when the Supreme Judicial Court held in *Adams* v. *Howe* [227] that it was bound by the legislature's construction of the constitution's religious provisions. As the court said:

> We must premise, that so much respect is due to any legislative
> act, solemnly passed, and admitted into the statute book, that a
> court of law, which may be called upon to decide its validity, will
> presume it to be constitutional, until the contrary clearly appears.
> So that in any case of the kind substantially doubtful, the law
> would have its force. The legislature is, in the first instance, the
> judge of its own constitutional powers; and it is only when
> manifest assumption of authority, or misapprehension of it, shall
> appear, that the judicial power will refuse to execute it. Whenever
> such a case happens, it is among the most important duties of the
> judicial power to declare the invalidity of an act so passed.[228]

Barnes and other earlier cases were held to be "correct" but distinguishable, since when they were decided "no legislative act had then been
passed, tending to vary or affect the natural and obvious meaning of the
terms of the articles of the declarations of rights. . . ."[229] Moreover,
even *Barnes*, according to the court, had recognized "the power of the
legislature . . . [to] 'grant any further relief in particular cases, which in
its discretion it may consider as deserving relief.' "[230]

Under the 1811 act and its subsequent amendatory legislation,[231]
a person who filed with his town clerk a certificate of membership in a
religious society was exempt from all religious taxation as long as he
maintained his membership, even if the society was an unincorporated
one and did not possess a full-time minister[232] and even if it was of
the same denomination as the established parish church.[233] If a
person wished to leave one religious society and join another, he had
merely to obtain a certificate from the society he proposed to
join,[234] which constituted conclusive evidence that he was no longer
a member of the former society.[235] If, despite this certificate, the
person who had obtained it was nonetheless taxed, his clergyman could
bring suit to recover the tax.[236] In short, every person was free to
join whatever religious society he wished, change societies whenever he
wished, and thereby avoid paying ecclesiastical taxes, as long as the
society of which he was currently a member chose to support itself by
voluntary contributions. Only atheists continued to suffer the burden
of being taxed to support a system of religion that they did not believe
in.

Taken together, the various libertarian changes in law discussed
above did far more than merely restructure institutions, safeguard the
procedural rights of criminal defendants, and grant equal rights to
certain previously underprivileged classes. Those changes contributed in
important ways to the breakdown of the ideal inherited from the
prerevolutionary period that communities should stand united in the
pursuit of shared ethical ends.

The breakdown of ethical unity began in the 1780s with the virtual cessation of criminal prosecutions for various sorts of immorality. During the fifteen years before the Revolution, as we have already seen, there had been an average of seventy-two prosecutions per year for sexual offenses, nearly all for fornication.[237] The first ten years after independence produced only a slight decline to fifty-eight cases each year. However, in 1786 the General Court enacted a new statute for the punishment of fornication, permitting a woman guilty of the crime to confess her guilt before a justice of the peace, pay an appropriate fine, and thereby avoid prosecution by way of indictment in the court of sessions.[238] The number of prosecutions for sexual offenses immediately declined to an average of eleven per year during 1786-1790 and to less than five per year during the four decades thereafter. It appears that after 1790 women simply stopped confessing their guilt of fornication,[239] apparently aware that even though they did not confess it was most unlikely that they would be indicted. Indeed, only four indictments for fornication were returned in the entire Commonwealth after 1790;[240] most sexual prosecutions after that date were for more serious offenses such as adultery,[241] public lewdness,[242] or the publication of obscene matter, such as the novel *Memoirs of a Woman of Pleasure*.[243]

Prosecutions for religious offenses also continued near the prewar rate of twenty-four per year until the mid-1780s.[244] But by the 1790s the number of cases had declined to about ten per year, except for the two-year period 1815-1816, when in a sudden burst of enforcement there were 109 cases in all. The decrease is explained by the fact that after the 1780s prosecutions for missing church on Sunday ceased;[245] prosecutions continued only for the offenses of working and traveling on Sunday.[246] Even the Sunday work and travel laws were less rigidly enforced, with the result that by the 1810s "the Laws . . . against profanations of the Sabbath, had fallen into general neglect . . . [and] thousands of violations occurred every year, with scarcely a single instance of punishment."[247]

The law's attitude toward adultery was also changing, although the number of prosecutions remained relatively constant. In 1793 the Supreme Judicial Court began regularly to grant divorces on the ground of adultery,[248] yet prosecutions for the crime remained rare.[249] Of course, the granting of such divorces is not indicative of a rise in the incidence of adultery; rather it suggests the development of an attitude of legal hypocrisy that made it possible, at least in divorce proceedings, for a court to acknowledge on the record the existence of sin without prosecuting it.

There was a parallel development in paternity litigation. As prosecutions for fornication ceased, it appears that a question arose whether an unwed mother not convicted of the crime could bring a paternity action against the putative father. One woman instituted such a suit in 1790[250] and gave bond to appear at the next term of court to prosecute it. At that term, however, a new condition was added to her bond—that she also appear to answer to a criminal charge of fornication.[251] Thus the first attempt by a woman to sue without first suffering the consequences of her own misdeed failed. Yet within five years a new attempt had succeeded,[252] and thereafter paternity suits by women not punished for their own sin succeeded regularly.[253] Allowing such suits was a step even more radical than granting divorce for adultery without prosecuting the adulterer. In the divorce cases, the courts merely took a neutral attitude toward the defendant sinner. In paternity cases, on the other hand, the courts not only overlooked the plaintiff's sinner status but also rendered the sinner affirmative help in obtaining relief from the consequences of her sin.

To many contemporaries the deemphasis of prosecution for sin appeared to be a decline in morals.[254] President Timothy Dwight of Yale traced the decline to the French and Indian War and especially to the Revolution, which, he said, had added "to the depravation still remaining [from the French War] . . . a long train of immoral doctrines and practices, which spread into every corner of the country. The profanation of the Sabbath, before unusual, profaneness of language, drunkenness, gambling, and lewdness were exceedingly increased. . . ."[255] Others also alluded to habits of card playing and gambling and to instances of social vice and illegitimacy.[256] Chief Justice William Cushing, for example, feared that "some men ha[d] been so liberal in thinking as to religion as to shake off all religion, & while they ha[d] labored to set up heathen above Christian morals, ha[d] shown themselves destitute of all morality. . . ."[257]

Notwithstanding these complaints, it does not appear that there was any deep-seated coarseness or general immorality during the closing years of the eighteenth century.[258] What was beginning to occur after the Revolution was not significantly more immorality but an abandonment of the prerevolutionary notion that government should act to enforce morality. Over time, however, the abandonment by government of its enforcement role would impair the notion that there was any one set of ethical standards that all men ought to obey.

The various other changes discussed in this chapter also contributed to the breakdown of the ideal of ethical unity. On the one hand, the process of change itself disrupted unity. At the turn of the century, for example, Massachusetts society was divided politically on the issue whether seditious libel could be prosecuted as a criminal offense,[259] and, as I have suggested, the division tended to impair social unity. The conflict over the law of seditious libel was followed almost immediately

by a far more substantial conflict over the continued existence of the
religious establishment. This dispute, essentially a battle over whether
ethical unity could be imposed by the state,[260] lingered almost
fifteen years into the nineteenth century. The very existence of this
political contention, following the earlier contention brought about by
the efforts of agrarian debtors in the 1780s to obtain amelioration of
their condition, severely strained whatever unity there had been at the
century's beginning.

The outcome of the conflicts over the law of libel and the religious
establishment contributed even more fundamentally to unity's destruction. Consider first the changes in the law of libel. As those changes
made political libels increasingly difficult to prosecute, political speech
became increasingly harsh and divisive. Speakers after 1800 not infrequently accused officials and candidates for office of earning their
"living by robbery and plunder"[261] or of using their office for
personal gain,[262] and on occasion they even compared them to
traitors such as Aaron Burr and Benedict Arnold.[263] Although many
still believed that in the small communities dominating Massachusetts in
1800 "friendship among all individuals . . . [was] highly necessary to
the happiness of the whole," it was becoming clear that "harsh and
provoking language" would continue to be used and that such language
would be destructive both of friendship and of community unity.[264]

The 1811 victory of the forces of disestablishment confirmed unity's
destruction. That victory marked the culmination of a trend that had
begun in the colonial period and gained momentum after the Revolution. The trend was away from having one set of ethical values laid
down by a single institution, which all inhabitants of a community were
compelled to join, toward having several sets of differing ethical values,
each represented by different organizations that individuals freely
elected to join. While the divergence in the ethical values of various
Protestant sects in early nineteenth-century Massachusetts was slight,
ethical divergence would soon become greater, when Roman Catholics
and radical Protestant sects like the Shakers began to appear in the
state. Effective disestablishment, however, was of some immediate
importance, for it marked the symbolic end of an age in which a single
institution or group of related institutions had legitimate authority to
impose one set of moral values on the community at large.

By the 1820s, in fact, not even a theological seminary had the power
to impose its values on members of its own community. In *Murdock,
Appellant*,[265] a professor of the Theological Institution of Phillips
Academy in Andover who had been discharged from office for *"gross
neglect of duty"* and for *"other just and sufficient cause"*[266]
appealed to the Supreme Judicial Court to have his discharge reversed.
Finding that the appellant had failed to deliver certain required

lectures, to conduct required classes, and to grade papers, the court affirmed his dismissal on the ground of neglect of duty, but it then proceeded to discuss in dictum whether the other charges against him constituted just and sufficient cause for his dismissal. It ruled that they did not. The other charges were that the appellant entertained "jealousies of the other members of the faculty," that "he had made representations to one of his colleagues, respecting another, of an unfavorable character," and that he had "discuss[ed] with the students subjects belonging to the departments of his colleagues, and in such discussions . . . [had] impugn[ed] the arguments which his colleagues ha[d] advanced."[267] In short, the appellant's conduct had shattered the unity and harmony of the theological seminary, but by the 1820s such conduct was no longer grounds for discipline or punishment.

The degree to which ancient ethical standards had been eroded by the early nineteenth century is also apparent in men's changing views on the meaning of an oath. As conservatives of the 1780s had feared, the oath, on which the legal system of colonial Massachusetts had rested, lost its divine sanction and hence, in the view of some men, its validity. The first step in that direction occurred in 1812, when the Supreme Judicial Court reversed the ancient practice of Massachusetts[268] and held that Quakers were not incapacitated from serving on grand juries by their unwillingness to take the usual oath; the "affirmation administered to them," according to the court, was "equivalent to the oath appointed to be taken by other persons."[269] This holding was consistent with statutes adopted in 1808 and 1811[270] for the relief of Quakers and with the constitutional provisions requiring that "every denomination of christians . . . be equally under the protection of the law" and prohibiting the "subordination of any one sect or denomination to another. . . ."[271] Nevertheless, to hold that an affirmation that by its own terms subjected a man only to " 'the pains and penalties of perjury' "[272] was equivalent to an oath was to alter one's conception of an oath—to view the primary sanction behind an oath as the penalty of perjury and not the punishment of Hell.

The next step was to hold that the penalty of perjury was the sole meaningful sanction behind an oath—which occurred six years later, when people who did not believe in a future state of rewards and punishments were held competent to testify. The argument against taking the step was the old, familiar one that "the use and object of an oath . . . [was] not to secure the temporal punishment of its violation, but that truth . . . [would] be manifested," because "the witness's sense of the obligation imposed on him . . . [would] make . . . it more improbable that he . . . [would] swear falsely."[273] To administer an oath to someone who did not believe in an afterlife would be, it was said, to perform "a lifeless ceremony ... over a dead carcase."[274] This argument, made in an 1817 slander case involving an accusation that an atheist had committed perjury, was rejected by the Supreme Judicial Court, however, which in the very next year held that a witness who did not believe in a future life could nonetheless be sworn and could testify.[275]

With the deemphasis of religion, old colonial rules of evidence, which had rested on the assumption that an oath taken by an honest, disinterested witness rendered his testimony true, also ceased to have any logical basis of support, and some of those rules accordingly began to change. Among them was the rule that conviction of a felony rendered the convict incompetent as a witness.[276] The courts also repudiated their old assumption that witnesses under oath would tell the truth when they ruled that a witness could be impeached by evidence of prior inconsistent statements without first being given an opportunity to show that those statements were in fact consistent with his statements under oath.[277] In fact, judicial assumptions about the veracity of sworn witnesses had turned full circle since the colonial period, for the courts now assumed that "witnesses about to be impeached ... [were] generally persons of a doubtful or unknown character; ... the wisdom of putting them upon their guard, and enabling them to forestall an answer to the opposing witness ... [was] not very discernible."[278] The courts, in short, no longer viewed fact finding as a clearcut process of believing testimony given under oath; fact finding was instead coming to be seen as "a difficult subject for a jury or a court," which often "presented ... a case for the discretion of the jury...."[279] Jurors were accordingly instructed to judge "the credit of the witness ... from the manner of his testifying, and other circumstances,"[280] and to interpret testimony "not only from the words themselves, but from the manner in which they may be spoken, and the circumstances to which they may relate."[281] Jurors were also instructed that they could rely on "presumption[s] ... drawn from other [undisputed or clearly proven] facts"[282] —a species of evidence that had been frowned on prior to the Revolution.[283] In short, jurors were no longer expected merely to accept testimony given under oath but were to weigh the credibility and inherent probability of that testimony in order to arrive at an understanding of truth that would reflect the community's understanding of human nature and worldly affairs. In arriving at such an understanding, jurors, of course, had much more freedom and leeway and hence power in finding facts than they had had during the colonial period.

Further symptoms of the breakdown of ancient religious standards were three cases holding enforceable contracts made on Sunday,[284] permitting mail carriers to travel on Sunday,[285] and otherwise

limiting the jurisdiction of justices of the peace over Sunday traveling.[286] However, "the most alarming symptom" of the breakdown
of ethical unity and social coherence was "the frequency and impunity
with which crimes against social order ... [were] increasing in large
cities. . . ."[287] Some men in the 1820s felt it proper, for example, to
disturb the worship of unpopular religious sects[288] and to disrupt
school sessions and "incite scholars" to disobedience.[289] They also
showed disrespect for militia officers and obstructed militia drills.[290]
Indeed, even a town meeting thought it permissible to refuse to make
an appropriation required by statute for an unpopular purpose—namely, militia expenses—and the selectmen, when sued by the militia
commander, successfully maintained that they were "not by the law of
the ... land in any manner bound to answer" for their town's breach of
the law.[291] Most disturbing of all were several post-1830 riots by
urban mobs, particularly the 1834 attack on the Ursuline Convent in
Charlestown and the 1835 assault on William Lloyd Garrison.[292]
Traditional forms of social deference and social restraint were, in short,
breaking down as individuals took it upon themselves to act in
accordance with their own ethical code rather than accept the one laid
down by the community at large.

Ultimately, perhaps, all of the changes discussed in this chapter—in
political institutions, in the law of seditious libel, in criminal procedure,
in the law of evidence, in the religious establishment, and in patterns of
interpersonal deference—were merely reflective of a more fundamental
change in men's understanding of the nature of truth. By the 1820s, if
not earlier, it was clear to most that the age of moral certainty had
passed and that truth could no longer be seen as a unitary set of values
formulated by God and readily ascertainable by man. Men now viewed
truth and morality as human values that might vary over time and place
and believed that nothing existed that could "not be plausibly argued
with ... much semblance of truth" on every side.[293]

This new understanding of the impossibility of finding ultimate
truths and ultimate ethical values required new institutional responses
in those areas where the state had previously been concerned with
finding truth or preserving values. In the litigation process, the new
response was to direct jurors, the agents of the community, to find
truth in accordance with the community's rather than with God's
standards—an essentially difficult task for which there were no legal
criteria and which the judges accordingly had not the slightest inclination to assume. In the area of religion, the new response was to
permit every man to find truth for himself. In politics, the new
response was to permit men to argue publicly about ethical values and
thereby attempt to persuade holders of power to enact particular values
into law. The emerging law of criminal procedure similarly sought to

give men every opportunity to persuade their peers of their factual or moral innocence.

The pursuit of liberty, in sum, transformed Massachusetts from a society where only men who claimed special wisdom in ascertaining a truth laid down by God could freely proclaim that truth into a society where all men were arbiters of ultimately human truths. When that transformation occurred, however, the inherited legal system of Massachusetts was deprived both of its ultimate justification—the preservation of a shared ethical unity—and of its sole means of resolving disputes—an appeal to that unity. The way was thereby opened for the legal system to take on an entirely new character.

7. Liberty and the Breakdown of Stability

The gradual breakdown of ethical unity in Massachusetts over a thirty-year period beginning in the 1780s did not mean that all the rules of law inherited from the prerevolutionary period were reversed. Some rules, notably the rules of property, which had protected the economic and social stability of colonial communities, were enforced with increasing rigor after independence was achieved. But, as we shall see, the social effects of enforcing those rules were quite different from what they had been before.

One area where concern for property continued to appear was in the criminal law. Indeed, concern for the protection of private property began to dominate the criminal law after the Revolution, and, as it did, it superseded the ethical concerns that had underlaid that body of law during the colonial period. The years after the Revolution brought forth vast changes in attitudes toward crime and the criminal when, during the 1780s there occurred a near cessation of prosecutions for various sorts of immorality and a dramatic increase in prosecutions for offenses in the nature of theft.

Like the decrease in prosecutions for sin, the increase in prosecutions for theft did not commence immediately after independence. From 1776 to 1781 there were an average of twenty-four cases per year, almost the same as the yearly average of twenty-three cases before the Revolution. But then the number of prosecutions for theft and similar offenses began to rise, to thirty-six in 1782, forty-one in 1783, sixty-five in 1784, and eighty-four in 1790. During the next four decades, out of a total of some 8,490 prosecutions for all crimes in the Supreme Judicial Court and the courts of sessions and of Common Pleas, 3,510—an average of eighty-eight prosecutions per year and 41 percent of all prosecutions—were for theft.

The decrease in prosecutions for sin and the increase in prosecutions for attacks on property, in combination, transformed legal and social attitudes toward crime and the criminal. Before the Revolution half of all prosecutions had been for immorality, and crime had been viewed as sin. By 1800, on the other hand, crime was prosecuted to "insure the peace and safety of society"[1] and to relieve the public from the "depradations" of "notorious offenders"[2] and the "tax levied on the community by . . . privateering" of thieves.[3] More than 40 percent of all prosecutions were for theft, only 7 percent for conduct offensive to morality. By the turn of the century, in short, the criminal was no longer envisioned as a sinner against God but rather as one who preyed on the property of his fellow citizens. Crime was thereafter prosecuted in order to protect the stability of society, but in the process of protecting that stability, one of the reasons for protecting it—the furtherance of community ethical values—and one of the key assumptions underlying it—that there was ethical and social coherence—came to be forgotten.

The transition from the attitude of 1760 to that of 1800 seems to have occurred largely during the decade following the conclusion of peace with Britain in 1783. But the first step in the change had been taken earlier, in the 1760s. During that decade and the first half of the following one, Massachusetts Tories carefully cultivated a fear that rebellion against British authority would lead ultimately to the destruction of all authority. The consequence of rebellion, they maintained, would be that "the bands of society would be dissolved, the harmony of the world confounded, and the order of nature subverted. . . ."[4] In a series of grand jury charges given during the 1760s, Chief Justice Hutchinson suggested how law should be used to prevent the destruction of society. Expressing his concern that "disorders are seldom confined to one Point" and that "people who begin with one View, seldom end there,"[5] Hutchinson urged the jurors "to point out and bring forward all Crimes and Offenses against the Tranquillity and Order of Society. . . ."[6] Hutchinson's argument essentially was that in order for society to protect itself, its better elements had to be watchful of attacks by mean, lawless, and ignorant men on order and authority and had to rely on law to punish and hence deter such attacks.

Many Whigs had similar apprehensions. John Adams was as concerned as Hutchinson when in 1765 a mob of rioters broke into a royal official's home. "[T]o have his Garden torn in Pieces, his House broken open, his furniture destroyed and his whole family thrown into Confusion and Terror, is a very atrocious Violation of the Peace and of dangerous Tendency and Consequence."[7] By the outbreak of hostilities between the British and Americans in 1774-1775, apprehension of the danger of possible lawlessness and mob rule had grown into an obsession shared by most colonists. An example is the conduct of the people of Groton in 1774 in sending supplies for the relief of Boston residents. With the supplies the town clerk of Groton sent a letter stating, "The inhabitants of this Town have . . . this day sent forty bushels of grain . . . and we earnestly desire you will use your utmost endeavor to prevent and avoid all mobs, riots, and tumults, and the insulting of private persons and property."[8]

This emerging fear of the mob seems to have been primarily of a political nature. Adams and Hutchinson were not worried that sinners would break into their homes and take away their property; nor did they fear an individual thief motivated by a longing for personal material gain. Rather, they dreaded organized groups of malcontents bent on the reconstruction of society. Yet they feared such political activity because they expected that it would be economically motivated. They were concerned that debtors would grow insolent[9] and that mobs would "invade private rights."[10] In short, their concern was that the economically underprivileged would seek material gain by banding together and destroying the ethical unity and social coherence on which stability and order in eighteenth-century Massachusetts rested.

Despite these new concerns, however, the old conception of the purpose of criminal law still prevailed at the outset of the Revolution. Thus in 1776 the General Court urged the people to "lead sober, Religious and peaceable Lives, avoiding all Blasphemies, contempt of the holy Scriptures, and of the Lord's day and all other Crimes and Misdemeanors, all Debauchery, Prophaneness, Corruption, Venality, all riotous and tumultuous Proceedings, and all Immoralities whatsoever. . . ."[11] In this statement, though, one can also see the beginning of a new apprehension of political and economic disorder. Although this anxiety was at first peripheral, by the early 1780s it was becoming a central one, as men came to view criminal law as having a dual function "to discourage [both] vice . . . and disorders in society. . . ."[12]

Although quite real, the new anxiety had little support in the events of the time. During the 1760s and early 1770s Massachusetts experienced relatively few violent attacks on property or serious breaches of ethical unity. The same was true during the Revolution itself. In the 1780s, however, fears previously unfounded became real, as a number of attacks on authority and property occurred. Between 1780 and 1785 there were in Middlesex County alone four prosecutions for rioting[13] and five for assaults on tax collectors,[14] in one of which eighteen codefendants had participated.[15] Conditions were even worse in the western counties. Between 1782 and 1785 there were two attempts in Berkshire to prevent the courts from sitting and transacting business and numerous attempts in several counties, successful and unsuccessful, to rescue prisoners.[16] On one occasion in 1782 authorities in Northampton had to release three hostages taken from insurgents, since they lacked the military power to resist an insurgent force camped in the nearby hills.[17] The culmination was reached in Shays's Rebellion in 1786, when for several months Massachusetts was engaged in a civil war in which rebel forces controlled most of Hampshire and Berkshire counties as well as parts of Worcester and Middlesex.[18]

Ending as they did in open rebellion, these seven years of violence undoubtedly heightened the fear of social breakdown and disorder. The simultaneous increase in the incidence of theft appears to have contributed to both a strengthening and a modification of the fear. Adams and Hutchinson, it will be recalled, had not been worried about thieves. A man living in 1786, however, must have viewed all attacks on property—by poverty-stricken mobs on the one hand and by poverty-stricken individuals on the other—as part of a single phenomenon. What was at stake, ultimately, was his security of property, which members of the lower classes were seeking to destroy. They used a variety of techniques: they rioted; they attacked courts and tax collectors; they refused to pay debts; and they entered men's homes and carried away their possessions. Logically their techniques could be broken into two categories. Some men—the thieves and the recalcitrant debtors—broke the law and infringed property rights and hence threatened social order and stability only indirectly. Others—the rioters and those who attacked the courts and the tax collectors—worked directly by trying to destroy the institutions of government, on which all order and stability rested. Governor Hancock perhaps best summed up this new view when in an address to the legislature in 1793 he suggested that the primary function of criminal law was to insure "the good order of Government . . . [and] the security of the people."[19]

Hancock's address, which said nothing about the preservation of religion and morality, is another indication that the ancient reasons for protecting property rights and preserving social stability were being forgotten. The protection of order and property was becoming an end in itself rather than merely a means to the pursuit of community morality—an end to which men with differing ethical ideals could adhere. Citizens of postrevolutionary Massachusetts, whether they believed in the preservation of the old, harmonious community structure or merely in their own economic well-being, could join in arguing that no man was "warranted by the laws of the land to make . . . havoc of private property"[20] and hence that every man had "a right to use his property as he please[d], provided by doing so he . . . [did] not injure another's. . . ."[21] At least in the context of the criminal process, protection of property and hence economic stability was becoming an important value in itself, completely separate from any lingering concern that law may have had for the protection of ethical unity.

Prerevolutionary rules regulating competition among resource users— a key element in the preservation of stability in the colonial era—were reaffirmed in the half century after the Revolution. Indeed, the rules were often extended in the postrevolutionary period to apply to new forms of wealth generated by changes in the economy. The law continued, for example, to confer on a man who had customarily exploited a particular economic resource an absolute and "despotic dominion" over it, "in total exclusion of the right of any other individual in the universe"[22]—a policy that, as we have seen, promoted the economic security of the individual. In suits between neighboring landowners that arose because one owner sought to use his land in a manner harmful to the other, this policy, as before the Revolution, meant that the older claimant's usage would be elevated to the level of a property right and that a more recent claimant would have to use his land so as not to interfere with the older right. A postrevolutionary plaintiff could thus recover damages for a nuisance if a defendant built a stable,[23] a blacksmith's shop,[24] or a factory that emitted noxious smells[25] next to an existing dwelling house or tavern; if he polluted water on or adjacent to the plaintiff's existing estate, causing the water to emit noxious smells,[26] pollute the plaintiff's well,[27] or be otherwise unfit for continued use;[28] if by constructing a drain[29] or a necessary house,[30] by failing to make due repair to his property,[31] or by placing gravel on his land[32] he caused noxious water to flow onto the plaintiff's land; if he obstructed the plaintiff's ancient drain, as a result of which water flowed back onto the plaintiff's land;[33] or if he drained a nearby pond, causing the plaintiff's immemorial well to dry up.[34] If, however, the defendant had an ancient prescriptive right older than the plaintiff's right, he would not be liable in damages.[35] That is, the courts would enforce whatever land use was older.

The same policy also underlay the increasing protection that the law accorded to mere possessory, as distinguished from proprietary, interests in land. As James Sullivan noted in 1801, American law viewed "the Estate by Occupancy . . . [as] a subject of philosophy, [rather] than of legal disquisition."[36] One who had possession of land without title thus had a property right good against all the world, except the state and the rightful owner[37]—a possession that would mature into title if it continued under proper conditions for thirty years.[38] Even if the rightful owner brought suit to recover the land before thirty years had elapsed, the possessor was not without rights: the owner had to pay him the value of any improvements he had made while occupying the land.[39] The courts also affirmed the importance of possession by holding that a grantee in open possession under an unrecorded deed could recover land as against a subsequent grantee under a recorded deed[40] and by holding that a deed would not be construed so as to destroy by implication an existing pattern of possession.[41] Indeed, possession was so important in the early nineteenth century's scale of social values that possessors of land were permitted to use mild force to eject people interfering with their enjoyment of it.[42]

Courts also continued to protect existing patterns of resource use in water rights and flooding cases. Thus a landowner who constructed a dam across a stream running through his land[43] acquired a property right in the stream's water and could bring suit for damages if an upstream owner diverted water needed to run the plaintiff's mill[44] or if a downstream owner built a dam and so raised the level of the stream that the plaintiff's mill wheels could not function properly.[45] The owner of a subsequently constructed dam was entitled to use only such water as would not interfere with the first owner's use.[46] Similarly, the owner of land along a stream could sue an upstream owner whose dam deprived him of water used for agriculture[47] or a downstream owner whose dam caused his land to be flooded.[48] In all these cases, however, a plaintiff could not recover if a defendant had an ancient prescriptive right older than the plaintiff's right[49] or if the plaintiff had suffered no damage,[50] as would occur if he had never improved the land for whose loss he was bringing suit.[51] In short, the law would confer a property right only on the prior user of an economic resource that others subsequently sought to use.[52]

Postrevolutionary property law did not, however, limit itself to protecting rights that had been protected in the colonial period; it also began to accord protection in cases where protection had not previously been given. For example, it treated rights in resources other than land as real property, which was "regarded as the most inviolable" form of property and hence received the greatest legal protection.[53] The courts not only continued to treat church pews as real property[54] but further held that the owner of a pew had a sufficient property interest in other portions of the church, such as "the windows . . . , or the walls, or the pulpit, or the singers' loft," to prevent a creditor of the church from attaching them and thereby interfering with the pew holder's "right of enjoying the house for public worship."[55] A grant to a man and his heirs forever of all standing timber on a particular close was likewise held to convey an estate of "inheritance in the trees, and an exclusive right in the soil of the close, as far as was necessary for their support and nourishment. . . ."[56] The Supreme Judicial Court, relying on a 1641 ordinance that had been repealed but had resulted in

"a usage . . . which now has force as our common law," also held that
the soil beneath tidal waterways on which wharves were built was
owned not by the public but by the owner of the adjoining land—
which, as the court expressly recognized, was contrary to the English
common law rule.[57] An owner of land along a nonnavigable stream
was even held to have property rights in the entire bed to the point of
midstream.[58]

Property rights were expanded and extended in a wide variety of
other instances. Consider, for example, the law of fisheries. Throughout
the postrevolutionary period it was settled that a riparian owner
possessing a right of property in the bed of a nonnavigable stream also
had a right to fish in the waters above that bed and to exclude all others
from those waters,[59] except those who had anciently appropriated
the exclusive right of fishing to themselves.[60] In navigable streams,
on the other hand, no one except a town[61] could own an exclusive
fishery, not even the owner of the adjoining land or flats,[62] for such
a fishery was "an uncertain custom" that "savor[ed] of arbitrary
power . . . [and was] in derogation of the rights of the subject . . ."[63] But while these rules on ownership of exclusive fisheries
remained constant throughout the half century after the Revolution,
the courts manipulated them in a manner that vastly increased the
number of exclusive fisheries, a form of private property. The manipulation consisted in changing the definition of a navigable stream: in
1779 a river such as the Connecticut, in which vessels could be
navigated but in which the tide did not ebb and flow, was deemed a
navigable river and hence incapable of supporting an exclusive fisher-
y;[64] by the turn of the century a river was held to be navigable only
if it was tidal, and hence the Connecticut and many other navigable
streams were treated as nonnavigable and thus proper subjects for
private property rights in their fish.[65]

The law relating to easements and profits was another body of rules
modified so as to make the acquisition of property rights easier. One
way this was done was to reduce the length of time required to obtain
an easement by prescription from sixty to twenty years.[66] Another
way was to accord recognition to new sorts of easements,[67] such as
easements of ancient light,[68] easements to pass over an adjoining
close not merely in one direction but in all directions,[69] and
easements to use ponds and wells on adjoining lands.[70] Finally, for
the first time in Massachusetts history, the courts upheld individual as
distinguished from common rights to take profits from another's
land.[71]

The courts also extended the legal protection accorded to holders of
various sorts of licenses. After the Revolution a person could not
become a ferryman, innkeeper, retailer of spirituous liquors, auctioneer,

or harbor pilot without first obtaining a license from state-created authorities.[72] In addition, many towns prohibited people from entering occupations such as butchering,[73] chimney sweeping,[74] acting as an intelligence officer,[75] selling tea or sugar or running a confectionary,[76] acting as a measurer or weigher of grain,[77] or producing plays[78] without first obtaining a license from town selectmen.[79] Licenses, of course, remained a sort of property right that sometimes conferred upon their holders monopolistic privileges that could be transmitted to others. As before the Revolution, ferry and liquor licenses could be conveyed as property[80] and would descend, upon their owners' deaths, to their heirs or successors.[81] Owners of land at which ferries had customarily docked induced courts to rule in several cases that the right to a ferry license was appurtenant to their land,[82] while owners of buildings that had customarily been licensed as inns obtained rulings that they had a legal right to have their licenses renewed even when town selectmen opposed renewal.[83] Holders of licenses could be deprived of their property right only if they failed to fulfill the various obligations to the public imposed on them by law—the obligation, for example, of charging a reasonable fee for their service.[84] As in the prerevolutionary period, the holder of a liquor license had no legal right to prevent competitors from entering into business if they could procure licenses,[85] but the holder of a ferry license did. In one case, for example, a licensed ferryman brought suit for a statutory penalty against an unlicensed competitor,[86] while in another a ferryman recovered damages against a bridge company that had drawn away some of his business, after the ferryman had given evidence that he was "seized in his own demesne as of fee" of the ferry.[87] Such recovery, in fact, would be denied only if a plaintiff had "no legal right to or property in [a] . . . Ferry. . . ."[88]

The important development in the postrevolutionary period was that the rules in the ferry cases were extended to cover analogous problems. Thus the owner of a turnpike was permitted to sue someone who built a road around his tollgate, thereby depriving him of his tolls.[89] Similarly, the owner of a fishing boat possessed a cause of action against the owner of another boat who intentionally operated it in a noisy and disorderly manner for the purpose of driving fish away from the plaintiff's vessel.[90] In fact, the courts appeared to be moving in the direction of developing a generic cause of action permitting an established businessman to recover damages against a new competitor who, as a result of his competition, had deprived the plaintiff of his business. Although the Supreme Judicial Court refused in 1783 to decide whether a millowner could maintain an action against a new competitor solely for "loss of custom," it did hold that such a claim could be joined to a claim for diversion of water.[91] Similarly, a businessman could recover for "loss of custom" resulting from a breach of contract; an employer, for example, could recover damages from an employee who, in leaving his employ, enticed his customers to leave him or otherwise caused him to lose business,[92] while an innkeeper could recover for "loss of custom" resulting from a supplier's fraudulent sale of noxious lemon juice.[93] In two cases remedies were even granted in the absence of a contract; in one a man sued someone for stealing his allegedly superior model for constructing ships,[94] while in the other a municipal judge, after refusing to entertain a criminal action, informed a complainant that municipal officials would assist him in preventing a competitor from passing off his product as the complainant's.[95] These cases, however, did not make clear whether the gist of the cause of action was the appropriation of a business or economic right or the interference with some other sort of right. Thus, although courts were moving in the direction of giving businessmen a right in the nature of property against increased competition from new entrants into their markets, the precise point at which they had arrived by the 1820s is unclear.

Results were much less ambiguous in an analogous series of cases holding that officeholders possessed rights in the nature of property in their offices. In one case, for instance, the Supreme Judicial Court spoke of an incumbent's "title to the office" of sheriff,[96] while in other cases plaintiffs successfully claimed that they had "Property" in military[97] and in merchant marine offices.[98] The Supreme Judicial Court, as we have seen, also held that a clergyman, "had an *estate for life* in his office. . . ."[99]

A similar trend can be seen in the rules of law regulating laborers. Although slaves in Massachusetts had been freed after the Revolution, the law continued to recognize the right of the head of a household to the labor and the wages of his "servants,"[100] his wife,[101] and his children.[102] It also continued to recognize the right of a master to the labor and wages of his apprentice and, in the event of default by the apprentice, not only would permit the master to sue the person from whom he had acquired the apprentice[103] or the person who had induced the apprentice to default,[104] but would even permit the master to invoke the criminal process to secure obedience from the apprentice.[105] Of course, a master also had authority to inflict corporal discipline on an apprentice without invoking the judicial process.[106]

In the nineteenth century the courts began to expand these rules to cover industrial laborers, whose economic position was quite different from that of children, apprentices, and traditional sorts of servants. Thus in one case a plaintiff recovered damages against a defendant who had induced minors employed at his factory to resign.[107] The gist of this action was not the modern remedy for tortious interference with contractual relations,[108] for although the employer could bring suit against one who interfered with his right to an employee, the employee possessed no action against a third party who sought to induce his employer to discharge him.[109] The analogy was rather to ancient concepts of property in children, apprentices, and servants; the courts slowly were coming to place factory workers under the same legal rubric as the older categories of servants, although in the 1820s they were not as yet prepared in Massachusetts to permit the invocation of the criminal process to insure that workers remained on the job.[110]

The reasons for the expansive application of property concepts in the postrevolutionary period are unclear. Part of the explanation might be that the courts were merely following traditions and applying rules inherited from the prerevolutionary period. This explanation is not, however, entirely satisfactory by itself, given the undeniable extension of prerevolutionary property doctrine by the courts.

Perhaps the extension of property doctrine may best be explained by a tendency of the postrevolutionary generation to equate the protection of property with the preservation of liberty. That generation often associated the "rights" of "life, liberty, and property"[111] with each other, arguing that "property must be secured, or liberty ... [could] not exist."[112] The association of property and liberty was so close that men classified property among their other fundamental "unalienable rights"[113] and viewed "the freedom of property from the indefinite despotism of sovereignty ... [as] the best security to be found against those laws by which social liberty ... [was] so often injured. ..."[114] As a result, challenges to property rights were labeled by litigants as "arbitrary and unprecedented ... in this free Country where property is held secure by the laws and constitution,"[115] and the courts, when confronted with an argument that to deny a claimed property right would undermine liberty, almost invariably granted the property right for which a claim was made.[116]

But while the concepts of private property and liberty may have been closely allied, the postrevolutionary rules allocating property did not result in increased individual liberty; they merely identified the individuals who would enjoy it. For every person who gained liberty by obtaining protection of a property right, some other person usually lost at least an equivalent amount of liberty. When one miller, for example, gained a property right to use water in a stream, another lost the right to use the same water. Likewise, when an employer obtained a right to prevent his employee from working for another, the employee effectively lost the liberty to improve his wages or working conditions by threatening to leave his master's employ. The effect of the postrevolutionary rules of property law considered above was simply to insure that the individuals who had possessed property and hence liberty in the past would continue to possess it in the future.

There is evidence that some members of the postrevolutionary generation consciously sought legal protection of property as a means of insuring economic and social stability. John Adams, for example, believed that it was essential to social order and stability that the property rights of the poor as well as the rich be protected.[117] Fisher Ames likewise thought that "the rights of property and the tranquillity of society" were related and that the duty of government was to secure both.[118] The very idea of property, in sum, may have become a code word for a broad constellation of genuine conservative values, including the preservation of upper-class wealth, community stability, and, perhaps, even ethical unity.

However, as ethical unity disintegrated, stability became a goal that often could not be attained. This is shown in a series of cases dealing with ownership of ecclesiastical wealth. The Religious Freedom Act of 1811 had, as we have seen, removed most legal restraints on religious liberty and left the churches of Massachusetts free to move toward the diversity and voluntarism that were rapidly becoming characteristic of religion elsewhere in America. Law no longer sought to impose unity on Christians or to restrain men from joining and directing that their taxes be paid to whichever Protestant sect they desired. Men were free even to secede from an existing sect and to form a new sect for any reason whatsoever.

Many men, in fact, did precisely that, particularly when, in the years after 1810, the ancient struggle between Calvinists and Arminians within the old Congregational establishment escalated into a controversy about the divinity of Christ, pitting Unitarians against Trinitarians and causing schisms in many a Congregational parish.[119] The legal system did nothing to prevent such schisms, for it had ceased to be concerned with men's religious beliefs. Nonetheless, it could not avoid involvement in the controversy when opposing factions in each parish laid claim to church wealth. Although similar disputes over church property had arisen before, notably after the Great Awakening had led to schism in the 1740s and in occasional cases thereafter,[120] the problem erupted in the 1820s with special urgency.

The two leading cases were *Baker* v. *Fales*[121] and *Stebbins* v. *Jennings.*[122] In the parishes in both cases, as in at least eighty other parishes in which schisms occurred,[123] the Unitarian faction obtained the support of the majority of the residents of the parish, the political subdivision established by the legislature to levy taxes for the support of a church, while the Trinitarians had the support of the majority of the membership of the church. Unitarians were able to control the parish while Trinitarians controlled the church because in the 1820s there were still vestiges of the establishment. Although all practicing Christians had complete freedom to join their own churches and thereby to avoid all association with the establishment, atheists and others who did not choose to join a different church automatically remained members of the parish in which they resided. They were not necessarily members of the parish church, however; church membership was determined by the church and usually required a certain standard of sincere belief and religious activism. At the moment of crisis, which would usually occur when the parish was exercising its claimed prerogative of selecting a minister for the church, nonmembers would usually join with the church's Unitarian members to select a Unitarian minister, even though the majority of the church members were Trinitarians. When this happened, the Trinitarian majority would secede from the parish's church, form a new church, and then lay claim to the original church's wealth, status, and records, claiming to be the true successor of the original church.

The way in which the Supreme Judicial Court handled these ecclesiastical disputes neatly illustrates the limitations of the judicial process. There were at least three ways in which the court could have analyzed the cases. One would have been to make some sort of equitable, pro rata distribution of the church's wealth, but the court took that approach only when all interested parties had agreed to a particular distribution.[124] A second possibility would have been to distribute the wealth in accordance with the intentions of those who had granted it to the church—at best a partial solution, since those intentions often could not have been determined. In one case, where the intentions of a grantor were unclear, the court did purport to follow them.[125] But in fact intentions were not determinative, as is clear from the case of *First Parish in Shapleigh* v. *Gilman*,[126] where land had been donated to a town "for a parsonage lot" with instructions that the town " 'endeavor that a *congregational* minister should be settled in said township within seven years . . . ,' "[127] and the court nonetheless held that the land could be used as a parsonage for a Baptist minister.

Instead the court adopted a third mode of analysis: it looked to traditional concepts of property law in order to ascertain which faction possessed the property in the church's wealth. The court's reliance on those concepts is evident in the words that permeated its opinions— words such as "vest"[128] and *"cestui que trust"*[129]—and in its conclusion that "in determining the question . . . we must look at the legal title, which is clearly in the parish."[130] The importance of the property concepts was that they induced the court to search for and identify some legal person capable of taking, holding, and transmitting absolute title to the property from the original grantor to one of the litigants.[131] Property concepts also precluded a pro rata distribution and, since courts found that Unitarian-dominated parishes were the only legal persons capable of taking and transmitting title, precluded resort to the intentions of grantors, except to ascertain whether a grantor had intended to contribute to a parish at the time he made his grant.

Deciding these cases by reference to property concepts, however, promoted neither stability nor unity. The cases overturned the earlier distribution of ecclesiastical wealth and did nothing to still the controversy arising out of the Unitarian schism. To laymen, property concepts appeared merely to be a ruse by which the Unitarian judges of the Supreme Judicial Court plundered the wealth of Trinitarian churches for Unitarian majorities. Trinitarians "submitted" to the decisions "as being technically the law of the land," but they "steadfastly believed" that the decisions "one day . . . [would] be legally set aside on account of the manifest injustice that . . . [was] in them."[132] By the 1850s even the Unitarians admitted that they did "not feel perfectly satisfied with the legal decisions . . . bearing upon the ownership of church property"[133] since they did "not seem equitable,"[134] and subsequent historians have seen the decisions as the final factor contributing to the 1833 constitutional amendment that formally abolished the religious establishment in Massachusetts[135] and thereby destroyed whatever had remained of the state's ancient religious unity and stability.

Property rules promoting stability also fared badly in a series of cases that arose when parishes decided to tear down old churches and construct new ones. The owners of pews within the churches, no longer subject to the restraints of ecclesiastical discipline, brought suit for the damage done to their pews. In deciding such cases, the Supreme Judicial Court qualified absolute property rights, holding that the rights of the owner of a pew were "necessarily subject to the right in the parish to take down and rebuild the meetinghouse, and make such alterations as the good of the society may require."[136] Indeed, if a meetinghouse had become "old and ruinous," the parish could tear it down without giving compensation to the owner,[137] although other improvements or alterations could be made only if compensation were given.[138] In sum, the owner of a pew, like other property owners, could use his property only to the extent that his use was consistent with the public interest.

Of much greater significance than the extension of the public interest concept to pew cases, however, was the fact that as libertarian ideas that law should reflect the will of the people continued to develop in nineteenth-century Massachusetts the public interest concept came to have a more restrictive impact on property owners than it had had in the immediate postrevolutionary period. A major challenge to property rights occurred, for example, when democratic majorities in the towns began in the decade and a half after the War of 1812 to struggle for temperance. As early as 1819 sessions courts were receiving petitions praying for a reduction in the number of liquor licenses being granted, on the ground that "great evils . . . [were] known to exist" in many licensed shops and houses, which were "nurseries of vice and debauchery," and on the ground that "the expenses for the support of the poor . . . [were] rapidly increasing . . . owing in a great measure to the undue use of ardent spirits."[139] In the early 1820s the courts were impervious to such petitions, ruling that existing holders of licenses had a right to have their licenses renewed and to remain in the business of selling liquor—a right in the nature of a property right—even when town selectmen had refused to sanction renewal[140] or a court of sessions had failed to grant it.[141] But in 1829 and 1830 some counties began to reverse their positions:[142] in Bristol County, twenty petitions for licenses were denied in 1830;[143] in Dukes, a petition from the "Society for the Suppression of Intemperance"[144] requesting that no licenses be renewed or approved led within two years to the termination of all but wine and beer licenses;[145] in Berkshire, the court directed town selectmen to indicate whether the public good required the approbation of all existing holders of licenses.[146] The principle that the holder of a liquor license had to use it in accordance with the public good rapidly became a truly restrictive limitation on what had been conceived of as a form of private property, and private property came to be seen as a value of less importance than promotion of the will of a democratic majority.

The notion that private property had to be used consistently with the public interest, even though the public paid no compensation to the owner for such use, emerged in a most interesting light in towns in which prisons were located. Property owners in those towns must always have encountered considerable difficulty with prisoners who possessed the liberty of the jail yard. As one woman informed the Middlesex Court of Sessions in 1793, she had been "deprived of the peaceable enjoyment of her garden and well of water because prisoners . . . [were] frequently trampling thro her garden leaving it exposed [and] drawing water out of her well . . . by reason of all which she . . . [was] greatly disturbed in her possessions[,] her house [was] exposed to profligate men[,] and she an helpless woman [was] exposed to insult. . . ." She conceived that the court had "never meant to give prisoners the liberty of abusing private property in the goal yard,"[147] and the court agreed when it ruled in 1796 that no "prisoner . . . shall have liberty to enter any dwellinghouse . . . included" within the limits of the yard.[148] At the turn of the century, as this ruling indicates, the absolute right to enjoy one's property without any outside interference was still of prime importance. As the Supreme Judicial Court said in 1808 in *Baxter* v. *Taber*,[149] which extended the Middlesex rule to the rest of the Commonwealth, the inclusion of private property within the limits of the jail yard would constitute an unconstitutional "appropriation of private property to public uses without compensation to the proprietors"; no agency of government could "make the private property of others, of which by law they have the exclusive use, a part of the county prison."[150] Courts of sessions throughout the Commonwealth, following the Supreme Court's opinion, accordingly began to redraw jail boundaries so as to exclude all private property.[151]

This exaltation of private property seriously impaired the ongoing development of other important social policies, however. One, which the court in *Baxter* v. *Taber* itself recognized, was that the law be "beneficial and humane to debtors. . . ."[152] As the Boston prisoners observed in a petition seeking restoration of thé old jail limits, they lived in a "deplorable" state "never . . . contemplated by the free and enlightened government" of the Commonwealth, in which they were deprived of all opportunity for employment.[153] Moreover, as they noted, there was another policy interest at stake: most counties, including Suffolk, had concluded that churches were a form of private property and had accordingly placed them outside the limits of the jail,[154] with the result, as the prisoners claimed, that they were "deprived of the privileges of public worship, of the free exercise of their religion guaranteed to them by the Constitution of the United States."[155]

Although the courts were unwilling to give heed to these other values, the legislature was, and in 1809 it provided by statute "that all boundaries of the goal yards . . . heretofore determined . . . shall be . . . rendered legal and valid to all intents and purposes. . . ." Seeking, however, to have the best of all worlds, the legislature added that nothing in the act should be "construed to affect the rights of any individuals owning real estate within such limits. . . ."[156] While this proviso probably assisted the Supreme Judicial Court in upholding the constitutionality of the legislation,[157] it had little other effect. Immediately after the statute, jail limits were extended in most counties to include houses of worship that had formerly been deemed private property,[158] and gradually other forms of private property, such as private homes,[159] blacksmith shops,[160] and all other unenclosed lands[161] were also included within the yard. The steps in the process of inclusion can be seen most clearly in Berkshire County. After an initial decision in 1810 that a private house formerly within the yard could not be included even under the 1809 statute,[162] the court in 1811 ruled that private property could be included within the limits, but only in accordance with the terms of that act, meaning apparently that prisoners could enter on private property only if they had been invited by the owner.[163] By 1815, however, that approach had been jettisoned, and the jail limits were explicitly drawn to "include any lands adjoining [said] roads belonging to individuals & which . . . [were] thrown open to public use or occupation & not exclusively occupied or fenced by individuals,"[164] while by 1820 debtors having the liberty were not barred from entering on any grounds or buildings included within the limits of the yard.[165] The policy of courts in the 1820s was aptly stated by a committee of the Berkshire court that recommended that the jail yard be further enlarged so "that persons confined for debt may have every possible facility for obtaining employment. . . ."[166] Even after these enlargements, owners of private property within the yard, of course, retained the same right to exclude prisoners from their land as they had to exclude other trespassers; what they lost was the aid of the state in bringing about that exclusion and compensation from the state for the depreciation in property values that resulted from the presence in their neighborhood of imprisoned debtors.

The direction in which the law of property was being pushed by a majoritarian democracy can be seen most clearly in the 1823 case of *Callender* v. *Marsh.*[167] The plaintiff, the owner of a house located on a hill in Boston, had brought suit against a surveyor of the highways who, without compensation to the plaintiff, had lowered the grade of a highway in front of the plaintiff's house, thereby weakening the foundation of the house and making access to the house more difficult. The plaintiff claimed that his property had been taken from him without compensation, in violation of the Massachusetts constitution, but the court ruled that no taking had occurred. The case, argued the court, was analogous to "the location of schoolhouses upon public land," which, although it might "materially diminish the value of an adjoining or opposite dwellinghouse, on account of the crowd and noise which they usually occasion," would not require "the public . . . to consult the convenience of the individual so far as to abstain from erecting the schoolhouse, or to pay the owner of the dwellinghouse for its diminished value."[168] The constitution required the public to pay for land physically taken from its owner but did not require compensation for a diminution in the value of the land resulting from a public improvement made without any actual taking.

What is most important about *Callender* v. *Marsh* is the court's analysis of the contending policy interests. On the one hand, as in the colonial period, there was the owner of private property. But since the colonial period the interest on the other side had changed. A selfish, rapacious, and authoritarian crown, which threatened the liberty and stability of Massachusetts communities, had been replaced by the majoritarian and egalitarian democracy of the Age of Jackson. The interests of community and of selfish individualism had changed sides. Absolute and total protection of the owner in his enjoyment of property no longer seemed necessary to the interests of community; instead, the individual now appeared as an obstruction to continued social progress, liberty, and equality—a perception that emerged with particular clarity in cases involving the limits of jail yards. By 1830, in short, private property was ceasing to be seen as an institution that promoted community values and was becoming instead a tool for the aggrandizement of the individual.

The corporation was another institution transformed in the early nineteenth century from a device furthering community values into one furthering the self-interest of individuals. Before and even immediately after the Revolution, the corporate form had been used largely by institutions like religious parishes and owners of common fields as a means of pooling the energies and resources of individuals in the pursuit of common ends.[169] By 1830, on the other hand, the typical corporation was the business corporation, in which individuals sought personal economic aggrandizement, often at the expense of others in the community.[170]

The key question in corporation law, the resolution of which resulted in the transformation of the corporation, was "whether the *private* property of any proprietors . . . [could be] held liable to satisfy the debts of the propriety, or the property of the Corporation only."[171] Men began to argue that to hold shareholders liable for a corporation's debts would be to take "a citizen's property . . . from under his own controul," contrary to "the best provisions of the constitution";[172] they also argued, rather emotionally, that "the great increase of corporations for almost every purpose . . . [was] seriously alarming" and threatened "the independence and integrity of every branch of . . . government."[173]

But at the turn of the century it was not yet clear whether such arguments would be accepted by the courts. For in the colonial and immediate postrevolutionary years, municipal and similar corporations had had unquestioned authority to levy taxes or assessments on their members in order to raise funds to discharge debts or for other authorized purposes.[174] The 1800 case of *Thompson* v. *Russell*[175] upheld the existence of a similar power on the part of private business corporations. The *Thompson* case was a suit in which the president of the Haymarket Theater Corporation recovered upon an assessment voted by the members of the corporation which the defendant had refused to pay. No agreement to pay the assessment was pleaded, and the fact that the suit was in debt rather than in case further suggests that the obligation to pay it arose not as the result of an agreement but as a matter of law from the defendant's membership in the corporation. The *Thompson* case, in short, rejected the doctrine of limited liability for shareholders of business corporations.

In the first decade of the nineteenth century, however, that doctrine triumphed.[176] Its victory was assured by the 1807 decision of *Ellis* v. *Marshall*,[177] which tested the validity of a claim by a street improvement corporation in Boston that a resident of the street whom the legislature had made a member of the corporation could not decline that membership. The corporation's argument, in substance, was that its members had a status analogous to that of residents of a municipal corporation, who could not decline the obligations imposed on them by the municipality.[178] The court, however, thought the two types of corporation different, since municipal corporations were created by "public acts, promotive of general convenience," while the street improvement corporation had been created by "a private act, obtained at the solicitation of individuals, for their emolument or advantage."[179] It therefore held that the private business corporation, unlike the municipal corporation, could not "press into service" unwilling individuals or their wealth.[180]

Two years later, in *Andover and Medford Turnpike Corporation* v. *Gould*,[181] the court took another step in holding that even a person who had voluntarily become a member of a business corporation could not be sued for unpaid corporate assessments unless he had expressly promised to pay them; the corporation's only remedy against a delinquent member was to sell his shares for whatever price they would bring on the market.[182] In reaching this decision, the court sought not only to protect private property but also to encourage investors to join corporations. It recognized that investors, who could no longer be forced to join, would be more willing to do so if they knew that when "assessments bec[a]me grievous, they [might] abandon the enterprise. . . ."[183] The central significance of the *Gould* case, however, lies in the transformation that it wrought in the underlying concept of shareholder liability. The *Thompson* case, it will be recalled, held that a shareholder was liable to pay assessments simply because he was a member of the corporation. That is, liability was imposed in *Thompson*, as it had been imposed pursuant to the colonial law of obligations, on account of a relationship rather than an agreement. *Gould*, however, put the emphasis on agreement; after *Gould*, not only the existence but even the scope of a shareholder's liability to pay assessments above and beyond the purchase price of his shares was determined by looking to the contract with the corporation by which he had purchased the shares.[184]

Having held that a corporation could not levy assessments on its members without their consent, the courts in 1808 found it easy to take the next step, which was to rule that "the bodies or private property of the individual members cannot be taken in execution to satisfy a judgment against the corporation. . . ."[185] This rule of limited liability to creditors followed from the rule of limited liability to the corporation. As Chief Justice Parsons explained, creditors of towns could seize property of individual inhabitants upon execution of a judgment obtained against the town, since the town itself had power to tax the inhabitants in order to pay the judgment. But a business "corporation ha[d] not this remedy." If it "assess[ed] on each share an equal proportion of the damages [recovered by its creditor], and . . . the owner . . . [did] not choose to pay, his share . . . [could merely] be sold, and . . . [might] bring much less than that proportion";[186] since the corporation lacked the power of assessment, its creditor also must lack that remedy. Parsons, analyzing the problem of liability through the shareholder's eyes, viewed a creditor as a mere subrogee of the corporation; of course, a shareholder could have no greater duty to the corporation's subrogee than to the corporation itself.

Thus, within a span of two years, the common law rules of shareholder liability had been rejected as inapplicable to the new species of corporation—the business corporation.[187] Although shareholders in some corporations, notably banks and manufacturing companies, continued to be held liable for corporate debts as a result of special legislation,[188] even that legislation was slowly rendered ineffective by the courts. In two 1819 cases the Supreme Judicial Court ruled that shareholders of banks that had been dissolved were no longer personally liable for debts owed by the bank.[189] The court reasoned that since "individuals were not answerable by the principles of the common law"[190] they could be made liable for corporate debts only if a provision for liability was made explicit by legislation. Similarly, the courts narrowed the liability of shareholders of manufacturing corporations. They held, for example, that a shareholder who sold his stock was no longer liable for the corporate debts,[191] even if the corporation was insolvent at the time of the sale,[192] unless the creditor could prove that the sale had been made "for the purpose of defeating the creditors of the company. . . ."[193] The Supreme Judicial Court also held that the estate of a deceased shareholder was not liable for corporate debts.[194] Finally, the court held that a shareholder could not be required to pay assessments levied by the corporation without his consent;[195] his special statutory liability was for the benefit of creditors alone and not of the corporation.

In the 1820s the legislature, in response to fears that the perpetuation of shareholder liability might drive business and capital to other states, began to move in the same direction as the courts. New charters ceased to impose shareholder liability,[196] and in 1827 the legislature even amended the act that rendered shareholders of manufacturing corporations fully liable by reducing the limitation period within which they could be sued.[197] Three years later the legislature repealed the act completely and expressly conferred limited liability on such shareholders.[198] By 1830, in short, the modern rule of limited liability was fully established in the law of business corporations.[199]

The statutory application of the rule of limited liability to manufacturing corporations marked the end in Massachusetts of the notion that coercive nongovernmental corporations could exist for the purpose of pooling individual resources for the common good. Thereafter people were free to join nongovernmental organizations only if they wished and to contribute to them only whatever resources they wished. And, as the subsequent history of the corporation in the nineteenth century shows, individuals would join largely to further their own economic well-being.

In contract as well as property and corporation law it became a postrevolutionary maxim that "a man ha[d] a right to use his property as he please[d], provided by doing so he . . . [did] not injure another's."[200] Two complementary principles followed. One was that a man ought to be permitted to enter into whatever contracts he wished and that the law ought to enforce all contracts he entered into. The other was that a man ought not to be compelled to enter into contracts when he did not wish to and that the law ought not to enforce liabilities to which parties had never given their consent. Over the course of several decades these two principles undermined the traditional customary and ethical basis of contract law and led to a new understanding of the essential nature of contract.

The former principle soon provided a basis for challenging the usury laws and the ethical concepts underlying them. As early as 1789 it was asked "with some degree of plausibility, why a man . . . [should] not set a price on his own money, as well as on his own goods. . . ."[201] Such a man, it was urged, was "not injured, if he voluntarily consent[ed] to . . . [a usurious] contract . . . , as no voluntary agreement . . . [could] be extorsive . . . ";[202] on the other hand, "no law . . . [could] be just or righteous, which . . . indulge[d] the subject in the violation of a contract into which he ha[d] *freely* and *voluntarily* entered. . . ."[203] By the 1820s this challenge had expanded beyond usury, and all "unnecessary, useless, and embarrassing restrictions" imposed by law on economic activity freely entered into were being questioned.[204]

The corollary principle that men ought not to be compelled to enter into contracts to which they did not consent received similar articulation. Courts thought it only "conformable to the principles of justice, and to the essential nature of contracts . . . [that] an obligation . . . [could] not be converted into a different engagement" from that which the parties had made.[205] That is, a party could not be subjected "to perils not undertaken by his contract."[206] The judges feared that to hold otherwise would put men "in an extremely unsafe situation, . . . [for their] property . . . [would be] bound by . . . irregular transactions. . . ."[207] Accordingly it seemed clear that relationship was not a sufficient basis for imposing contractual liability[208] — that an agent who had failed to obtain insurance for his principal was not subject to liability in the absence of an express promise to obtain the insurance[209] and that an owner of a vessel was not liable to a supplier of his vessel for supplies furnished to its master in the absence of evidence of authority on the part of the master to bind the owner.[210]

To hold explicitly that individuals should themselves determine whether to undertake contractual liability did not, however, effect any fundamental change in existing law, for even in the colonial period persons other than slaves, children, and servants were rarely held to liability without their consent. The postrevolutionary changes in contract law were more marginal, being concerned chiefly with questions about the scope and the terms rather than the existence of contractual liability. In the colonial period, as we have seen, the terms of contracts were usually determined by reference to customary usage, but after the Revolution the intentions of the parties at the time of their entry into a contract became key. The new approach was an inevitable consequence of the new underpinnings of contract law. As one judge explained, the rule that a contract could "not be carried *beyond* the intent of the parties *at the time of entering into it* . . . [was] clear from the nature of its constitution; one essential ingredient being, that it is entered into freely, of the parties' own accord."[211] The essential point, of course, is that the terms of contractual liability are as important as its existence; a requirement that a contract conform to certain customary terms and that it contain no others can effectively impose liabilities on individuals to which they have never given their consent and can effectively bar them from making contracts that they seek to make.

Such a requirement can be especially burdensome in periods of rapid change, when custom makes no provision for new kinds of commercial relationships and for new and unanticipated business needs. In early nineteenth-century Massachusetts, the breakdown of traditional ethical standards combined with rapid economic development was having precisely this effect, and the courts as a result found themselves confronted by many issues that were "not determined by uniform usage and practice" on the part of the commercial community[212] or by past judicial decisions.[213] In one case involving the "duty of an agent of a hat manufacturing company," for example, the court observed that the duty could "not be well ascertained by usage, because probably this was the first company of the kind ever established in this commonwealth"; thus it was necessary to decide the case by inquiring into "the essential nature of contracts. . . ."[214] Or, as the court said in another case in which there were "no authorities directly in point . . . [,] the action must then be determined by the meaning" of the contract made by the parties.[215] Indeed, there was little else besides the meaning of the parties to which the courts could look. To have attempted to search for custom that in fact did not exist would only have given juries free reign to impose liabilities incapable of prior anticipation. This, in turn, would have made economic planning impossible and would, in the minds of contemporaries, have rendered property insecure. Hence it became settled that "in every contract, the first and most important consideration . . . [was] to discover the intention of the parties"[216] and "to effectuate . . . [that] intention"[217] "if consistent with the rules of law. . . ."[218]

Courts determined the parties' intentions not only by reference to their express declarations, however, but also by inferences drawn from their course of conduct and from the facts and circumstances surrounding their relationship.[219] Evidence of a usage or custom of trade was thus admissible to aid in construction of the parties' contract, provided that the usage or custom was known to the parties[220] or was "of so general a nature as to furnish a presumption of knowledge."[221] Evidence of usage and custom was admitted not because, as in the colonial period, usage and custom constituted rules of law for the decision of a case,[222] but because usage and custom were "useful, in many cases, to explain the intent of the parties. . . ."[223] Contracting parties were therefore free to reject customary usage as the basis of their contract, and, when they had in fact rejected a usage, they would not be bound by it.

Whitwell v. *Wyer*[224] was one case in which the parties were held to have rejected usage. In *Whitwell* the seller had agreed to deliver twenty-five hogsheads of rum to the buyer at an agreed price per gallon in casks to be furnished by the seller. Rum was customarily delivered in casks containing 108 to 112 gallons, but the seller, after a rise in the price of rum, delivered in 97-gallon casks. The buyer, after initially accepting the smaller casks without objection, subsequently claimed that he had a right to the larger ones, arguing that the contract had contemplated casks of customary size. The court, however, disagreed, holding that his receipt of the smaller casks constituted a manifestation of an intention that customary usage be displaced.

Kettell v. *Wiggin*,[225] a marine insurance case, marked another occasion on which the courts gave effect to the apparent intentions of the parties, even though their decision contributed to the disruption of economic patterns that had prevailed since the colonial era. Colonial mercantile ventures rarely had followed carefully planned or otherwise preordained trade routes: colonial sea captains did not leave Boston with a cargo of rum knowing that they would sell the rum in Africa for slaves, that they would then sell the slaves in Jamaica for molasses, and that they would finally return to Boston and sell the molasses to a distiller of rum. Commerce was much more haphazard and flexible. A sea captain might leave Boston with a cargo of rum that he planned to sell in Jamaica, but if on his arrival in the Caribbean he learned that the market was unfavorable in Jamaica or that some other market was more favorable, he would go to that other market. In fact a vessel might stop at several ports other than that originally planned before unloading its cargo and might pick up a return cargo at one or several of these ports or even at different ports.[226] The vessel in *Kettell* v. *Wiggin* was engaging in precisely this kind of trade. Its insurance provided that the vessel should proceed first to Gibraltar, where the outward cargo would be sold; then to one of the Cape Verde Islands for a cargo of salt; and finally back to Boston. The vessel did in fact sail to Gibraltar and then to the Cape Verdes, but upon its arrival at one of the islands the captain learned that seventeen vessels were waiting in port for salt and that he would not be able to obtain a cargo for approximately five weeks. Being short on provisions, the captain concluded that he could not wait. The island's governor, however, offered to expedite the loading of a cargo of salt if the captain would first take the vessel to a neighboring island on a mission for the governor, and the captain agreed. As a result, he was able to load his vessel considerably sooner, but his early departure from the Cape Verdes for Boston led to the vessel's being captured by pirates on the return voyage. When the owners sought to recover their loss from their insurers, the insurers contended that the mission on behalf of the governor amounted to a deviation from the voyage, which invalidated the insurance, and the court agreed, holding that the voyage on which the vessel had sailed was not the same as the voyage that the defendants had insured and hence "was not within the terms of the policy,"[227] even though the voyage had, according to the jury, been in accordance with the customary usage of merchants trading in the Cape Verde Islands. Thus the colonial doctrine that "a Voyage performed in the usual manner doth not affect ye Insurance"[228] was overruled; usage had simply come to be of less weight in the scales of justice than the right of a promissor to enforce the explicit terms of his promise and not to be held liable to contractual provisions to which he had not freely consented.

In upholding the principle in *Kettell* that a party could not be held to contractual liability beyond the terms of his express promise, the court actually did far more than merely adhere to the intentions of the parties. It had, in fact, made a significant policy judgment about who should bear the burden of loss in a case where the parties had had no intentions. The parties in *Kettell* had not and, indeed, could not have anticipated the need for the deviation that the captain later made; the real question in the case was whether liability would be imposed when the parties had made no provision either for or against it. The plaintiff's position, in effect, was that liability flowed from the fact that the vessel's deviation was sanctioned by customary usage not inconsistent with the express contract of the parties. The court, however, held that usage that had not been incorporated into an express contract could not be the basis of legal obligation in a case where parties had entered into such an agreement. By making an express contract the parties "suspended" rights in the nature of quasi contract that might otherwise have existed on the basis of customary usage.[229]

In cases like *Whitwell* and *Kettell*, in short, the Supreme Judicial Court worked out a new relationship between custom and agreement. Many other cases explicated that relationship. One set of cases articulated more precisely than had been necessary in the colonial period the dominance of express over implied contract, establishing the principle that the law would "not imply a promise, where there was an express promise," because the express promise would be "repugnant to any implication of a promise."[230] Thus, if a workman agreed to perform a job and then quit in the middle of the task[231] or performed the task so deficiently that his work was not of value to the defendant,[232] he could not recover upon his express contract, on account of his breach, nor upon an implied contract, since the express contract had superseded it. Similarly, a creditor who took the personal promise of one partner to pay the debt of a partnership could not hold the other partners liable.[233] Once an express contract had been made, recovery could be had upon an implied contract only if the express contract was invalid,[234] if it was rescinded,[235] if the plaintiff had been prevented from performing the contract by inevitable accident,[236] or if the parties had never intended the express contract to be their sole remedy.[237] This same doctrine—that a person who made an express agreement could be bound only in accordance with its terms and not beyond them—also led to the reversal in the 1790s of the colonial rule implying a warranty of merchantability in all cases involving sales of goods and the rule prohibiting a common carrier from limiting its liability to less than what custom would impose.[238]

A second set of cases established the modern doctrine of impossibility of performance. While the cases recognized that contingencies that were difficult to foresee, such as wars, trade embargoes, fires to rented premises, and changes in market prices, might make the performance of a contract undesirable, they held that mere undesirability as distinguished from impossibility of performance was no defense.[239] As the Supreme Judicial Court observed, "parties must be bound by their contracts; if they will not provide against contingencies, as they may...."[240] It warned men to "be more cautious in making their contracts, and not [to] rely upon the hardship of their cases to relieve them, when they are brought into difficulty,"[241] adding that it had to assume that "risks, equally known to the parties..., must... have been considered by them, when making their contract."[242] The law, in short, would not relieve parties of burdens that they had voluntarily undertaken. Nor would it impose burdens for which no provision had been made by "the express contract of the parties... "[243]—a rule that was applied in many cases to preclude recovery by plaintiffs who had failed to make express provision for it in their contracts.[244]

A third set of cases reversed the colonial rule that a plaintiff's performance of his promise was a condition precedent to his maintenance of a suit for the defendant's failure to perform—a rule having a substantial capacity for defeating intention. By the 1810s that rule had been effectively abolished, and the courts were determining whether a provision of a contract constituted a condition by looking to "the evident intent and meaning of the parties, as expressed in the instrument...."[245] While "principles which regulate covenants which are mutual and dependent" remained relevant in determining the effect of such covenants,[246] those principles were ignored when "other circumstance[s] appear[ed], showing... [a contrary] intention of the parties...."[247] As Chief Justice Parker declared, the more recent cases "all show[ed] a disposition, on the part of the judges, to break through the bonds which some old cases had imposed upon them, and to adopt what Lord *Kenyon*, in one of the cases, call[ed] the common sense doctrine,—that the true intent of the parties, as apparent in the instrument, should determine whether covenants or promises are mutual or conditional, instead of any technical rules, of which the parties were totally ignorant, and the application of which would, in most cases, utterly defeat their intention."[248] Indeed, nearly all technical rules arising as a matter of law from the nature of a transaction ought, it was thought, to "be controlled by the agreement of the parties."[249]

Once it had been determined that the conditional or unconditional nature of a promise was to be decided by reference to the intentions of the parties rather than to old rules of law, it followed that a promissor could require whatever degree of performance he wished from a promissee as a condition to his own duty to perform. If the parties so intended, they could require either full performance by the promissee, tender of performance by the promissee, or merely readiness to perform as a condition to the promissor's performance.[250] Indeed, if the parties manifested an intention to do so, they could make a purely executory contract binding. As a result, the colonial rule was reversed, and a seller of goods could recover the benefit of his lost bargain when a buyer repudiated his duty to pay for the goods even though the seller had not yet delivered them at the time of the repudiation.[251]

The new rules of law permitting parties to ignore custom and usage and to enforce executory contracts undermined but did not totally destroy prerevolutionary ethical standards. Indeed, a few of those standards persisted throughout the postrevolutionary period.[252] In *Boynton* v. *Hubbard*,[253] for instance, the Supreme Judicial Court vigorously reaffirmed ancient moral standards in holding that an individual could not make a contract for the sale of an inheritance that he expected to receive in the future from an ancestor who was living at the time the contract was made. It reasoned that if such contracts were upheld,

> . . . Heirs, who ought to be under the reasonable advice and direction of their ancestor, who has no other influence over them than what arises from a fear of his displeasure, from which fear the heirs may be induced to live industriously, virtuously, and prudently, are, with the aid of money speculators, let loose from this salutary control, and may indulge in prodigality, idleness, and vice; and taking care, by hypocritically preserving appearances, not to alarm their ancestor, may go on trafficking with his expected bounty, making it a fund to supply the wastes of dissipation and extravagance. Certainly the policy of the law will not sanction a transaction of this kind, from a regard to the moral habits of the citizens.[254]

Likewise the legislature throughout the period had rejected pleas that the usury laws violated the right of individuals freely to make and enforce contracts;[255] "the experience of mankind," as one commentator noted, demonstrated the necessity of preventing "the horrid oppression of usury,"[256] for usury would "ripen . . . into a disease that . . . [would] gangrene . . . the whole course of money transactions."[257] Similarly, the courts continued to hold wagering contracts void and unenforceable, despite arguments that "men . . . [were] masters of their own property" and that the law ought "not enquire minutely into the value of the consideration, which may induce them to part with it."[258] The contrary argument—that "every man of experience, and [with] a knowledge of the human character" knew "that it would be hostile to the welfare of society, that . . . such contracts, should be protected by judicial authority"—carried much greater weight, since many men still believed that " 'the practice of gaming . . . pervert[ed] the activity of the mind, taint[ed] the heart, and deprave[d] the affections.' "[259]

The important effect of the postrevolutionary changes in contract law was the undermining not of the ethical standards but of economic and social stability. The new rules of contract undermined stability primarily by giving individuals freedom to make economic bargains purely in their own interest. Postrevolutionary bargainers no longer needed to assume that they should receive only a fair equivalent in return for their goods or services; they no longer needed to assume that hard work resulting in the production of goods or services was the only legitimate means of accumulating wealth. Instead, the new law of contract permitted men to accumulate wealth by turning a sharp bargain or by anticipating the fluctuations of the market. Whereas prerevolutionary contract law had rested on an assumption that economic values and economic relationships were fixed and unchanging and had impeded efforts by individuals to alter their inherited place in the economy, postrevolutionary law assumed that a fluctuating market-place was the central institution in the economy and left individuals free to manipulate its workings so that they rather than their neighbors would most benefit from it.

The shift in the philosophy of contract was merely one part, however, of a broader shift in men's understanding of the role of law in the economy. In the prerevolutionary period the function of law had been to render the distribution of wealth stable by granting individuals property rights in that wealth and by making it difficult for them to lose it in exchange transactions. After the Revolution property ceased to be viewed as a man's stable portion of the community's resources. Instead, his property became his starting stake in a rapidly changing economy—which he could use as he wished, by combining with other entrepreneurs or by making sharp bargains so as to promote his own aggrandizement. Massachusetts, in short, had been transformed from a society where men with stable places in the economy concentrated on pursuing ethical ends to a society where economic place was uncertain and many men used their wealth chiefly for the purpose of acquiring even greater wealth. The prerevolutionary legal system, in which community was the primary social value, had largely been destroyed. A new system emphasizing rugged individualism as its fundamental value had begun to take its place.

A new legal system did not emerge fully developed merely by virtue of the destruction of the old system, however. Although the destruction of the colonial system finally settled the question whether the state could impose ethical values on individuals who did not freely accept them, it did not settle the question of how resources would be distributed among individuals possessing different values; that is, it did not settle whether some values would be favored over others in a distributional scheme. The decline of the colonial legal system and the establishment of a system permitting individuals to select their own values did not produce the classical nineteenth-century laissez-faire state with its emphasis on competition and material well-being. Competition and materialism came to be favored not only because old traditions and old patterns of stability broke down but also because Massachusetts law after the Revolution developed a concern for economic development.

The process by which the law of Massachusetts was transformed after independence can be seen in microcosm in the law of contract. In prerevolutionary Massachusetts contracts had been enforced through a series of discrete writs, the most frequently used of which had encouraged the exchange of goods at fair prices, but others of which had permitted parties to set their own price. The lack of a substantive conception of contract kept the inconsistencies among the writs hidden. But with the postrevolutionary changes in the law of pleading and the resulting emergence of a substantive law of contract, a unitary conception of contract had to emerge. The breakdown of traditional ethical standards had its analog in contract in the breakdown of notions of fair price and equal exchange[260] —a breakdown that undermined one of the prerevolutionary conceptions of contract. Meanwhile, the emerging social theory that individuals should be allowed to use their property as they wished furthered the concept of contract as a free bargain and insured that the emerging law of contract would be individualistic in its orientation. None of the developments so far discussed lent credence, however, to the idea that contract law should serve the needs of the business community. That idea, on the contrary, was the result of the law's concern for economic growth, the subject to which we must now turn.

8. Economic Growth and the Law

The Revolutionary War and the attainment of national independence transformed the economic expectations of many inhabitants of Massachusetts. Like most wars, the War of Independence produced a great deal of both economic dislocation and economic opportunity. On the one hand, it destroyed established trading patterns with England and other British colonies, along with some of the merchants who had gained their livelihood exploiting them. On the other hand, a few enterprising individuals who were able to sell substitutes for English goods or to open new markets for Massachusetts goods made great profits. Just as the war opened new opportunities for some individuals, so too did the attainment of independence. It brought about the removal of many of the colonial era's economic restrictions: restrictions, for example, on the manufacture of American goods, on the trade routes of American ships, and on settlement of and speculation in western lands. Independence enabled Americans to establish their own banks, regulate their own currency, and enact trade legislation.[1] In short, independence made it possible for some entrepreneurs to structure the economy in their own interest, while the Revolution showed that huge profits could be earned as a result.

The urge of individuals to alter the structure of the economy to their own benefit was complemented by a broader, ideological urge for national greatness. As soon as the peace treaty with England was signed there was an outpouring of pamphlets and other publications bearing such titles as *The United States elevated to Glory and Honor*[2] and observing that Americans now had "an empire to raise and support."[3] The resources of the new nation seemed limitless: America, as its citizens proudly noted for the next half century, had an "abundance of the means of subsistence,"[4] "a sturdy, independent, and intelligent people," and "a territory as exhaustless in moral and physical treasures, as it is wide in its expanse."[5] It seemed that the nation's vast resources had only to be organized in order to attain an unprecedented level of economic well-being.

In Massachusetts, at least, economic growth was nonetheless severely limited at first. During the 1780s the state's economy, mired in a depression, only returned to its prerevolutionary level. Although the first bank in the state was chartered in 1784 and some growth occurred in the iron, leather, and paper industries, in 1789 the principal industries—agriculture and maritime activity—had not yet fully recovered from the war. Shipbuilding and whaling, for example, remained at one-third of their prewar rates.[6] Beginning in the 1790s, however, there was a dramatic increase in economic growth. For two decades expansion was most visible in the maritime industries and in an improved internal transportation network, but after 1810 manufacturing industries grew rapidly as well.

The phenomenal growth of maritime industries after 1790 was a result in part of the adoption of the federal constitution and in part of the beginning of the Napoleonic Wars in Europe. Statistics tell much of the story. In the first four years of the 1790s the total fishing tonnage of Massachusetts more than doubled, and between 1790 and 1807 American exports, a substantial portion of which were carried in Massachusetts bottoms, increased eightfold. Perhaps most revealing of all is that during 1803, 1804, and 1805 the United States was the largest carrier of goods between various ports in Europe and that more than 40 percent of the American vessels occupied in the European carrying trade were owned by Massachusetts merchants. Statistics, however, tell only part of the story; another part consists in the extraordinarily successful efforts of Massachusetts seamen to open trade routes in new parts of the world, notably the Pacific Northwest and China.[7]

Equally great was the growth of the state's internal transportation network, which consisted chiefly of turnpikes and other roadways. Beginning in the 1790s there were a flood of petitions seeking the construction of new highways—a flood that did not thereafter cease. Petitioners sought new highways for many reasons, among them the improvement of access to markets[8] and to "gristmill[s] & Saw Mill[s],"[9] the increase of "private business,"[10] and the promotion of "extensive manufactories."[11] One petition pointed out that a minor alteration in the course of a winding road would save "more than fifteen thousand miles extra travel in one year."[12] Another, pointing to New York, "the great mart of Trade for this Country," as worthy of emulation, observed that "the integrity & wealth of a State greatly depend on the social & commercial intercourse of its citizens." Roads and highways, it concluded, were "the veins & arteries of a state" and were "always a primary object with a wise government. . . ."[13]

Measured by this standard the government of Massachusetts was wise indeed, for by the early years of the nineteenth century transportation in the state had been significantly improved. By 1830 over sixty turnpikes had been built, twelve of them radiating from Boston to various other towns and cities.[14] Between 1825 and 1832 the number of stagecoach lines doubled. As a result, travel time between cities was significantly reduced; by 1830 it was possible to go from Boston to Worcester in less than six hours.[15] This land transportation system was supplemented by two canals—the Middlesex, which connected Boston and Lowell, and the Blackstone, which linked Providence and Worcester—and by navigational improvements along the Connecticut and Merrimac rivers.[16]

Improved transportation contributed substantially to the progress of manufacturing.[17] The two decades after 1810 saw the beginnings of the factory system in the state; some 137 factories, exclusive of printing establishments, had been founded by 1831. The principal manufacturing industries were in textiles and leather goods, although others, particularly in machine tools, were also important. Perhaps the best index of the extent of industrial growth was the town of Lowell, which grew from a rural farm district of about 200 families in 1822 into an industrial town of about 2,500 inhabitants, nearly all mill operatives, by 1826.[18]

Thus in the forty years after 1790 the economy of Massachusetts was transformed from an essentially agrarian, subsistence economy, in which commercial activity was generally restricted to a small number of coastal towns, into an industrialized, market economy that reached into the interior of the state. Following such a transformation in the economy, change was inevitable in the rules of law. Some of it was planned, but much was unanticipated.

One of the consequences of the economic transformation was a series of changes in the law of debtor and creditor resulting in rules more suited to the increasingly commercial nature of the marketplace. These changes occurred slowly, however. One reason for the slowness was that debtor-creditor law throughout the postrevolutionary period was a politically divisive subject, and both debtor- and creditor-oriented interest groups were able to mobilize significant power in the legislature to block proposed changes in the law to which they were opposed.[19] But there was another reason: simply that men for a long time were unable to contemplate the outlines of a body of law that would be new and fundamentally different from colonial debtor-creditor law. Indeed, it was only after the new body of law had in large part come into existence that men were able to describe it and that they began to question the underlying assumption of colonial debtor-creditor law, that a debtor was under an ethical obligation to make full payment for all benefits he had received from his creditor, even "if by Mismanagement he . . . [was] unable to discharge his debts. . . ."[20]

During the 1780s, when rural debtors mounted a sustained campaign for legal reform, no one seriously questioned the colonial assumption. General bankruptcy and insolvency laws were not proposed, nor, in fact, was the practice of imprisonment for debt challenged. This is not surprising in view of the nature of the postrevolutionary economy. Bankruptcy and insolvency laws and the abolition of imprisonment for debt are sensible legal arrangements in an industrialized society, in which personal skills are a man's primary economic resource, for a man does not lose those skills when he enters into bankruptcy, nor can he use them while he is imprisoned for debt. But in a predominantly agrarian economy, from which Massachusetts in the 1780s was not yet far removed, land is the most important resource; land, it must be remembered, can remain productive while a man is imprisoned for debt but is taken from a man who enters into bankruptcy. A debtor in such an economy may thus be better off imprisoned. In an economy in which there is a limited market for the sale of land, a creditor—rather than seizing and trying to sell land—may also be better off imprisoning a debtor in the hope that friends or other creditors will pay his debt. For these reasons it appears that although debtor-creditor law was a subject of great controversy in the 1780s, radical modification of its substance was not then proposed.[21]

Despite the absence of a radical challenge to existing law, some reforms beneficial to debtors were enacted. But many of the reforms were only of a temporary nature; they represented attempts on the part of the legislature to alleviate distress without making permanent changes in the legal system. One temporary reform was the Confession Act of 1782,[22] which permitted debtors to acknowledge their debts before a justice of the peace, after which a creditor, without a formal suit, could obtain execution on the day the debt was due—a device that considerably reduced the legal costs that debtors were required to pay. In the same year a temporary personal property tender law allowed debtors to pay their debts in personal property at appraised values rather than in specie.[23] Four years later another temporary statute permitted tender at appraised values of both real and personal property.[24] All of these laws had expired, however, by the 1790s, and none were ever enacted on a permanent basis. Other legislation was temporary in the sense that it applied only to debts already in existence on certain specified dates but not to subsequently arising debts. One such act required creditors to whom paper money had been tendered prior to January 1, 1777, to accept payment in paper;[25] another suspended the statute of limitations on all personal actions until

November 1, 1788,[26] thereby letting creditors opt to exercise forbearance.

Other legislation enacted during the 1780s was permanent but initially wrought only piecemeal reform. One act established procedures by which a judgment debtor, who since the rendition of judgment had paid his debt, could obtain judicial relief from further harassment by his creditor.[27] Two others that improved the position of debtors were a 1784 act on executions[28] and a 1787 act for the relief of poor people imprisoned for debt.[29] The 1784 statute continued the old rule that a creditor could levy execution on the goods and chattels of his debtor,[30] excepting necessary food,[31] clothing,[32] and tools of trade,[33] and, in the absence of goods and chattels, on his debtor's land.[34] As in the prerevolutionary period, land could be taken only at an appraised value determined by three indifferent appraisers, one each to be appointed by the creditor, the debtor, and the sheriff.[35] The change that the 1784 act brought about was that it deprived the creditor of his option to seize chattels at an appraised value;[36] henceforth goods that were seized had to be sold at a public auction at which people in addition to the creditor had an opportunity to bid.[37] Otherwise, though, the law governing levy of execution remained the same.[38]

The 1787 act for the relief of poor prisoners had a somewhat more significant impact. Whereas debtors having no property could be imprisoned under prerevolutionary law if their creditors provided an allowance for their support,[39] the act of 1787 provided for the release of such prisoners upon their taking an oath as to their poverty.[40] Once he had been released, a debtor could never be rearrested for the same debt,[41] although any property that he subsequently acquired remained liable to execution.[42] On the whole, the act was liberally construed by the courts: they applied it not only to prisoners committed upon debts arising out of contracts but to all prisoners committed upon civil judgments and even upon quasi-criminal judgments for statutory penalties awarded for failure to perform duties such as appearing at a militia muster.[43] Moreover, in 1821 the legislature abolished the requirements of an oath and of notification to the creditor and permitted an impecunious debtor to secure a discharge merely by making an informal statement of his poverty to his jailer.[44]

The courts also improved the situation of indigent debtors by holding a jailer liable only for nominal damages when an indigent prisoner escaped as a result of either negligent or intentional conduct by the jailer.[45] This rule encouraged the "humane or mistaken officer" to be lenient with prisoners whose escape would put their creditors "in no worse situation than ... [they] would have been in had the officer done his duty . . . ";[46] even if such an officer intentionally failed to arrest or, after an arrest, released an indigent debtor, he was not liable.[47] The law, in effect, urged officers to release poor prisoners on their own initiative, although we have no way of knowing the frequency with which officers did so. In any event, the exemption of officers from liability must have encouraged them to apply the statutes for the release of poor prisoners more liberally and must thereby have assisted in putting an end to civil imprisonment of indigents.

Meanwhile, statutes and judicial decisions were alleviating the condition of other prisoners who were confined for debt. As had been true in the prerevolutionary period, imprisoned debtors who possessed sufficient wealth to obtain bond were released during the daytime from close confinement and could then remain anywhere within the liberties of the jail yard.[48] Postrevolutionary courts broadened this privilege in a number of ways. Sessions courts, for instance, extended the boundaries of jail yards "for the conveniency of Debtors who . . . [had] given bond . . . '"[49] and the Supreme Judicial Court construed the word "daytime" broadly "to mean that portion of the twenty-four hours in which a man's person and countenance are distinguishable."[50] After much judicial confusion on the question of the closeness of the confinement in which prisoners were to be kept in the nighttime[51]—confusion that is seen in contradictory decisions on the question whether during the night prisoners could use a necessary house that was not physically attached to the prison[52]—the legislature intervened and provided that prisoners who had given bond could enjoy the liberties of the yard during the night as well as during the day.[53] The result, as Chief Justice Parker noted with only slight exaggeration, was that "imprisonment of a debtor . . . [became] merely nominal," for he could "sleep in his own bed, eat at his own table, and carry on business at his usual place, notwithstanding he is legally in jail."[54] By the 1820s no debtor needed to remain in jail;[55] indigents could obtain unconditional release, while other prisoners could reside anywhere within the jail's by then extensive liberties. As a result of a series of piecemeal reforms, imprisonment for debt had largely been abolished, although final statutory abolition did not occur for another three decades.[56]

Pressures from debtors produced other changes beneficial to them. The law of mortgages[57] was judicially modified to prohibit the recovery by a creditor of mesne profits arising during the interval between the commencement and the termination of a foreclosure proceeding—a modification that the Supreme Judicial Court recognized as an exception to the usual common law rule favoring recovery of mesne profits.[58] Debtors, on the other hand, could upon redemption of their land recover profits accruing during any period in which their creditors held their lands on foreclosure to the extent that those profits exceeded the sum due on the mortgage.[59] The legislature also enacted rules of mortgage law favorable to debtors. When the courts, for example, held that a debtor who wished to pay his mortgage following foreclosure could not maintain a bill in equity to redeem his land[60] without tendering the sum of money actually due to the creditor—a sum that the debtor had to ascertain at his peril[61]—the legislature immediately made statutory provision requiring the creditor to inform the debtor, upon demand, of the sum that was in fact due.[62]

Pressures for favorable legal change came, however, from creditors as well as debtors. They sought and obtained legislation that increased their remedies against the real estate of deceased debtors,[63] remedies that became increasingly valuable as the land market matured. But far more important were judicial decisions permitting creditors to use the old colonial trustee process to attach debtors' goods and credits that were in the hands of third parties—not only when, as in the colonial period, their debtors had absconded and left Massachusetts but even when the debtor remained within the state. This change commenced with a 1788 statute[64] making the trustee process available to judgment creditors whose debtors were still in the Commonwealth. The next step occurred when the Common Pleas courts in the early 1790s extended the benefits of the new rule even to creditors who had not yet recovered judgment;[65] these cases were then confirmed by the Supreme Judicial Court in a 1793 case[66] giving the 1758 trustee statute a "liberal construction," since its purpose was "to counterwork fraud & advanced equity. . . ."[67] Two years later the legislature enacted a comprehensive revision of the trustee act which codified the recent court decisions and remained the basis of the trustee process for the next half century.[68] Pursuant to the trustee process,[69] which lay in all personal actions except suits for personal torts[70] or for specific recovery of chattels[71] and against all persons except aggregate corporations[72] and persons such as sheriffs whose liability arose solely from the law,[73] a creditor could attach personal property[74] of his debtor that was in the hands of another[75] and credits or other contract rights owed to the debtor by another.[76] This other person was deemed a trustee, against whom judgment would be rendered whenever his answers upon his examination[77] disclosed the existence of a legally enforceable right on the part of the debtor.[78] The trustee, however, would not be held unless the debtor, in order to obtain his rights, still had to bring a legal proceeding in which the trustee could interpose defenses.[79] This rule was necessary since a judgment by the creditor terminated the trustee's liability to the debtor[80]—a termination that could only be enforced, however, if there was still some proceeding at which the trustee could interpose the termination as a defense.[81]

Taken together, these specific changes in debtor-creditor law, themselves the product of interest-group pressures, reveal that a more general legal development had begun to occur. That development was the increasing emphasis in debtor-creditor law on remedies to help creditors actually collect debts from debtors able to pay them and the growing recognition of the inappropriateness and futility of creditors' other remedies. Debtors, men came to see, ought not to be placed at the mercy of their creditors and, in effect, punished for their inability to pay their debts; men were coming to realize that "poverty . . . [was] no crime. . . ."[82] Yet they wanted law to provide greater assistance to creditors seeking to extract every last penny out of their debtors' actual assets. Thus, while creditors were losing their power to subject their debtors to rigorous imprisonment, they were gaining new remedies against the real estate of deceased debtors and against a wide spectrum of property held by third persons for their debtors' benefit. Such was the direction in which debtor-creditor law continued to move during the nineteenth century. Yet the modern body of law, which emphasizes an economically efficient credit system rather than the punishment of defaulting debtors, was not to be achieved for some time.

The key to such a body of law is a general bankruptcy act that insures fair distribution of available assets by preventing preferences of particular creditors[83] and that "makes the bankrupt a new" and hence an economically productive "man, by discharging him from all debts which might have been proved under the commission."[84] Some men saw the need for a bankruptcy act at an early date, and the first such American act was passed by Congress in 1800.[85] Although it was enacted largely in response to pressures from creditor-oriented interests, whose aim was to prevent preferences,[86] the act also aided debtors, provided that they had been engaged in commerce, for it barred a levy of execution on their person or property once they had obtained a discharge.[87] This act remained on the statute books, though, for only three years.[88]

With its repeal in 1803, the Massachusetts courts tried to continue many of its policies through manipulation of the common law doctrine of creditors' compositions. As the common law had developed in Massachusetts, a debtor was permitted to assign all or part of .his property in trust to all or some of his creditors; such an assignment was valid in the absence of fraud as long as one or more of the creditors, whose debts were sufficient to absorb the property assigned, assented to the assignment.[89] The property assigned was thereafter exempt from attachment by any creditors,[90] both assenting and nonassenting. Assenting creditors, moreover, were barred from arresting the debtor or attaching his other property, even if it was subsequently acquired,[91] although nonassenting creditors were not subject to such bars.[92] Creditors' compositions fulfilled the functions of a general bankruptcy law only partially, however, for they conferred discharges only as against the claims of assenting creditors and did not prevent preferences of those creditors.

The need for general bankruptcy legislation thus continued, and as the economy developed it became increasingly apparent. The key events that pointed up the lack were the panics of 1819 and 1837. As the American economy became increasingly industrialized, interdependent, and tied to international markets, larger numbers of men, farmers as well as merchants and urban laborers, became dependent on the mechanisms of the market, with the result that downturns in the economy brought unprecedented hardship. The panic of 1819 resulted, according to contemporaries, in "an universal complaint of the want of employment and ... a consequent reduction of the wages of labor. ..."[93] Nor were the effects of the panic limited to those who by mismanagement were unable to discharge their debts; the "distress pervade[d] every part of the Union, every class of society, all ... [felt] it[,] ... all must inhale it and none ... [could] escape it. ..."[94] The panic of 1837 was even worse. During its course "the problem of unemployment ... [became] general, and ... some cities ... [even] caused relief work to be instigated by public bodies."[95] Indeed, it seemed to Daniel Webster "inconceivable that conditions ... [could] ever right themselves enough to have prosperous times ... again."[96]

The effect of these perceptions of unparalleled distress was finally to undermine the assumption that colonial debtor-creditor law had rested on—namely, that debtors who failed to pay their debts were, in effect, guilty of sin. As Joseph Story wrote in 1837, "[A] change ... [came] over the public mind. ..."[97] Borrowing, it seemed, no longer occurred because men sought to avoid "the Humiliations of a *Low and a Mean Condition*" by living beyond their station in life[98] but because they sought to improve that station by entering into the mainstream of a developing market economy. Similarly, defaults seemed the result not of breaches of trust but of circumstances in the marketplace beyond debtors' control. Many men, in short, had become hopelessly sunk in debt simply because they had sought to participate in the dream of national economic development. Such men were not sinners who deserved the punishment of a prison but were, like their creditors, victims of an impersonal market who deserved an equitable readjustment of their liabilities and the opportunity to participate again in the nation's continuing growth. In 1841 the general bankruptcy legislation needed to achieve these results became law, but again the legislation was soon repealed. In fact, the nation had to wait until 1898 before a bankruptcy law was permanently enacted.[99]

The direction of change was clear, however, by a much earlier date—probably by the time of the panic of 1819 and surely by that of 1837. By then it was already clear that the increasingly materialistic nature of society required major modifications in the law of debtor and creditor. In Massachusetts those changes had already begun to occur.[100] It was also becoming apparent that the ideal man was no longer an essentially spiritual being who devoted himself to the pursuit of religious ends; he was coming instead to be viewed as an essentially economic being who devoted himself to the pursuit of material ends.

Freedom of contract, the dominant concern of early nineteenth-century contract law, did not, as we have seen, always further entrepreneurial activity. In the case of *Kettell* v. *Wiggin*,[101] for example, the Supreme Judicial Court undermined a commercially useful pattern of trade so that an insurer would not be held to terms to which he had not consented. In the early years of the century, when the law was strongly influenced by the ideology of property rights, the result in *Kettell* seemed sound. Other values, however, never entirely disappeared from contract law, even in the early 1800s. One such value was that the rules of the marketplace should be structured so as to promote economic development.

As the nineteenth century wore on, courts in contract cases thus turned with increasing frequency to an analysis of the economic needs of the business and mercantile communities. The judges were, as they themselves said, "necessarily led to consider the effect of a different opinion on the commerical part of the community,"[102] for they realized that if they adopted rules disadvantageous to business "there would soon be an end of ... very extensive class[es] of commercial enterprises."[103] Thus they adopted the practice of construing all contracts "liberally for the security and promotion of commerce"[104] and of affording "no facility ... [to] practice[s] ... injurious to commerce."[105]

One of the commercial community's greatest needs was for certainty and predictability in the law. The courts recognized that if the rules of law were "unknown and uncertain among those concerned in ... [a] branch of commerce, ... the effects of that uncertainty could not fail to be embarrassing and mischievous."[106] A businessman had to know the rules applicable to his business, for "his calculations depend[ed] not infrequently on [such] a knowledge. ..."[107] In the absence of this knowledge, it was "out of the power of ... [the businessman] to calculate with any certainty upon the extent of [and the best possible investments for] his funds; his commercial enterprise . . . [would thus] be checked and his plans embarrassed and defeated."[108]

The case of *Baxter* v. *New England Marine Insurance Company* will illustrate.[109] The issue in that case was whether a shipowner whose vessel had been condemned in a foreign court for breach of the foreign nation's trade laws—a breach which, if it actually occurred, was also in violation of the vessel's insurance policy—was precluded by the foreign judgment from introducing evidence that the foreign laws and hence the insurance policy had not been violated. The court, recognizing the need for certainty and predictability, thought it "less important, perhaps, what the rule . . . [was], than that it should be established and known," for, as the court explained, any rule would affect insurance rates: "if foreign sentences . . . [were] conclusive . . . , the premium of insurance . . . [would] be less; if they . . . [were] not conclusive . . . , the premium . . . [would] of course be greater." The court's economic analysis went even further, however, in holding the foreign judgment conclusive, not on an analysis of the res judicata effect of foreign judgments in general, but because such a rule would induce shipowners to defend their vessels in the foreign proceedings and hence would "be most beneficial to neutral commerce, and most for the interest of neutral nations," of which the United States was the leading one.[110]

It was, of course, vital not only that the rules of contract be known but also that once known they be followed in the courts with consistency. Thus in *Robinson* v. *Jones*[111] the Supreme Judicial Court expressly followed the *Baxter* case, noting that "the question as to the conclusiveness of decrees of admiralty courts . . . must be considered as settled by that decision" and that it was "probable that our mercantile contracts have been generally entered into with a view to that law. . . ."[112] Contracts, that is, had to be enforced in accordance with precedent because the parties had acted against the background of precedent. They had given meaning to their contracts "by virtue of certain words, which may be considered technical . . . [and which were] well understood by all who concern[ed] themselves in commerce. It would," as the court accordingly noted, "be dangerous to give to any other form of words that meaning, where any doubts may exist as to the intention to give them that effect"[113] or otherwise to change a rule that had been sanctioned by "very respectable writers . . . whose works [had] become popular, and by whose authority merchants regulate[d] their conduct. . . ."[114] In short, the courts felt a need to adhere to precedent both because contracting parties manifestly intended to incorporate it into their contracts and because the rational economic world of the entrepreneur could function only if the rules by which it had to function were known and certain.

There was, of course, one other reason for following precedent—namely, that most precedent came either from England or from other American jurisdictions. It was appropriate to "adopt the principles of the English courts" since it was "very desirable that, in maritime law, there should be a uniformity among all great commercial nations."[115] Similarly, Massachusetts respected the decisions of the federal and of other state courts because it was "highly interesting to commerce, that the same rule of decision . . . should pervade the whole country."[116] However, the most important reason for adherence to precedent remained the commercial community's need for certainty and predictability so that it could engage in rational economic planning and resource allocation.

Throughout the early nineteenth century the courts rarely had difficulty in simultaneously giving effect to the intentions of the parties and facilitating commercial operations and economic growth. Usually the two objectives were consistent, and hence there was considerable overlap between them. One of the most important issues on which they overlapped was whether a party to an oral contract could testify to its contents. It will be recalled that the colonial rule barring testimony from a party had made it nearly impossible to prove and hence enforce terms on which the parties had agreed when those terms differed from customary usage.[117] The colonial rule, however, was inconsistent not only with giving effect to the intentions of the parties but also with "considerations of necessity and great public convenience, for the sake of trade, and the common usage of business."[118] Accordingly, at the turn of the century cracks began to appear in the ancient rule, and "the modern cases often [began to] contradict the ancient ones. . . ."[119] For example, people with joint interests in a matter were sometimes permitted to testify on behalf of each other. Thus sailors were allowed to speak on each other's behalf in a series of suits involving common issues brought by them against their vessel for wages, while insurance underwriters who were sued severally were permitted to testify in suits other than the ones against themselves, even though those who lost suits were liable to contribute to a common loss.[120] Similarly, officers and members of corporations, even business corporations, were sometimes permitted to testify in suits in which their corporation was a party.[121] Most important, an agent who had made an oral contract on behalf of his principal was allowed to testify to its contents, thus making the terms of oral contracts provable whenever parties acted through agents,[122] on the theory that such contracts were "often for the benefit of trade" and that the agents, "who alone can possibly have knowledge of the fact, may *ex necessitate rei*, be called as witnesses to prove it. . . ."[123] By the 1820s so many exceptions had been carved into the rule rendering persons interested in the outcome of litigation incompetent that one commentator doubted whether that "strict rule ... of evidence ... extended to mercantile transactions,"[124] although it was not until 1857 that the rule was abolished by statute.[125] Thus, long before the middle of the nineteenth century, the needs of the business community had furthered the efforts of parties seeking to make contracts on terms other than those sanctioned by custom.

On occasion, however, the needs of business and the principles of free contract seemed inconsistent, and then judicial concern for economic development and commercial convenience sometimes triumphed over the doctrine that a person should be held to contractual liability only under terms to which he had given his free consent. The first important case where this occurred was in 1808 in *Stetson* v. *Massachusetts Mutual Fire Insurance Company*,[126] a suit by the owner of a building against his insurer seeking to recover for a loss caused by a fire. The owner in that case had, since the making of the contract, improved his building, and the defendant insurer, by analogy to cases of deviation from marine insurance contracts, such as *Kettell* v. *Wiggin*,[127] contended that the improvements invalidated the contract. His position was that whereas in marine insurance contracts "the party contracting ... voluntarily substituted another voyage, for that which was insured,"[128] and so lost the benefit of the contract, the plaintiff here had substituted a building for that which the defendant had agreed to insure, and so ought not be permitted to recover. Analytically the defendant's argument was a sound one, but its practical results were unacceptable. To accept it would seemingly have impeded real estate improvements and, as the court observed, rendered "contracts of this kind ... so inconvenient, as wholly to prevent them."[129] The argument was therefore rejected, and recovery by the plaintiff was allowed.

Economic analysis was carried even further in the 1827 case of *Thorndike* v. *Bordman*,[130] the facts of which were analogous to those in *Kettell* v. *Wiggin*.[131] The plaintiff in *Thorndike* brought suit to recover for the loss of his vessel, which had been insured for a voyage to as many ports as it wished to proceed in the Indian seas in order to discharge its outbound cargo and procure a new one. After selling the outbound cargo, the vessel had proceeded "to Cochin China, and ... to the port of Saigon, up a river of the country, where no American vessels had been before,"[132] in order to purchase a cargo of sugar. Able to obtain only a portion there, the master next brought the vessel to Batavia in Java, where he learned that prices were higher than at the neighboring Javanese port of Samarang, to which he decided to proceed. Local law prohibited him from carrying sugar from Batavia to Samarang, however, and accordingly he sold the sugar that he had obtained at Saigon. He then proceeded to Samarang, purchased a full cargo of sugar, and began his voyage home, during which the vessel was wrecked in a storm.

The defendant insurer, relying on *Kettell* v. *Wiggin*, contended that the sale of a portion of the inbound cargo at Batavia constituted a deviation from the voyage that he had originally insured and hence invalidated the insurance contract. The Supreme Judicial Court, over a dissenting opinion by Justice Putnam, rejected this contention and held for the plaintiff. Chief Justice Parker, writing for the court, tried unpersuasively to distinguish the *Kettell* case, but the real reasons for the court's decision emerge only after analysis of the dissent. Putnam's opinion dramatizes how in the decade after 1815 men's ambitions and concerns had changed. For Putnam did not argue, as the court in *Kettell* v. *Wiggin* had, that holding the defendant to liability would deprive him of sacred property rights without his consent, for property rights, as we shall see, were ceasing to have such connotations. Putnam's argument, instead, was an economic one: he pointed out that the defendant "must have relied" on the requirement in the insurance contract that the plaintiff merely sell his old and acquire a new cargo in order "to calculate the duration of the voyage . . . [and] the premium adequate to the risk."[133] In short, the social value that Putnam was seeking to protect was not the conception that a man ought not to have his property taken without his consent but the economic conception that businessmen could operate only in a rational economic world where legal relationships were certain and predictable. As against this value, however, the ambition of opening "various markets in . . . [an] extensive region . . . almost new to the commerce of this country"[134] —an inherently hazardous and uncertain enterprise in which risks could not be perfectly calculated—was certain to triumph.[135]

By the 1820s, then, contract law reflected a variety of different and sometimes conflicting policies. On the one hand, prerevolutionary ethical standards continued to have some impact on the law, chiefly in the rules concerning usury and wagering contracts but also in the principle that in the absence of a contract a man should receive fair compensation for services rendered. A far more important influence was the law's concern that men be held only to contractual liability to which they had consented and that they be held to that liability in strict accordance wtih the terms of their consent. But in contract law, as in debtor-creditor law, the courts were beginning to develop an increasingly commercial and materialistic view of man, and as they did a practical concern for business needs also began to influence contract rules.

The growing judicial concern for economic development also manifested itself in property law. The Supreme Judicial Court observed that it was "the wise policy of government, in this state, to facilitate the alienation of lands, and to encourage their cultivation,"[136] and accordingly refused to adopt rules that "would operate as a clog upon estates, designed to be the subject of transfer. . . . ."[137] Similarly, it sought to keep open the paths of inland commerce.[138] The most important way in which nineteenth-century courts promoted economic development in property cases, however, was to overturn inherited rules that had conferred monopolistic privileges on initial users of valuable economic resources.

The cases decided pursuant to the various acts to encourage the construction of mills were one of the earliest indications of the judiciary's willingness to sacrifice ancient property rules to the promotion of economic development.[139] Although Massachusetts had had a mill act throughout the eighteenth century,[140] that act became important only in 1814, when the Supreme Judicial Court construed a 1796 amendment to the act[141] as preempting a millowner's common law remedies for interference with his water rights.[142] The legislature, according to the court, had found that the common law remedies would "burthen the owner of a mill with continual lawsuits and expenses" when he overflowed his neighbor's land;[143] hence the common law actions for damages and to abate a milldam as a nuisance, along with the injunctive remedy that would have existed once equity jurisdiction had been conferred on the Massachusetts courts in the nineteenth century, were done away with.[144] The only remedy remaining to the owner of land that was flooded by the raising of a mill was the statutory remedy, which provided for compensation by way of annual rather than lump-sum damages and hence compelled the landowner to make an enforced loan of the capital value of his land to be repaid over a period of years by the entrepreneur who constructed the mill. In a society suffering from a scarcity of capital, such forced loans appeared to be of considerable value to the economic developers. Of course, such loans amounted to an invasion of sacred rights of property, but that invasion was nonetheless tolerated, since "the encouragement of mills ha[d] always been a favourite object with the legislature. . . ."[145]

Similar favoritism was shown in the 1827 case of *Avery* v. *Van-Dusen*,[146] where the issue was whether a landowner who received greater benefit than harm from a newly constructed milldam that partially flooded his land could still recover damages for the harm he had suffered. The court held that he could not.[147] The real significance of the case, however, lay not in its result but in its implicit recognition of a new theory of property, for in holding that an

enforced benefit that increased productivity could outweigh any equivalent injury, the court in effect was no longer viewing landed wealth as
a legally protected source of individual security but as a commodity
whose price in the market depended on its productivity.

Analogous developments had begun, meanwhile, to occur elsewhere.
Colonial and postrevolutionary law, it will be recalled, had granted a
property right to a person who for some period of time had been using
water in a stream that another person subsequently sought to use.[148]
The question that had been left unsettled in the colonial period was the
length of time for which the prior user had to have existed in order for
a property right to have matured. That question was settled immediately after the Revolution in the case of *Shorey* v. *Gorrell*,[149] which
held that one could not gain title to water by prior use unless he proved
that he had actually used the water for the full prescriptive period.[150] By 1800 it had become clear that the prescriptive period in
water cases was sixty years—a period which, unlike the prescriptive
period in other cases, was never reduced during the first three decades
of the century.[15i] Although it is unlikely that the Supreme Judicial
Court had a consciously developmental purpose when it decided the
Shorey case in 1783, its decision, by rendering the acquisition of
property rights in water difficult, ultimately would have had such an
effect in two sets of circumstances. The first would occur when an
entrepreneur sought to construct a large mill using water previously
used by several smaller mills. If the prior users had a property right, the
entrepreneur would have to negotiate to purchase their rights, perhaps
at an artificially high price brought about by competition among the
prior users to be the last to sell and thereby obtain a holdout price;
indeed, the costs of buying out such holdouts or other costs involved in
multiparty negotiations might be so high that the entrepreneur might
abandon his project of constructing a large mill. Similarly, if an
entrepreneur were seeking to buy water rights that would enable him to
enter into competition with a monopolist, he might, as we have seen,
find the monopolist's price artificially high, and as a result a valuable
economic improvement might be deterred. By making the acquisition
of property rights in water difficult, *Shorey* minimized the frequency
with which the two situations would arise.[152]

The issue of monopoly versus free competition also came before the
Supreme Judicial Court in the case of *Boston Glass Manufactory* v.
Binney,[153] and again the forces of competitive development triumphed. The gist of the plaintiffs' action was that the defendant,
"intending to wrong, injure and damnify the Pl[ain]t[i]ffs in their
business ... did ... entice and seduce and persuade ... the [plaintiffs'
workers] to quit and foresake, leave and abandon the service
and business of the plaintiffs ... by the allurement of higher

wages. . . ."[154] The action was not one for tortious interference with contractual relations,[155] for no contract between the plaintiffs and their workers was proved; rather, the suit was an attempt by the plaintiffs to extend the concepts of property with which the courts analyzed cases involving apprentices, children, and other servants to a new legal category—that of industrial laborers. The plaintiffs, in short, were attempting to extend rules inherited from the economically restrictive medieval guilds to the newly arising industries of nineteenth-century America. The court refused to do so, however, arguing that the plaintiffs' position "would lead to the most mischievous consequences, and would operate injuriously both to labourers and their employers."[156] The court, in short, preferred the unrestrictive model of the free competitive market.

The conflict between monopoly and competition culminated two years later when the proprietors of the Charles River Bridge, connecting Boston and Charlestown, sought to enjoin the construction of the parallel Warren Bridge. The facts of the *Charles River Bridge* case[157] dramatize the extent to which monopoly facilities were by the 1820s beginning to prove inadequate to handle expanding economic activity. When the Charles River Bridge was built in 1785 the population of Boston had amounted to 17,000 people, that of Charlestown to only 1,200. By 1827, when the Massachusetts legislature authorized the erection of the Warren Bridge, Boston's population had increased to more than 60,000, Charlestown's to 8,000, with the surrounding suburbs enjoying a like growth. As a result of these changes, Chief Justice Parker pointed out, "the profits of the bridge ha[d] been great beyond the example of any similar institution in this country;"[158] on an initial investment of $51,000, plus a subsequent outlay of $19,000, the bridge had been collecting annual tolls of $30,000 by the time the Warren Bridge was chartered.[159]

Although Justices Morton and Wilde, on the basis of whose opinions the injunction sought by the Charles River Bridge was denied, conceded that certain monopolistic rights had been granted in the past, they thought such a position "now generally exploded." For the legislature had in many instances "established new turnpikes, some nearly parallel with and diverting travel to the injury and sometimes ruin of former ones"; to hold that the proprietors of the earliest turnpikes possessed exclusive monopolies would have meant, Justice Morton argued, that subsequent entrepreneurs "ha[d] been acting and expending their money on the faith of void charters. . . ." Moreover, to recognize an exclusive monopoly over an entire line of travel, as the Charles River Bridge wanted the court to do, "would [have] amount[ed] to a stipulation, that the channels of communication and course of business, and in fact the state of society and of the country itself, should remain stationary." While Morton recognized that "exclusive rights for short periods sometimes encourage[d] enterprises of public usefulness," he nonetheless believed that "generally their tendency . . . [was] to impede the march of public improvement, and to interrupt that fair and equal competition which it ha[d] ever been the policy of our country to encourage."[160] As against monopolistic rights of property, Morton thought the doctrine of encouraging competition and public improvement ought to triumph.

When the Charles River Bridge appealed to the United States Supreme Court, Chief Justice Taney, affirming the Massachusetts court's denial of an injunction, adopted an approach similar to that of Morton and Wilde. Perhaps the most decisive influence on both courts was the advent of the railroad. Both Massachusetts and New York had chartered railroads in 1826, and within the next eight years fifty-one additional railroads had been chartered.[161] To hold that existing transportation facilities had exclusive monopolies would have saddled virtually every railroad with an unmanageable burden of costly damage actions as well as exposed them to injunctions. "Let it once be understood," Chief Justice Taney explained, that existing facilities possessed such rights, and "you will soon find the old turnpike corporations awakening from their sleep, and calling upon this Court to put down the improvements which have taken their place. The millions of property which have been invested in railroads and canals, upon lines of travel which had been before occupied by turnpike corporations, will be put in jeopardy."[162] Recognition of exclusive property rights in accordance with traditional doctrines would have made economic development impossible, now that scarcity of resources and new forms of technology had produced an economy in which initial developers were not always utilizing economic resources in the manner most profitable to society as a whole; accordingly the traditional doctrines were rejected.

The dissenting judges in both the Massachusetts and the federal courts were equally interested in economic development and equally willing to overturn old property concepts, but their model of development was a different one. For Justice Putnam of the Massachusetts court and Justice Story of the Supreme Court, for instance, the essential preconditions of economic progress were certainty of expectations and predictability of legal consequences. With these conditions satisfied, Putnam predicted that "men of capital and energy would embark their funds in enterprises of a public character, in the hope that their own fortunes might be advanced with the public prosperity . . . [,] but let the reverse of this be suspected, and public credit will be paralysed."[163] Story similarly could "conceive of no surer plan to arrest all public improvements, founded on private capital and enterprise, than to make the outlay of that capital uncertain, and questionable both as to security, and as to productiveness."[164] Neither Story nor Putnam used any of the old rhetoric about liberty and social stability in arguing for the Charles River Bridge; indeed, no one connected with the case ever argued that the property of the owners of the bridge had to be secured so that liberty could continue to exist. Although men such as Story himself[165] and John Taylor of Caroline[166] sometimes looked backward and persisted in using such rhetoric in their speeches and writings, the fact is that the rhetoric was of little use in solving the concrete problems of the 1820s, and hence it was becoming rare. Thus men such as Nathaniel Chipman and Thomas Cooper, who in the 1790s had put forth libertarian analyses of property,[167] were by the 1820s observing that property was "sanctioned by the principle of utility"[168] and that concern for the "rights attached to property . . . [was] one of the most efficient means of promoting national prosperity."[169] The nineteenth century's basic concern, as Cooper articulated it, was that if the law "intermeddle[d] needlessly in the honest acquirement of wealth, by legislative directions, restrictions or prohibitions," it would "detract in the same proportion from the stimulus to industry and exertion."[170] The concern of both judges and text writers, in short, was that unsound doctrines of property would lead to the destruction not of order or liberty but of the economic and industrial climate necessary for national development. Their differences were differences only as to the appropriate means of achieving the goals of development on which they agreed. For all of them, property law had become a subject for economic rather than political analysis, and landed wealth had become merely one of several commodities in the marketplace rather than the keystone of a well-ordered community.

The majority of the judges in *Charles River Bridge* and similar cases also advocated that the market function in a competitive way. They sought to encourage men to compete for control over land and other forms of wealth, believing that in a free market such competition would best promote the growth of the economy as a whole. Thus they formulated rules of law that legitimated competition. With that legitimation, the transformation of a society of well-ordered communities united in the pursuit of ethical ends into a society of individuals engaged in competition for material goods was complete. While individuals were free, like Henry David Thoreau, not to participate in the competitive, materialistic society that law was helping to create, they could do so only at the cost of leaving to those who remained most opportunities for worldly goods.

In summary, two fundamental shifts occurred in the legal and social structure of Massachusetts between 1760 and 1830. One was a shift from a set of essentially religious, other worldly values to a set of materialistic, worldly values. The other was a shift in the extent to which individuals were required to accept the values favored by the bulk of society. In the colonial period the expectation had been that all men would share the same values, and criminal prosecutions were frequently brought against those who refused to abide by the values that the community accepted. By the nineteenth century few expected all men to embrace the same values, and criminal prosecutions were rarely brought for breach of ethical codes. Nonetheless, while individuals were free to choose their own values, the law was not value-blind: it allocated resources and structured distributional rules, like the rules of debtor and creditor, in favor of those who decided to pursue earthly riches rather than those who accepted older, more religious values. The law of nineteenth-century Massachusetts was not, nor would it ever become totally neutral in its values.

9. Toward a Modern American Jurisprudence: Judges and Legislators as Makers of Law

The increasing preoccupation of nineteenth-century Massachusetts with economic development, which resulted in modification of the doctrines of property, contract, and debtor-creditor law, also led men to question the power of the jury to find and hence to make law. To lodge such power in juries became unsatisfactory in the nineteenth century, for the certainty and predictability of substantive rules that a commercial economy required would be of little avail if juries remained free to reject those rules or to apply them inconsistently. Owners and prospective builders of milldams, for example, were disturbed at the possibility of having their rights and liabilities determined by "the fluctuating estimates of juries,"[1] who under the mill act were authorized to determine the extent to which the owner of a milldam could flood a complainant's land in the future. Their power, as the owners of one dam argued, was often exercised in a manner that was "utterly indefinite and uncertain" and that provided defendants with "no rule for their future conduct," with the result that "uncertainty . . . would lead them to endless litigation. . . ."[2] Nor was the problem limited to flooding cases; in contract cases as well litigants pointed out the need "to establish some precise rules, which may make this branch of litigation less troublesome than it has hitherto been,"[3] and urged "that juries ought by the court to be restrained and kept within the proper and established rules. . . ."[4] Indeed, in all instances in which trial by jury had been practiced so as to give juries power to find the law, it was claimed that "neither expedition, certainty nor system ha[d] prevailed."[5]

The difficulty of having juries as lawfinders was compounded by the continuing breakdown of the state's ethical unity. In prerevolutionary Massachusetts juries had been able to arrive at verdicts in individual cases and to apply law consistently over a long series of cases largely because men selected to juries shared a common set of ethical values and assumptions that facilitated the attainment of unanimity and consistency in the application of the rules of common law. But once ethical unity broke down and jurors could no longer agree whether a community gained or lost when, for instance, a millpond flooded a meadow, jury verdicts indeed became "fluctuating estimates" that were "utterly indefinite and uncertain," and it became essential to transfer to the judiciary the power of finding law.

Effective judicial control over the law-finding function remained impossible, though, as long as trials were conducted before the full bench of the Supreme Judicial Court. The key problem was the court's seriatim charge to the jury. As long as each judge was free to state to the jury his opinion of the law and each jury was free to select the opinion it preferred, adherence to past verdicts was at best fortuitous, and legal certainty and predictability were unobtainable.[6] Another difficulty was that questions of law often arose for final determination during the very course of trial, when they had to be "decided by the judges without consultation, or with only a hasty one . . . [and without] time . . . for deliberation or research."[7] Mechanisms for preserving legal questions for reconsideration after trial were virtually nonexistent.

By the beginning of the nineteenth century, however, multiple trials before full judicial benches had become a luxury that Massachusetts could no longer afford. "[A] great accession of wealth and increase of population" had created overcrowded dockets and "render[ed] it necessary to revise the judiciary system. . . ."[8] During the period from 1804 to 1809 several jurisdictional reforms were enacted; those reforms, in turn, made possible a reduction in the power of the jury.

Much of the jurisdictional legislation dealt with the Courts of General Sessions of the Peace, which in a series of acts were completely abolished. The first step was to transfer all of sessions's criminal jurisiction to the Courts of Common Pleas,[9] thereby leaving sessions with jurisdiction only over the "erecting and repairing . . . [of] County buildings;[10] allowing & settling County accounts";[11] raising "County taxes;[12] granting licenses,[13] & laying out, altering & discontinuing highways. . . ."[14] General Sessions also retained power to approve and disapprove town bylaws, and as a result it continued to have vast administrative powers over local communities.[15] Of course, the individual justices of the peace still had petty civil and criminal jurisdiction. Three years later, however, another reform act completely abolished the ancient Court of General Sessions and replaced it by a new Court of Sessions, consisting of from three to seven justices per county;[16] this new court was in turn abolished two years later and its jurisdiction transferred to Common Pleas.[17] For the next two decades Massachusetts experimented with a variety of small Courts of

Sessions and with giving sessions's jurisdiction to Common Pleas,[18] until in 1828 the concept of a court supervising local government was rejected and an administrative agency—the County Commissioners, which remains in existence today—was established.[19] The key fact about the County Commissioners was that they lacked power to summon and hence sat without a jury; a party seeking to present to a jury a matter before the commissioners had to bring an action in the Court of Common Pleas in order to do so. The commissioners were accordingly able, on the many matters of local significance that came before them, to formulate and carry into effect coherent and consistent administrative policies.

The years 1804 and 1805 also saw a major overhauling of the system of appellate jurisdiction,[20] the object of which was to eliminate the wasteful system of a de novo trial before the full bench of the Supreme Judicial Court following a full trial in Common Pleas. First, the legislature prohibited appeals in personal actions where the amount in controversy did not exceed fifty dollars—a figure subsequently raised to one hundred dollars.[21] In such cases review could be had in the Supreme Court only upon a writ of error, which brought only points of law and not points of fact before the court.[22] Meanwhile, another act provided that trials before the Supreme Court were no longer to be conducted before the full bench but only before one of its judges; provision was made, however, for the reservation for the full court, by means of a bill of exceptions, of questions of law that arose during such trials.[23]

This legislation had far greater consequences than the mere simplification of the state's judicial structure, for it facilitated the development of a coherent body of case law. The process was a two-step one: first, a mechanism had to be found for compelling judges, upon questions as to the admissibility of evidence and the propriety of instructions, to make a single authoritative ruling consistent with prior rulings rather than a series of individual rulings inconsistent with each other; second, a mechanism had to be found for compelling juries to adhere to the instructions given them.

By providing for the trial of cases before a single judge rather than the full bench of the Supreme Court, the 1804-1805 legislation insured that juries would receive a single coherent statement of the law from that judge rather than a variety of potentially contradictory instructions from several judges. The legislation also made possible uniform and hence consistent control by the Supreme Judicial Court of all trials held in the state by providing that litigants could move for new trials or otherwise take an exception to "any opinion, direction, or judgment" of a trial court and thereby preserve points of law for determination by the full Supreme Court.[24] Although litigants prior to 1804 theoreti-

cally could and occasionally did move for new trials or otherwise object
to alleged errors in the admission or rejection of evidence or in the
giving of instructions,[25] such motions had been rare and had not
been hospitably received by the courts. As a general rule, a court would
decline to consider such a motion when the evidence had "been
admitted [or rejected or an instruction approved or denied] by a
quorum of the court"[26] —that is, a court would normally decline to
reopen and reconsider a decision that it had only recently made. After
the 1804-1805 legislation, however, the initial decision on an instruction or a point of evidence was made by a single judge. The old reason
for declining to undertake posttrial consideration of evidence and
instruction questions thereupon disappeared; indeed, such reconsideration was essential if the full court was to keep control of its nisi prius
judges. After 1804 exceptions and motions for new trials challenging
trial court determinations as to the admissibility of evidence[27] and
the propriety of instructions[28] became commonplace and frequently
led to careful, deliberative opinions settling important points of law.
When in 1804 provision was also made by statute for the publication of
those opinions,[29] the development of a modern system of case law
was given further impetus.

The second step in rationalizing the litigation process—finding a
mechanism for compelling juries to follow the instructions given
them—began when the Supreme Judicial Court in the 1808 case of
Coffin v. *Coffin*[30] held for the first time that the judge who tried a
case was required to instruct the jury on every material point at issue.
This case marked the beginning of a subtle shift in the judge-jury
relationship. Although the court in *Coffin* recognized that "the jury
must decide the law and the fact," it simultaneously observed that "to
enable them . . . truly [to] decide the law, they were entitled to the
assistance of the judge."[31] Such assistance was necessary because the
litigants had a right to have the jury decide the law correctly; in order
to secure that right, a litigant was entitled to "claim, from a judge
trying his case, the benefit of his instructions to the jury. . . ."[32]

The law, however, did not long remain at the point of requiring a
judge to assist the jury in finding the law correctly without requiring
the jury to accept the judge's assistance. For as soon as men perceived
that there was only one correct view of the law, rather than the seriatim
views of five judges, and that juries, even with the aid of instructions
from the court, sometimes returned verdicts contrary to the correct
view, they began a search for mechanisms to control erroneous verdicts.
The mechanism they found was the motion for a new trial on the
ground that a verdict was contrary to law and to the instructions of the
court. Although such motions had been used occasionally prior to the
1804-1805 jurisdictional legislation[33] and on one occasion had been

granted,[34] they became frequent only thereafter.[35] Once they
became frequent—which occurred by 1810—it was clear that the
instructions of the court, originally advisory, had become mandatory
and therefore that juries no longer had the power to determine the law.
Courts and litigants quickly perceived the transformation that had
occurred and soon began to articulate a new principle—that "point[s]
of law ... should ... be ... decided by the Court,"[36] while points
of fact ought to be decided by the jury.[37]

The significance of the transfer between 1804 and 1810 of the
law-finding function from the jury to the judge can best be illustrated
by comparing the 1820 case of *Baker* v. *Fales*[38] with the 1793 case
of *French* v. *Read*.[39] Both cases raised the same issue: how to
determine the disposition of the property of a parish that had
undergone a religious schism. But they resolved that issue very differ-
ently. *Baker* v. *Fales*, which came to the court upon a motion for a new
trial on the ground of error in the trial judge's instructions, ended in a
determination that as a matter of law those in control of the parish
corporation were entitled to the property—a determination that ultimately was applied in some eighty other parishes,[40] usually without
resort to litigation but also without a jury's taking into account local
needs and circumstances in its rendition of a verdict. The *French* case,
on the other hand, was decided purely as a question of fact; following a
plea by the defendant that the property belonged to the minister and
the congregation of the church and a replication by the plaintiff that
the property belonged to the parish corporation, the jury found for the
defendant. In so finding, the jury undoubtedly took local needs and
circumstances into account; what it did not do, however, was to frame
a rule capable of prospective application. The *French* case, in short,
preserved the local control of the legal system that was so central a
feature of eighteenth-century law; *Baker*, on the other hand, facilitated
the certainty and predictability that were so essential to the economic
developers of the nineteenth.

The transfer of the law-finding function from jury to judge was also
significant since it necessitated increased judicial supervision of the
fact-finding process as well. In order to insure that juries followed their
instructions, courts were also required to formulate rules as to the
quantum of evidence needed for the validity of a verdict. Analytically it
made no sense to require a jury to adhere to a rule of law in deciding a
case if the jury could circumvent that requirement by deciding the case
without any regard to the evidence. Consider, for example, an action of
debt on a bond in which a defendant introduced evidence, which the
plaintiff never rebutted, that the bond had been obtained by fraud—
which, as the court would charge the jury, constituted a good defense
to the action.[41] If, despite such a charge, the jury was permitted to

ignore the evidence and return a verdict for the plaintiff, there would be no way of policing the jury so as to insure that it adhered to the court's instructions; indeed, in the case which has been put, as in most such cases, it would be impossible to know whether the jury had ignored the instructions or ignored the evidence. In order to insure adherence to the instructions, it was thus necessary to require adherence to the evidence. This was done by a vastly increased use of the motion, which had existed since the colonial period, to set aside a verdict that was contrary to the evidence or to the weight of the evidence. In fact, in every case in which a litigant moved to set aside a verdict as contrary to the instructions of the court, such a motion was joined[42] and in cases where the verdict was "so manifestly wrong as to satisfy the Court that the jury could not have understood the case rightly," the courts became willing to grant such motions.[43] Thus, whereas eighteenth-century courts would set aside a verdict only if it had no support whatsoever in the evidence and not if it was merely against the weight of the evidence and, even then, would do so only sparingly,[44] courts in the nineteenth century were more liberal. By the 1810s the colonial rule had been reversed, and it was clear that a verdict would be set aside if it was "manifestly against the weight of the evidence."[45] Although the court looked with jealousy on such motions, since it was necessary that "disputes ... be settled and finished" and since the "law and constitution ... [had] given the ultimate decision upon the facts to the jury,"[46] nonetheless it thought it "absolutely necessary ... [to] have a control over verdicts, for sometimes they seem[ed] to be given unaccountably against the manifest justice of the case."[47] It was hoped, however, that "the increasing intelligence and respectability of our juries ... [and] their respect for the Court and the good understanding subsisting between them and the Court" would "diminish the ... frequency" of such motions.[48] Meanwhile, however, the courts continued to grant postverdict motions and to develop other mechanisms to enable them to supervise the fact-finding process, such as rules permitting the drawing of certain conclusive presumptions from facts otherwise proven,[49] rules regulating the burden of persuasion,[50] and a rule for nonsuiting litigants who failed to present evidence on issues material to their claims.[51]

Within a mere decade, then, of the initial jurisdictional reforms, the role of the jury as a finder both of law and of fact had been totally transformed. The jury had ceased to be an adjunct of local communities which articulated into positive law the ethical standards of those communities and which in doing so completely dominated the legal system's decision-making processes. It had become instead the adjunct of the court and had been left only with those fact-finding tasks, such as determining the credibility of witnesses and weighing the inherent probability of competing testimony, for which courts lack special expertise.

This change in the role of the jury paralleled a change in the role of the courts in making and applying law. In the colonial and postrevolutionary periods nearly everyone had agreed that it was the duty of judges to avoid making law by deciding cases in accordance with precedent. By the beginning of the nineteenth century, however, judges were abandoning the notion that they should adhere rigidly to precedent. It is impossible to specify precisely when or how that abandonment occurred, for the process was not sharp and clear-cut but slow and, even then, only partial. But it began early, when, within a few years of independence, the courts began on occasion to ignore precedent, as the cases that brought about the abolition of slavery in the 1780s indicate. Even as late as the 1820s, however, precedent remained important, and courts followed it in most cases simply because the interests of justice, rational social planning, and economy of judicial resources required that like cases have like results. The change that occurred between the 1780s and the 1820s was less in what the courts did than in their understanding of what they properly could do. That is, the change was in men's answer to the question whether judges must adhere to precedent when, on balance, other considerations of social policy dictated a departure. In the 1780s and the early 1790s nearly all men agreed on the necessity of adherence, whereas by the 1820s many accepted the propriety of departure.

The shift in attitude was brought about in part by the transfer from the jury to the court of ultimate law-finding power. As long as juries had found the law in verdicts that had no binding effect on and in fact were not even known to other juries deciding similar cases in the future, adherence to precedent had imposed little burden on the legal system, for the doctrine had had an impact only on questions of pleading, procedure, and evidence. But once the law-finding power passed to judges, who began to exercise it by rendering written opinions that remained available for all to read, precedent threatened to impose a straitjacket on future legal development and to bar all future legal change. Rigid adherence to precedent thus became impossible.

A second factor that contributed to the abandonment of precedent was the frequency of legal change in postrevolutionary Massachusetts, much of it judicially administered. By the early nineteenth century judicially administered change had become an abiding and unavoidable feature of the legal system, and for judges to have said that they were merely applying precedent in bringing about such change would have been to ignore reality.

It was at the turn of the century that judges and other legal commentators first became aware of the extent to which judicial modification of the legal system was occurring. The first man with such an awareness was James Sullivan, who perceived that judges had in fact become "legislators," for in interpreting any principle of law the courts in "every . . . trial . . . furnish[ed] a new comment upon it . . . [and] explained [it] more to our purpose. . . ."[52] As the century progressed, Sullivan's realization became widespread. Thus the Supreme Judicial Court recognized that some of the cases that came before it were "applications[s] of an entirely new impression"[53] or were "raised for the purpose of having the rule in such cases settled, rather than on account of any real controversy" between the parties.[54] The courts recognized that the existence of such cases caused them to adopt "different principle[s than had] . . . heretofore governed . . . in actions" of the same sort.[55] As Chief Justice Parker explained, while the fundamental "principles of the common law . . . [would] undoubtedly apply" at all times, the application of these principles may be different now, from that which was made several hundred years ago, when the rule was laid down."[56] Commentators were even more explicit. Recognizing that many of "the cases which . . . [came] before the Judges . . . [were] new either in principle or in circumstance,"[57] they saw what their predecessors in the revolutionary era had failed to see—that the "true glory"[58] of the common law was that "it must for ever be in a state of progress, or change, to adapt itself to the exigencies and changes of society. . . ."[59] They saw that "the expansion of a country, the increase of its wealth, its . . . new acquisitions moral and physical . . . and the changes consequent on these, all tend[ed] to produce a revolution in its jurisprudence. . . ."[60] By 1830 lawyers were coming to see all law as "essentially variable, extending and contracting itself according to the condition of the nation, accommodating its flexible character to the manners, habits, and employments of the people . . .";[61] law, they now thought, "must necessarily vary with the varying tempers of ages and nations . . . ,"[62] since "the grand law of human life [was] mutability."[63]

Not only were men beginning to realize the inevitability of legal change, but they were also beginning to see that the direction of change was a matter of choice from among competing policies rather than deduction from shared first principles. Judges of the early nineteenth century sensed that "policy is a science of calculations and combinations, arising out of times, places, and circumstances," which "cannot be reduced to absolute simplicity and certainty."[64] They were disturbed by the difficulty of making policy judgments because they knew that different men had different ideas about which policies were right. Nonetheless, the judgments had to be made.

The early nineteenth-century shift in the roles of the jury and the court suggests that yet a third shift had occurred in the ability of the institutions of government to enforce the law both in Massachusetts and elsewhere in the nation. The occurrence of the latter shift is confirmed by other evidence, such as the suppression of Shays's Rebellion in Massachusetts in 1786-1787 and the suppression of subsequent rebellions like the Whiskey Rebellion in the 1790s. For reasons beyond the scope of this book, government was becoming increasingly able to compel recalcitrant minorities to obey rules of law that they found objectionable. Shays's Rebellion was suppressed with considerable effort, the Whiskey Rebellion with somewhat less effort, and the antirent movement in New York in the 1830s and 1840s with hardly any effort at all. Indeed, by the middle of the nineteenth century government was able to suppress a rebellion by an entire section of the nation.

The New York antirent movement best illustrates the government's changing power of enforcement.[65] Prerevolutionary Massachusetts sheriffs, it will be recalled, were powerless to enforce court orders in communities that were willing to band together to resist enforcement. When New York sheriffs, on the other hand, began in the late 1830s to serve process on rent-withholding tenants in eastern New York, the result was quite different. There were some cases of violence and resistance to officers, but most violent resisters were apprehended and punished, and whenever large-scale resistance occurred it was readily suppressed by military force. The New York antirenters, however, did not give up their goal of abolishing the tenurial system that required them to pay rents; they organized politically and mounted a statewide propaganda campaign that brought them some success in the legislature.

The New York antirent movement illustrates how the locus of power and the mode of resolving social controversies had changed, at least in the northeastern states. Social controversies were no longer resolved in local communities by a process of consensus building that assured nearly unanimous support for whatever decision was reached. Instead, statewide political and legal institutions became the focus of the decision-making process. These new institutions, moreover, did not attempt to secure the acquiescence of the entire state in their decisions; they secured only as much support for a decision as was necessary to make the decision politically acceptable and militarily enforceable.

The changes in the power of the jury to make law, in judges' understanding of their power to change law, and in the ability of legal institutions to enforce law suggest that a final, fundamental change had occurred in the nature and social function of law. Whether it was made by courts or legislatures, law in nineteenth-century America had ceased to be a mechanism for the preservation of local power and the building of local consensus or to be a mirror of stable and widely shared ethical values. In part it had become a mechanism for giving individuals liberty to choose their own ethical values and for enforcing the choices they made. More often, however, the function of the law was to resolve disputes among individuals seeking control over a particular economic resource. In resolving those distributional disputes, the law came to be a tool by which those interest groups that had emerged victorious in the competition for control of law-making institutions could seize most of society's wealth for themselves and enforce their seizure upon the losers.

Bibliography of Manuscript Sources, Notes, Index

Bibliography of Manuscript Sources

JUDICIAL MATERIALS

Apart from three sets of published cases—the one volume of Josiah Quincy, Jr., *Reports of Cases Argued and Adjudged in the Superior Court of Judicature of the Province of Massachusetts Bay, between 1761 and 1772*; volumes 1-17 of the *Massachusetts Reports*, covering the period 1804-1822; and volumes 1-10 of *Pickering's Reports* (also numbered as volumes 18-27 of the *Massachusetts Reports*), covering the period 1822-1830—clerks of court kept voluminous official records of judicial proceedings throughout the period 1760-1830. There are four principal sets of records, as follows:

1. The extended record of the Supreme Judicial Court, known prior to 1780 as the Superior Court, is bound in a total of 134 volumes covering the period 1760-1830. All cases that progressed to final judgment before the court are recorded in the bound volumes, with only occasional omissions. In a typical case, the record consisted of the clerk's transcription of the parties' pleadings and motions, the jury's verdict, and the court's judgment. Until 1797 these records were kept in Boston by the clerk of the court, but beginning in that year they were kept in the various county seats to which the court traveled on its circuit.

2. The extended records of the Courts of Common Pleas, known prior to 1780 as the Inferior Courts, are bound in hundreds of volumes located in the various county seats of the Commonwealth. All cases progressing to final judgment are recorded, again with only occasional omissions. A record in a typical case contains the same material as in a case before the Supreme Judicial Court.

3. The extended records of the Courts of General Sessions, known by various names between 1760 and 1830, are also found in volumes located in the county seats. To the extent that these records contain transcriptions of civil or criminal litigation, their content is similar to that of the Supreme Judicial Court and Common Pleas records. However, the sessions records are in large part transcriptions of administrative proceedings which often report those proceedings in great detail—detail that is of interest to the social and economic as well as to the legal historian.

4. In addition, papers and documents submitted to the various courts during the course of litigation have been preserved with varying degrees of care in the different counties. The researcher is liable to find innumerable sorts of documents in sifting through file papers, although most of the papers are pleadings, depositions, petitions, and the like. The papers are generally filed by court term, but, except for the pre-1797 papers of the Supreme Judicial Court, are otherwise unindexed.

The manuscript sources that have been preserved in each of the counties are as follows:

Berkshire. Seven volumes of post-1797 Supreme Judicial Court records, 56 volumes of Common Pleas records, and 4 volumes of sessions records are available at the Berkshire County Courthouse in Pittsfield. The last set of records is located in the County Commissioners' office; the first two sets are in the custody of the clerk of courts. No file papers have been preserved for the period 1760-1830.

Bristol. Five volumes of post-1797 Supreme Judicial Court records, 25 volumes of Common Pleas records, 5 volumes of sessions records, and 6 boxes of sessions file papers covering the years 1760-1764 are available at the Bristol County Courthouse in Taunton. The clerk of courts has custody of all the above records.

Dukes. One volume of Common Pleas records, one volume of sessions records, and two volumes containing records of both courts have been preserved in the office of the clerk of courts in the courthouse at Edgartown. No other records have been preserved.

Essex. Fifteen volumes of post-1797 Supreme Judicial Court records, 70 volumes of Common Pleas records, and 7 volumes of sessions records are available at the Essex County Courthouse in Salem. In addition, there are an indeterminate number of boxes of file papers; the clerk of courts will retrieve papers either by case name or by date but will not permit access to the vault in which they are stored. The clerk of courts also has custody of the other records.

Franklin. Ten volumes of Common Pleas and two volumes of sessions records, both covering only the period 1812-1830, are in the custody of the clerk of courts at the county courthouse in Greenfield. No other records have been preserved. Cases arising prior to 1812 are included in the Hampshire County records.

Hampden. Two volumes of Supreme Judicial Court records, 13 volumes of Common Pleas records, and 2 volumes of sessions records, all covering the period 1812-1830, are in the custody of the clerk of courts at the county courthouse in Springfield. No file papers have been preserved. Cases arising prior to 1812 are included in the Hampshire County records.

Hampshire. The following records covering the entire period from 1760 to 1830 are in the custody of the clerk of courts at the county courthouse in Northampton—4 volumes of Supreme Judicial Court records for the years following 1797, 36 volumes of Common Pleas records, 5 volumes of sessions records, 4 volumes containing both Common Pleas and sessions records, 295 boxes of Common Pleas file papers, and 35 boxes of sessions file papers.

Middlesex. The clerk of courts at the county courthouse in Cambridge has custody of 12 volumes of post-1797 Supreme Judicial Court records and 7 volumes of sessions records covering the entire period 1760-1830. There are 25 volumes of Common Pleas records from 1760 to 1806, but only 4 post-1806 volumes, covering less than four complete years, have been preserved. However, the researcher can learn the content of the missing volumes by examining 85 post-1806 volumes of Common Pleas docket books, which contain the clerk's preliminary notes from which, along with file papers, he pieced together the final extended record. Middlesex possesses perhaps the best preserved set of file papers—a total of 715 boxes of Common Pleas files and 120 boxes of sessions files covering every year between 1760 and 1830.

Nantucket. The clerk of courts in Nantucket has in his custody three volumes containing both Common Pleas and General Sessions records for the period 1760-1807, four volumes of Common Pleas records covering 1807-1830, and one volume of sessions records covering the same period. No records of the Supreme Judicial Court and no file papers have been preserved.

Norfolk. Seven volumes of post-1797 Supreme Judicial Court records, 28 volumes of post-1793 Common Pleas records, and 2 volumes of post-1793 sessions records are in the custody of the clerk of courts at the county courthouse in Dedham. No file papers have been preserved. Cases prior to 1793 are included in the Suffolk County records.

Plymouth. Four volumes of post-1797 Supreme Judicial Court records are in the custody of the clerk of courts at the county courthouse in Plymouth. One post-1817 volume of sessions records is in the custody of the County Commissioners, whose office is also at the courthouse. Four volumes of sessions records covering the period from 1760 to 1817 and 21 volumes of Common Pleas records, covering 1760-1830, are at Pilgrim Hall, a private historical museum also located in Plymouth.

Suffolk. The greatest bulk and widest variety of records have been preserved in Suffolk, although few of the sets are complete. Indeed, only the Supreme Judicial Court records are complete for all years between 1760 and 1830. Thirty-two volumes, covering cases prior to 1797 in all the counties of Massachusetts, are in the custody of the clerk of the Supreme Judicial Court in the Suffolk County courthouse in Boston; all 32 volumes are also available on microfilm at the clerk's office and at the Massachusetts Historical Society. The clerk also has custody of 38 volumes of Supreme Judicial Court records covering cases in Suffolk County after 1797; the first 3 volumes have also been microfilmed. The clerk has also preserved an immense collection of pre-1797 file papers, which have been indexed and filed by index number in some 1,700 bound volumes. The indexed papers are also available on microfilm.

In addition, 148 volumes of Common Pleas records for the years 1780-1830 are available in vault five of the Suffolk County Superior Court files; access to the vault can be obtained from the clerk of the Superior Court, Civil Division, whose office is at the county courthouse. Eight Common Pleas docket books for the years 1764-1772 and 1776-1780 are stored in vault one of the Superior Court files, to which access can be obtained from the clerk. Vault one also contains some 450 boxes of Common Pleas file papers covering the period 1760-1830, with occasional gaps.

Sessions records for Suffolk are incomplete. The clerk of the Supreme Judicial Court has custody of two sessions docket books covering 1764-1773 and one folder containing a small number of eighteenth-century file papers. Five volumes of sessions records covering 1797-1817 are also available in vault five of the Superior Court files.

Two sets of records not available for other counties are available for Suffolk. One is the nine-volume set of the Criminal Records of Boston Justices of the Peace, covering 1806-1822, which is now part of the Adlow Collection at the Boston Public Library. The other is an eight-volume set of Boston Police Court Dockets from 1824 to 1830, which is in the custody of the criminal clerk of the Boston Municipal Court, whose office is in the Suffolk County Courthouse. Both sets contain notes of dispositions of petty criminal cases, interspersed with remarks of the justices, the complainants, and the defendants.

Worcester. The clerk of courts at the county courthouse in Worcester has custody of 8 post-1797 volumes of Supreme Judicial Court records and 69 volumes of Common Pleas records. The County Engineers, whose office is also in the courthouse, have custody of seven volumes of sessions records. No file papers have been preserved for Worcester County.

In addition to the records located in the various county seats, there are two other volumes of official court records—Samuel Curwen's Justice of the Peace

Book, located in the Essex Institute in Salem, and the Plymouth Notary Public Records, 1768-1830, located in Pilgrim Hall in Plymouth. They contain various records kept by a justice of the peace and a notary public.

Notes of various lawyers and judges who regularly attended the proceedings of the Supreme Judicial Court have also been preserved. The notes consist largely of the trial testimony of witnesses, but they often report other matters, such as argument of counsel, instructions by the court, and other comments from the bench.

I have used the following notes. The legal papers of Robert Treat Paine are a three-volume set covering the years 1760-1789, when Paine attended many sessions of court, first as a young attorney and then, after 1780, as attorney general; the Paine Papers are in the custody of the Massachusetts Historical Society in Boston. William Cushing, who was a judge of the Superior and Supreme Judicial Courts from 1772 to 1789, took notes on many of the cases, which are available in typescript in the Harvard Law School Library in Cambridge; Cushing's notes generally consist of complete texts of judicial opinions or jury instructions delivered from the bench. Judge Increase Sumner took three volumes of Notes of Evidence over the period 1782-1794, which are preserved at the Massachusetts Historical Society. The society also has custody of the voluminous Minute Books of Francis Dana, another judge, covering cases from 1788 to 1806; Dana's Minutes consist chiefly of trial testimony, but they also contain well over two hundred summaries of opinions delivered from the bench. Finally, the Essex Institute in Salem has custody of the Court Minutes of Nathaniel Peaslee Sargeant, the judge who took notes covering the years 1777 to 1794. In all, there is thus at least one set of notes covering every year of the Supreme Judicial Court's activity between 1760 and the beginning of the publication of the *Massachusetts Reports* in 1804.

LEGISLATIVE MATERIALS

I have not systematically examined any legislative materials apart from the two published sets—*The Acts and Resolves, Public and Private, of the Province of the Massachusetts Bay*, 5 vols., Boston, 1869-1922, and the *Acts and Laws of the Commonwealth of Massachusetts, Passed by the General Court*, which has been published in several editions.

OTHER MANUSCRIPT MATERIALS

Cushing Papers, ca. 1710-1790, 2 vols., Massachusetts Historical Society, Boston. This collection contains the letters and legal and miscellaneous papers of three generations of Cushings who sat on the benches of the Superior and Supreme Judicial Courts.

Luther S. Cushing, Appendix, in Asahel Stearns, Lectures on Law, ca. 1825, Harvard Law School Library, Cambridge. The appendix is a 90-page handwritten draft of a treatise on the Massachusetts trustee law.

Gerry II Papers, ca. 1775-1815, Massachusetts Historical Society, Boston. Two boxes of the letters and other papers of Elbridge Gerry.

Samuel Howe, Lectures on the Practice of Courts, ca. 1825, Harvard Law School Library, Cambridge. This 450-page manuscript contains Judge Howe's notes for a course on civil procedure that he taught to law students in Northampton during the 1820s.

Paine Papers, ca. 1755-1805, Massachusetts Historical Society, Boston. A voluminous collection of letters, legal documents, and other loose papers, stored in folders, of Robert Treat Paine.

Theophilus Parsons, Memorandum Book, ca. 1770, Essex Institute, Salem. This single, 100-page volume contains Parsons's notes from his days as a student.

Theophilus Parsons, Notes of Jury Instructions, Nov. 10, 1806, in Taft Papers, Massachusetts Historical Society, Boston.

Theophilus Parsons, Precedents, ca. 1775-1790, Harvard Law School Library, Cambridge. This single, 100-page volume contains copies of writs drawn by or otherwise known to Parsons in the early years of his legal practice.

Sargeant Papers, ca. 1775-1794, Essex Institute, Salem. This miscellaneous collection of loose papers stored in boxes contains occasional legal papers drawn by Nathaniel Peaslee Sargeant.

Sullivan Papers, ca. 1770-1808, Massachusetts Historical Society, Boston. A voluminous collection of letters, legal documents, and other loose papers, stored in folders, of James Sullivan.

Edmund Trowbridge, Law Cases and Law Notes, ca. 1750-1790, in Dana Papers, folders 612-700, Massachusetts Historical Society, Boston. Several folders of legal opinions and miscellaneous notes of Edmund Trowbridge.

Notes

ABBREVIATIONS FOR COURT RECORDS

Citations to official manuscript court records are given in a special form. The name of the case is followed by abbreviations for the county in which the case was begun, the court in which it was heard, and the month and year. For example, a citation to Smith v. Jones, BeCP, 7–63, would refer to the case of Smith against Jones, heard in the Berkshire County Court of Common Pleas in July 1763. A citation to Smith v. Jones, HSJC, 11–09, would refer to the case of Smith against Jones in the Hampshire County Supreme Judicial Court in November 1809. (The number before the hyphen stands for the month, while the next number stands for the year, with the numbers 40 to 99 representing the years 1740 to 1799 and the numbers 00 to 39 representing the years 1800 to 1839).

The abbreviations for the various counties are as follows:

Ba	Barnstable
Be	Berkshire
Br	Bristol
C	Cumberland
D	County of Dukes
E	Essex
F	Franklin
H	Hampshire
Hd	Hampden
L	Lincoln
M	Middlesex
N	Nantucket
Nf	Norfolk
P	Plymouth
S	Suffolk
W	Worcester
Y	York

The following abbreviations are used for the courts in which cases were heard:

Boston Justice Ct.	Boston Justice of the Peace Court
Boston Police Ct.	Boston Police Court

CC	County Commissioners
CP	Court of Common Pleas
GS	Court of General Sessions
SC	Superior Court of Judicature
SJC	Supreme Judicial Court

Citations only by county, court, and date can be found in the appropriate place in the extended record of the court or, if no extended record is available, in the appropriate docket book. For example, Smith v. Jones, MGS, 9–85, is a citation to the case of Smith against Jones to be found in the extended record or docket book of the Middlesex Court of General Sessions in September 1785. On the other hand, citations to "Files" can be found only in loose file papers. Thus, Smith v. Jones, MGS Files, 9–85, refers to material in the case of Smith against Jones to be found in the file papers of the Middlesex Court of General Sessions for September 1785. Citations to Suff. Files are to material in the file papers of the Superior and Supreme Judicial Courts in the custody of the Clerk of the Supreme Judicial Court for Suffolk County. The cases are cited by file number, county, and year, although all papers are filed in Suffolk. The following abbreviations for counties are used in such citations: Barns., Berk., Bris., Cumb., Dukes, Frank., Hamp., Hampd., Linc., Msex., Nan., Norf., Ply., Suff., and Worc.

OTHER ABBREVIATIONS

Many standard legal abbreviations have been used in the notes. For their meaning, consult *A Uniform System of Citation*, published by the Harvard Law Review Association, Cambridge, Mass., in several editions, or the table of abbreviations in the appendix to *Black's Law Dictionary*, also published in several editions by the West Publishing Co., St. Paul, Minn. In addition, the following abbreviations are used in the notes:

Cushing	William Cushing, Notes of Cases Decided in the Superior and Supreme Judicial Courts of Massachusetts, 1772–1789, Harvard Law School Library, Cambridge (typescript)
Cushing Papers	Cushing Papers, Massachusetts Historical Society, Boston
Dana, Minute Books	Francis Dana, Minute Books, Massachusetts Historical Society, Boston
HLS	Harvard Law School Library, Cambridge
MHS	Massachusetts Historical Society, Boston
Paine, Minutes	Robert Treat Paine, Minutes of Trials and Law Cases, Massachusetts Historical Society, Boston
Paine Papers	Paine Papers, Massachusetts Historical Society, Boston
Parsons, Memorandum Book	Theophilus Parsons, Memorandum Book, Essex Institute, Salem
Parsons, Precedents	Theophilus Parsons, Precedents, Harvard Law School Library, Cambridge
Quincy	Josiah Quincy, Jr., *Reports of Cases Argued and Adjudged in the Superior*

Sargeant Papers
Sullivan Papers

Trowbridge, Law Cases

Trowbridge, Law Notes

Court of Judicature of the Province of Massachusetts Bay, between 1761 and 1772 (Boston, 1865)
Sargeant Papers, Essex Institute, Salem
Sullivan Papers, Massachusetts Historical Society, Boston
Edmund Trowbridge, Law Cases, in Dana Papers, Massachusetts Historical Society, Boston
Edmund Trowbridge, Law Notes, in Dana Papers, Massachusetts Historical Society, Boston

Chapter 1. Law in a Changing Social Order

1. Quoted in T. Harry Williams, Richard N. Current, and Frank Freidel, *A History of the United States* (New York, 2d ed., 1965), I, 390 (emphasis in original).

2. A total of nine colleges had been founded by 1776. See Bernard Bailyn, *Education in the Forming of American Society* (Chapel Hill, N.C., 1960), 87. Some sixty colleges were founded between 1780 and 1820, half of which are operating today. See Harry G. Good, *A History of American Education* (New York, 2d ed., 1962), 95.

3. *American Jurist*, first published in 1829.

4. On the vast power of juries in prerevolutionary Massachusetts, see Chapter 2. It has been suggested that modern juries disagree with judges on the law in less than one out of every five cases and that even when they do disagree they rarely do so openly. See Harry Kalven and Hans Zeisel, *The American Jury* (Boston, 1966), 494-495.

5. Accord, Michael Zuckerman, *Peaceable Kingdoms: New England Towns in the Eighteenth Century* (New York, 1970); Michael Zuckerman, "The Social Context of Democracy in Massachusetts," *William and Mary Quarterly*, 3d ser., XXV (1968), 523-544. Contrary to the view of David G. Allen, "The Zuckerman Thesis and the Process of Legal Rationalization in Provincial Massachusetts," *William and Mary Quarterly*, 3d ser., XXIX (1972), 443, 455-459, the fact of both intertown and intratown litigation does not imply that consensus based on shared ethical values had ceased to be the ideal toward which Massachusetts communities strived. On the continuity of ideals between the seven-

teenth and eighteenth centuries, see Edward M. Cook, Jr., "Social Behavior and Changing Values in Dedham, Massachusetts, 1700 to 1775," *William and Mary Quarterly*, 3d ser., XXVII (1970), 546, 548-553, 579-580. Nor does the fact of litigation suggest that consensus did not, on the whole, exist. That an ideal is not always attained does not mean that the ideal is not frequently attained. See Stephen Foster, *Their Solitary Way: The Puritan Social Ethic in the First Century of Settlement in New England* (New Haven, 1971), 151-160. It appears, moreover, that litigation did not always disrupt but sometimes strengthened social unity and stability. See David T. Konig, "Social Conflict and Community Tensions in Essex County, Massachusetts, 1672-1692" (Ph.D. Diss., Harvard University, 1973), 55-80, 112-166. Most important, the lawsuits that were brought could not have been resolved if they had been destructive of the underlying ethical consensus in Massachusetts. While breaches in social unity and stability occurred and sometimes lasted for several years, those breaches were ultimately healed. See Cook, "Changing Values in Dedham," 553-557. For further support of the position taken in the text, see Foster, *Their Solitary Way*, 11-64, 99-126, 155-172; Robert Zemsky, *Merchants, Farmers, and River Gods: An Essay on Eighteenth-Century American Politics* (Boston, 1971), 64-74.

6. See Chapter 3.

7. See Chapter 4.

8. See Cook, "Changing Values in Dedham," 565-573.

9. See Chapter 5.

10. See Chapter 6.

11. See Chapter 7.

12. See Chapter 8.

13. See Chapter 9.

14. Constitution of 1780, Part II, ch. 6, art. 6, in Oscar Handlin and Mary F. Handlin, eds., *The Popular Sources of Political Authority: Documents on the Massachusetts Constitution of 1780* (Cambridge, Mass., 1966), 452.

15. Sackett v. Sackett, 8 Pick. 309, 316 (1829).

16. 16 Mass. 480 (1820).

17. Two statements in abridgments that were directly on point were Knightley D'Anvers, *A General Abridgment of the Common Law* (London, 1705), I, 715; Charles Viner, *A General Abridgment of Law and Equity* (London, ca. 1740), IV, 109.

18. Coppin v. _____, 2 P. Wms. 496, 24 Eng. Rep. 832 (Ch. 1728); Christ's Hospital v. Budgin, 2 Vern. 683, 23 Eng. Rep. 1043 (Ch. 1712).

19. Brooks v. Dorr, 2 Mass. 39, 48 (1806).

20. 10 Pick. 295 (1830).

21. See Morton J. Horwitz, "The Transformation in the Conception of Property in American Law, 1780-1860," *University of Chicago Law Review*, XL (1973), 248, 264n52.

22. 15 Mass. 164 (1818).

23. Ibid., 166-167.

24. But cf. White v. Willis, 7 Pick. 143 (1828). It followed from Conner that a widow was not entitled to dower in land that was wild when alienated by her husband and subsequently brought into cultivation by his grantee. See Webb v. Townsend, 1 Pick. 21 (1822). Cf. Ayer v. Spring, 9 Mass. 8 (1812). See also Sargent v. Towne, 10 Mass. 303 (1813), holding that a devise of wild, uncultivated land carries a fee without words of inheritance.

25. 6 Pick. 187 (1828).

26. See Pierce v. Bartrum, 1 Cowper 269, 98 Eng. Rep. 1080 (K.B. 1775); The Chamberlain of London's Case, 5 Co. Rep. 62b, 77 Eng. Rep. 150 (K.B. 1591).

27. See Dodwell v. University of Oxford, 2 Ventris 33, 86 Eng. Rep. 292 (C.P. 1681). See generally John Comyns, *A Digest of the Laws of England* (London, 1762), I, 617-619.

28. 12 Mass. 220 (1815).

29. See Leader v. Moxton, 3 Wils. K.B. 462, 95 Eng. Rep. 1157 (K.B. 1773); Smith v. Martin, 2 Wms. Saund. 394, 85 Eng. Rep. 1206 (K.B. 1672); Jones v. Powell, Palmer 536, 81 Eng. Rep. 1208 (K.B. 1628); Slingsby v. Barnard, 1 Rolle 430, 81 Eng. Rep. 586 (K.B. 1617); William Aldred's Case, 9 Co.

Rep. 57b, 77 Eng. Rep. 816 (K.B. 1612); Henry Rolle, *Un Abridgment des Plusieurs Cases et Resolutions del Common Ley* (London, 1668), I, 140-141; Edward Coke, *The First Part of the Institutes of the Laws of England* (London, 1628), 56.

30. Slingsby v. Barnard, 1 Rolle 430, 81 Eng. Rep. 586 (K.B. 1617).

31. 12 Mass. at 227.

32. See Morton J. Horwitz, "The Historical Foundations of Modern Contract Law," *Harvard Law Review*, LXXXVII (1974), 917, and "Damage Judgments, Legal Liability and Economic Development before the Civil War" (unpublished paper in the possession of Professor Horwitz, Harvard Law School).

33. See Chapter 2, especially notes 165-166.

34. See Chapter 6, notes 140, 146, and accompanying text.

35. See Chapter 3, notes 17, 19.

36. See Chapter 3, text at notes 74, 84.

37. See Chapter 8, notes 46, 87. See also Morton J. Horwitz, "The Transformation in the Conception of Property in American Law," *University of Chicago Law Review*, XL (1973), 248-290.

38. As the material cited in note 37 above indicates, English property law did not take the prodevelopmental turn that American law took in the 1820s. See Chapter 8.

Chapter 2. The Legal Restraint of Power

1. See Bernard Bailyn, ed., *Pamphlets of the American Revolution, 1750-1776* (Cambridge, Mass., 1965), I, 38-41.

2. Draper v. Bicknell, Quincy 164, 165 (1765).

3. On the legal powers of the General Court, see Albert B. Hart, ed., *Commonwealth History of Massachusetts* (New York, 1928), II, 10; Emory Washburn, *Sketches of the Judicial History of Massachusetts* (Boston, 1840), 137-138, 151. On the unavailability of ungranted land, except in Maine, see Frederick S. Allis, ed., *William Bingham's Maine Lands, 1790-1820* (Boston, 1954), I, 24, 32, which indicates that after the Revolution, when the General Court sought to sell ungranted land in order to raise money, very little land was available other than in Maine. On the inability of government in eighteenth-century Massachusetts to raise substantial sums through taxation, see Oscar Handlin and Mary F. Handlin, *Commonwealth: A Study of the Role of Government in the American Economy—Massachusetts, 1774-1861* (Cam-

bridge, Mass., rev. ed., 1969), 14, 36-37, 64-86.

4. See generally Gordon S. Wood, *The Creation of the American Republic, 1776-1787* (Chapel Hill, N.C., 1969), 259-268. Of course, seventeenth-century legislation, at least in Massachusetts, had made substantial changes in the common law. See Mark DeW. Howe, "The Sources and Nature of Law in Colonial Massachusetts," in George A. Billias, ed., *Law and Authority in Colonial America* (Barre, Mass., 1965), 1; George L. Haskins, "Reception of the Common Law in Seventeenth-Century Massachusetts: A Case Study," ibid., 17, "The Beginnings of Partible Inheritance in the American Colonies," *Yale Law Journal*, LI (1942), 1280 and "The Beginnings of the Recording System in Massachusetts," *Boston University Law Review*, XXI (1941), 281. Few men had given any consideration to the theoretical implications of that legislation, however. But see Wood, *American Republic*, 263-264. Hence it was only during the imperial debate of the 1760s that Americans began to articulate their doubts about the limits of legislative power.

5. James Otis, "The Rights of the British Colonies Asserted and Proved," in Bailyn, *Pamphlets*, I, 454.

6. *The Crisis, Number XI* (New York, 1775), 81-87, quoted in Wood, *American Republic*, 266.

7. See Laws of 1761, chs. 1, 3-4, 13, 15-17, 22-25, 27-29, 39-40, 44, 48-50.

8. See ibid., chs. 6-10, 12, 18, 20, 30, 33-38, 42-43, 45-47, 51.

9. See ibid., chs. 5, 11, 14, 19, 26, 31.

10. See e.g., Resolves of 1761, chs. 3, 210. See also Resolves of 1760, ch. 235, in which the Court granted a witness at a committee hearing protection from arrest during the proceedings. Frequently the Court also granted liquor licenses, see, e.g., Resolves of 1760, ch. 460, and gave fiduciaries permission to sell assets or otherwise act on behalf of their trust. See, e.g., Resolves of 1761, ch. 188. In the preceding year, the Court in several instances had also stayed actions pending against bankrupts. See, e.g., Resolves of 1759, ch. 446.

11. Laws of 1761, ch. 21.

12. Ibid., ch. 2.

13. Ibid., ch. 32.

14. See Hart, *Commonwealth History*, II, 8, 11-13, 591-592; Washburn, *Judicial History*, 137-138.

15. For examples of the types of bylaws passed by town meetings, see Boston Record Commissioners, *Boston Town Records 1701-*

1728 (Boston, 1882), 9-17; Boston Record Commissioners, *Boston Town Records 1758-1769* (Boston, 1886), 76-77. See generally Charles Francis Adams, *Three Episodes of Massachusetts History* (Boston, 1892), II, 822-824; Kenneth Lockridge, *A New England Town: The First Hundred Years* (New York, 1970), 120-124; Michael Zuckerman, *Peaceable Kingdoms: New England Towns in the Eighteenth Century* (New York, 1970), 165.

16. See Adams, *Three Episodes*, 812-824; Lockridge, *New England Town*, 120-124; Zuckerman, *Peaceable Kingdoms*, 125-148.

17. See Adams, *Three Episodes*, 819; Lockridge, *New England Town*, 121-124; John Fairfield Sly, *Town Government in Massachusetts 1620-1930* (Hamden, Conn., 1930), 81-83; Zuckerman, *Peaceable Kingdoms*, 165-186.

18. This and the following three paragraphs are based on L. Kinvin Wroth and Hiller B. Zobel, eds., *Legal Papers of John Adams* (Cambridge, Mass., 1965), I, xxxviii-xliv.

19. See Reed v. Purrinton, PCP, 10-71; Murray v. Greenwood, WCP, 8-67; Sever v. Leach, PCP, 4-60.

20. See, e.g., Younglove v. Freeman, BeCP, 4-65, holding that an appeal could not be heard if one of the judges constituting the Common Pleas quorum had been the justice of the peace who had originally tried the action.

21. See, e.g., Taggart v. Smith, HGS, 8-67, overruling a motion to dismiss on the ground that no appeal lies from a justice's conviction for failure to work on highway repairs.

22. See, e.g., Order re Highway thro Shirley, MGS, 9-62 (bridge case); Southampton Highway, HGS, 8-60 (road case). See also Order re Naponsit River Bridge, SGS, 7-70 (court had power to determine whether it or town had duty to repair bridge). But see Petition of Chelmsford, MGS, 5-61 (only legislature had jurisdiction over bridges across navigable streams).

23. See Littleton By-Law, MGS, 9-62 (rejecting bylaw, "provision being made in that Regard by a Law of this Province").

24. If a person could not support himself and had no parents, children, or grandchildren, cf. Petition of Concord, MGS, 11-73 (holding that a grandson was liable for one-half of the support of his maternal grandmother, even though four of his grandmother's daughters, including the respondent's own mother, were still alive), or, if he were a servant or slave and had no master capable of supporting him, see Petition of Stoughton,

MGS, 11-70; Petition of Stickney, EGS, 3-69, the town in which he had his "settlement" became liable for his support. Under the statutes in force until 1767, a person gained a settlement by remaining in a town for twelve consecutive months without being warned by the selectmen to depart. See Wroth and Zobel, *Legal Papers*, I, 289. After 1767 a person could gain a settlement only by being born in a town or being approbated by the selectmen. See Laws of 1766, ch. 17. Much litigation arose between towns concerning which one was liable for the support of particular paupers. The most frequent issue in such litigation was whether a justice of the peace who was an inhabitant of a town could participate in the process by which a nonresident was warned to depart. See Wroth and Zobel, *Legal Papers*, I, 294, 297, 299; Petition of Pratt, SGS, 8-69; Petition of Natick, MGS, 3-68; Framingham Petition, MGS Files, 9-65. The initial rule was that a justice could not participate, but that rule was reversed by statute in 1772. See Laws of 1772, ch. 4. The effect of formal defects in warrants of warning and removal was another frequent issue, see Wroth and Zobel, *Legal Papers*, I, 294; Petition of Selectmen of Brookline, SGS, 11-68, the courts holding, of course, that the removal of a pauper without a proper warning was illegal. See Petition of Reading, MGS, 12-63. Pauper cases also raised many other interesting procedural issues, such as the status of a pauper who had been warned but not removed from a town within one year of his arrival, see Wilmington v. Reading, MGS, 9-66, the effect of a warning issued to "John Mucklewain with his wife and family" on a daughter by a former marriage of his wife, see Petition of Woburn, MGS, 3-68, the effect of a warning on a pauper who was too old to be moved, see Petition of Bridges, MGS, 3-65, and the effect of a warning issued in 1743 on a pauper who left town but returned a decade later and stayed for over a year. See Petition of Charlestown, MGS, 5-70. Finally, questions arose about which county court had jurisdiction to hear a case involving towns in two counties. See Upton v. Westfield, HGS, 5-74.

25. See Selectmen of Northampton v. Lee, HGS, 11-67; Petition of Lee, HGS, 8-67.

26. See, e.g., Order re County Tax, BeGS, 9-61. See also Order Assessing Town of Granby, HGS, 11-71, ordering the town to pay a portion of the back taxes of a district of which it was a part when the taxes were levied.

27. See, e.g., Order re Concord Goal, MGS, 11-69 (order to build new jail).

28. Such as hearing petitions to divide common fields. See Petition of Worthington, HGS, 5-66. But see Petition of Williams, HGS, 11-63 (dismissing petition to divide common field for want of jurisdiction).

29. See Petition of Marston, EGS, 9-69 (implying that court lacked power to direct a quarantine).

30. See Vote re Petitions for Highways, MGS, 9-69.

31. See Vote re Licenses, MGS, 9-65.

32. See Question re Depositions, PGS, 4-66 (denying access).

33. See Petition of Dren, PGS, 10-61.

34. See Clap v. Sprague, PCP, 12-70. Each inferior court tried only actions having some tie to the county in which it sat. Actions involving title to land were required to be tried before the inferior court of the county where the land lay; trespass vi et armis, in the county where the trespass had been committed; debt on a bond, in the county where the bond had been executed. See Laws of 1749-1750, ch. 9; Laws of 1699, ch. 2; Ingersoll v. Johns, BeCP, 9-68. Cf. Poor v. Doble, Quincy 86 (1763) (action of case for rescue must be brought in county where rescue committed); Rex v. Gleason, WGS, 1-70 (criminal action quashed for want of jurisdiction since place of crime not averred). Other personal actions were brought in the county where either of the parties resided. See Laws of 1749-1750, ch. 9; Fowler v. Smith, BeCP, 4-65. In transitory actions, a plaintiff was also required to allege fictionally that his cause of action had arisen within the county in which he was suing, so that "a Jury might be called proper to try the same. . . ." Goodwin v. Whitemore, MCP Files, 12-65. Failure to make the allegation was ground for abatement, see Russell v. Diamond, MCP Files, 5-69; Banister v. Ward, WCP, 1-69; Thurstin v. Hobson, ECP, 9-67; Calef v. Rust, ECP, 7-66; although the allegation, once made, was nontraversable and hence fictional. See Perley v. Hidden, ECP, 7-67. Nonresidents could be sued in any county. See Laws of 1749-1750, ch. 9. Claims of improper venue had to be raised by way of a plea in abatement or were forever waived. See Ward v. Carter, Suff. Files nos. 147932, 148089 (Msex. 1773), rejecting a plea in bar to the effect that neither party was an inhabitant of the county in which the suit was commenced.

35. There were some matters, however, in which appellants did not obtain a trial de novo in the Superior Court. The losing party, for example, could not appeal from the judgment of Common Pleas entered on an appeal

originally taken from a judgment of a justice of the peace, but he could obtain review of the legal issues by bringing a writ of error in the Superior Court. Only two litigants did this during the fifteen years before the Revolution. See Hulet v. Dix, Cushing 4 (1773); Macumber v. Godfrey, SSC, 8-69. And while an appeal de novo did lie from a criminal conviction in General Sessions, see Baldwin v. King, WSC, 9-68; a criminal conviction, if rendered by a justice of the peace, could be reviewed only on certiorari. See Talbut v. Scott, SSC, 2-62. The regulatory decisions of General Sessions likewise could be reviewed on certiorari, see Inhabitants of Blanford v. Morton, HSC, 9-68, or on a writ of error. See Charlestown v. Medford, MSC, 4-73. The scope of review on certiorari was not altogether clear. In Massachusetts, unlike England, the writ did permit review of mere errors of law, see Jones v. Jones, HSC, 9-61 (paternity proceedings quashed since neither complainant nor judgment below set forth place of child's birth), while it is equally clear that the writ did not permit the reviewing court to inquire into new evidence not presented to the court below. See Pond v. Medway, Quincy 193 (1765). The best study of the scope of review on certiorari in Massachusetts, which takes full note of the complexities of the problem, is Wroth and Zobel, *Legal Papers*, I, 301-304, 321-322.

36. Scollay v. Dunn, Quincy 74, 81 (1763).

37. See, e.g., Scollay v. Dunn, Quincy 74 (1763); Dudley v. Dudley, Quincy 12, 25n9 (1762); Hancock v. Bowers, SSC, 8-66.

38. See Joseph H. Smith, *Appeals to the Privy Council from the American Plantations* (New York, 1950), 160-163.

39. See ibid., 163-165, 328-335. The common law courts were supplemented by other specialized tribunals. One such set of tribunals was the county probate courts. Testate and intestate distribution of personal property was within the jurisdiction of probate courts, although testate and intestate descent of real estate remained under the control of the common law courts. See "Question: Is the Probate of a Will of Land by ye Judge of Probates, etc.," in Edmund Trowbridge, Law Notes, folder 696. However, if the personalty of an estate was insufficient to pay the debts and legacies, the common law courts, upon presentation of a certificate from the probate judge, would make an order permitting sale of as much of the real estate as necessary to make such payments. Appeal from county judges of probate lay to the governor and

council, sitting as the Supreme Court of Probate; the governor and council also constituted the province's divorce court. Prerevolutionary Massachusetts also had courts with admiralty jurisdiction. It lacked a court of equity, although the common law courts by statute possessed certain equitable powers. See generally Wroth and Zobel, *Legal Papers* I, xliv; II, 68-395; L. Kinvin Wroth, "The Massachusetts Vice-Admiralty Court," in Billias, *Law and Authority*, 32; William L. Curran, "The Struggle for Equity Jurisdiction in Massachusetts," *Boston University Law Review*, XXXI (1951), 269; Edwin H. Woodruff, "Chancery in Massachusetts," *Law Quarterly Review*, V (1889), 370.

40. See Petition of Selectmen of Boxford, EGS, 3-71.

41. See Rex v. Wait, EGS, 9-61.

42. Suits could be maintained only if a tax collector had taken actual steps to collect the tax and if the complainant had applied to an appropriate local officer for a refund. See Thompson v. Libbey, CSC, 6-64 (writ abated for failure to allege time and place of distress); Petition of Woodcocke, PGS, 7-68 (petition dismissed since application for refund never made).

43. See Phillips v. Marble, HGS, 5-62; Petition of Royall, MGS, 12-60; Petition of Richmond, BrGS, 12-60; Sherer v. Assessors of Palmer, HGS, 8-60. See also Warren's Complaint, WGS, 8-63.

44. See Blodgett v. Assessors of Brimfield, HGS, 8-63.

45. See Luce v. Town of Edgartown, DGS, 2-65.

46. See Cotton v. Delano, PSC, 5-67.

47. See Zuckerman, *Peaceable Kingdoms*, 130.

48. See Tyng v. Fletcher, MSC, 10-66. Cf. Ruddock v. Gordon, Quincy 58 (1763).

49. See Keith v. Leonard, BrSC, 10-62; Richmond v. Walker, BrCP, 2-70, appeal dism., BrSC, 10-70; Stacy v. Rand, BrCP, 8-65. See also Petition of Sherman, PGS, 10-68 (petition for relief by Baptists dismissed on petitioners' default).

50. See Bass v. Knight, ECP, 3-73, aff'd, ESC, 6-73; Washburn v. Green, WSC, 9-69. Dissenters could not, however, obtain exemption from religous taxation without procuring certificates, nor could their ministers obtain the special exemption from all taxation given to orthodox ministers. See Clark v. Smith, HCP, 8-71 (Baptist minister denied clerical exemption); Phillips v. Marble, HGS, 5-62 (plea that inhabitant for whom tax exemption claimed was a settled minister denied). In-

deed, all religious exemptions were construed narrowly by the courts. Thus a dissenting apprentice who had been a member of a dissenting family at the time the family had obtained an express legislative exemption from religious taxation was held to have lost that exemption upon the expiration of his apprenticeship. See Pearson v. Tollansbee, ESC, 6-68.

51. The only officials who were immune from suit were legislators and judges. See Wroth and Zobel, *Legal Papers*, II, 23. Judicial immunity, however, did not extend to justices of the peace, who were subject to suits for official misconduct, such as failing to take recognizances from defendants who were to appear before them in the future. See Merry v. Collins, ESC, 6-60.

52. See e.g., Fowler v. Williams, HSC 9-72. Three allegations were essential in order for a plaintiff to establish a cause of action in such cases—first, that the plaintiff lost his recovery from a judgment; second, that the loss occurred as a result of the neglect or misfeasance of the sheriff or his deputy; and third, that the sheriff against whom he had brought suit was responsible for that neglect or misfeasance. Giddings v. Hall, ECP Files, 9-66; Bait v. Tidey, YSC, 6-66.

53. See Williams v. Jones, HSC, 4-71; Miller v. Williams, BeCP, 4-64.

54. See Mayhew v. Basset, DCP, 10-63, appeal dism., BaSC, 5-64. Cf. Keeler v. Jones, BeCP, 9-64 (suit against sheriff for deputy's false return that he had arrested the plaintiff). Often the real issue in such cases was the validity of the arrest. See Mayhew v. Basset, supra. Cf. Rex v. Gay, Quincy 91 (1763).

55. See Richmond v. Walker, BrCP, 9-70, appeal dism., BrSC, 10-70. In many trespass actions for wrongful seizure of property, the principal issue was not the legality of the official's procedures but whether the plaintiff possessed the property right which he claimed; that is, officials usually defended such actions by pleading that they were rendering public property—usually public highways—available for public use. See Lee v. Craige, WCP, 3-72; Bigelow v. Rice, WCP, 5-69. See also Burt v. Williams, BrCP, 9-71 (plea by private subject that land he was accused of trespassing on was common highway).

56. See Erving v. Cradock, Quincy 553 (1761).

57. See Mayhew v. Basset, DCP, 10-63, appeal dism., BaSC, 5-64 (jury verdict that officer not guilty "If This Warrant be Lawfull in This Case," but guilty otherwise). Cf. Rex v. Gay, Quincy 91 (1763).

58. Ainsley v. Williams in Trowbridge, Law Cases, folder 695.

59. Mayhew v. Basset, BaSC, 5-64, in Robert Treat Paine, Minutes, vol. 1.

60. See Thurston v. Pingry, ESC, 6-69; Gould v. Holland, WSC, 9-60. Such suits had to be brought for the full amount of any penalty. See Powers v. Hazen, MCP Files, 9-64, aff'd by referees, MSC, 8-64.

61. See Chandler v. Shattuck, MSC, 8-61.

62. See Graffam v. Elder, CSC, 6-73.

63. Also liable to statutory penalties were men who absented themselves from militia duty, see Harrington v. Eastman, WSC, 9-64; engaged in illegal fishing, see Ripley v. Williams, BrSC, 10-73; or failed to maintain required partition fences. See Keen v. Turner, SSC, 8-70.

64. "A Letter to the People of Pennsylvania," in Bailyn, *Pamphlets*, I, 268.

65. Ibid., I, 262.

66. Charge to the Grand Jury, Quincy 306, 307 (1769).

67. Ibid., 308.

68. Charge to the Grand Jury, Quincy 241, 243 (1767).

69. John Adams, *Diary and Autobiography*, ed. L.H. Butterfield (Cambridge, Mass., 1961), I, 167.

70. This is my conclusion from a brief, unsystematic glance at early eighteenth-century Massachusetts court records.

71. See Wroth and Zobel, *Legal Papers*, III, 282.

72. See ibid., III, 242.

73. See ibid., I, 99-100, 132-134, 253-254; II, 418-424; III, 93, 144, 226, 302, 310.

74. Pateshall v. Apthorp, Quincy 179, 185 (1765).

75. The various sorts of matters that were ground for abatement are discussed in detail in Chapter 5.

76. See Wroth and Zobel, *Legal Papers*, I, xlv. Nor would the running of the statute of limitations during the pendency of a suit that was subsequently abated be likely to do injustice, since courts almost invariably decided whether an action would be abated within several weeks or at most several months of its commencement.

77. That pleas in abatement could not raise questions going to the merits of litigation, see Ruddock v. Gordon, Quincy 58 (1763). On occasion, however, pleas in abatement could raise factual questions, such as whether a party was a yeoman or a gentleman or whether a party resided in the town named by the plaintiff or in some other town. When such an issue did arise, it was resolved by the court sitting without a jury. See Wise v. Hight,

YSC, 6-67; Allin v. Whaples, BeCP, 9-63, appeal dism., HSC, 9-63; Hickok v. Jacobs, BeCP, 4-63. But see Remington v. Crawley, MCP, 9-68 (factual issue of whether plaintiff an executor resolved by jury).

78. Bishop v. Brig Freemason, Quincy 387, 388 (1763). See also Wroth and Zobel, *Legal Papers*, I, 293; II, 167-168, 195-196, 322-325.

79. Dudley v. Dudley, Quincy 14, 19 (1762).

80. Poor v. Dougharty, Quincy 1, 2 (1762). See also Hall v. Miller, Quincy 252 (1767).

81. See Symes v. Hill, Quincy 318, 322 (1771); Banister v. Henderson, Quincy 119, 143-144 (1765); Whitney v. Whitney, Quincy 117 (1765); Elwell v. Pierson, Quincy 42, 45 (1763).

82. See Pateshall v. Apthorp, Quincy 179 (1765); Russel v. Oakes, Quincy 48, 50 (1763); Derumple v. Clark, Quincy 38, 39 (1763).

83. See Wroth and Zobel, *Legal Papers*, II, 54, 55-57.

84. See ibid., II, 30-31.

85. See ibid., II, 322-325.

86. See ibid., II, 134-144; Paxton's Case, Quincy 51 (1761).

87. Of the 77 cases reported in the main body of Quincy's Reports—a selection of cases containing noteworthy legal issues—only the nine cases cited from Quincy in notes 74 and 78-81 above and the case of Box v. Welch, Quincy 227 (1766), contain arguments based on anything but precedent. In the four cases in which litigants sought to have precedent overruled, they were unsuccessful.

88. See Baker v. Mattocks, Quincy 69, 73-74 (1763), where the Massachusetts rule was followed despite the understanding of some of the judges that the common law rule was to the contrary. Accord, Rex v. Mangent, Quincy 162 (1765). But see Baker v. Mattocks, supra at 74, where Chief Justice Hutchinson had some difficulty with the question whether the custom of Massachusetts could prevail against the common law, and Pateshall v. Apthorp, Quincy 179, 181 (1765), where counsel implied a distinction between the common law, which would be binding in Massachusetts, and the mere custom of England, which would not be binding.

89. Watts v. Hasey, Quincy 194, 195 (1765).

90. Ballard v. McLean, Quincy 106, 107 (1764).

91. "Resolves of Middlesex County Convention, August 1774," in Lemuel Shattuck, *A History of the Town of Concord* (Boston,

1835), 84.

92. Charles F. Adams, ed., *The Works of John Adams* (Boston, 1850-1856), III, 481.

93. Wroth and Zobel, *Legal Papers*, I, 229.

94. See ibid., I, xvi, xlix, 158; III, 18.

95. See ibid., I, xlix.

96. See Toppan v. Bartlet, ECP, 9-71.

97. Wroth and Zobel, *Legal Papers*, II, 392.

98. Thus, although evidence of a promise to pay within a specified number of months would be admitted under an allegation of a promise to pay on demand, provided the specified number of months had elapsed, see Hall v. Miller, Quincy 252 (1767), evidence that a dam was built in 1762 would not be admissible under an allegation that construction had occurred in 1766. See Wroth and Zobel, *Legal Papers*, I, 274.

99. Wroth and Zobel, *Legal Papers*, II, 392.

100. See generally A. W. B. Simpson, "The Penal Bond with Conditional Defeasance," *Law Quarterly Review* (1966), LXXXII, 392.

101. See Wroth and Zobel, *Legal Papers*, I, 15. A defendant, on the other hand, could not put in evidence of a partial failure of consideration. See Noble v. Smith, Quincy 254 (1767).

102. See Wroth and Zobel, *Legal Papers*, I, 188.

103. See ibid., I, 157.

104. For an illustration of the confusion surrounding this question, see ibid., I, 266.

105. See Gardiner v. Purrington, Quincy 59 (1763).

106. These are the conclusions of Wroth and Zobel, *Legal Papers*, I, 28-29, which have been thoroughly confirmed by my research. For one of the rare examples in prerevolutionary Massachusetts of special pleading beyond the replication, see Theophilus Parsons, Precedents, no. 71.

107. See John P. Reid, "Civil Law as a Criminal Sanction: The Use of the Jury in the Coming of the American Revolution," in Edward M. Wise and G.O.W. Mueller, eds., *Studies in Comparative Criminal Law* (forthcoming).

108. Apthorp v. Eyres, Quincy 229, 231 (1766).

109. Norwood v. Fairservice, Quincy 189, 190 (1765).

110. Ibid., 190. See also Pateshall v. Apthorp, Quincy 179, 182 (1765).

111. Geoffrey Gilbert, *The Law of Evidence* (London, 1756), 122.

112. Wroth and Zobel, *Legal Papers*, III, 232 (argument of counsel for defendant).

113. Gilbert, *Evidence*, 122.

114. Wrentham Proprietors v. Metcalf, Quincy 36 (1763).

115. Allison v. Cockran, Quincy 94, 99n3 (1764).

116. Barnes v. Greenleaf, Quincy 41 (1763).

117. Rex v. Jackson, PCP, 7-67, in Paine, Minutes, vol. 1.

118. See Wroth and Zobel, *Legal Papers*, II, 36-37n8.

119. Wrentham Proprietors v. Metcalf, Quincy 36, 37 (1763).

120. Rex v. Pourksdorff, Quincy 104, 105 (1764).

121. For cases in which witnesses testified as to out-of-court statements made by others, see Wroth and Zobel, *Legal Papers*, I, 87, 97-99; II, 68, 88; Stoughton Petition, MGS Files, 11-70. For cases in which depositions taken out of court were admitted into evidence, see Stoughton Petition, supra; Reading v. Framingham, MGS Files, 12-63. On the admissibility of such depositions, see Laws of 1695, ch. 15.

122. Gilbert, *Evidence*, 151-153.

123. Ibid., 156-157.

124. Ibid., 157, cited in Wroth and Zobel, *Legal Papers*, II, 68, 90.

125. See Matthew Hale, *Historia Placitorum Coronae: The History of the Pleas of the Crown* (London, 1736), II, 289.

126. While the papers of lawyers and judges which have been preserved contain many examples of grand jury charges and petit jury charges in criminal cases, few civil charges remain. This suggests that fewer such charges may have been delivered.

127. James Sullivan to Elbridge Gerry, Dec. 25, 1779 (in MHS).

128. Wroth and Zobel, *Legal Papers*, I, 230.

129. Grand Jury Charge, 1759, Cushing Papers, vol. 1.

130. See, e.g., Wroth and Zobel, *Legal Papers*, III, 226-282.

131. See ibid., I, 141, 149, for a case in which John Adams was barred from arguing the law to the jury. Adams's anger at being barred suggests that such a step was unusual.

132. See Pateshall v. Apthorp, Quincy 179 (1765); Bromfield v. Little, Quincy 108 (1764); Hanlon v. Thayer, Quincy 99 (1764); Derumple v. Clark, Quincy 38 (1763); Jackson v. Foye, Quincy 22 (1762).

133. See Rex v. Needham, HGS, 11-61. See also Rex v. Robinson, SSC, 2-63 (defendant pardoned before motion decided).

134. See King v. Hodge, SSC, 8-66, overturning a wife's conviction of larceny as a codefendant with husband on the theory that she was subject to his control and so lacked the free will requisite for the crime.

135. See Rex v. Phelps, HGS, 8-70.

136. See Hussey v. Parker, YSC, 6-66; Wroth and Zobel, *Legal Papers*, II, 70n8.

137. See ibid., I, 142n10.

138. See Smith v. Fuller, ESC, 11-71; Moffit v. Gibbs, HCP, 8-67; Sharpe v. Buckminster, HCP, 8-62.

139. See Lincoln Motion, MGS, 5-70.

140. See Lansing v. Baldwin, WSC, 9-66 (copy of contract delivered to jury differed from one contained in court files).

141. See Leonard v. Cooper, Suff. Files no. 157569, 157570 (Hamp. 1769).

142. See Reed's Contempt, MCP, 3-60. A party who tampered with or insulted a juror was also liable to a contempt charge. See Order re Baker's Conduct, SSC, 8-62; Reed's Contempt, supra.

143. See King v. Abel, BrGS, 12-73, where a verdict in a prosecution for dancing and reveling was set aside since the jury foreman had been a member of the grand jury that had returned the indictment.

144. See Wroth and Zobel, *Legal Papers*, II, 406-408, 426-430 (verdict upheld although final juror had agreed to it only on condition that court would not accept it if it were contrary to law).

145. Bartlett v. White, ESC, 6-69; Wroth and Zobel, *Legal Papers*, II, 36-37n8. See also Box v. Welch, SSC, 3-67 (motion for a new trial granted on indeterminate grounds). The case is reported on another point in Quincy 227 (1766). Motions for new trials were also made and denied in several other cases. See Woodbridge v. Miller, HSC, 4-71; Rex v. Ross, SSC, 8-69, 3-70; Tollansbee v. Pearson, ESC, 11-69; Bailey v. Williams, CSC, 6-69; Dodge v. Brown, WCP, 8-69. See generally Wroth and Zobel, *Legal Papers*, I, 176n8, 210-216.

146. See Angier v. Jackson, Quincy 84, 85 (1763). See also Phelps v. Colton, HCP, 8-62 (denying motion not to enter judgment after verdict).

147. See Goodspeed v. Gay, Quincy 558 (1763); Erving v. Cradock, Quincy 553, 556-557n (1761).

148. Wroth and Zobel, *Legal Papers*, II, 36-37n8.

149. Lyon v. Cobb, BrCP, 11-69, in Paine, Minutes, vol. 1.

150. Quincy v. Howard, BrCP, 10-70, in Paine, Minutes, vol. 1.

151. Wroth and Zobel, *Legal Papers*, I, 230.

152. Quoted in Zuckerman, *Peaceable Kingdoms*, 39. See generally ibid., 38-41.

153. Box v. Welch, Quincy 227 (1766).

154. Watts v. Hasey, Quincy 194 (1765).

155. Derumple v. Clark, Quincy 38, 40 (1763). Accord, Tyler v. Richards, Quincy 195 (1765); Bromfield v. Little, Quincy 108 (1764).

156. Baker v. Mattocks, Quincy 69, 71 (1763).

157. Ibid., 73.

158. Wroth and Zobel, *Legal Papers*, II, 68, 76.

159. Colden v. Stockbridge, PCP, 4-72, PSC, 5-72, in Paine, Minutes, vol. 1.

160. Derumple v. Clark, Quincy 38, 39 (1763).

161. Baker v. Mattocks, Quincy 69, 74 (1763).

162. Derumple v. Clark, Quincy 38, 41 (1763).

163. See Baker v. Mattocks, Quincy 69 (1763); Derumple v. Clark, Quincy 38 (1763); Zuckerman, *Peaceable Kingdoms*, 38-43.

164. See notes 2, 65, above.

165. See George W. Pepper, *Pleading at Common Law and under the Codes* (Northport, N.Y., 1891),476-477. For examples of cases in which special pleas were entered in eighteenth-century England, see Charles Viner, *A General Abridgment of Law and Equity* (London, 2d ed., 1793), XXI, 69-78.

166. See Bright v. Eynon, 1 Burr. 390, 97 Eng. Rep. 365 (K.B. 1757); Wood v. Gunston, Style 462, 82 Eng. Rep. 864 (K.B. 1655). As Lord Mansfield explained in Bright v. Eynon, one reason that English law courts found it necessary to grant new trials was that equity would always set aside jury verdicts that did injustice. In Massachusetts, however, the courts faced no such pressure, since no equity court existed. See note 39 above. In view of the fact that English judges would grant new trials when juries failed to follow their instructions, it is not surprising that English lawyers believed that juries had no power to determine questions of law. See Viner, *Abridgment*, XXI, 384.

167. Quincy 553 (1761).

168. See George L. Haskins, *Law and Authority in Early Massachusetts* (New York, 1960), 130.

169. See ibid., 213.

170. See ibid., 119-140.

171. Of course, some judges, such as Thomas Hutchinson, were close political allies of the executive.

172. Selectmen of Newton, Mass., to Selectmen of Boston, Mass., in Samuel F. Smith, *History of Newton, Massachusetts* (Boston, 1880), 326.

173. Resolves of the Middlesex County Convention, Aug. 1774, in Shattuck, *Town of Concord*, 85.

174. Bailyn, *Pamphlets*, I, 48-49.

175. Washburn, *Judicial History*, 160-162, 298, 301-302.

176. See Oliver M. Dickerson, *The Navigation Acts and the American Revolution* (Philadelphia, 1951), 209, 225, 252.

177. See Washburn, *Judicial History*, 293-317; Wroth and Zobel, *Legal Papers*, I, xcv-cxiv.

178. See Washburn, *Judicial History*, 318-400.

179. See George L. Haskins, *The Growth of English Representative Government* (Philadelphia, 1948), 27-29, 46-53; Sidney Webb and Beatrice Webb, *English Local Government from the Revolution to the Municipal Corporations Act: The Parish and the County* (London, 1906), VI, 309-310. Government in seventeenth-century Massachusetts was somewhat more centralized than it was in contemporary England or than it would be in eighteenth-century England or Massachusetts; nonetheless traditions of localism remained strong in the Puritan Bay Colony. See Haskins, *Law and Authority*, 68-79.

180. See Edmund S. Morgan and Helen M. Morgan, *The Stamp Act Crisis: Prologue to Revolution* (New York, rev. ed., 1963), 159.

181. Quoted in Morgan and Morgan, *Stamp Act Crisis*, 65.

182. See ibid., 168-169.

183. Quoted in Zuckerman, *Peaceable Kingdoms*, 87 n.

Chapter 3. The Law of a "Civil and Christian State"

1. Rex v. Root, BeGS, 3-62.

2. Order re Licenses, PGS, 10-72.

3. Cotton Mather, *Fair Dealing between Debtor and Creditor* (Boston, 1716), 13.

4. Grand Jury Charge, NSC, 8-46, in Cushing Papers, vol. 1.

5. On the criminal law of Puritan Massachusetts, see generally George L. Haskins, *Law and Authority in Early Massachusetts* (New York, 1960), 174-177, 204-212; Edwin Powers, *Crime and Punishment in Early Massachusetts, 1620-1692* (Boston, 1966).

6. The 2,784 prosecutions occurred in seven Massachusetts counties, the only counties for which complete or nearly complete statistics are available for the entire period from 1760 to 1830. Those counties are Berkshire, Hampshire (later divided into Hampshire, Hampden, and Franklin), Worcester, Middlesex, Essex, Bristol, and Plymouth.

7. See King v. Hodgkins, EGS, 3-71.

8. Slocum v. Turner, BrGS, 5-69.

9. See Edmonds v. Edmonds, PGS, 10-73; Gardner v. Pinkham, NGS, 10-61.

10. William Blackstone, *Commentaries on the Laws of England* (Oxford, 1765-1769), IV, 41.

11. See note 6 above.

12. See Rex v. Eaton, MSC, 10-70.

13. See King v. Goodenow, MSC, 4-68, affirming MGS, 11-67.

14. See King v. Leach, PGS, 10-65.

15. See King v. Coy, EGS, 9-70.

16. See King v. Jernat, EGS, 3-68.

17. In England fornication was not an offense cognizable in the temporal courts and appears to have gone largely unpunished in the spiritual courts. See Blackstone, *Commentaries*, IV, 64; John Comyns, *A Digest of the Laws of England* (Dublin, 1785), IV, 164.

18. See King v. Peter, EGS, 12-70 (prosecution dismissed for want of indictment).

19. In England the mother of an illegitimate child was punished by imprisonment in the house of correction if she was unable to support the child, but not otherwise. See Blackstone, *Commentaries*, I, 458. Thus illegitimacy proceedings in England seem to have had the sole function of minimizing municipal liability for support of illegitimate children. Arthur P. Scott, *Criminal Law in Colonial Virginia* (Chicago, 1930), 280-281, reaches this same conclusion for Virginia.

20. See King v. Mallet, MGS, 5-60.

21. See King v. Marshall, SGS, 4-65.

22. See Streeter v. Blunt, WGS, 11-60.

23. See Rex v. Warrin, BeGS, 9-65; Rex v. Hubbard, HGS, 11-61; King v. Paterson, MGS, 3-61.

24. Compare, e.g., King v. Munro, MGS, 11-70 (5-shilling fine), with King v. Paterson, MGS, 3-61 (same fine).

25. See King v. Hayward, MGS, 3-73 (not attending church); King v. Cutler, MGS, 11-69 (traveling on Sunday); King v. Osborne, MGS, 12-62 (working on Sunday). Cf. Robinson v. Tisdale, BrCP, 8-65, in Robert Treat Paine, Minutes, vol. 1 ("note was not good for it was given on Saturday night").

26. See King v. Prat, PSC, 5-68.

27. See King v. Hannover, EGS Files, 1767; Coffin v. King, NGS, 10-64; King v. Creacy, EGS Files, 1762; Rex v. Rich, WGS, 5-60.

28. See the cases in note 27 above. But see King v. Morslander, NGS, 3-62.

29. See Rex v. Brooks, WGS, 8-61.

30. See Rex v. Williams, SGS, 4-65.

31. See Rex v. Jennison, WGS, 8-61.

32. See Rex v. Wait, EGS, 9-61.

33. See King v. Stephen, EGS, 7-62; King v. Hussey, NGS, 3-62.

34. King v. Clark, NGS, 10-60.

35. Rex v. Root, BeGS, 3-62.

36. See Rex v. Man, WGS, 3-71.

37. King v. Tucker, PGS, 1-64.

38. See Petition of Selectmen of Boxford, EGS, 3-71.

39. See King v. Gardner, SGS, 7-66.

40. See Process against Maynard, MGS, 9-71.

41. Rex v. How, HGS, 8-69.

42. Taylor v. Fowler, HGS, 2-73. See also Rex v. Burghardt, HGS, 8-60 (contempt for failure to appear as a witness).

43. King v. Haynes, EGS, 7-68.

44. Waters v. Rex, EGS Files, 9-63.

45. Barter v. Kirby, EGS Files, 12-70.

46. Rex v. Hall, SGS Files, 2-62.

47. See Rex v. Mcintier, WGS, 11-61; Dodge v. Town, WGS, 8-60.

48. See Rex v. Flagg, WGS, 8-67. See also Rex v. Brittan, BrGS, 5-68; Howard v. Britton, BrGS Files, 5-68 (criminal charge of defamation for woman's saying that the complainant "offered to force me . . . and Pulled out his Naked yard so that I felt it and attempted to pull up my coats" dismissed when complainant was indicted for assault upon the woman).

49. Babbit v. Robinson, BrGS, 6-63. Accord, Bacon v. King, EGS, 7-62; Rex v. Hall, SGS Files, 2-62.

50. Grand Jury Charge, NSC, 8-42, in Cushing Papers, vol. 1.

51. Grand Jury Charge, NSC, 8-46, in ibid.

52. Jonathan Sewall to John Adams, Oct. 5, 1765, in Paine Papers. See also S. Howard, "A Sermon Preached Before the Honorable Council and the Honorable House of Representatives of the State of Massachusetts-Bay, in New-England, May 31, 1780," in John W. Thornton, ed., *The Pulpit of the American Revolution* (Boston, 1860), 355, 382-383, 393-394.

53. Michael Foster, *A Report on Some Proceedings on the Commission of Oyer and Terminer and Goal Delivery for the Trial of Rebels in the Year 1746 in the County of Surry, and of other Crown Cases* (Oxford, 1767), v-vi.

54. Blackstone, *Commentaries*, IV, 2.

55. See S. Langdon, "Government Corrupted by Vice, and Recovered by Righteousness, Sermon to the Congress of the Massachusetts Bay Colony, May 31, 1775," in Thornton, *Pulpit*, 227, 247-248.

56. See William E. Nelson, "Emerging Notions of Modern Criminal Law in the Revolutionary Era: An Historical Perspective," *New York University Law Review*, XLII (1967), 450, 455.

57. See King v. Wheeler, HSC, 9-63 (20 years of hard labor for counterfeiting); King v. How, MSC, 1-62 (same sentence).

58. On the English background of tort law, see C. H. S. Fifoot, *History and Sources of the Common Law: Tort and Contract* (London, 1949), 126-137; S. F. C. Milsom, *Historical Foundations of the Common Law* (London, 1969), 333-340; Frederick Pollock and Frederic W. Maitland, *The History of English Law before the Time of Edward I* (Cambridge, 2d ed., 1911), II, 536-537. During the eighteenth century, rudimentary doctrines of privilege were creeping into the law. In Massachusetts participants in legislative and judicial proceedings were granted an absolute privilege as a matter of public necessity. See L. Kinvin Wroth and Hiller B. Zobel, eds., *Legal Papers of John Adams* (Cambridge, Mass., 1965), II, 23. In England absolute privilege in judicial proceedings was first established in Cutler v. Dixon, 4 Co. Rep. 14b, 76 Eng. Rep. 888 (K.B. 1585) and Buckley v. Wood, 4 Co. Rep. 14b, 76 Eng. Rep. 888 (K.B. 1591). Absolute privilege in legislative proceedings did not fully develop until Lake v. King, 1 Lev. 240, 83 Eng. Rep. 387 (K.B. 1669). Concepts of qualified privilege were also appearing in Massachusetts. See Wroth and Zobel, *Legal Papers*, II, 23-24; Green v. Stimpson, MCP, 12-60. In England qualified privilege developed during the period between Lake v. King, supra, and Weatherston v. Hawkins, 1 T.R. 110, 99 Eng. Rep. 1001 (K.B. 1786).

59. Theophilus Parsons, Precedents, no. 32. Accord, Wroth and Zobel, *Legal Papers*, II, 20. Defamatory words, that is, had to be "false words" in order for a plaintiff to recover damages. See Morrison v. Stewart, HCP, 5-66 (special verdict finding defendant "guilty of speaking these false words"). Truth was a defense. See Whitney v. Herbert, WCP, 5-65; Green v. Stimpson, MCP, 12-60.

60. See Morey v. Fairbank, BrCP, 6-63, appeal dism., BrSC, 10-63; Wroth and Zobel, *Legal Papers*, I, 142.

61. Hubbard v. Bush, BeCP, 4-64.

62. Morison v. Stewart, HCP, 5-66.

63. Mason v. Cole, BrCP, 2-69, in Paine, Minutes, vol. 1.

64. Stetson v. Bourne, PCP, 1-63.

65. Aiken v. Richards, PCP, 7-64.

66. Wroth and Zobel, *Legal Papers*, I, 47n46. English law was substantially in accord with that of Massachusetts. See Farmer v. Darling, 4 Burr. 1971, 98 Eng. Rep. 27 (K.B. 1766). In defamation it was common to allege that a defendant had spoken the words in order to cause the plaintiff "to be brought

under the penalties & punishments by the law provided. . . ." Parsons, Precedents, no. 33. Accord, ibid., nos. 32, 34.

67. See Waters v. Prescott, ESC, 11-67. A plaintiff could recover judgment as long as he was vindicated at any stage of the malicious proceedings—whether his vindication occurred before a petit jury after a grand jury had indicted him, see Wroth and Zobel, *Legal Papers*, I, 47n46, before the grand jury itself, see Hart v. Tyler, WCP, 8-67, or as a result of the defendant's giving up his malicious suit. See Allen v. Spooner, WCP, 8-69. The plaintiff did, however, have to prove his ultimate vindication: that is, the defendant's malicious charge had to be proved false before the plaintiff could maintain a malicious prosecution suit.

68. See the cases cited in notes 69-72 below. In England the essence of a cause of action for fraud was also that a seller had knowingly made a false affirmation at the time of sale. See Comyns, *Digest*, I, 178. In Massachusetts, however, a plaintiff did not have to prove that the false affirmation was made knowingly at the time of sale provided either that he could show a subsequent intent to defraud the plaintiff, see Taylor v. Fowler, HSC, 9-64, or some subsequent tortious conduct amounting to a fraud, see Jones v. Root, HSC, 9-71 (defendant, a witness in suit, subsequently put in false bill of costs), or that he could maintain a suit in contract for breach of warranty rather than in tort for the fraud. See Cummings v. Fish, BrCP, 3-64. Suits for breach of warranty were brought in a wide variety of circumstances. See, e.g., Sears v. Davis, PSC, 5-68 (warranty in sale of fish); Stevens v. Brooks, WSC, 9-66 (warranty in sale of horse); Wait v. Nichols, WSC, 9-64 (warranty as to third party's credit); Wheeler v. Dewey, HSC, 9-63 (unworkmanlike construction of dam). The difference between the suit for fraud and the suit for breach of warranty was that the former was a tort action to which the defendant pleaded not guilty as a general issue; the proper general issue in a suit for breach of warranty was never promised, indicating that the gist of the cause of action was contract.

69. See Nightingall v. Curtis, SSC, 2-68. Cf. Badcock v. Underwood, MSC, 4-65 (sale of standing timber).

70. See Oliver v. Sale, Quincy 29 (1762).

71. See Chase v. Prentice, WSC, 4-71.

72. See Hill v. Clark, WSC, 9-70. Cf. Nurss v. Bardwell, HSC, 4-73 (affirmation that slave was healthy); Quincy v. Oliver, SSC, 3-65 (same affirmation).

73. See Laws of 1693, ch. 1. Usury was a

complete defense to an action in assumpsit. See How v. Church, MSC, 8-64; Chapin v. Harwood, WCP, 5-60. However, it was not a defense to an action of debt on a bond, since it could not be pleaded specially. See Tuffts v. Bartlett, ECP, 3-65. Even in assumpsit the plea of usury was not a particularly efficacious one, for a plaintiff could avoid it merely by swearing that he did not receive over 6 percent interest; upon his taking such an oath, the court gave judgment for him without granting a trial by jury. See How v. Church, supra; Chapin v. Harwood, supra.

74. Smith v. Upham, MCP, 9-60 (rejecting quoted plea).

75. See "On a National Bankrupt Law," *American Jurist*, I (1829), 35, 40.

76. See Richmond v. Davis, Quincy 279, 297 (1768).

77. See ibid., 279-296.

78. See Laws of 1772, ch. 12.

79. See Hill v. Brown, BrSC, 10-68; Blackstone, *Commentaries*, III, 421.

80. See Blackstone, *Commentaries*, III, 421. A judgment that had been reversed or improperly rendered or was less than a year old could not, of course, be revived. See Allen v. Goodrich, BeCP, 9-70; Tucker v. Eddey, BrCP, 6-70.

81. See Kellog v. Baily, BeCP, 9-69.

82. Twenty years was the limitation period applicable to a writ of scire facias on a judgment, but apparently there was no limitation period for a writ of debt. See Blackstone, *Commentaries*, III, 307.

83. See Hanlon v. Thayer, Quincy 99 (1764); Richmond v. Davis, SSC, 3-68.

84. See Springer v. Potter, CSC, 6-64 (defendant not liable in trespass for entering on land as the administrator of intestate owner); Salter v. Phillips, SSC, 2-60 (title of claimant under probate order superior to title of purchaser from coheir). See generally Wroth and Zobel, *Legal Papers*, I, 255; Thomas E. Atkinson, "The Development of the Massachusetts Probate System," *Michigan Law Review*, XLII (1943), 425.

85. See Minot v. Prout, Quincy 9 (1762).

86. See ibid.

87. See Hanlon v. Thayer, Quincy 99 (1764).

88. See Gould v. Stevens, Quincy 34 (1762), holding that even an executor who committed an actionable wrong was liable only to the extent of the goods of the estate in his hands.

89. See Mendall v. Rowe, WSC, 9-73. A creditor without a judgment, however, could not maintain suit against an insolvent estate.

90. See Warner v. Brunson, BeCP, 9-66.

91. See Mansis v. Hickling, ECP, 3-69.

92. See Lindsey v. Hale, ESC, 6-63.

93. Laws of 1758, ch. 10.

94. See Wyman v. Baldwin, MSC, 10-66; Putnam v. Andrew, ECP, 3-68; Gray v. Scott, SCP, 10-66.

95. See Deblois v. Coffin, SCP, 10-66.

96. Willard v. Whiting, BeCP, 9-68.

97. Buttar v. Ouchterlony, SSC, 3-68.

98. Whitney v. Whitney, Quincy 117 (1765). Accord, John Tisdall, *Laws and Usages Respecting Bills of Exchange and Promissory Notes* (Philadelphia, 1775), 3.

99. See Selkrig v. Erskine, SSC, 2-72 (suit on bill against distant endorser); Griffiths v. Hallowell, SSC, 3-69 (suit on note by distant endorsee against payee on payee's endorsement). See also Weld v. Grant, HSC, 9-63 (suit on note against plaintiff's immediate endorser).

100. See Elwell v. Fletcher, ESC, 6-71 (endorsee against maker).

101. See Malcolm v. Gleason, Quincy 251 (1767) (endorsee against acceptor); Bartlett v. Kennedy, ESC, 11-67 (endorsee against maker); Barney v. Ridden, BrCP, 9-63 (endorsee against maker).

102. See Eaton v. Tollansbe, fragment in Sargeant Papers (ca. 1779).

103. See Blackstone, *Commentaries*, II, 446; Tisdall, *Laws and Usages*, 18. See also Noble v. Smith, Quincy 254 (1767).

104. See Tuttle v. Willington, Quincy 335 (1772); Russel v. Oakes, Quincy 48 (1763).

105. Laws of 1764, ch. 35, as amended, Laws of 1765, ch. 2; Laws of 1757, ch. 12.

106. See Laws of 1757, ch. 12 (note at end of text); Laws of 1766, ch. 5.

107. See Laws of 1766, ch. 5; Laws of 1760, ch. 16. See also Henshaw v. Chandler, SSC, 2-68; Holman v. Heywood, MCP, 9-62; Estes v. Jones, ECP, 3-61.

108. See Brown v. Hill, MSC, 4-69.

109. See Watts v. Hasey, Quincy 194 (1765).

110. See Hooton v. Grout, Quincy 343 (1772); Symes v. Hill, Quincy 318 (1771); Hubbart v. Rogers, SSC, 3-70; Lord v. Junkins, YSC, 7-69; Marston v. Story, SSC, 9-60.

111. Laws of 1764, ch. 35, as amended, Laws of 1766, ch. 5.

112. See Robert E. Brown, *Middle-Class Democracy and the Revolution in Massachusetts, 1691-1780* (Ithaca, N.Y., 1955), 63-66. During the years immediately before the Revolution, every town was entitled to one representative in the General Court—towns of more than 120 freeholders were entitled to two; Boston was entitled to four. See Robert J. Taylor, ed., *Massachusetts: Colony to Com-*

NOTES TO PAGES 44-49

monwealth (Chapel Hill, N.C., 1961), 3-4. See also Henry R. Spencer, *Constitutional Conflict in Provincial Massachusetts* (Columbus, Ohio, 1905), 50-51.

113. The traditional view among historians has been that colonial legislatures were controlled by debtors. See William Douglass, *A Summary, Historical and Political, of the First Planting, Progressive Improvements, and Present State of the British Settlements in North America* (London, 1760), I, 310; Bray Hammond, *Banks and Politics in America* (Princeton, 1957), 17; Herbert L. Osgood, *The American Colonies in the Eighteenth Century* (New York, 1924), II, 372; Horace White, *Money and Banking* (Boston, 2d ed., 1902), 103-111.

114. Theophilus Parsons, Memorandum Book.

115. Cotton Mather, *Fair Dealing between Debtor and Creditor* (Boston, 1716), 13.

Chapter 4. Rules of Unity and Stability

1. See James A. Henretta, "Economic Development and Social Structure in Colonial Boston," *William and Mary Quarterly*, 3d ser., XXII (1965), 75-92; Kenneth Lockridge, "Land, Population and the Evolution of New England Society, 1630-1790; and an Afterthought," in Stanley N. Katz, ed., *Essays in Politics and Social Development: Colonial America* (Boston, 1971), 466-491. While titles such as esquire, gentleman, and laborer may not have been marks of precise economic distinction, see Robert E. Brown, *Middle-Class Democracy and the Revolution in Massachusetts, 1691-1780* (Ithaca, N.Y., 1955), 18-19, the fact that men bore such titles surely indicates that they had a hierarchical conception of society.

2. Thomas B. Chandler, *The American Querist* (New York, 1774), 4.

3. Susan M. Kingsbury, ed., *Records of the Virginia Company* (Washington, D.C., 1906-1935), III, 231-232.

4. Thomas B. Chandler, *A Friendly Address to All Reasonable Americans* (New York, 1774), 5.

5. Francis Hutcheson, *A System of Moral Philosophy*, II, 240-266, quoted in Caroline Robbins, *The Eighteenth Century Commonwealthman* (Cambridge, Mass., 1959), 190. Excerpts were reprinted in *Massachusetts Spy* (Boston), Feb. 13, 1772, p. 1, col. 4. See generally Bernard Bailyn, *Pamphlets of the American Revolution, 1750-1776* (Cambridge, Mass., 1965), I, 52; Isaac Kramnick, *Bolingbroke and His Circle* (Cambridge, Mass.,

1968), 76-83; Robbins, *Commonwealthman*, 190-191, 242, 314-315.

6. Viscount Bolingbroke, *The Craftsman*, no. 57, Aug. 5, 1727 (London, 1731-1737), II, 84-85.

7. See Boltwood v. White, HSC, 9-64 (ejectment by brothers and sisters of intestate owner). See generally George L. Haskins, "The Beginnings of Partible Inheritance in the American Colonies," *Yale Law Journal*, LI (1942), 1280.

8. See Baker v. Mattocks, Quincy 69 (1763).

9. See Jacobs v. Little, PSC, 5-65. On the seventeenth-century background of dower in Massachusetts, see George L. Haskins, *Law and Authority in Early Massachusetts* (New York, 1960), 180-182, 215.

10. Complaint of Tracey, EGS, 9-66.

11. Complaint of Orrinzo, DGS, 2-65. In England masters also had to make adequate provision for the needs of their apprentices and servants. See Rex v. Easman, 2 Str. 1013, 93 Eng. Rep. 1003 (K.B. 1743); Rex v. Inhabitants of Hales Owen, 1 Str. 99, 93 Eng. Rep. 410 (K.B. 1718).

12. On the poor law, see Chapter 2, note 24.

13. See J.B. Black, *The Reign of Elizabeth, 1558-1603* (Oxford, 2d ed., 1959), 264-266.

14. Robinson v. Brayton, BrSC, 10-71, in Robert Treat Paine, Minutes, vol. 1.

15. See Anonymous, Quincy 370, 377 (1770).

16. See Hathaway v. Strange, BrSC, 10-70 (upholding right of tenant to take crops according to terms of lease existing at time of sale of land).

17. See Burghardt v. Wood, HSC, 4-72 holding that a grant by the General Court was superior to a prior grant whose terms had not been complied with, except as to land actually and constructively occupied by first grantee.

18. See Green v. Gordon, SSC, 8-65.

19. See French v. Cobb, BrSC, 10-63, in Paine, Minutes, vol. 1. Of course, some cases arose in which priority of possession was not an issue. A large number of such cases involved the validity or construction of written documents, especially wills. See, e.g., Banister v. Henderson, Quincy 119 (1765); Elwell v. Pierson, Quincy 42 (1763); Dudley v. Dudley, Quincy 12 (1762). Other cases involved deeds. See, e.g., Walker v. Walker, BrSC, 10-70; Boucher v. Stearns, MSC, 8-62.

20. See Perkins v. Merrill, YSC, 6-70; Pope v. Church, BrSC, 10-68. In England pews were also treated as a form of real estate. See

William Blackstone, *Commentaries on the Laws of England* (Oxford, 1765-1769), II, 429; John Comyns, *A Digest of the Laws of England* (Dublin, 1785), III, 194.

21. A landowner was permitted to maintain trespass against one who entered his land and cut down his trees, see Hallowell v. Springer, CSC, 6-70; Morrill v. Cutts, YSC, 6-70, provided that he could at least prove his title to the trees, see Pier v. Reed, BeCP, 9-63, and could prove the quantity of trees taken away. See Shae v. Warnsley, DCP, 3-74. The law also gave a landowner protection against animals that came on his land and damaged it: he could either sue the owner of the animals for his damages, see French v. Briggs, BrSC, 10-69, or could seize the animals themselves. See Pearson v. Hale, ECP, 9-74 (jury verdict for defendant in writ of replevin upon plea of plaintiff's horse damage feasant). See also Brunson v. Spoor, BeCP, 9-68 (jury verdict for plaintiff upon same plea). In Brunson, it should be noted, the plaintiff's replication to the plea of damage feasant was that title to the land on which the animals were seized was in the plaintiff, which suggests that replevin was thus used as a tool for trying title to land. However, a landowner did not have these remedies if animals entered his land through his own neglect of his fences. See Balch v. Cree, ECP, 3-69. But see Dodge v. Raymond, ESC, 6-65 (replication of defective fence ignored by jury in returning verdict). Finally, a landowner could hold his neighbor to absolute liability if the neighbor permitted his fire to spread form his own property. See Richard B. Morris, *Studies in the History of American Law* (New York, 1930), 242-244; Morton J. Horwitz, "Damage Judgments, Legal Liability and Economic Development before the Civil War," 58 (unpublished paper in the possession of Professor Horwitz, Harvard Law School). If in the spread of the fire the defendant physically invaded the plaintiff's land, he was liable in trespass, see Jones v. Cook, CSC, 6-70; in the absence of a physical invasion, liability was in case. See Potter v. Mosely, WCP, 8-65, appeal dism., WSC, 9-66; Jones v. Persey, BeCP, 4-63; Heywood v. Taylor, WCP, 11-62. But a landowner had no remedy against a person who took fish from a stream crossing his freehold. See Winslow v. Clark, BaCP, 12-67 (argument of counsel), in Paine, Minutes, vol. 1.

22. See Minott v. Prince, SSC, 2-73; Burt v. Williams, BrSC, 10-72; Russell v. Dupee, SSC, 8-69; Belcher v. Capen, SSC, 3-68; Bleigh v. Curtis, SSC, 8-66.

23. See Ridgeway v. Lille, SSC, 8-62 (right to set foot on adjoining land when necessary

to make repairs to own house).

24. See Bartlett v. Terry, HSC, 9-63.

25. See Bartlett v. Watson, PCP, 4-72. In one situation, however, the courts did refuse to enforce customary rights—namely, allegedly customary rights in common to fish or to dig clams up to the high-water mark of navigable streams. See Patch v. Herrick, ESC, 6-72; Bartlet v. Morrell, ECP, 3-73.

26. See Morton J. Horwitz, "The Transformation of the Conception of Property in American Law, 1780-1860," *University of Chicago Law Review*, LX (1973), 248, 262n40. See also James Sullivan, *The History of Land Titles in Massachusetts* (Boston, 1801), 272-274; Wroth and Zobel, *Legal Papers*, I, 68n90. Horwitz maintains that the Massachusetts rule of prior appropriation was not uniformly followed either in England or in the rest of the American colonies. See Horwitz, "Conception of Property," 249-253, 262n40.

27. The only real question was how long a proprietor of a dam had to have used the water in a stream before his priority matured into a property right. Many declarations alleged possession from time immemorial or from some ancient time. See Manley v. Gay, BrCP, 9-64 ("time immemorial"); Sprague v. Howard, MSC, 8-63 ("time out of mind"); Minot v. Wheat, MCP, 12-62 ("ancient"time). See also Wroth and Zobel, *Legal Papers*, I, 82n108. This suggests that a plaintiff had to demonstrate a prescriptive title in order to recover, but the evidence introduced in Prescott v. Priest, see Wroth and Zobel, *Legal Papers*, I, 266, 272, stated the length of time for which the plaintiff had been in actual possession of the dam and mill; thus a plaintiff's usage may sometimes have been ancient but never sufficiently immemorial to create a title by prescription on a theory of lost grant. But the law always sanctified some past usage. Usually recovery in suits involving competing water use was had in case. See Bennett v. Bennett, PCP, 12-73; Manley v. Gay, BrCP, 9-64; Williams v. Drury, BeCP, 9-63. Indeed, trespass could not be maintained for obstructing or diverting water, see Sawyer v. Farnham, ESC, 6-65, unless there was an allegation that the defendant had entered the plaintiff's close and built a dam touching the plaintiff's land. See Pejepscot Props. v. Willson, CSC, 6-65; Sprague v. Howard, MSC, 8-63. See generally Wroth and Zobel, *Legal Papers*, I, 275n8.

28. See Wroth and Zobel, *Legal Papers*, I, 242, 274.

29. See ibid., I, 274.

30. See ibid, I, 242, 274.

31. In addition to his common law action

in trespass or case, as appropriate, see the cases cited in notes 28-30 above, an owner whose land was flooded could, under the mill act, Laws of 1713, ch. 15, petition the court of sessions to appoint a jury to assess the yearly damages that he suffered from the flooding. See Cobb v. Miller, PGS, 10-66; Petition of Drake, BeGS, 9-62. The petition had to request a jury determination of damages and would be dismissed for making a request to the court. See Hunt Petition, BrGS Files, 3-62.

32. Petition of Bartlet, EGS, 7-61.

33. Amesbury v. Currier, ESC, 6-67. See also Order re Ferryman, DGS, 3-66 (court order empowering ferryman to prosecute competitors). Horwitz, "Conception of Property," 248, 264, maintains that in England collection of a toll for a ferry could ripen in time into a right to exclude competition. On the ambiguities of English law, see Churchman v. Tunstal, Handres 162, 145 Eng. Rep. 432 (Ex. 1659), suggesting that English courts, at least in some areas, were concerned with monopolies and restraint of trade in the context of ferry cases.

34. See Cottle's License, EGS, 9-74; Petition of Herrick, EGS, 7-64.

35. See Petition of Flagg, WGS, 6-71.

36. See Petition of Ingalls, EGS, 9-65; Petition of Tyler, EGS, 9-65; Petition of Martin, EGS, 12-62.

37. See Petition of Wood, HGS, 8-72. Accord, Petition of Partridge, HGS, 8-69.

38. See the cases cited in note 37 above.

39. Oliver v. Sale, Quincy 29, 30 (1762) (argument of counsel for plaintiff). See generally Allison v. Cockran, Quincy 94-98n1 (1764).

40. See Rogers v. Noble, HSC, 9-61, holding that the warranty was breached by the outstanding interest at the time of the sale of one who had purchased the slave for a term of years of servitude imposed by a court as a punishment for crime.

41. See Newell v. Gyles, SSC, 9-60.

42. See Inhabitants of Stoughton Petition, MGS Files, 11-70.

43. See Inhabitants of Stoneham v. Inhabitants of Lincoln, MGS Files, 5-66.

44. Brown v. Switser, SSC, 9-60.

45. "A Letter to the People of Pennsylvania," in Bailyn, Pamphlets, I, 262.

46. See Dunten v. Richards, Quincy 67 (1763). Contracts could be modified by a mutual agreement made subsequent to the original contract. See Naunaumphtaunt v. Bernent, BeCP, 9-71.

47. See Complaint of Dehon, SGS, 1-65 (holding that child not bound as apprentice if parent or guardian failed to sign indenture); Dogget v. Dykes, NGS, 3-61 (holding that child cannot bind himself). Infants, of course, could not make contracts of any sort, see Hill v. Emory, YSC, 6-66; Wyer v. Haley, MCP Files, 12-63, except for goods or services that "were necessary for" the infant "and fitting to his degree," Wyer v. Haley, supra, and had to be sued and could themselves sue only through their parents or guardian. See Gleason v. Gilpatrick, SCP Files, 1-65. Thus a parent was entitled to any wages earned by a child and could bring suit for them. See Coffin v. Barnard, NCP, 3-74. A parent, of course, could not apprentice a child beyond his twenty-first birthday. See Crocker v. Gorham, BaCP, 3-63, in Paine, Minutes, vol. 1 ("Inden. not good because for more than 21 yrs.").

48. For a physical abduction, the owner could maintain trespass. See Freeman v. Thompson, SSC, 2-72 (apprentice); Gorham v. Sturgis, BaSC, 5-61 (apprentice). Trespass was also the usual writ for testing whether someone was a freeman or a slave. This result was achieved by the alleged slave's bringing trespass for assault or false imprisonment and by the defendant's then pleading that the plaintiff was his own proper slave—a plea which, if a jury found it true, constituted both a procedural bar to the plaintiff's maintaining suit, see Tillage v. Jacobs, PCP, 4-72; Colden v. Stockbridge, PCP, 4-72; and a defense to the suit on the merits. See Wroth and Zobel, Legal Papers, II, 55. Issues often arising in these suits were whether the defendant had purchased the plaintiff from a seller who had been the plaintiff's rightful owner, see ibid.; Webster v. Jasper, MSC, 1-63; and whether the plaintiff was the child of a free woman and hence free himself. See Lewis v. Dodge, ESC, 11-69; Wroth and Zobel, Legal Papers, II, 52. Trespass was not, however, the only possible remedy for a slave; he could also bring a writ of de homine replegiando to obtain his freedom, see Muzzy v. Margaret, MSC, 10-70, or a writ of case for wages, upon which his freedom would be put in issue by the defendant. See Hill v. Hayward, PCP, 7-73.

49. In the absence of physical abduction, the owner could maintain case. See Prat v. Millard, BrSC, 10-67 (indentured servant); Wallingford v. Emery, YSC, 6-67 (slave); Southworth v. Leavitt, CSC, 6-65 (indentured servant); Holloway v. Chace, BrSC, 10-63 (daughter); Frobisher v. Roffe, SSC, 9-60 (apprentice).

50. See Barker v. Mooney, NGS, 3-61 (servant ordered to do work provided for in

his indenture). Justices of the peace in England had similar broad powers to compel apprentices and artisans to fulfill the terms of their contracts, see An Act for Better Regulating Apprentices and Persons Working Under Contract, 6 Geo. 3, ch. 25 (1765), and to compel common laborers to work during hay or harvest time. See Comyns, *Digest*, IV, 91.

51. See Petition of White, EGS, 9-72; Petition of Osgood, EGS, 3-60. Roads that were no longer necessary would be discontinued. See Petition of Oliver, MGS, 11-72. Usually the determination of a road's necessity and convenience was made by a committee appointed by General Sessions for that purpose, but a dissatisfied party had a right to have the determination made by a jury. See Petition of Peaslee, EGS, 3-61.

52. Petition of Osgood, EGS, 3-60.

53. See, e.g., How's Petition, MGS Files, 11-71 (petitioner's farm cut in two by road, separating main portion from spring).

54. Sometimes farmers whose land was cut in half were permitted to maintain gates across the highway so as to minimize their damage, as long as those gates would not "be disadvantageous to the Publick." Petition of Stebbins, HGS, 5-69. But gates could be maintained only with court leave; if that leave was withdrawn, the gates were then deemed an obstruction of the highway. See ibid. Like any other obstruction, they could be abated as a nuisance, and their existence would render their owner liable to indictment for a nuisance. See Rex v. Wild, HGS, 11-69. Cf. Mantor v. Cottle, DGS, 4-60 (gristmill obstructing a highway abated as a nuisance).

55. See, e.g., Petition of Headley, MGS, 12-62. Lack of title barred recovery of damages. See Petition of White, EGS, 9-72.

56. See King v. Moulton, SGS, 4-67 (indictment for establishing bakery in building not previously so used and "not being in such part of said Town, as the Justices of the peace, & Selectmen of said Town . . . have determined convenient . . ."). Cf. Salem By-Laws, EGS Files, 9-62 (coopers required to build chimneys of brick or stone).

57. See Marblehead By-Laws, EGS Files, 12-62; Salem By-Laws, EGS Files, 9-62.

58. See Salem By-Laws, EGS Files, 9-62.

59. See Petition of Concord, MGS, 11-73; Petition of Richardson, MGS, 9-61.

60. See Petition of Paine, MGS, 9-68.

61. See, e.g., Petition of Tyng, MGS, 5-60.

62. See King v. Mulliken, EGS, 7-64 (fine for using unsafe boat leading to drowning of passenger).

63. See Petition of Rowell, EGS, 9-61 (ferryman ordered to maintain two boats, one for each side of the river).

64. See Petition of Cogswell, EGS, 3-74.

65. See Petition of Herrick, EGS, 3-68.

66. Complaint of Orrinzo, DGS, 2-65.

67. See Chapter 2, note 24.

68. See Order re Licenses, PGS, 10-72, directing that the town approve the granting of licenses only to necessary houses, since too many would lead to debauchery.

69. See Petition of Pomeroy, HGS, 8-71; Petition of Flagg, WCP, 8-73. A private citizen could also bring a complaint against a licensee who was "suspected of hard drinking spiritous liquors" and so was "unfitted" to keep an inn. Fowler v. Staunton, HGS, 8-60.

70. See Petition of Wilson, HGS, 8-71.

71. See Resolution re Public Houses, MGS, 5-62.

72. See Order re Votes of Harvard College, MGS, 12-64.

73. Indebitatus assumpsit lay, for example, to recover on an account for goods furnished or labor performed, as on an account for food given by a town to the promissor's wife. See Brown v. Culnon, Quincy 66 (1763). But see Knap v. Pernan, ECP, 9-66, ruling that a husband was not liable for the debts of his dissolute wife, who had deserted him, as long as he posted public notice in the town indicating that he would not pay them. Another example would be an account for lodging given by the promissee to some other person whom the promissor had to support. See Carney v. Bailey, SSC, 8-63. See also Hall v. Miller, Quincy 252 (1767). Indebitatus assumpsit also lay to recover money paid by a plaintiff to the use of a defendant, as when a debtor procured an agent to settle his affairs with his creditors; the debtor was then under an obligation to reimburse the agent for the money he expended. See Murray v. Walker, WSC, 9-67. See also the notes opposite Rex v. Loring, PSC, 10-64, in Paine, Minutes, vol. 1 (conveyance of all one's goods "implies secret trust & confidence yt the donee shall deal favorably with the donor"). Finally, indebitatus assumpsit was often used to recover money had and received by a defendant, as in cases of receipt of money upon promises to serve as the promissee's substitute in the draft, see Allen v. Shipman, HSC, 9-61, or to purchase insurance for the promissee's ship. See Molineaux v. Stephens, SSC, 8-63.

74. Suits arising out of such relationships were frequent. They were brought, for ex-

ample, against executors and administrators for withholding legacies and distributions, see Libby v. Libby, CSC, 6-71; Gay v. Simpson, SSC, 8-67; Anthony v. Luther, BrSC, 10-66; Brayton v. Robinson, BrSC, 10-63; Wroth and Zobel, *Legal Papers*, I, 63; Theophilus Parsons, Precedents, no. 29; against innkeepers for failing to keep travelers' chattels safely, see Smith v. Bush, BeCP, 4-64, against bailees who negligently cared for their bailors' animals, see Phillips v. Gains, HCP, 5-73; Hinsdale v. Williams, BeCP, 4-63; Ryan v. Griswold, BeCP, 9-62, against common carriers, see Holland v. Mosely, CSC, 7-74, and other shippers and bailees, see Needham v. Hall, SSC, 8-73; Bacon v. Barker, HSC, 9-72; Collins v. Bryant, SSC, 2-72; Higgins v. Dwight, HSC, 9-71; Langdon v. Barber, SSC, 8-71; for not returning the plaintiff's goods, and against servants who through negligence or other breaches of duty exposed their masters to loss of profit, see Proctor v. Oaks, ESC, 6-61, or to other damage. See Hickling v. Holland, SSC, 8-69 (captain overloading ship); Paine v. Paine, MSC, 4-65 (captain engaging in smuggling); Balstone v. Gridley, SSC, 2-61 (negligence); Cloutman v. St. Barbe, ECP, 9-64 (seaman's smuggling leading to captain's imprisonment).

75. Indebitatus assumpsit lay when and only when an action of debt also lay. See Glover v. LeTestue, Quincy 225 (1770); Wroth and Zobel, *Legal Papers*, I, 37. Failure to plead the precedent debt or obligation was cause for abatement of the writ. See Paxton v. Gray, SSC, 8-61; Doty v. Stone, WCP, 2-64; Gibbs v. Marsh, HCP, 8-63; Hartman v. Staunton, HCP, 5-60.

76. See S. F. C. Milsom, *Historical Foundations of the Common Law* (London, 1969), 304-308; Theodore F. T. Plucknett, *A Concise History of the Common Law* (Boston, 1956), 644-646.

77. A variety of indebitatus assumpsit, known as insimul computassent, lay on behalf of a party to whom a balance was owing after two parties had balanced their accounts. See Apthorp v. Shepard, Quincy 298 (1768). But see Clap v. Griffith, PCP, 7-62, overruling a plea in abatement in insimul computassent for bringing suit for a balance of accounts when only one party owed money on the account. That assumpsit lay in lieu of account, see Clap v. Leonard, HCP, 8-64; Thompson v. Watson, PCP, 4-62.

78. Cf. Bromfield v. Little, Quincy 108 (1764).

79. See John Adams's Pleadings Book, in Wroth and Zobel, *Legal Papers*, I, 37n31, 38. Examples would be suits brought by a doctor to recover for visits and medicines, see Glover v. LeTestue, Quincy 225 (1770), overruling Pynchon v. Brewster, Quincy 224 (1766), or by a teacher to recover what he reasonably deserved to have for his instruction. See Campbell v. Lillie, WSC, 9-68.

80. See Blackstone, *Commentaries*, III, 161. In addition to its use in sale of goods cases, quantum meruit lay against a father to recover the reasonable value of food and lodging furnished to his son at the plaintiff's boarding school. See Tyler v. Richards, Quincy 195 (1765). Occasionally both quantum meruit and quantum valebant were available to a plaintiff. For example, a lessor seeking to recover compensation from his lessee in the absence of an agreement as to rent could bring either writ. Compare Sherman v. Britnall, MSC, 1-62, with Parsons, Precedents, no. 65. A plaintiff could bring these various forms of assumpsit jointly in the alternative, even though they were inconsistent with each other. See Barker v. Jacobs, PCP, 12-71; Wroth and Zobel, *Legal Papers*, I, 37-38. See also Thomas v. Wing, PCP, 7-73. But see Temple v. Walles, MSC, 4-67 (writ abated for setting forth two separate and repugnant contracts for same goods).

81. Cushing 1, 92, 98-99 (1772).

82. Many contracts were enforced in special assumpsit—between two parties who had recovered judgments against each other and had mutually agreed to forbear levying execution, see Nash v. Smith, HSC, 9-65; Gay v. Goodspeed, SSC, 8-64; Wiswall v. Hall, SSC, 8-62, between two parties who had agreed to submit a dispute to arbitration, see Russell v. Dupee, SSC, 8-65, between a promissor who had agreed to deliver a cargo to a vessel within fourteen days and a promissee who had agreed in return to pay for it, see Preble v. King, CSC, 6-64, and between children who had agreed to contribute proportionally to their father's support. See Freeman v. Freeman, BrCP, 6-74.

83. See Paxton v. Gray, SSC, 8-61; Newhall v. Bartlett, ECP, 9-72; Russell v. Diamond, MCP Files, 5-69; Woodbridge v. Minck, BeCP, 9-68; Farwell v. Dodge, MCP Files, 3-65; Sumner v. Hammond, MCP Files, 9-64; Fonda v. King, BeCP, 4-64; Marsh v. Graves, HCP, 5-62; Maynard v. Skinner, MCP Files, 12-61. The promise that the plaintiff alleged had to be one capable of performance. See Kimball v. Somes, ECP, 3-61, rev'd on default, ESC, 6-61. A plaintiff did not have to

allege the time at which the promise was made. See Peirce v. Brown, BrCP, 9-71; Cole v. Ingalls, ECP, 7-60.

84. See Shutless v. Howard, Suff. Files no. 142362 (Ply. 1770); Sargent v. Webb, ECP, 12-74; Brown v. Rowley, BeCP, 9-70; Davell v. Millard, BrCP, 9-70; Rowley v. Sheldon, BeCP, 2-70; Ingersoll v. Read, BeCP, 12-66; Stanton v. Ingersoll, BeCP, 9-63.

85. See Pixley v. Alford, BeCP, 11-73; Newhall v. Bartlet, ECP, 9-72; Fonda v. Barrett, BeCP, 4-65, rev'd on default, HSC, 9-65. In the event that a defendant breached a contract wherein performance was due at some time in the future, the plaintiff had to plead the time at which performance would have been due. See Jones v. Read, Suff. Files no. 145319 (Bris. 1767).

86. See Jenison v. Marsh, WSC, 9-63; Jenison v. Marcy, WSC, 9-63; Smith v. Dodge, MCP Files, 9-73; Hickok v. Downing, BeCP, 9-68; Kimball v. Somes, ECP, 3-61, rev'd on default, ESC, 6-61. But see Bernent v. Burghart, Cushing 1 (1772) (request not necessary in suit on promise to produce debtor in court). It was also unnecessary for a plaintiff to plead the time at which he requested the defendant to perform. See Ford v. Boardman, ESC, 6-69, reversing ECP, 9-68.

87. See Montague v. Alvord, HCP, 8-65.

88. See Smith v. Boyd, Suff. Files no. 152263 (Worc. 1767); Smith v. Dodge, MCP Files, 9-73; Anderson v. Gilbert, HCP, 11-66, rev'd on default, HSC, 9-67; Breck v. Noble, BeCP, 9-62; Chace v. Chace, BrCP, 9-60, aff'd, BrSC, 10-60.

89. Cotton Mather, *Theopolis Americana: An Essay . . . against the CORRUPTIONS of the Market-Place* (Boston, 1710), 19-20.

90. By statute, Massachusetts not only made the recovery of gambling debts illegal but also gave a cause of action to a debtor who had paid such debts to recover his payments. See Laws of 1742, ch. 27, as amended, Laws of 1749, ch. 16; Laws of 1759, ch. 34; Laws of 1769, ch. 12; Laws of 1772. ch. 52.

On the possible religious origins of a number of contract doctrines, including the doctrines of consideration and mutuality of obligation, see Jerome A. Cohen and William E. Nelson, eds., "Development of Law and Legal Institutions," II-100—II-109 (unpublished class materials on file in HLS); John D. Eusden, *Puritans, Lawyers and Politics in Early Seventeenth-Century England* (New Haven, 1958), vii-viii, 29-30; Milsom, *Historical Foundations*, 213; Frederick Pollock and Frederic W. Maitland, *The History of English*

Law before the Time of Edward I (Cambridge, 2d ed., 1911), II, 189-199, 208-209; A. W. B. Simpson, "The Penal Bond with Conditional Defeasance," *Law Quarterly Review*, LXXXII (1966), 392, 412-414, 419-422.

91. Wroth and Zobel, *Legal Papers*, I, 20.

92. Ibid., I, 4-5. Accord, ibid., I, 21.

93. See Parsons, Precedents, nos. 50-51. But see Porter v. Second Parish in Ipswich, ECP, 3-64 (overruling plea in abatement for failure to plead performance of condition precedent). Ministers could also sue for support in General Sessions. See Petition of Hovey, PGS, 10-69. But a contract with the town was a bar to such a suit. See Morton v. Inhabitants of Blanford, HGS, 5-67. But see Petition of Hovey, supra, where such a contract was alleged.

94. See Smith v. Moody, HSC, 9-67. In requiring a plaintiff to aver his performance of his part of the bargain, Massachusetts appears to have been following English law, see Callonel v. Briggs, 1 Salk. 112, 91 Eng. Rep. 104 (Q.B. 1703); Peeters v. Opie, 2 Wms. Saund. 351, 85 Eng. Rep. 1144 (K.B. 1671), although there is some evidence that purely executory contracts were enforceable in eighteenth-century England. See Comyns, *Digest*, I, 132; V, 46. In Massachusetts it appears that while a plaintiff had to plead some significant performance on his part, he did not have to plead perfect performance. See Gale v. Hunt, MSC, 4-67 (buyer held liable for damages for breach of contract for sale of goods despite special finding by jury that seller had not made delivery on date required by contract); Paine v. Eldridge, BrCP, 8-65, rev'd on default, BrSC, 10-65 (suit on arbitration contract abated for plaintiff's failure to allege performance or readiness to perform); Pynchon v. Williams, BeCP, 9-63 (jury verdict for plaintiff in suit on bill of exchange for military pay following pleas in bar that regiment never mustered out and defendant never received money to pay over).

95. See Ayer v. Gardiner, SSC, 8-73 (note given on condition maker could have easement over payee's land; endorsee pleaded payee's performance); Smith v. Moodey, HSC, 9-67 (contract to exchange goods specifying certain conditions); Paine v. Eldridge, BrCP, 8-65, rev'd on default, BrSC, 10-65.

96. See Porter v. Inhabitants of 2d Parish in Ipswich, ECP, 3-64.

97. See Morey v. Hodges, BrCP, 9-60, rev'd on other grounds, BrSC, 10-60. See also Barker v. Jacobs, PCP, 12-71 (count in special

assumpsit joined to count in quantum
meruit); Hartman v. Staunton, HCP, 5-60
(count in special assumpsit joined to count in
indebitatus assumpsit).

98. See Obrian v. Millikin, YSC, 7-62. Cf.
Smith v. Moodey, HSC, 9-67 (contract to sell
oxen for money and rum; seller pleaded delivery of oxen); Turner v. Elliot, PCP, 4-73,
aff'd, PSC, 5-73 (contract to exchange horses;
plaintiff pleaded own performance). See also
Crocker v. Brown, PCP, 5-60 (contract to sell
goods; seller pleaded delivery; unclear whether declaration was in special or in indebitatus
assumpsit).

99. See Collins v. Bryant, SSC, 2-72; Higgins v. Dwight, HSC, 9-71; Vassall v. Billings,
MSC, 10-68; Lansing v. Baldwin, WSC, 9-66;
Bush v. How, HCP, 8-67. Cf. Temple v. Curtis,
MSC, 4-72 (plaintiff pleaded that he attended
auction, bid, and won but that defendant
failed to honor promise to deliver goods);
Preble v. King, CSC, 7-64 (plaintiff pleaded
that he readied ship to receive goods but that
defendant failed to honor promise to deliver
goods); Molineaux v. Stephens, SSC, 8-63
(plaintiff pleaded payment for insurance but
that defendant failed to honor promise to
obtain it).

100. See Beard v. Wright, HCP, 8-73; Hill
v. Bliss, BrCP, 8-68; Smith v. Nash, HCP,
2-65. Cf. Gay v. Goodspeed, SSC, 8-64 (plaintiff pleaded default in own suit against defendant but that defendant breached promise
to forbear levying execution in another suit);
Dix v. Shepard, HCP, 8-67 (plaintiff pleaded
payment of settlement money to defendant
but that defendant breached promise to forbear suit).

101. See Tirrell v. Gay, SSC, 2-62; Chadwick v. Foster, HCP, 2-70; Soule v. Soule,
PCP, 7-69; Emerson v. Marsh, WCP, 8-66. Cf.
Fowler v. Fowler, HCP, 8-71 (plaintiff
pleaded own execution of bond to submit to
arbitration but that defendant was unwilling
to execute bond).

102. See Bangs v. Snow, BaSC, 5-72; Hale
v. Willet, ESC, 11-66; Homans v. Paxton, SSC,
2-62.

103. See Freeman v. Freeman, BrCP, 6-74.

104. See Tucker v. Slocum, BrCP, 3-71.

105. See Aldrich v. Daniels, WCP, 2-64;
Russell v. Slocum, BrCP, 9-60. Cf. Daniels v.
Bowin, WSC, 9-64 (writ abated when plaintiff
married another man after commencement of
action).

106. See Noble v. Welch, BeCP, 9-65; Williams v. Powers, BeCP, 9-65; Williams v. Fisk,
BeCP, 9-65.

107. Williams v. Fisk, BeCP, 9-65.
108. See text at notes 39-50 above.
109. See Parsons, Precedents, nos. 50-51.
110. Wroth and Zobel, *Legal Papers*, I, 63.
111. Edson v. Parkhurst, BrCP, 8-60, in
Paine, Minutes, vol. 1. But see the notes
opposite Rex v. Loring, PSC, 10-64, ibid., vol.
1 ("a Sale can never be without a good
consideration").
112. Brown v. Culnon, Quincy 66 (1763).
113. Wroth and Zobel, *Legal Papers*, I, 33.
Accord, ibid., I, 35. Thus interest was not
allowed as an element of an account for
which recovery was sought in indebitatus
assumpsit, when there was no custom among
Massachusetts merchants so to allow it. See
Bromfield v. Little, Quincy 108 (1764).
114. Folger v. Worth, NCP, 10-73.
115. Bower v. White, BrCP, 12-70, in
Paine, Minutes, vol. 1.
116. See Derumple v. Clark, Quincy 38
(1763). A tenant could also become liable to
pay the taxes as a result of a customary
course of dealing between the parties. See
Jackson v. Foye, Quincy 26 (1762).
117. For suits brought on such warranties,
see Whiting v. Dinmore, BeCP, 9-68; White v.
Winsor, PCP, 12-67; Dewey v. Wheeler, BeCP,
4-63. Analogous suits were brought against
doctors for negligent malpractice, see Credi-
ford v. Allen, YSC, 6-70; Leonard v. Cooper,
HSC, 9-69, as well as against sellers of goods
for breaches of their implied warranty of
merchantability, which arose on all sales of
merchandise by means other than sample. See
Oliver v. Sale, Quincy 29 (1762); Baker v.
Frobisher, Quincy 4 (1762). But see Cummins
v. Fish, BrCP, 3-64, in Paine, Minutes, vol. 1
(witness testified that he was "Present at the
Sale No Warranty").
118. White v. Winsor, PCP, 12-67, in
Paine, Minutes, vol. 1.
119. Bromfield v. Little, Quincy 108
(1764).
120. Pynchon v. Brewster, Quincy 224
(1766).
121. Tyler v. Richards, Quincy 195
(1765).
122. Hall v. Richardson, WCP, 8-68.
123. Younglove v. Williams, HCP, 5-60.
124. See Robinson v. Tisdale, BrCP, 8-65,
in Paine, Minutes, vol. 1 ("note was not good
for it was given on Saturday night").
125. See Barnes v. Greenleaf, Quincy 41
(1763); Barney v. Cottle, BrCP, 12-70, in
Paine, Minutes, vol. 1.
126. See note 94 above and accompanying
text.

127. It is unclear whether the statute of frauds, which requires certain contracts to be in writing, was in full effect in prerevolutionary Massachusetts. The defense of the statute was raised successfully in Cushing v. Tabour, BrSC, 10-60, but unsuccessfully in Smith v. Nash, HCP, 2-65.

128. See Apthorp v. Shepard, Quincy 298 (1768), overruling Pateshall v. Apthorp, Quincy 179 (1765).

129. Whaples v. Moor, HCP, 5-70.

130. See Noble v. Smith, Quincy 254 (1767).

131. See Wroth and Zobel, *Legal Papers*, I, 37-39; Parsons, Precedents, nos. 35, 64.

132. See Arthor v. Coffin, NCP, 3-61 (suit for price of rum; defendant stated he did not buy rum but received it on account for a share of a whaling venture).

133. See Geoffrey Gilbert, *The Law of Evidence* (London, 1756), 122. See also Chapter 2, text at notes 111-119.

134. See Affidavit re Swan's Barrgain, Dec. 28, 1764, in Samuel Curwen, Justice of the Peace Book (in Essex Institute, Salem, Mass.); Oath of John Ross re being shipped on board the ship Merger, Sept. 7, 1761, ibid; Promissory Note from Joseph Pendleton to Joseph Bartlett, Plymouth Notary Public Records, 1768-1830, p. 51 (in Pilgrim Hall, Plymouth, Mass.).

135. Aldrich v. Nobby, NCP, 3-70.

136. In addition to the various writs discussed in the text, the writ of account was sometimes used. See Eldridge v. Spooner, BrSC, 10-67; McKenzie v. Mallbone, SSC, 8-61; Bates v. Ripley, PSC, 5-60.

137. Cf. Tuffts v. Bartlett, ECP, 3-65, holding that usury or illegality of consideration could not be pleaded in defense to an action of debt on a bond. See also Chapter 3, note 73.

138. See Gilbert, *Evidence*, 73.

139. See Dole v. Loomis, BeCP, 3-73 (sustaining demurrer for failure to allege making of covenant); Fonda v. Holland, BeCP, 9-70 (writ abated for failure to plead condition precedent and to allege making and delivery of contract in accordance with parties' intent).

140. See Pollard v. Stevens, SSC, 8-63. See also Stephens v. Bollan, BrSC, 10-61 (holding on special verdict that lease cannot be extended at expiration except with consent of lessor or his successor).

141. See Temple v. How, WSC, 9-68; Ingersoll v. Sikes, HSC, 9-62. In cases involving warranties in the conveyance of land in fee,

lawsuits on the sealed instrument could subsequently arise alleging breach of the defendant's warranties, cf. the cases in note 140 above, for which a plaintiff could recover damages provided that the warranties were personal as distinguished from real—that is, provided that they were covenants that bound the parties personally rather than covenants that ran with the land. See Hamlin v. Hopkins, BeCP, 11-72 (demurrer sustained on ground that action of covenant cannot be maintained on real covenant); Wright v. Searl, BeCP, 9-67 (writ abated for joining claims on real and personal covenants). Another remedy was to bring a writ of warrantia cartae against the warrantor to compel him to warrant or to pay damages in lieu thereof. See Percy v. Fowler, HCP, 3-67, appeal dism., HSC, 9-68; Sharpe v. Ball, HCP, 3-62; Parsons, Precedents, no. 88. Of course, a warrantor could also come in voluntarily and defend in a suit brought against his grantee. See Taggart v. Percy, HCP, 3-68. Deeds under seal were also commonly used to create and transfer property interests in slaves, apprentices, and other servants. See notes 46-47 above and accompanying text. Conveyances of land in fee simple had to be recorded. See Hooton v. Grout, Quincy 343 (1772); Anonymous, Quincy 370 (1770); Arnold v. Hook, ECP, 3-64. See generally George L. Haskins, "The Beginnings of the Recording System in Massachusetts," *Boston University Law Review*, XXI (1941), 281; Mark DeW. Howe, "The Recording of Deeds in the Colony of Massachusetts Bay," ibid., XXVIII (1948), 1.

142. There are no known cases in prerevolutionary Massachusetts of debt on an unsealed contract; plaintiffs preferred to bring indebitatus assumpsit. See notes 75-77 above and accompanying text.

143. See Stow v. King, BeCP, 9-71; Wroth and Zobel, *Legal Papers*, I, 48; Parsons, Precedents, no. 2. See also Davis v. Merrill, MSC, 4-69 (parties allowed to modify bond by reexecution and redelivery thereof).

144. See Corliss v. Pingry, ECP, 3-70.

145. See Wroth and Zobel, *Legal Papers*, I, 13, 48-49n49.

146. See generally A. W. B. Simpson, "The Penal Bond with Conditional Defeasance," *Law Quarterly Review*, LXXXII (1966), 392.

147. See Dwight v. Bostwick, BeCP, 4-65.

148. See Hall v. Cudworth, SSC, 8-67.

149. See Blood v. Blood, MSC, 5-68.

150. See Brooks v. Blanchard, MCP, 9-60; Wroth and Zobel, *Legal Papers*, I, 48-49n49. To be able to sue in debt on a bond was of

significant value to a plaintiff since it minimized his problems of proof; production of the sealed instrument alone would generally entitle him to recovery. However, John Adams's statement that the defendant in debt on a bond could not plead the general issue was incorrect. See Wroth and Zobel, *Legal Papers*, I, 18. As to the fact that the general issue of non est factum could be pleaded, see Wheeler v. Taylor, MCP, 3-70; Blackstone, *Commentaries*, III, 305. Nonetheless Adams's point was of significance—a defendant by so pleading merely raised the issue of due execution of the instrument. Other defenses, such as performance by the defendant, see Spooner v. Dennie, BrSC, 10-64; Symonds v. Aborn, ECP, 7-73, illegality, see Lee v. Pell, BeCP, 2-70 (jury verdict on plea that bail bond executed with design that prisoner go at large); McLean v. Burbank, HCP, 8-61 (jury verdict on plea of usury); accord and satisfaction, see Ingersoll v. Smith, BeCP, 2-71, or nonperformance of a condition precedent to the defendant's duty to perform had to be pleaded specially. See Blood v. Blood, MSC, 5-68; Kenwick v. Rogers, BaSC, 5-63; Moultin v. Blanchard, SSC, 2-61; Meriman v. Mighill, HCP, 11-72; Hutchins v. Willard, WCP, 9-72; Wheeler v. Taylor, MCP, 3-70; Thayer v. Taft, WCP, 5-66, rev'd on default, WSC, 9-66; Lomis v. Curtis, HCP, 5-62; Putnam v. Putnam, WCP, 8-60. See also Woodman v. Plummer, CSC, 6-69 (arbitrators' rendition of award sufficient performance of condition precedent even if not delivered to parties). This, of course, placed the burden of proof on the defendant. As in medieval England, a plea merely of payment was not a defense. See Chadwick v. Fowler, BeCP, 9-66.

The Postrevolutionary Legal System Introduction

1. See Erving v. Cradock, Quincy 553 (1761); Lawrence H. Gipson, *The Coming of the Revolution, 1763-1775* (New York, 1954), 208-209; L. Kinvin Wroth and Hiller B. Zobel, eds., *Legal Papers of John Adams* (Cambridge, Mass., 1965), I, 201-202.
2. There were a few exceptional counties in which the courts were still open at the end of 1774. The Boston courts, for example, remained open until the British occupation of the city was ended in the spring of 1775. The most notable exception was the Essex Court of General Sessions, which sat continuously through 1774, 1775, and 1776 while being reconstituted as a state court.

3. Berkshire (1780) and Nantucket (1783).
4. See generally Oscar Handlin and Mary F. Handlin, "Revolutionary Economic Policy in Massachusetts," *William and Mary Quarterly*, 3d ser., IV (1947), 3.
5. Quoted in J. Franklin Jameson, *The American Revolution Considered as a Social Movement* (Princeton, 1926), 20.
6. Charles F. Adams, ed., *The Works of John Adams* (Boston, 1852), VII, 160-161. See generally Elisha P. Douglass, *Rebels and Democrats* (Chapel Hill, 1955), 13-14; Gordon S. Wood, *The Creation of the American Republic, 1776-1787* (Chapel Hill, 1969), 48.
7. Adams, *Works of John Adams*, VII, 161.
8. Benjamin Austin [Honestus], *Observations on the Pernicious Practice of the Law* (Boston, 1794), 12, 41.
9. Jesse Root, "Introduction to Connecticut Reports," in Perry Miller, ed., *The Legal Mind in America from Independence to the Civil War* (New York, 1962), 39. See generally Wood, *American Republic*, 300-301.

Chapter 5. The Reform of Common Law Pleading

1. Constitution of 1780, Part I, art. 11, in Oscar Handlin and Mary F. Handlin, eds., *The Popular Sources of Political Authority: Documents on the Massachusetts Constitution of 1780* (Cambridge, Mass., 1966), 444-445.
2. Benjamin Austin [Honestus], *Observations on the Pernicious Practice of the Law* (Boston, 1794), 3-4.
3. Reed v. Davis, 4 Pick. 216, 219 (1826).
4. Austin, *Observations*, 3-4.
5. See generally ibid.; Oscar Handlin and Mary F. Handlin, *Commonwealth: A Study of the Role of Government in the American Economy—Massachusetts, 1774-1861* (Cambridge, Mass., rev. ed., 1969), 41; Robert J. Taylor, *Western Massachusetts in the Revolution* (Providence, 1954), 134-136.
6. See Laws of 1785, ch. 23.
7. See Laws of 1789, ch. 58.
8. See Gerard W. Gawalt, "Massachusetts Lawyers: A Historical Analysis of the Process of Professionalization, 1760-1840" (Ph.D. diss., Clark University, 1969), 36-62.
9. Laws of 1785, ch. 23.
10. See Regulae Generales, 6 Mass. 382 (1810); Court Rule, PCP, 8-98 (requiring all suits to be argued pro se or by a duly admitted attorney).

11. See Chapter 2, notes 176-177 and accompanying text.

12. See William Sullivan, *An Address to the Members of the Bar of Suffolk, Massachusetts, at their Stated Meeting on the First Tuesday of March, 1824* (Boston, Mass., 1825), 41-42; Massachusetts Bar Association, *The Supreme Judicial Court of Massachusetts, 1692-1942* (Boston, 1947), 51.

13. Petition of Worcester County Convention, Oct. 1786, in *Worcester Magazine* (Worcester, 1786-1788), II, 334. Accord, Petition of Middlesex County Convention, Oct. 3, 1786, ibid., II, 358; Petition of Hampshire County Convention, Aug. 1786, in George R. Minot, *The History of the Insurrections in Massachusetts in the Year Seventeen Hundred and Eighty Six and the Rebellion Consequent Thereon* (Boston, 2d ed., 1810), 34; *Independent Chronicle* (Boston) June 8, 1786, p. 2, col. 2, reporting Dedham instructions.

14. See Petition of Worcester County Convention, Apr. 9, 1782, in *Massachusetts Spy* (Worcester), Apr. 18, 1782, p. 3, col. 3; Taylor, *Western Massachusetts*, 113-115.

15. *Independent Chronicle* (Boston), June 29, 1786, p. 1, col. 2. Accord, Petition of Worcester County Convention, Oct. 1786, in *Worcester Magazine*, II, 334.

16. Laws of 1783, ch. 42. See also Order Continuing All Defaulted Actions under £ 4, HCP, 8-84; Order re Suits Where Damages under £ 4, HCP, 11-84. Suits begun before justices which subsequently came to involve title to realty were removed to Common Pleas. See Russell v. Wheeler, MCP Files, 11-95.

17. Laws of 1786, ch. 21. The act gave the referees no jurisdiction over questions of title to real estate, see Fowler v. Bigelow, 8 Mass. 1 (1811), required that submission of the case be made before a justice of the peace, see Jones v. Hacker, 5 Mass. 264 (1809), and required the report of the referees to be approved by the Common Pleas judges. See ibid. No appeal lay from the report, as so approved, to the Supreme Judicial Court, see Noyes v. Noyes, MSJC, 10-96, although a writ of error did. See Short v. Pratt, 6 Mass. 495 (1810). The statute required the suit to be heard by three referees, see Monosiet v. Post, 4 Mass. 532 (1808), two of whom had to concur in the report. See Short v. Pratt, supra.

18. See Laws of 1786, ch. 43; Laws of 1788, chs. 26, 67. These acts, which permitted either party to elect to have the suit heard in Common Pleas, also contained provisions directing justices to endeavor to have the parties submit their dispute to referees. See Heywood v. Temple, MCP Files, 9-96, rev'd on default, MSJC, 4-98.

19. *Boston Gazette*, May 13, 1782, p. 1, col. 2.

20. Ibid., col. 1.

21. Austin, *Observations*, 29.

22. Ibid., 9.

23. James Neale to Robert Treat Paine, June 6, 1794, in Paine Papers.

24. *Boston Gazette*, May 13, 1782, p. 1, col. 1.

25. Ibid., May 6, 1782, p. 1, col. 3.

26. Hubbell v. Hoose, BeCP, 2-24.

27. *Boston Gazette*, May 13, 1782, p. 1, col. 2.

28. Various costs of litigation are discussed in detail in L. Kinvin Wroth and Hiller B. Zobel, eds., *Legal Papers of John Adams* (Cambridge, Mass., 1965), I, lxix-lxxi.

29. Writs that were technically insufficient were abated, but abatement normally did not bar reinstitution of a suit by the filing of a new and technically sufficient writ. See ibid., xlv.

30. See Ingersol v. Sikes, HSC, 9-62 (mention made of prior writ of novel disseisin); Reed v. Riddan, ECP, 12-61 (recout). Some writs, however, served different functions in Massachusetts from what they had served in England. Entry, which had become obsolete in eighteenth-century England, see Theodore F. T. Plucknett, *A Concise History of the Common Law* (Boston, 5th ed., 1956), 373, became in Massachusetts an all-purpose writ in the nature of case for the recovery of land, see Asahel Stearns, *A Summary of the Law and Practice of Real Actions* (Boston, 1824), 507-508, while replevin, which lay in England only for wrongful distress, see Plucknett, *Concise History*, 368-369, had become a general writ for litigating property in chattels. See Scott v. Tirrell, SSC, 8-73; Sixley v. Brown, BeCP, 9-67.

31. Watson v. Bliss, BrCP, 12-64.

32. Atkins v. Roby, SCP Files, 1-67.

33. Hunt v. Fay, MCP Files, 11-71.

34. See Sawyer v. Farnham, ESC, 6-65.

35. See Bush v. Fellows, BeCP, 11-71.

36. See Owen v. Lee, HCP, 8-61.

37. See Ross v. Willson, BeCP, 9-66; Fonda v. Lee, BeCP, 4-65, rev'd on default, HSC, 9-65. See also Bicknall v. Draper, BrSC, 10-61 (abated for calling writ "plea of review of plea of debt" instead of "plea of review of plea of review of plea of debt").

38. See Boyce v. Spear, PCP, 12-66.

39. Clap v. Stockbridge, PCP, 4-68.

40. Barker v. Elmes, PCP, 4-68.

41. See generally Wroth and Zobel, *Legal Papers*, I, xlvi.

42. The absence of special pleading in the prerevolutionary period noted by Wroth and Zobel, *Legal Papers*, I, 28-29, has been thoroughly confirmed by my research. For one of the rare examples in prerevolutionary Massachusetts of special pleading beyond the replication, see Theophilus Parsons, Precedents, no. 71. For examples of special pleading during the first decade after the Revolution, see Trear v. Bacon, BeSJC, 10-88; Murray v. Farley, ESJC, 11-87; Allen v. Bruce, WSJC, 5-87; Clark v. Holmes, MSJC, 11-86; Sexton v. Parker, HSJC, 11-85; Commonwealth v. Raymond, MSJC, 4-85; Commonwealth v. Otis, SSJC, 3-85; Peters v. Wilkins, ESJC, 6-83.

43. See Sacket v. Sacket, HCP, 11-71.

44. See Prouty v. Bryant, PCP, 12-69 (plea in debt on administration bond that arbitrators made no award); Phelps v. Cotton, HCP, 8-62 (plea that defendant never warranted primary obligee's ability to pay).

45. See Allen v. Spooner, WCP, 6-72, appeal dism., WSC, 5-73.

46. See generally William Blackstone, *Commentaries on the Laws of England* (Oxford, 1765-1769), III, 306-313.

47. See ibid., 309-311.

48. Ibid., 309.

49. See Lapham v. Corving, PCP, 7-66; Hyland v. Clap, PCP, 7-63; Partridge v. Hinds, HCP, 5-61. Cf. Stiles v. Leete, HCP, 11-64 (plea that defendant never signed note rejected).

50. See Crowfoot v. Percey, BeCP, 9-63.

51. See Talmage v. Strong, BeCP, 9-69, appeal dism., HSC, 9-69.

52. See Ingersol v. Sikes, HSC, 9-62 (mention made of prior writ of novel disseisin).

53. See Stearns, *Summary*, 507-508; Wroth and Zobel, *Legal Papers*, I, 261.

54. See Stoddard v. Goodrich, HSC, 4-73; Hills v. Brown, BrSC, 10-71; Wilson v. Linton, BrSC, 10-66; Rochester Proprietors v. Hammond, PSC, 5-64; Ruggles v. Barrows, PSC, 5-64. Bare title in the plaintiff alone was insufficient to make out an allegation of seisin; a plaintiff also had to allege that he was in possession of the land, see Powers v. Powers, WCP, 12-76 (writ abated for failure to allege possession in addition to bare title), or that he was taking its profits. See Moor v. Spencer, BeCP, 2-69 (writ abated for failure to allege taking of profits). See also Spaulding v. Green, MSC, 10-71 (writ containing allega-

tion of taking of profits). Not all writs, hcwever, contained this allegation. See Warren v. Apthorp, SSC, 2-72.

55. On the 30-year limitation period, see Stoddard v. Goodrich, HSC, 4-73; Lindale v. Cudworth, BrCP, 9-60. In addition to his allegation of seisin, a plaintiff also had to describe by metes and bounds the close to which title was being litigated. See Rochester Proprietors v. Hammond, Quincy 159 (1765); Ruggles v. Barrows, PSC, 5-64; French v. Cobb, BrSC, 10-63, in Robert Treat Paine, Minutes, vol. 1; King v. Averill, BeCP, 9-67.

56. In addition to trespass quare clausum fregit, trespass was frequently used in two other forms in prerevolutionary Massachusetts—trespass to the person and trespass de bonis asportatis. Trespass to the person lay for assaults, see Wroth and Zobel, *Legal Papers*, I, 106, 151, 157, for wrongfully imprisoning the plaintiff "against the Custom of England and this province," Hendricks v. Ashley, HSC, 9-72, even if the imprisonment occurred pursuant to legal process, see Martin v. Welch, SSC, 8-63; Perkins v. White, HCP, 11-67, and for having sexual intercourse with the plaintiff's wife. See Dougherty v. Little, MSC, 5-68; Staple v. Hammet, YSC, 6-63. Cf. Fairbanks v. Morey, BrCP, 6-60, aff'd, BrSC, 10-61 (abduction of plaintiff's wife, but no allegation of intercourse). Trespass de bonis asportatis lay for taking money, see Wroth and Zobel, *Legal Papers*, I, 149, or valuable documents belonging to the plaintiff, see Bradford v. Crowningshield, ESC, 6-63, for taking or wounding the plaintiff's animals, see Wise v. Hight, YSC, 6-67; Wentworth v. Willum, YSC, 7-65, for taking the plaintiff's ship, see Bailey v. Williams, CSC, 6-69; Treat v. Preble, BrSC, 10-64, modified, SSC, 8-65, and for destroying the plaintiff's fishing net. See Buck v. Runnels, ESC, 10-63. In order to bring any writ of trespass, a plaintiff had to prove that the defendant's use of "force and arms," Briggs v. Foster, BrCP, 3-73, was "against the peace of his Present Majesty. . . ." Ingersoll v. Johns, BeCP, 9-69. It was not necessary, however, for the plaintiff to prove any actual injury in order to recover damages. Cf. Gibbs. v. Higgins, HCP, 8-63 (sustaining declaration that set forth injuries only by way of recital instead of by positive averment). He could recover merely for being "robb'd and deprived of that peace, Satisfaction & Security [to] which every one of the leige Subjects had a right &c," Howell v. Pearson, CSC, 6-67, and for his "disgrace." Tyng v. Henshaw, SSC, 8-61. Accord, Martin

v. Welch, SSC, 8-63. A plaintiff could also recover in trespass for consequential as distinguished from immediate damages; damages were awarded, for example, for loss of wages due to injuries sustained from an assault, see Spooner v. Allen, WSC, 4-73, for the loss of a lawsuit as a result of the defendant's theft of the plaintiff's documents, see Bradford v. Crowningshield, supra, or for profits from a voyage lost as a result of the defendant's wrongful seizure of the plaintiff's ship. See Bailey v. Williams, CSC, 6-69; Treat v. Preble, BrSC, 10-64, modified, SSC, 8-65; Winslow v. Capen, SSC, 8-62.

57. Wroth and Zobel, *Legal Papers*, I, 84; Parsons, Precedents, no. 71. As in the plea of land, a plaintiff in trespass also had to describe the close by metes and bounds. See Fowle v. Wyman, Quincy 336 (1773); Sartell v. Parkhurst, MSC, 4-65; Foster v. Bradford, PCP, 12-67; Bagley v. Ring, ECP, 7-63. See also Ingersoll v. Hamlin, BeCP, 9-69 (writ abated for alleging that trespass occurred at two different places).

58. See Jordan v. Miller, CSC, 6-72; Bowdoin v. Branch, CSC, 6-70; Bowdoin v. Springer, CSC, 6-69; Case v. Ingersoll, BeCP, 4-64.

59. The execution that issued on a writ of trespass to which a defendant had pleaded proper soil and freehold gave only money damages and did not put the plaintiff back in seisin of the land. See the cases in note 58 above.

60. See Bryant v. Inhabitants of Chesterfield, HGS, 11-68. A plaintiff could elect the means by which he wanted process served, but once he had made his choice, service had to be by that means. A suit commenced by a capias, for example, would be dismissed if the officer making the service could find neither the defendant's estate nor his body, see Rogers v. Whitehand, ECP, 12-64, or if, instead of arresting the defendant, the officer merely summoned him and took security for his appearance. See Mansis v. Butters, ECP Files, 12-71. Cf. Barnes v. Greenleaf, Quincy 41 (1763). Service by capias was also insufficient if the officer attached real instead of personal property. See Sargent v. Bishop, ECP Files, 12-68. An action against an executor could not, of course, be commenced by a capias directing attachment of the fiduciary's personal estate or body. See Sprague v. Wing, PCP, 10-69. Service by summons, on the other hand, was defective if the summons itself was defective in that it failed to state the plaintiff's cause of action, see Gilbert v. Ulitt, WCP, 10-63; Newcomb v. Newland,

BrCP, 6-63, and the amount of damages demanded, see Gilbert v. Ulitt, supra, or in that it was not duly authenticated by the court. See Cheney v. Child, WCP, 10-63. A misnomer, however, did not invalidate a summons. See Ingales v. Hill, BrCP, 9-64, appeal dism., BrSC, 10-64. Service by summons was also defective if a valid summons was not properly served. Proper service required that the summons be left with the defendant at his residence or last usual place of abode. See Story v. Sawyer, ECP Files, 3-69; Page v. Nurse, WCP, 5-63. It was not sufficient for the officer merely to read the summons to the defendant. See Robinson v. Geyer, SCP Files, 10-72; Stow v. Wyman, MCP Files, 5-70.

61. See, e.g., Potamia v. Gould, MCP Files, 11-67; Boucher v. Stearns, MCP Files, 12-60; Wroth and Zobel, *Legal Papers*, I, 34, 36, 37, 42, 43, 51, 58, 60, 62, 65, 80.

62. See Hedden v. Noyes, ECP Files, 9-70; Farrow v. Wilson, MCP Files, 5-65; Wroth and Zobel, *Legal Papers*, I, 39, 41, 45, 47, 48, 55, 59, 63, 68, 79, 81, 84, 85. An officer could not be commanded to attach goods without also being commanded to take the defendant's body should no goods be found. See Eaton v. Hart, ECP, 3-66. A search through the pleadings book of John Adams, in Wroth and Zobel, *Legal Papers*, I, 31-86, and the pleadings book of Theophilus Parsons, in HLS, indicates that a plaintiff's attorney had the option in all writs of using a summons or a capias. See Laws of 1699, ch. 2. See also Hanlon v. Thayer, Quincy 99n2 (1764). Of 23 actions of debt recorded in the two books, for example, 12 were begun by a capias and 11 by a summons; of 63 actions of case, 51 by capias and 12 by summons; of 10 actions of trespass, 6 by capias and 4 by summons; and of 23 actions for the recovery of land, 1 by capias and 22 by summons. All 7 writs of convenant in the Parsons book were begun by capias, while the 3 actions of account in the two books were begun by summons. In actions of case one can find, in addition to practice by the bar, judicial statements and holdings sanctioning service either by summons alone, see Bartlett v. Kennedy, ECP, 3-67 (overruling plea that service by summons without attachment was defective), or by attachment alone. See Leonard v. Stetson, PSC, 5-65 (overruling plea that service by attachment without summons was defective); Blanchard v. Torney, MCP, 12-65 (noting that service on defaulting defendant was of the sort "where Estate only was attached . . .").

63. See Holden v. Holman, BeCP, 9-62.

Usually that officer was a sheriff or his deputy, but in suits under £ 10 a plaintiff could direct that service be made by a town constable instead. A constable, however, could not be used if the suit was for £ 10 or more. See Bragg v. Norwood, ECP, 3-71; Barry v. Mason, BrCP, 9-70, aff'd, BrSC, 10-70; Dike v. Alexander, ECP, 9-66, rev'd on default, ESC, 11-66; Brewer v. Brown, WCP, 2-64. If a sheriff or deputy was party to a suit, service was required to be made by a constable, but see Dewey v. Sackett, BeCP, 4-62, or if the suit was for more than £ 10, by a county coroner. See Nickols v. Wait, WSC, 9-64; Rowlee v. Sanford, BeCP, 2-69, rev'd on default, HSC, 9-69. See also Briggs v. Bennett, BrCP, 5-65 (writ abated since directed to improper officer). But a deputy sheriff resident in a town that was a party to an action could serve process. See Hopkins v. Inhabitants of Great Barrington, BeCP, 9-69.

64. A writ directed to one sheriff, for example, could not be served by another. See Willson v. Proprietors of Pejepscott, CSC, 6-67; Williams v. Fairfield, ECP, 7-69. A writ directed to a sheriff could not be served by a constable. See Reed v. Purrinton, PCP, 10-71; Norwood v. Pulcifer, ECP, 9-68. And a writ directed to a coroner could not be served by a deputy sheriff. See Jennison v. Stone, Suff. Files no. 152271 (Worc. 1767); Whitney v. Adams, BeCP, 2-69. A writ could, however, be directed to more than one officer if there was need to do so; such a need would arise, for example, in cases involving joint defendants living in different counties. See Williams v. Fosse, BrCP, 8-65.

65. See Laws of 1699, ch. 3, § 4. See generally Wroth and Zobel, Legal Papers, I, lxviii.

66. See Hodges v. Gilmore, BrSC, 10-65; Harwood v. Cragin, BeCP, 3-74; Ely v. Burbank, HCP, 5-67; Dole v. Tollansbee, ECP, 9-64. But see Fowler v. Barber, HCP, 5-62 (writ not abated when proper term of court was stated therein, but that term was slightly misdated).

67. A claim of improper joinder could be raised only by a plea in abatement, and failure to make such timely objection constituted a waiver thereof. See Keep v. Prescott, Cushing 7 (1773).

68. See Banks v. Jordan, CSC, 6-67; Ingersoll v. Baker, BeCP, 5-73; Ingersoll v. Read, BeCP, 9-66. Principal and surety could be sued as joint promissors. See Porter v. White, ECP, 3-63. Coexecutors and coadministrators were required to be joined. See Rogers v.

Orne, ECP, 3-64. It was not necessary, however, for the goods of all promissors to be attached. See Tripp v. Durfey, BrSC, 10-61 (reversing prior decision on undetermined grounds).

69. See Kent v. Pratt, HCP, 8-64, appeal dism., HSC, 9-64.

70. Wroth and Zobel, Legal Papers, I, 18.

71. See Daniels v. Bowin, WSC, 9-64.

72. See Wroth and Zobel, Legal Papers, II, 59, 61.

73. See ibid., I, 266, 268; Pennel v. Small, YSC, 6-64; Marston v. Coombs, ECP Files, 7-72; Fowler v. Sacket, HCP, 8-66. If one tenant in common died during the pendency of the action, the action survived to the remaining tenants. See Prescott v. Priest, Cushing 4 (1773).

74. See Choate v. Severy, ECP, 3-65.

75. See Perkins v. Goldthwait, HCP, 11-66.

76. See Graves v. King, BeCP, 9-68.

77. See Burns v. Flagg, CSC, 6-73; Swan v. Adams, ECP, 3-68.

78. See Hart v. Eaton, ESC, 11-66; Rex v. Sprague, HGS, 5-68.

79. See Flint v. Ingersoll, HCP, 8-63. Contra, Morey v. Richardson, BrCP, 9-62.

80. See Wheeler v. Cole, BrCP, 5-67. But see King v. Collins, EGS, 3-66, a criminal case in which the court refused to abate a writ containing a misnomer. English rules on misnomers were substantially the same as those in Massachusetts. See generally Henry Stephen, A Treatise on the Principles of Pleading in Civil Actions (London, 1824), 319.

81. See Atwater v. Merwin, BeCP, 5-74.

82. See Parsons v. Waunchnauncet, BeCP, 5-73; Mace v. Rogers, HCP, 8-67; Aldridge v. Prat, BrCP, 5-67; Cullar v. Wood, WCP, 11-64.

83. See Housatonneck Proprietors v. Williams, HSC, 9-71, affirming BeCP, 9-71.

84. For cases in which writs were abated because counties were not stated, see Younglove v. Fonda, BeCP, 9-70; Burghardt v. North, BeCP, 9-66; Fellows v. Campbell, WCP, 5-64; Lee v. Lee, ECP, 7-63. For cases in which the names of counties were misstated or misspelled, see Watson v. Ulley, HSC, 9-61; Bliss v. Mason, HCP, 8-70; Duboys v. Gelusiah, BeCP, 9-63. For cases in which the names of towns were misstated or misspelled, see Ballard v. McLean, Quincy 106 (1764); Brown v. Will, PSC, 5-60; Seymour v. Way, BeCP, 9-70; Griffin v. Hilyer, BeCP, 2-70, rev'd on default, HSC, 9-70; Perrigo v. Howard, PCP, 10-69; Hickok v. Spoor, BeCP, 9-69; Latham v. Turner, PCP, 12-66, rev'd on

default, PSC, 5-67; Blankinship v. Holmes, PCP, 10-66; Fonda v. Fitch, BeCP, 9-66; Cobb v. Soper, BrCP, 8-65; Flint v. Ingersoll, HCP, 8-63; Fuller v. Clark, MCP, 12-62; Fosbury v. Fuller, BeCP, 9-62, appeal dism., HSC, 9-63; Roberts v. Church, BeCP, 4-62. Cf. Warner v. Ramsdell, HCP, 8-69 (residence misstated); Russell v. Diamond, MCP Files, 5-69 (town and county not stated); Briggs v. Bennett, BrCP, 5-65 (county not stated and town misstated). But see Jackson v. Munro, BrCP, 11-66, where a writ in which the province was misspelled was not abated. The English rule, again, was the same as that in Massachusetts. See Turvil v. Aynsworth, 2 Ld. Raym. 1515, 92 Eng. Rep. 483 (K.B. 1728).

85. See Levi v. Page, ECP, 7-72, in which a plea in abatement to the effect that the defendant's residence was misstated with the result that he was not properly served was waived by consent.

86. See Cobb v. Soper, BrCP, 8-65 (dismissal for improper venue). On the requirement that at least one party in a transitory action be a resident of the county in which suit was brought, see Ward v. Carter, MCP, 9-71. See also Chapter 2, note 34.

87. See Wise v. Hight, YSC, 6-67 (plaintiff should be called gentleman, not yeoman); Homan v. Tucker, ECP, 12-66 (no allegation that plaintiff an administrator); Willmot v. Gray, BeCP, 9-63 (plaintiff should be called yeoman, not gentleman); Phelps v. Kellogg, HCP, 5-63 (plaintiff should be called gentleman, not esquire); Sumner v. Dudley, BeCP, 4-62 (plaintiff should be called yeoman, not gentleman).

88. Bromfield v. Lovejoy, Quincy 237 (1767) (defendant should be called gentleman, not yeoman); Pickard v. Lowell, ESC, 11-67 (defendant should be called tanner, not blacksmith); Pell v. Fellows, BeCP, 9-70 (defendant should be called gentleman, not yeoman); Wheelock v. Goodspeed, WCP, 8-69 (defendant should be called yeoman, not gentleman); Whiting v. Naunaumphtaunk, BeCP, 2-69 (defendant should be called gentleman, not yeoman); Rotch v. Brock, NCP, 3-68 (defendant should be called mariner, not gentleman); Ames v. Lathrop, SCP Files, 1-67 (defendant should be called blacksmith, not husbandman); Storer v. Twiss, ECP, 12-66 (defendant should be called administratrix, not executrix); Hickok v. Sheldon, BeCP, 9-65 (defendant should be called gentleman, not yeoman); Lee v. Martin, BeCP, 4-65 (defendant's addition not stated); Eames v. Hayward, MCP, 5-64, appeal dism., MSC, 4-65 (defendant should be called yeoman, not gen-

tleman); Cheney v. Child, WCP, 8-63 (defendant should be called laborer, not yeoman); Burbank v. Worster, HCP, 8-61 (defendant should be called spinster, not widow); Bumpas v. Whitten, PCP, 10-60 (defendant should be called laborer, not yeoman); Walker v. Colby, WCP, 5-60 (defendant should be called husbandman, not housewright). The rules concerning additions were applied even more strictly in England, where "names of dignity" as well as additions had to be written in proper form. See Stephen, Treatise, 320-321.

89. See King v. Miller, EGS, 3-74 (defendant should be called gentleman, not yeoman). For civil cases, see notes 87-88 above.

90. See Blower v. Campbell, Quincy 8 (1763).

91. See Bromfield v. Lovejoy, Quincy 237 (1767).

92. See Whiting v. Whiting, BeCP, 9-67 (plaintiff's testator should be called esquire, not gentleman).

93. See Zuill v. Bradley, Quincy 6 (1762); Goodspeed v. Gay, BaSC, 5-63; Trefrey v. Thaxter, SCP Files, 7-68; Fearing v. Pearce, PCP, 4-67; Thayer v. Brown, WCP, 8-62. In cases where two unrelated persons in the same town had the same name but the plaintiff failed to style one of them "the younger," see Ely v. Smith, HCP, 8-62, or "the second of that name," see Willson v. Luther, Suff. Files no. 145402 (Bris. 1768); Thomson v. Woolcot, Suff. Files no. 152195 (Worc. 1766), the possibility of confusion was as great as in cases involving identically named fathers and sons. The courts, however, were never clear as to whether the misnomer rule applied in such cases. In two cases they held it did, see Gifford v. Butter, BrCP, 12-72; Leonard v. Porter, BrCP, 5-67, but in others they ignored the purpose of the rule, applied existing custom rather narrowly, simply because it was custom, and refused to extend it to an analogous case. See Ballard v. McLean, Quincy 106 (1764). See also Willson v. Luther, supra; Thomson v. Woolcot, supra; Ely v. Smith, supra. Likewise, a court refused to abate a writ in which a plaintiff gave a defendant an improper alias, see Wheeler v. Cole, Suff. Files no. 145315 (Bris. 1767); here too there was potential for confusion, but the court again declined to look at whatever underlying rationale the misnomer rule may have had.

94. See Willson v. Luther, BrCP, 8-67; Deboys v. Bement, BeCP, 9-63. Cf. Leonard v. Porter, BrCP, 5-67 (abated for calling defendant "the second" when he was in fact "the third").

95. HGS, 5-71.

96. See Thyot v. Whitman, EGS, 7-70; Wroth and Zobel, *Legal Papers*, I, 320.

97. See Waldo v. Haskell, YSC, 7-65; Daniels v. Smith, SSC, 8-64; Dodge v. Manning, ECP, 9-67; How v. Manning, ECP, 3-66; Eday v. Phelps, BeCP, 4-64; Green v. Jones, WCP, 5-62. An endorsement by the defendant's rather than the plaintiff's attorney was insufficient. See Blood v. Blood, MCP, 3-62. In replevin a plaintiff also had to give a bond to prosecute his action. See Davis v. Smith, WCP, 11-61.

98. See Ingraham v. Cook, Quincy 4, 5 (1762) (new endorser required whenever "it could be made to appear to the Court that there was Danger the present Indorser could not answer Costs").

99. See Smith v. Moody, HSC, 9-64; Clark v. Moody, HSC, 9-64; Dwight v. Spencer, HCP Files, 2-60. Cf. Volentine v. Stephens, BrCP, 12-64 (abated for improper date of teste).

100. See Bacon v. Hayward, WCP, 5-67; Brown v. Rowley, BeCP, 9-64.

101. See Powell v. Pettit, HSC, 9-60, reversing HCP Files, 2-60.

102. See Hayward v. Lothrop, BrSC, 10-68; Wroth and Zobel, *Legal Papers*, I, 33n22.

103. See Hayward v. Lothrop, BrSC, 10-68; Gilbert v. Chace, BrCP, 12-73; Thayer v. Thayer, WCP, 5-62, appeal dism., WSC, 9-62. But see Spencer v. Cooley, HCP Files, 5-61, appeal dism., HSC, 9-61.

104. See Smith v. Moody, HSC, 9-64 (abated for saying in one part of writ that cattle "distrained" and in another part that cattle "detained"); Clark v. Moody, HSC, 9-64 (abated on same ground); Bowen v. Kelley, BrCP, 3-74 (abated for variance between writ in account and declaration in case); Rowley v. Sheldon, BeCP, 2-70 (abated for repugnancy in description of land).

105. See Paddock v. Pratt, PCP, 10-68. But see Gager v. Mattoon, HCP, 11-60, and HCP, 2-61, appeal dism., HSC, 9-62 (overruling plea alleging variance).

106. See Cobb v. Barstow, BrCP, 12-60. Cf. Burnal v. Gwin, NCP, 3-70 (abated since no account annexed to writ).

107. See Ashley v. Ashley, BeCP, 2-71, appeal dism., HSC, 4-71. However, if there was a constructional issue whether a will was consistent with a writ, the will was admitted into evidence so that the jury could construe it. See Gibbs v. Gibbs, Quincy 251 (1767).

108. Taylor, *Western Massachusetts*, 103-115, 128-136.

109. The chief effect of technical pleading rules was the reinstitution of suits. See note

29 above and accompanying text. But this did not produce any significant added income for lawyers, since lawyers' fees were quite low. For a discussion of various costs of litigation, see Wroth and Zobel, *Legal Papers*, I, lxix-lxxii.

110. Court Rule, WSC, 9-76, copied in note appended to Briscoe v. Gale, MSJC, 10-89, in Francis Dana, Minute Books.

111. See Gage v. Noyes, ECP, 4-84, plea in abatement withdrawn, ESJC, 6-84 (abated for improper addition); Gerrish v. Carr, ECP, 4-82 (abated on same ground); Mackintire v. Jones, WCP, 12-81 (abated on same ground); Parks v. Sacket, HCP, 11-83 (abated for improperly describing self as administrator of the "Rights & Credits" rather than the "Goods & Chattels" of decedent and for senseless language in writ and failure to aver date of note); Hammond v. Delano, PCP, 4-83 (abated for not pursuing register of writs).

112. Laws of 1784, ch. 28, §14.

113. Rules on joinder of parties remained exceedingly complex and technical. See generally the editor's note in Converse v. Symmes, 10 Mass. 377, 379 (1813). Some of the basic rules were as follows. (1) In contract actions, joint promissors and joint promissees all had to be joined, see Drury v. Baxter, SCP, 4-25; Belcher v. Ward, WCP, 3-25, appeal dism., WSJC, 10-26; Shaw v. Bottom, WCP, 3-25; Allen v. Wing, PCP, 8-16, aff'd by referees, PSJC, 10-16; Adams v. Savage, SCP, 7-16; Kearney v. McCullock, SCP, 9-12, even if the plaintiff had no knowledge of the existence of the joint promissor. See Niles v. Prescott, WSJC, 9-02. (2) However, administrators had to be sued in their representative rather than their personal capacity, see Francis v. Wynn, ECP, 7-82, appeal dism., ESJC, 6-83, and therefore an administrator could not join with a surviving promissee to recover on a contract right of the decedent. Smith v. Franklin, 1 Mass. 480 (1805); Walker v. Maxwell, 1 Mass. 104, 112-113 (1804). (3) Persons with a subsidiary interest in a contract right could not join with the principal promissee to enforce the right. Grozier v. Atwood, 4 Pick. 234 (1826); Baxter v. Rodman, 3 Pick. 435, 438-439 (1826). (4) Joint tortfeasors did not have to be joined in a single action, see Mitchell v. Keith, PCP, 10-89, and they could not be joined if only one of them had actually committed the tort and the other's liability was of a derivative nature. Campbell v. Phelps, 1 Pick. 62, 66-67 (1822). (5) Joint victims of a personal tort could not join, since their injuries were of a separate rather than joint nature. Baker v. Jewell, 6 Mass. 460 (1810)

(dictum). (6) Coowners of property, on the other hand, were required to join in suits brought to recover for tortious damage to the property. See Daniels v. Daniels, 7 Mass. 135 (1810); Derby v. Harraden, ECP, 7-79. See also Thompson v. Hoskins, 11 Mass. 419 (1814). (7) Tenants in common, however, could not join to recover the property itself, see Inhabitants of Rehoboth v. Hunt, 1 Pick. 224, 228 (1822); other joint owners could but did not need to join in suits to recover their property. Oxnard v. Proprietors of Kennebeck Purchase, 10 Mass. 179 (1813). (8) Joint guardians could maintain suit together. Shearman v. Akins, 4 Pick. 282, 291-292 (1826). (9) Parties who had once been joined could not thereafter be severed for causes such as want of evidence of their joint liability, see Converse v. Symmes, 10 Mass. 377 (1813), Brett v. Proprietors of West Shore, PSJC, 5-90; disability, see Oxnard v. Proprietors of Kennebeck Purchase, supra, or death. Cutts v. Haskins, 11 Mass. 56 (1814). A settlement by a defendant with one of several joint plaintiffs did not, however, preclude the maintenance of suit by the others. Baker v. Jewell, 6 Mass. 460 (1810).

114. Baker v. Jewell, 6 Mass. 460, 462 (1810).

115. See Sherman v. Proprietors of Connecticut River Bridge, 11 Mass. 338 (1814).

116. See Kincaid v. Howe, 10 Mass. 203 (1813); Holcomb v. Root, HCP, 5-92. Cf. Atkins v. Sawyer 1 Pick. 351, 353-354 (1823) (dictum) (permitting amendment of judgment rendered "against the administrator" to read "against the goods and estate of the intestate").

117. See generally Samuel Howe, Lectures on the Practice of the Courts, 115-116 (in HLS).

118. All such motions of which there is a record were denied. See Clark v. Lowe, 15 Mass. 476 (1819); Little v. Putnam, WCP, 6-06; Hooper v. Clark, WCP, 6-06; Brimmer v. Hussey, ECP, 9-90; Lynde v. Eppes, ECP, 9-85.

119. See Bowers v. Brown, BrCP, 6-80.

120. See Blood v. Harrington, 8 Pick. 552 (1829).

121. See Richmond v. Shearman, BeCP, 8-06, appeal dism., BeSJC, 9-06; Howe, Lectures, 118, citing Ripley v. Warren, 2 Pick. 592 (1824). Contra, Hall v. Jones, 9 Pick. 446 (1830); Richardson v. Mooney, MCP Files, 3-18.

122. See Danielson v. Andrews, 1 Pick. 156 (1822). But see Yale v. Oliver, MCP Files, 9-25.

123. See Holmes v. Holmes, 2 Pick. 23 (1823) (error in allegation of length of seisin); Cumings v. Rawson, 7 Mass. 440 (1811) (error in description of close). Mere technical informalities often did not even require amendment. See Kennedy v. Carpenter, SCP, 7-28 (failure to allege notice of assignment of lease); Arey v. Wetmore, SCP, 1-97, aff'd, SSJC, 2-97 (failure to allege consideration for promise or time at which payment promised); Jenks v. Ward, ECP, 9-89 (failure to allege that plaintiff in trespass was in the peace of the Commonwealth when assault occurred).

124. See Swan v. Nesmith, 7 Pick. 220, 224-225 (1828); Clark v. Lamb, 6 Pick. 512, 515 (1828); Ball v. Claflin, 5 Pick. 303, 304-305 (1827); Tappan v. Austin, 1 Mass. 31 (1804); Howe, Lectures, 113-114. Cf. Parker v. Parker, 17 Mass. 376, 379 (1821); Cane v. Wetmore, HSJC, 9-94, in Dana, Minute Books (permitting plaintiff to introduce evidence without necessity of amending declaration to conform it thereto, since declaration gave adequate notice of claim). The mere addition of a new count would not discharge the bail or deprive the plaintiff of his priority over subsequent attaching creditors, see Miller v. Clark, 8 Pick. 412 (1829) (dictum); Ball v. Claflin, supra, at 305, unless the count was for a new cause of action. See Putnam v. Hall, 3 Pick. 445 (1826); Willis v. Crooker, 1 Pick. 204 (1822).

125. See Pratt v. Bacon, 10 Pick. 123, 128 (1830); Vancleef v. Therasson, 3 Pick. 12 (1825); Holbrook v. Gould NfCP, 9-28. Thus amendment would be denied if the original writ contained no count or declaration, see Rathbone v. Rathbone, 5 Pick. 221 (1827); Brigham v. Este, 2 Pick. 420, 424-425 (1823); Gates v. Whitney, SCP, 10-25, appeal dism., SSJC, 11-25, or if the proposed count was one that could not originally have been joined to the existing count. See Mason v. Waite, 1 Pick. 452 (1823) (by implication).

126. See Briscoe v. Gale, MSJC, 10-89, in Dana, Minute Books. See also Petition of Gardner, NCP, 10-29, overruling an objection to a proposed amendment of a writ of execution on the ground that substantive rights would be affected thereby.

127. Stanwood v. Scovel, 4 Pick. 422 (1827); Williams v. Hingham & Quincy Bridge & Tpke. Corp., 4 Pick. 341, 349 (1826).

128. Babcock v. Thompson, 3 Pick. 446, 449 (1826) (dictum). See also Ball v. Hopkinton Cotton Mfg. Co., MSJC, 10-20 (amendment ordered in eminent domain case of description of land in jury venire).

129. See Adams v. Hill, 1 Pick. 461

(1823); Thatcher v. Miller, 13 Mass. 270, 271 (1816) (dictum); Welles v. Battelle, 11 Mass. 477, 481 (1814) (dictum); Campbell v. Stiles, 9 Mass. 217 (1812); Hearsey v. Bradbury, 9 Mass. 95 (1812); Swan v. French, SSJC, 2-89, in Dana, Minute Books. But amendments by officers did not affect the rights of persons not party to the suit if those rights were acquired prior to the amendment. Emerson v. Upton, 9 Pick. 167 (1829). Cf. Williams v. Brackett, 8 Mass. 240 (1811) (officer could not amend return in suit between parties other than the ones involved in the former action). Of course, a technical defect was still fatal if the officer failed to amend his writ. See Ward v. Brigham, MCP Files, 3-09; Reed v. Morris, WCP, 9-03, rev'd on default, WSJC, 9-03; Brown v. Vorce, WCP, 8-93, Clark v. Clark, MCP, 3-90. See also Commonwealth v. Parker, 2 Pick. 550, 561 (1824) (constable permitted to amend jury venire); Badlam v. Tucker, 1 Pick. 389, 391, 395-396 (1823) (use of trustee writ in which name of trustee left blank not fatal in suit brought only against original debtor).

130. See Lane v. Vernon, SSJC, 2-87, overruling an exception to a verdict on the ground that the deputy sheriff who served the writ had taken his oath of office before one justice of the peace instead of two justices quorum unus.

131. Basic rules as to service of process were not changed, however, in the postrevolutionary period. Normally actions had to be commenced either by summons or capias, see Laws of 1784, ch. 28; Whitney v. Bigelow, WCP, 12-24, aff'd, WSJC, 10-26, although in exceptional cases the two forms of writ could be combined into one. See Cooke v. Gibbs, 3 Mass. 193 (1807) (opinion of Parsons, C.J.); Bullard v. Ware, MCP Files, 12-17. Contra, Peirce v. Cody, WCP, 8-93, appeal dism., WSJC, 9-93. If the service was by attachment, it was essential that actual valuable property of the defendant was attached; otherwise the service was invalid. For examples of such invalid service, see Bridge v. Marshall, MCP Files, 5-98, aff'd, MSJC, 4-00 ("a hat the property of the within named" defendant attached); Harrington v. Reed, MCP Files, 3-93 ("a log of wood" attached); Baker v. Baker, SCP Files, 4-84 (heir's interest in undistributed realty attached); Sprague v. Mansfield, SCP Files, 4-80 ("a certain note of hand" attached); Warren v. Mansfield, SCP Files, 1-80 ("public bills of credit of the United States" attached); Maynard v. Rice, MCP Files, 3-79 (goods "reputed to be Estate of" defendant attached). Moreover, service by

attachment had to be accompanied by actual notice to the defendant. See Farr v. Barrows, LSJC, 7-94. If service was by summons, it was insufficient simply to read the summons, see Spaulding v. Inhabitants of Charlestown, MCP Files, 9-90; it was necessary to leave the summons at the defendant's last usual and permanent abode, see Richardson v. Judd, SCP Files, 4-24 (leaving summons at temporary abode and mailing it to permanent abode unsatisfactory), even if the building had been destroyed, see Brown v. Hurlbut, BeCP, 3-90, but not if the defendant was an absent and absconding debtor in a suit pursuant to the trustee act. See Gold v. Stone, BeCP, 9-88. A return on a writ that the defendant could not be found within the server's precinct was, of course, an insufficient return, see Sullivan v. Gragg, MCP Files, 9-90; Otis v. Claflin, SCP Files, 7-83; Wait v. Fecham, SCP Files, 4-83; Phillips v. Farewell, SCP Files, 4-83; Hatch v. Newell, SCP Files, 4-83; as was a return that the defendant upon arrest paid the debt in full, see Cunningham v. Felton, SCP Files, 4-83, or was released at the creditor's command upon a part payment. See Webster v. Waite, SCP Files, 1-80.

132. Shearer v. Tappan, BeCP, 4-98. Such notice was a requisite of "natural justice" as well as of legislation. Clap v. Joslyn, 1 Mass. 129 (1804) (opinion of Sedgwick, J.). Accord, Inhabitants of Lancaster v. Pope, 1 Mass. 86 (1804).

133. See Taunton & Boston Tpke. Corp. v. Whiting, BrCP, 3-10.

134. See Foster v. Baldwin, 2 Mass. (Supp.) 569 (1786); Legate v. Porter, Cushing 80 (1786); Swan v. French, SSJC, 2-89, in Dana, Minute Books; Bright v. Henderson, MCP, 11-85.

135. See Barden v. Crocker, 10 Pick. 383, 390-391 (1830). Cf. Thompson v. Crocker, 9 Pick. 59 (1829).

136. Briggs v. Nantucket Bank, 5 Mass. 94, 96 (1809).

137. Kincaid v. Howe, 10 Mass. 203, 205 (1813).

138. Ripley v. Warren, 2 Pick. 592, 594 (1824). Accordingly, the court held that "all dilatory pleas, or those which amount only to an exception to the form of the process, are required to be exposed to the view of the court in the first stage," ibid., 594, when the plaintiff still had a right to amend, and that failure to make timely objection constituted a waiver thereof. See Prescott v. Tufts, 7 Mass. 209 (1810); Gilbert v. Nantucket Bank, 5 Mass. 97 (1809); Cleveland v. Welsh, 4 Mass. 591 (1808); Livermore v. Boswell, 4 Mass.

437 (1808); Whiting v. Hollister, 2 Mass. 102 (1806); Barrell v. Farley, MSJC, 4-89. Cf. Smith v. Bowker, 1 Mass. 76 (1804). But see Rathbone v. Rathbone, 4 Pick. 89 (1826) (objection of which defendant lacked notice not waived by delay).

139. See Haggins v. Henderson, SSJC, 2-93, 8-93 in Dana, Minute Books; Williams v. Gore, SSJC, 2-92, ibid.; Henderson v. Bethume, SSJC, 2-91, ibid.

140. Watson v. Robinson, HCP, 8-89.

141. See Harris v. Fullam, WCP, 3-07 (demurrer for joining count in tort for injuring plaintiff's horse and count in contract for not paying for it sustained); Barker v. Burrell, SCP, 7-05 (plaintiff in trespass nonsuited for joining to writ declaration lying in case); Schermerhorn v. Willard, BeCP, 1-97, appeal dism., BeSJC, 10-98 (demurrer for joining claims on bond and promissory note sustained); Codman v. Henderson, SCP, 7-89, rev'd on default, SSJC, 2-90 (abated for joining counts against sheriff in tort for not serving writ and in contract for breach of promise to serve it). But two varieties of the same form of action, such as trover, a variety of case, and case, could be joined. See Ayer v. Bartlett, 9 Pick. 156, 161 (1829).

142. See Lienow v. Ritchie, 8 Pick. 235 (1829); Jones v. Hoar, 5 Pick. 285 (1827); Lane v. Smith, 2 Pick. 281 (1824); Hayden v. Shed, 11 Mass. 500 (1814); Agry v. Young, 11 Mass. 220 (1814); Bangoree v. Hovey, 5 Mass. 11, 24-26 (1809); Adams v. Hemmenway, 1 Mass. 145 (1804). But cf. White v. Moseley, 8 Pick. 356 (1829); Wiswall v. Austin, WCP, 3-88, rev'd on other grounds, WSJC, 9-88 (debt proper form of action for statutory penalty for usury).

143. Lovell v. Francis, NCP, 3-03.

144. Bigelow v. Barker, NCP, 5-16.

145. As to lateness of objection, see Whitney v. Russell, MSJC, 12-82 (motion in arrest of judgment overruled in "plea of taking imprisoning and detaining" the plaintiff); Sacket v. Bishop, HdCP, 11-22 (overruling motion in arrest for suing in case rather than trespass in wagon collision case); Maynard v. Currant, SCP, 7-06 (overruling motion in arrest for joining causes of action for breach of contract and for statutory penalty). But see Paul v. Frazer, SCP, 1-07, aff'd, SSJC, 3-07 (granting motion in arrest for failure to state a cause of action).

146. Coe v. Cornwall, HCP, 8-01, appeal dism., HSJC, 5-02.

147. Lumbart v. Washbourn, DCP, 10-97.

148. King v. Sykes, HCP, 5-83. Accord, Shaw v. Billings, HCP, 5-95; Phelps v. Munroe,

HCP, 1-93; Pearce v. Bucklin, BrCP, 9-81, rev'd on default, BrSJC, 10-81.

149. See Corsa v. Noble, BeSJC, 10-99; Lumbert v. Hoyt, NCP, 10-04; Porter v. Atwater, HCP, 11-98; Sumner v. Lackor, HCP, 9-98.

150. Remington v. Palmer, HSJC, 9-11. Accord, Barney v. Mason, BrSJC, 10-99; Wheelock v. Tupper, NCP, 10-83. See also Divol v. Gibbs, BrSJC, 11-82 ("Case for trover").

151. Nosavet v. Stat, DCP, 10-88.

152. Athearn v. Hancock, DCP, 10-93.

153. Sewell v. Sawyer, HCP, 5-04.

154. See Ewer v. Handy, NCP, 10-01; Luce v. Volintin, DCP, 4-98; Sears v. Easton, HCP, 2-85.

155. See Jenkins v. Brewster, HSJC, 9-17; Williams v. Sampson, SSJC, 8-87; Parkman v. Jefferson, SCP, 10-21; Swett v. Poor, ECP, 9-13, aff'd, ESJC, 11-14; Hinckley v. George, NCP, 3-00; Taylor v. Eustis, SCP, 7-98, aff'd, SSJC, 8-99. Cf. Clary v. Parling, WSJC, 4-85 (case on an agreement "in imitation of a Penal obligation").

156. See Norton v. Norton, DCP, 4-94; Harris v. Fuller, HCP, 8-78.

157. See White v. Jewett, HCP, 1-99, rev'd on default, HSJC, 9-00. Cf. Wood v. Vose, NCP, 3-93 (case for assault); Bradford v. Stark, BrCP, 9-77 (case for assault), rev'd on other grounds, BrSC, 10-78 (where writ was labeled as trespass).

158. See Penniman v. Shaw, SCP, 4-10 (joining counts against sheriff for tort for not serving writ and for breach of promise to serve it). Cf. Mixer v. Johnson, WCP, 12-90 (joining debt and case for recovery of statutory penalty).

159. Jones v. Hoar, 5 Pick. 285n (1827).

160. Some of the departures, however, can be attributed to their carelessness. See, e.g., Parkman v. Jefferson, SCP, 10-21 (writ of case on a bond, to which the defendant pleaded that he owed nothing, the proper plea to a writ of debt on a bond); Lumbart v. Washbourn, DCP, 10-97 ("Plea of the for the Recovery" of certain nails). In the former action, a clerk probably substituted the word "case" for "debt"; in the latter, a clerk probably left out the name of the action.

161. See, e.g., Coe v. Cornwall, HCP, 8-01, appeal dism., HSJC, 5-02 ("a plea of Grievous complaint" brought by George Bliss, Esq.); King v. Sykes, HCP, 5-83 ("a Plea for not performing his promise" brought by Moses Bliss, Esq.).

162. SCP, 7-98, aff'd, SSJC, 8-99.

163. See note 183 below.

164. See Chapter 9, note 30.

165. See Richards v. Killam, 10 Mass. 239 (1813); Kimball v. Tucker, 10 Mass. 192 (1813); Bangoree v. Hovey, 5 Mass. 11, 24-26 (1809) (dissenting opinion).

166. See Bangoree v. Hovey, 5 Mass. 11, 26-33 (1809) (dissenting opinion).

167. See Reed v. Davis, 8 Pick. 514, 516 (1829) (dictum); Peirce v. Spring, 15 Mass. 489 (1819).

168. See Reed v. Davis, 8 Pick. 514 (1829); Jeffrey v. Blue-Hill Tpke. Corp., 10 Mass. 368 (1813); Bigelow v. Cambridge & Concord Tpke. Corp., 7 Mass. 202 (1810).

169. See Peabody v. Hoyt, SCP, 4-11, rev'd on other grounds, SSJC, 3-13; Scales v. Williams, MCP, 12-05, appeal dism., MSJC, 10-06; Brooks v. Stow, WCP, 8-90.

170. See Bigelow v. Jones, 10 Pick. 161, 165 (1830) (dictum).

171. See Cole v. Fisher, 11 Mass. 137 (1814) (by implication).

172. See Jones v. Harraden, Cushing 62 (1784).

173. See M'Millan v. Eastman, 4 Mass. 378, 382 (1808).

174. See Grinnell v. Phillips, 1 Mass. 530, 538 (1805) (allowing trespass as a remedy). See also Campbell v. Phelps, 1 Pick. 62, 69 (1822) (dictum that Grinnell v. Phillips was the first instance in which trespass instead of case was held a proper remedy). But see Campbell v. Phelps, 17 Mass. 244 (1821) (holding trespass to be the sole remedy), criticized at 246n8.

175. 11 Mass. 137 (1814).

176. Ibid., 139. Accord, Cummings v. Noyes, 10 Mass. 433, 436 (1813).

177. Boodin v. Ellis, 7 Mass. 507, 508-509 (1811).

178. Constitution of 1780, Part I, art. 11, in Handlin and Handlin, *Popular Sources*, 444.

179. Cooke v. Gibbs, 3 Mass. 193, 196 (1807).

180. For an example of pleading without writ, see Hubbard v. Hubbard, 6 Mass. 397 (1810). See also Ross v. Ross, NCP, 10-93, a suit in which a wife without writ "complain[ed] against" her husband that he beat and threatened her, forcing her to flee. The suit was apparently transferred to General Sessions, which committed the husband to the house of correction. See generally Howe, Lectures, 22-24.

181. Third Parish in Dedham v. Gay, NfCP, 9-96.

182. See Eddy v. Oliver, LSJC, 6-95 (jury verdict of guilty in part); Metcalf v. Rawson,

SSJC, 2-89 (jury verdict of guilty); Davenport v. Lamson, WCP, 12-03, appeal dism., WSJC, 4-06 (jury verdict of not guilty); Pearley v. Bagley, ECP, 10-99, aff'd, ESJC, 11-00 (plea of not guilty upheld below and jury verdict of not guilty on appeal); Thayer v. Wallack, SCP, 1-91, aff'd, SSJC, 8-91 (same plea upheld below and same verdict on appeal); Barker v. Story, SCP, 1-89, appeal dism., SSJC, 8-89 (plea of not guilty upheld); Winslow v. Sears, WCP, 9-87, rev'd on other grounds, WSJC, 9-87 (plea of not guilty upheld below and then waived on appeal, where jury found defendant was indebted).

183. Stilson v. Tobey, 2 Mass. 521 (1807). One difference between the pleas was that on a plea of not indebted the jury awarded the penalty, whereas the court did so on a plea of not guilty. Commonwealth v. Stevens, 15 Mass. 195 (1818).

184. See Allen v. Carter, WSJC, 9-92 (jury verdict of not guilty); Hatch v. Hatch, SCP, 7-04 (plea of not guilty upheld). But see Joselyn v. Hudley, PCP, 4-93 (plea of not guilty rejected).

185. See Storer v. Stowell, SCP, 7-94, aff'd, SSJC, 8-95 (plea of not guilty upheld below; jury verdict of not indebted on appeal). Cf. Holker v. Bulfinch, SCP, 1-94 (plea of never promised upheld in writ of debt).

186. Compare Willard v. Flagg, WCP, 6-74 (case; plea of never promised upheld); Loring v. Loring, PCP, 10-72 (debt; plea of not indebted upheld); with Atkins v. Russell, ECP, 9-68 (case; plea of not by law chargeable rejected); Parsons v. Kinsman, ECP, 12-74 (debt; plea of never requested to pay rejected).

187. See Besom v. Grant, ECP, 4-94. Cf. Wilkins v. Wilkins, ECP, 10-97, appeal dism., ESJC, 6-98 (plea of payment upheld).

188. See Rogers v. Adams, PCP, 8-00, rev'd on other grounds, PSJC, 6-01 (plea of not guilty upheld below; jury verdict that defendant took goods on appeal); Howe v. Symmes, SCP, 4-99, rev'd on other grounds, SSJC, 2-00 (plea of not guilty upheld below; jury verdict of property in plaintiff on appeal); Soul v. Winthrop, SCP, 7-93, aff'd, SSJC, 8-93 (plea of not guilty upheld below; jury verdict of property in defendants on appeal).

189. That plaintiffs retained the right to plead to the specific form of action, see Miller v. Hartshorne, SSJC, 2-99 (jury verdict in replevin that property not in plaintiff); Kirkwood v. Prout, CSJC, 6-93 (jury verdict in writ of debt that defendant was indebted); Butman v. Hutson, ESJC, 6-92 (jury verdict in

replevin that property was not in third person as alleged by defendant); Benson v. Bell, SCP, 1-06 (upholding plea in replevin of never took); Rice v. Brigham, WCP, 8-00, appeal dism., WSJC, 9-00 (jury verdict of not guilty in writ of case for statutory penalty); Dutch v. Mighill, ECP, 4-99, appeal dism., ESJC, 6-99 (upholding plea of never promised in writ of case against executor); Townsend v. Fayerweather, MCP, 3-99, rev'd on default, MSJC, 4-01 (upholding plea of never promised to similar writ).

190. See Winsor v. Rich, PSJC, 10-10; Stearns v. Barrett, SCP, 10-21; Peck v. Jackson, SCP, 10-99, appeal dism. SSJC, 8-00; Winsor v. Edes, PCP, 4-99; Vaughan v. Woods, SCP, 7-98, rev'd by referees, SSJC, 2-99; Wady v. Tallman, BrCP, 3-92.

191. See Kent v. Woodward, SCP, 1-04; Sullivan v. Blake, SCP, 1-00, rev'd on default, SSJC, 8-00. Cf. Pynes v. Allen, PCP, 4-14, appeal dism., PSJC, 10-14 (plea of never promised upheld in action of account).

192. See Frothingham v. Soley, SCP, 1-99, appeal dism., SSJC, 2-00; Coffin v. Folger, NCP, 3-97; Bordman v. Stewart, SCP, 10-91, rev'd on default, SSJC, 2-92; Moore v. Titcomb, ECP, 4-88; Rogerson v. Howard, SCP, 1-88; Winslow v. Pitcher, PCP, 4-82. Cf. Devens v. Bryant, SCP, 1-89, rev'd on default, SSJC, 2-89 (plea of non est factum upheld).

193. See Alden v. Milikan, CSJC, 6-93.

194. See Quincy v. Shaw, SCP, 7-95.

195. Apparently, however, there was some recognition during the 1790s of subcategories within the general category of contract. In particular, it appears that debt, covenant, and indebitatus assumpsit were regarded as one subcategory distinct from another subcategory of special assumpsit, for while pleas of not guilty became proper in writs of debt, see Lindsey v. House, PCP, 4-00, appeal dism., PSJC, 6-01; Storer v. Stowell, SCP, 7-94, aff'd, SSJC, 8-95 (plea of not guilty upheld below; jury verdict of not defendant's deed on appeal), covenant, see Drew v. Edes, PCP, 4-01, appeal dism., PSJC, 6-01; Beals v. Barrow, SSJC, 8-91 (jury verdict of guilty); Bolter v. Proprietors of Hay market Theater, SCP, 4-98, appeal dism., SSJC, 2-99; Smith v. Knoepsel, SCP, 7-97, aff'd, SSJC, 2-98 (plea of not guilty upheld below; special verdict on appeal); Villiers v. Tyler, SCP, 7-95; Shaw v. Jackson, SCP, 7-95, aff'd, SSJC, 8-96 (plea of not guilty upheld below; jury verdict of did not keep covenant on appeal); and indebitatus assumpsit, see Barnard v. Hulbert, BeCP, 1-03,

appeal dism., BeSJC, 5-04; Walter v. Guppy, SCP, 7-99, rev'd by referees, SSJC, 2-00; Endicot v. Sumner, SCP, 7-89, aff'd, SSJC, 2-90 (plea of not guilty upheld below; jury verdict of never promised on appeal), where no promise on the part of the defendant needed to be proved by the plaintiff and where, consequently, a plea of never promised would have been inappropriate on the facts. Pleas of not guilty were throughout the 1790s held inappropriate on writs of special assumpsit, see Frothingham v. Patten SCP, 1-94; Storer v. Wilder, SCP, 1-93; Read v. Shearman, BrCP, 3-91, where a promise on the part of the defendant did have to be proved by the plaintiff and a plea of never promised was therefore appropriate.

196. See Wheeler v. Russell, 17 Mass. 258, 281 (1821); Russell v. DeGrand, 15 Mass. 35 (1818); Allen v. Shearman, BrCP, 12-07.

197. See Knapp v. Lee, 3 Pick. 452, 457 (1826).

198. Fowler v. Shearer, 7 Mass. 14, 22 (1810). Accord, Boutell v. Cowdin, 9 Mass. 254 (1812); Bliss v. Negus, 8 Mass. 46 (1811). See also Hill v. Buckminster, 5 Pick. 391 (1827), holding that a note given in renewal of a note that was void for want of consideration was also void; Whitcomb v. Williams, 4 Pick. 228 (1826), permitting a maker of a note who failed to raise a defense of want of consideration in a suit on the note to maintain a new suit to recover the money paid on the note. Contra, Stackpole v. Arnold, 11 Mass. 27, 32 (1814).

199. See Chapter 3, notes 102-103 and accompanying text.

200. See Hemmenway v. Hickes, 4 Pick. 497, 500 (1827).

201. Micah v. Clap, HSJC, 5-92, in Dana, Minute Books. See also Lyman v. Leavitt, HSJC, 9-99, ibid., where the defendant maker of a promissory note argued that "the want of such Cons[ideration] prevent[ed] the Indorsee the Pl[ain]t[iff]: from recovering in this Action."

202. Sumner v. Williams, 8 Mass. 162, 191 (1811).

203. See Grew v. Burditt, 9 Pick. 265 (1830); Bartlett v. Skinner, WCP, 8-30.

204. See Page v. Trufant, MCP, 9-00.

205. Parker v. Mather, MSJC, 4-92, in Dana, Minute Books.

206. See Pierce v. Woodward, 6 Pick. 206 (1828); Palmer v. Stebbins, 3 Pick. 188, 193 (1825); Perkins v. Lyman, 9 Mass. 522, 530 (1813); Pierce v. Fuller, 8 Mass. 223, 226

(1811).

207. See Davenport v. Mason, 15 Mass. 85, 92 (1818); Sumner v. Williams, 8 Mass. 162, 188 (1811).

208. Stearns v. Barrett, 1 Pick. 443, 448-449n (1823).

209. Upham v. Smith, 7 Mass. 265, 266 (1811). Accord, Mitchell v. Kingman, 5 Pick. 431, 433 (1827) (by implication).

210. Page v. Trufant, 2 Mass. 159, 162 (1806) (opinion of Parsons, C.J.).

211. Ibid., 162.

212. See note 208 above and accompanying text.

213. See Harris v. Newell, 8 Mass. 262 (1811); Caswell v. Wendell, 4 Mass. 108, 110 (1808); Bickford v. Page, 2 Mass. 455, 461 (1807); Marston v. Hobbs, 2 Mass. 433, 440 (1807).

214. See Munroe v. Perkins, 9 Pick. 298, 303-305 (1830); Randall v. Rich, 11 Mass. 494 (1814). See also Bacon v. Kingman, BeCP, 9-83 (new agreement pleaded in protestando, but plea never brought to issue).

215. See Howe v. Mackay, 5 Pick. 44, 50 (1827).

216. See Pepoon v. Porter, HSJC, 9-95 (jury verdict that deputy not guilty); Greenleaf v. Sibley, WSJC, 4-92 (jury verdict that deputy guilty); Brown v. Henderson, SSJC, 2-92 (jury verdict that deputy guilty of neglect of duty); Hurd v. Henderson, SSJC, 2-88 (jury verdict that deputy guilty in part); Hills v. Baldwin, MSJC, 10-87 (jury verdict that deputy guilty); Brown v. Hyde, BeSJC, 10-85 (jury verdict of not guilty in writ of case against sheriff that included allegation that the sheriff had promised to serve an execution); Brooks v. Burroughs, SCP, 1-99 (plea of never promised upheld); Sloane v. Henderson, SCP, 10-91 (plea that sheriff not liable for deputy's promises and that deputy never promised upheld).

217. See Wood v. Wood, SSJC, 11-08 (jury verdict that defendant promised); Child v. Merry, SSJC, 2-99 (same verdict); Fisk v. Caldwell, WSJC, 4-98 (jury verdict of guilty); Niles v. Prince, SSJC, 2-94 (jury verdict that defendant promised); Hulbert v. Houghton, FCP, 8-15 (jury verdict of not guilty on plea of never promised); Pinkham v. Griffin, SCP, 7-07 (jury verdict of not guilty); Pope v. Godshall, ECP, 6-05 (plea of never promised upheld); Cushing v. Davis, 3-05, appeal dism., ESJC, 4-05 (plea of not guilty upheld); Niles v. Capt, SCP, 10-96, appeal dism., SSJC, 2-97 (same plea upheld); Evans v. Linkon, BrCP,

12-84 (jury verdict on plea of not guilty).

218. See Wilson v. Dunlap, ESJC, 6-97 (jury verdict of not guilty); Steel v. Billings, BeSJC, 10-95 (same verdict); Webb v. Cross, CSJC, 6-95 (jury verdict of guilty); Gray v. Bordman, SSJC, 2-95 (jury verdict of not guilty); Smith v. Whitney, HdCP, 8-24 (jury verdict that defendant promised); Briggs v. Atwood, PCP, 11-07 (jury verdict of guilty); Denny v. March, WCP, 9-05, appeal dism., WSJC, 9-06 (jury verdict of not guilty); Newhall v. Eaton, BrCP, 4-05, appeal dism., BrSJC, 10-06 (same verdict); Fennelly v. Lee, SCP, 1-05, rev'd on default, SSJC, 11-06 (plea of never promised upheld); Martins v. Walter, SCP, 1-05, appeal dism., SSJC, 11-06 (plea of not guilty upheld); Welsh v. Gridley, SCP, 10-99, appeal dism., SSJC, 8-01 (plea of never promised upheld); Vernon v. Gay, SCP, 10-97, appeal dism., SSJC, 2-99 (same verdict); Foster v. Pope, BeCP, 9-97, appeal dism., BeSJC, 10-99 (jury verdict of guilty); Train v. Henshaw, WCP, 12-83 (jury verdict of not guilty).

219. See Ferre v. Wallis, HCP, 11-08, appeal dism., HSJC, 4-10; Wells v. Chase, ECP, 6-04; Twiss v. Perry, ECP, 9-85, appeal dism., ESJC, 6-86.

220. For other examples of pleas to suits on the borderline between tort and contract, see Hurd v. Silk, BaSJC, 5-92 (jury verdict of guilty on writ of case for defendant's failure to pay plaintiff wages due for hiring of his servant); Tufts v. Apthorp, SSJC, 2-88 (jury verdict that defendant never promised on writ of case for breach of promise made by defendant's agent); Abrahams v. Hays, LSJC, 6-87 (jury verdict of not guilty on writ of case for failure of broker to deliver insurance policy to plaintiff); Maccarty v. Fifth Mass. Tpke. Corp., WCP, 3-05, appeal dism., WSJC, 9-05 (plea of not guilty upheld on writ of case for defect in turnpike encountered after paying toll); Thomas v. Lunt, ECP, 9-85 (jury verdict of guilty in plea of case alleging negligence on part of defendant contrary to his promise). See also Hill v. Inhabitants of Shutesbury, HSJC, 5-86 (jury verdict that defendant not guilty but did promise on writ of case by minister for salary).

221. White v. Snell, 5 Pick. 425, 427 (1827). But see Remick v. Wyatt, ECP, 12-13 (denying motion to arrest judgment for improper joinder of tort and contract).

222. Baker v. Jewell, 6 Mass. 460, 462 (1810).

223. Meagher v. Bachelder, 6 Mass. 444

(1810). On joinder of parties, see generally note 113 above.

224. For one of the few prerevolutionary cases to use the term "tort" or "contract," see Walker v. Murray, WCP, 8-66.

225. But see VanSchaack v. Watson, HCP, 1-12, appeal dism., HSJC, 4-12 (defendant's plea rejected because interposed only for delay).

226. See Hayward v. Weston, PCP, 4-02, appeal dism., PSJC, 6-03.

227. See Hinds v. Raymond, PCP, 11-00, appeal dism., PSJC, 6-01.

228. See Hussey v. Coffin, NCP, 10-96.

229. See Barnes v. Peck, SCP, 7-10, rev'd on other grounds, SSJC, 11-10 (jury verdict on appeal that defendant did promise).

230. See Sewall v. Mattoon, SCP, 10-11, rev'd on default, SSJC, 3-13.

231. Compare, e.g., Goodwin v. Woodbridge, BeCP, 9-97 (plea of never promised rejected), with Allen v. Lathrop, SCP, 7-05, rev'd on default, SSJC, 11-06 (plea of never promised upheld).

232. Compare Hutchins v. Low, SCP, 4-17; Jenkins v. Hanley, BeCP, 1-03, appeal dism., BeSJC, 5-03 (pleas of not guilty rejected), with Phelps v. Adams, ECP, 3-14, appeal dism., ESJC, 11-14; Bond v. Blackmore, SCP, 4-08; Brown v. Spaulding, SCP, 10-07; Farrar v. King, WCP, 3-07, appeal dism., WSJC, 4-07; Wendell v. McMullen, SCP, 10-06, appeal dism., SSJC, 11-06; Scott v. Hodge, SCP, 10-05; Dwight v. Webster, BeCP, 9-97, aff'd, BeSJC, 10-97 (pleas of not guilty upheld).

233. See Griffin v. Brown, BeCP, 10-22, aff'd, BeSJC, 5-26. See also Parker v. Thompson, SCP, 10-24, rev'd on other grounds, SSJC, 3-25; Davis v. Winegar, BeCP, 2-21, aff'd, BeSJC, 9-24; Marsh v. Gold, BeCP, 2-21, aff'd, BeSJC, 5-24; Perkins v. Wetherell, PCP, 8-14, aff'd, PSJC, 10-14; Curtis v. Curtis, NfCP, 12-12, appeal dism., NfSJC, 10-14; Windsor v. Rich, PCP, 4-10, aff'd, PSJC, 10-10. Cf. Chapman v. Eldredge, BeCP, 2-26, modified, BeSJC, 9-26 (parties agreed without joining issue on merits that jury might assess damages).

234. See Briggs v. Braley, PCP, 8-28, rev'd on default, PSJC, 5-30 (jury verdict in case for defamation of guilty on plea that defendant was "not of the premises"); Sunkes v. Russell, SCP, 10-27 (jury verdict in assumpsit on plea of not guilty that defendant promised); Fellows v. Dwight, BeCP, 2-91 (jury verdict in assumpsit on plea of not guilty that defendant never promised); Warner v. Gus-

tine, HCP, 11-82, 2-83 (same jury verdict in indebitatus assumpsit on same plea). But see Gerrish v. Train, SCP, 1-25, appeal dism., SSJC, 3-27 (jury verdict of not guilty on immaterial issue in trespass rejected).

235. Wheeler v. Train, 3 Pick. 255, 258 (1825). See Williams v. Woodman, 8 Pick. 78 (1829); Whiting v. Cochran, 9 Mass. 532 (1813). Cf. Barnard v. Whiting, 7 Mass. 358 (1811); Patten v. Gurney, 17 Mass. 182, 187 (1821).

236. Clark v. Lamb, 8 Pick. 415, 418 (1829). Accord, Porter v. Rummery, 10 Mass. 64, 66 (1813); McMasters v. Parsons, ESJC, 6-94 (verdict "in favor of the Plaintiffs"); Wilbur v. Reed, BrCP, 6-29 (verdict for plaintiff on plea of tender which failed to award damages); Wilbour v. Howard, BrCP, 9-26 (verdict in assumpsit of not guilty on plea of never promised); Hakes v. Hubbell, BeCP, 10-22, aff'd, BeSJC, 9-23 (verdict in case for defamation on plea of not guilty that defendant was indebted).

237. See Russell v. Kinney, BrCP, 12-21 (verdict in assumpsit of not guilty on plea of not guilty); Lowden v. Lowden, PCP, 11-07 (same verdict).

238. See Eaton v. Strong, 7 Mass. 312, 314 (1811).

239. Ropps v. Barker, 4 Pick. 239, 242 (1826).

240. See Gerrish v. Train, 3 Pick. 124, 127 (1825); Newburyport v. Adams, ESJC, 6-85 (verdict failed to disclose land taken for road and thus damages could not be determined).

241. See Laws of 1783, ch. 42. The statute is considered in Waters v. Lilley, 4 Pick. 145 (1826). See also Lynch v. Rosseter, 6 Pick. 419 (1828), as to the general rule that a defendant could not introduce matters involving title to land into evidence in trespass actions commenced before justices of the peace.

242. See Laws of 1783, ch. 38, construed in Foster v. Abbot, 1 Mass. 234 (1804).

243. See Laws of 1792, ch. 41, construed in Bangs v. Snow, 1 Mass. 181 (1804). The statute was also applied in Drake v. Hewins, NfSJC, 2-19; Stearns v. Merwin, HdCP, 11-26; Whipple v. Chamberlain, SCP, 10-15; Lamson v. Calley, ECP, 12-13.

244. See Howe, Lectures, 181-182.

245. See Pierce v. McCrellis, HSJC, 4-00; Hall v. Fletcher, MCP, 9-92. But see Kellogg v. Ingersoll, 1 Mass. 5 (1804) (special matter not allowed in evidence under plea of non est factum to writ of covenant).

246. See Merry v. Gay, 3 Pick. 388

(1826); Baker v. Prescott, SSJC, 3-26; Sanderson v. Henderson, SSJC, 2-92; Breed v. Hurd, SCP, 10-27, rev'd on other grounds, SSJC, 3-28; Stratton v. Whitney, WCP, 9-16; Raymond v. Braman, BrCP, 9-05, appeal dism., BrSJC, 10-06. But see Martin v. Woods, 6 Mass. 6 (1809) (defendant could not plead in special plea a fact that he already had to prove under general issue to which special plea was joined); DeLuce v. DeGuiscard, SSJC, 8-83 (overruling motion in writ of case for defamation for leave to plead general issue and special justification).

247. See Merry v. Gay, 3 Pick. 388, 389n1 (1826).

248. Howe, Lectures, 141.

249. See Hildreth v. Winslow, WSJC, 4-90; Chase v. Patterson, YSJC, 6-88; Wood v. Stevens, CSJC, 6-86; Wood v. Hinckley, SCP, 7-21, aff'd, SSJC, 11-21; McElwain v. Lyon, HCP, 8-01; Freeman v. Norman, SCP, 7-85, rev'd on default, SSJC, 2-86; Howe, Lectures, 199-200.

250. Hodges v. Raymond, 9 Mass. 316 (1812).

251. A basic rule of special pleading that so survived was that a defendant could not plead specially facts that merely "amounted to the general issue"—that is, "facts . . . [that] would be proper evidence under" such an issue. Inhabitants of Freeport v. Inhabitants of Edgecumbe, 1 Mass. 459, 462 (1805). Accord, Ely v. Granger, HCP, 9-94. Since in most writs "the defendant [could] give in evidence under the general issue any matter that contradict[ed] the allegations which the plaintiff [was] bound to prove," a defendant had to plead specially "matter[s] of excuse or justification" and other special defenses. Rawson v. Morse, 4 Pick. 127 (1826). For examples of matters that were admissible under the general issue and hence could not be pleaded specially, see Poor v. Robinson, 10 Mass. 131, 134 (1813) (all evidence with exception of collateral warranty in writ of right); Proprietors of Monumoi Great Beach v. Rogers, 1 Mass. 159, 160 (1804) (dictum) (evidence of title in trespass q.c.f.); Hayward v. Parris, PCP, 11-99 (evidence in assumpsit that contract never made); Campbell v. Jones, HCP, 5-79 (same evidence); Boardman v. Barton, SCP, 1-93 (evidence in trespass for assault that defendant did not wound plaintiff); Waitt v. Clap, ECP, 9-88 (evidence of fraud in indorsement of note). One common sort of evidence that was not admissible under the general issue and hence could be pleaded specially was payment, discharge, or accord

and satisfaction. See Noble v. Talcot, BeSJC, 10-96; Padelford v. Cobb, PSJC, 5-90; Weld v. Needham, HCP, 11-09, appeal dism., HSJC, 4-10; Parry v. Daman, SCP, 1-06; Parker v. Grout, SCP, 10-00; Allen v. Minot, SCP, 7-90; Saltmarsh v. Willington, ECP, 9-87; VanDusen v. Williams, BeCP, 9-84. Another was tender. See Bates v. Googins, ESJC, 11-92; Robbins v. Luce, BeCP, 4-06, aff'd, BeSJC, 9-08; Drury v. Knowles, SCP, 7-85. Still another was fraud or duress. See Almy v. Bacon, BrSJC, 4-26; Stevenson v. Edey, SCP, 3-13; Holmes v. Allen, HCP, 1-09; Cornish v. Allen, BeCP, 9-94. For examples of other matters not admissible under the general issue, see Pray v. Pierce, 7 Mass. 381 (1811); Wolcott v. Knight, 6 Mass. 418, 420 (1810); Kelleran v. Brown, 4 Mass. 443 (1808); M'Farland v. Baker, 1 Mass. 153 (1804); Poor v. Downer, ESJC, 6-86 (justification in defamation); Cunningham v. Barnes, SCP, 7-87, appeal dism., SSJC, 2-88 (justification for assault); Hooper v. Putnam, ECP, 4-85 (performance of conditions of bond). But see Dawes v. Gooch, 8 Mass. 488 (1812). Another rule that survived was that a defendant could not plead parole evidence which varied a written contract, nor could he put such evidence in under the general issue. See Sibley v. Brown, 4 Pick. 137 (1826); Jacobs v. Putnam, 4 Pick. 108 (1826); Townsend v. Weld, 8 Mass. 146 (1811); Barnard v. Titcomb, ECP, 7-90. On the limits of the parole evidence rule, see generally Comstock v. VanDusen, 5 Pick. 163 (1827); Leland v. Stone, 10 Mass. 459 (1813).

252. Laws of 1836, ch. 273, §2.

253. Sampson v. Coy, 15 Mass. 493, 494 (1819). Accord, Hemmenway v. Woods, 1 Pick. 524 (1823).

254. See *Monthly Law Reporter*, XIII (1850-1851), 481.

255. See *Law Review and Quarterly Journal of British and Foreign Jurisprudence*, XIV (1851), 143.

256. See Laws of 1851, ch. 233, §1. The 1851 law was repealed in 1852 and was replaced by Laws of 1852, ch. 312, §1, which retained the 1851 reforms and added certain other reforms. For a discussion of the additions in the 1852 law, see *Monthly Law Reporter*, XV 91853), 112.

257. See *A Report of the Commissioners Appointed to Consider and Report upon the Practicability and Expediency of Reducing to a Written and Systematic Code the Common Law of Massachusetts, or Any Part Thereof* (Boston, 1837), in William W. Story, ed., *Miscellaneous Writings of Joseph Story* (Bos-

ton, 1852), 728. Justice Story headed the commission that finally recommended not the codification of the law of pleading but its reduction to a more simple form.

258. Laws of 1836, ch. 273, §1.

259. Howe, Lectures, 336.

260. See Parker v. Standish, 3 Pick. 288 (1825); Standish v. Parker, 2 Pick. 20 (1823), for cases in which the Supreme Judicial Court, in great confusion, struggled with this question. Its problem was that the appropriate mode for determining the existence and scope of a prior judgment was for the court to inspect the record. See Bellows v. Hosmer, MCP Files, 9-20, rev'd on default, MSJC, 10-20. But cf. Hayden v. Shed, MSJC, 11-14, where the jury returned a verdict for the plaintiff in a trespass suit for seizing property after a prior suit involving the same cause of action.

261. Kelton v. Butler, SCP, 1-01.

262. Howe, Lectures, 336.

263. Vining v. Whiting, SSJC, 2-96, in Dana, Minute Books.

264. Sylvester v. Bailey, PSJC, 5-90, ibid.

265. Blackstone, *Commentaries*, III, 306, quoted in *Boston Gazette*, May 13, 1782, p. 1, col. 1. See also Taylor v. Parsons, ECP, 12-16; Quirk v. Mingus, NfCP, 9-10; Mason v. Payson, MCP, 3-05; in which movants for new trials claimed surprise but were unable to make sufficient demonstrations thereof on the facts.

266. See Chatfield v. Lathrop, 6 Pick. 417 (1828); Niles v. Bracket, 15 Mass. 378 (1819); Starbuck v. Coffin, NCP, 10-25. See also Bond v. Humphrey, SCP, 7-28; Sylvester v. Wood, BrCP, 9-14; Taylor v. Stone, MCP Files, 12-13; Paddock v. Holbrook, WCP, 3-11; Ford v. Haley, MCP Files, 12-08; Hager v. Weston, MCP Files, 12-07, rev'd on other grounds, MSJC, 10-10; where litigants sought new trials on the basis of newly discovered evidence but failed to make the requisite showing therefor; Petition of Coffin, NCP, 10-05, where an application for a new trial was not disposed of. See generally Howe, Lectures, 376-383.

267. See Tuttle v. Cooper, 5 Pick. 414 (1827).

268. See Chatfield v. Lathrop, 6 Pick. 417, 418 (1828) (dictum); Gardner v. Mitchell, 6 Pick. 114, 116 (1828).

269. See Bond v. Cutler, 7 Mass. 205 (1810); Hammond v. Wadhams, 5 Mass. 353 (1809).

270. Howe, Lectures, 376. Of course, new trials continued to be granted for various sorts of misconduct on the part of jurors or be-

cause juries were improperly composed. See Commonwealth v. Hussey, 13 Mass. 221 (1816); Knight v. Inhabitants of Freeport, 13 Mass. 218 (1816); Prescott v. Spring, MSJC, 4-97 (juror absent during part of deliberations); Commonwealth v. Cooms, ESJC, 11-86 (jurors separated during deliberations); Wait v. Boston & Roxbury Mill Corp., NfCP, 12-21 (juror related to plaintiff); Commonwealth v. Godfrey, NfCP, 9-21 (no jury foreman chosen); Hubbard v. Hartwell, BeCP, 2-21 (juror discussed case with nonjurors prior to verdict); Youlin v. Cogswell, ECP, 12-17 (juror in paternity case a resident of town in which plaintiff was a pauper); Petition of Newhall, EGS, 10-06 (jurors improperly summoned); White v. Bodwell, ECP, 9-05 (jury in road case held before deputy sheriff instead of sheriff); Saxon v. Vinall, SCP, 10-02 (jurors had out-of-court conversation prior to verdict). Cf. Highway in Cambridge, MGS, 9-03 (report of road committee rejected since one member was "not a disinterested freeholder, he having real estate" in town paying for road). But see Washburn v. Inhabitants of Middleboro, PCP, 11-28 (overruling motion on ground officer in charge of jury was inhabitant of defendant's town); Wood v. Souther, MCP Files, 3-25 (overruling motion on ground that magistrate in paternity case to whom complaint was made was inhabitant of plaintiff's town); Anthony v. Briggs, BrCP, 9-20 (overruling motion on ground juror was nephew of plaintiff); Butterfield v. Mason, MCP Files, 3-20 (overruling motion on ground juror was related to defendant); Hincher v. Howland, WCP, 12-19 (overruling motion after hearing on ground juror absent during evidence, argument, and deliberations); Petition of Lovell, NfGS, 9-13 (overruling motion on ground juror a proprietor in defendant corporation); Batterman v. Bell, SCP Files, 12-12 (overruling motion on ground jurors separated during deliberations); White v. Leonard, NfCP, 4-11 (overruling motion on ground jurors in paternity case residents of plaintiff's town). Other objections to the composition of juries were valid only if seasonably made. See Commonwealth v. Knapp, 10 Pick. 477, 479-480 (1830) (name of juror not in jury box); Commonwealth v. Knapp, 9 Pick. 496, 499 (1830) (discussion of propriety of challenges for cause on basis of jurors' prior knowledge from newspapers about facts of criminal case); Inhabitants of Amherst v. Inhabitants of Hadley, 1 Pick. 38 (1822) (juror's name drawn more than 20 days before court sitting).

271. For other such rules, see Dunham v. Baxter, 4 Mass. 79 (1808) (new trial granted when defendant prevented by court's ruling from presenting relevant evidence); Leadbetter v. Lovewell, MCP Files, 9-23 (new trial granted when defendant suddenly taken seriously ill and therefore unable to attend court); Patten v. Richardson, NfCP, 12-21 (new trial granted when judgment on default entered for "mistake and accident"); Hall v. Walker, BeCP, 1-19 (new trial granted when attorney of out-of-state defendant forgot return date of writ); Brooks v. Davis, WCP, 11-13 (new trial granted when defendant ill and failed to attend court in belief that nominal party in interest would answer); Brown v. Keith, WCP, 6-13 (new trial granted to nonresident who had no knowledge of suit); Petition of Gilbert, HCP, 5-92 (new trial granted when defendant did not know of suit). Cf. Highway in Cambridge, MGS, 11-93 (decision on report of road committee postponed when party "unexpectedly deprived of an opportunity of showing his reasons against the acceptance" thereof). But see Inhabitants of Worcester v. Allen, WGS, 3-25 (new trial denied when agent of defendant failed to make arguments which defendant had ordered him to make); Brown v. Bigelow, WCP, 12-23, (new trial denied when defendant unable to write plea owing to lack of attorney); Jewett v. Lane, WCP, 6-18 (new trial denied when bad roads prevented timely arrival of out-of-state litigant); Petition of Chase, ECP, 6-13 (new trial denied on claim that original trial held so quickly that defendants lacked opportunity to prepare); Richardson v. Truman, SCP Files, 10-07 (new trial denied to defendant when plaintiff, after putting documents in evidence, failed to give copies to defendant to enable a rebuttal).

272. The common law system continued in England throughout the first third of the nineteenth century. While the demand for reform developed early in the century, the first actual reforms were the Hilary Reforms of 1834. They abolished the technicalities in the commencement and the conclusion of pleas, simplified the form of demurrer and joinder in demurrer, specified the scope of general issues in the different forms of action, specified when several pleas could be used, and clarified when several counts would be employed in the declaration. See Edson R. Sunderland, *Cases and Materials on Code Pleading* (Chicago, 2d ed., 1940), 3. The effect of the reforms appears to have been minimal; one commentator argued that the new rules retarded the progress of reform by postponing the real reform of common law pleading for another 20 years. See Charles McGuffy Hepburn, *The Historical Development of Code Pleading In America and England* (Cincinnati, 1897), 76-77. The major reforms of English pleading came with the Common Law Procedure Acts of 1852, 1854, and 1860 and the Supreme Court of Judicature Acts of 1873 and 1875, with the 1873 Act "sweeping away the English system of common law pleading even more completely than our codes have swept it away." Charles McGuffy Hepburn, "The Historical Development of Code Pleading in America and England," in Association of American Law Schools, ed., *Select Essays in Anglo-American Legal History* (Boston, 1908), II, 680. Accord, Joseph H. Koffler and Alison Reppy, *Handbook of Common Law Pleading* (St. Paul, Minn., 1969), 3. English procedural reform seems to have come about largely through American influence, as is evidenced by the attention paid by English legal journals to American procedural reforms of the mid-nineteenth century. See *Law Review and Quarterly Journal of British and Foreign Jurisprudence*, XIV (1851), 143-144, 284; XXI (1855), 140, 184, 185; XXII (1855), 185, 399, 431.

Chapter 6. Law as the Guardian of Liberty

1. Return of Braintree, June 5, 1780, in Oscar Handlin and Mary F. Handlin, eds., *The Popular Sources of Political Authority: Documents on the Massachusetts Constitution of 1780* (Cambridge, Mass., 1966), 769.

2. "The Letters of 'A Republican Federalist,' " in Cecelia M. Kenyon, ed., *The Antifederalists* (Indianapolis, 1966), 122.

3. Return of Groton, June 5, 1780, in Handlin, *Popular Sources*, 649. See generally ibid., 29.

4. Williams v. Hinsdale, BeCP, 10-21.

5. " 'Republican Federalist,' " 118.

6. "The Essex Result, 1778," in Handlin and Handlin, *Popular Sources*, 329.

7. Peter Force, ed., *American Archives*, 4th ser., V (1851), 807, quoted in Handlin and Handlin, *Popular Sources*, 17.

8. Robert Treat Paine to James Neale, Dec. 1794, in Paine Papers.

9. Simeon Howard, "A Sermon Preached before the Honorable Council and the Honorable House of Representatives of the State of Massachusetts Bay in New-England, May 31, 1780," in John W. Thornton, ed., *The Pulpit*

of the American Revolution (Boston, 1860), 390-391.

10. James Neale to Robert Treat Paine, June 6, 1794, in Paine Papers.

11. Wyman v. Royall, MSC, 10-78.

12. Commonwealth v. Foster, 1 Mass. 488, 494 (1805) (dictum).

13. Commonwealth v. Green, 17 Mass. 515, 517 (1822) (argument of counsel).

14. Commonwealth v. Daly, Boston Police Ct., 1825, no. 1151.

15. Crocker's Petition, MCP, 6-05.

16. Commonwealth v. Sosa, Boston Police Ct., 1827, no. 382.

17. *Baltimore Journal*, Apr. 13, 1787, quoted in Gordon S. Wood, *The Creation of the American Republic, 1776-1787* (Chapel Hill, 1969), 386.

18. Commonwealth v. Fowler, 10 Mass. 290, 302 (1813).

19. Ibid., 302.

20. *Baltimore Journal*, Feb. 20, 1787, quoted in Wood, *American Republic*, 371.

21. *Baltimore Journal*, Aug. 3, 1787, quoted ibid., 371.

22. Constitution of 1780, Part II, ch. 1, §1, art. 4, in Handlin and Handlin, *Popular Sources*, 449.

23. See William E. Nelson, "Continuity and Change in Constitutional Adjudication," *Yale Law Journal*, LXXVIII (1969), 500, 508-510.

24. Laws of 1780, ch. 32.

25. Laws of 1778, ch. 49.

26. New York Laws of 1779, ch. 25.

27. Laws of 1783, ch. 24.

28. Ibid., ch. 36.

29. Ibid., ch. 52.

30. Laws of 1785, ch. 1.

31. Laws of 1786, ch. 45.

32. See Laws of 1782, ch. 10.

33. See Laws of 1783, ch. 57.

34. See Nathaniel Peaslee Sargeant to ———, Jan. 22, 1786, in Sargeant Papers.

35. Ingraham v. Doggett, 5 Pick, 451, 452 (1827).

36. Cf. Dodds v. Henry, 9 Mass. 262, 265 (1812).

37. See Laws of 1792, ch. 41. See also ibid., ch. 32.

38. Bangs v. Snow, 1 Mass. 181, 185 (1804) (opinion of Sedgwick, J.).

39. Ingraham v. Doggett, 5 Pick. 451, 452-453 (1827).

40. See Laws of 1823, ch. 138, § 5.

41. See Fisher v. Billings, NfSJC, 10-10.

42. See Noyes v. Carter, MSJC, 10-98; Whitney v. Wait, MCP, 12-25.

43. See Dawes v. Jackson, 9 Mass. 490

(1813); Freeman v. Otis, 9 Mass. 272 (1812); Brown v. Austin, 1 Mass. 208 (1804).

44. See Whitney v. Peckham, Cushing 78 (1785); Motion of Blake, SSJC, 2-01.

45. See, e.g., Sterne v. Lyman, WCP, 3-99, appeal dism., WSJC, 4-00.

46. See, e.g., Knox v. Balchellor, WSJC, 9-00.

47. See Stacy v. Webber, ECP, 3-14.

48. See Richards v. Tisdale, NfSJC, 2-02.

49. See Jackson v. Wilson, SCP, 10-27, appeal dism., SSJC, 11-27.

50. See Gardner v. Whitaker, HdSJC, 4-30; Gooch v. Avery, LSJC, 7-96; Briggs v. Wardwell, BrCP, 9-12; Davis v. Howe, WCP, 6-12, appeal dism., WSJC, 9-13.

51. Commonwealth v. Foster, 10 Mass. 290, 302 (1813). But see Howard v. Gage, 6 Mass. 462 (1810).

52. See Bridge v. Lincoln, 14 Mass. 367 (1817).

53. See Williams v. Whiting, 11 Mass. 424 (1814); Putnam v. Johnson, 10 Mass. 488 (1813).

54. See Brown v. Austin, MCP, 5-99.

55. See Goodwin v. Rice, LSJC, 6-91. Cf. Henshaw v. Foster, 9 Pick. 312 (1830).

56. William Cushing to John Adams, Feb. 18, 1789, in Cushing Papers. The letter and Adams's reply are published in Frank W. Grinnell, ed., "Hitherto Unpublished Correspondence between Chief Justice Cushing and John Adams in 1789," *Massachusetts Law Quarterly*, XXVII (1942), 12.

57. See Leonard W. Levy, *Legacy of Suppression: Freedom of Speech and Press in Early American History* (Cambridge, Mass., 1960), 13-14.

58. William Blackstone, *Commentaries on the Laws of England* (Oxford, 1765-1769), IV, 152.

59. Commonwealth v. Clap, 4 Mass. 163, 170 (1808).

60. Dodds v. Henry, 9 Mass. 262, 265 (1812).

61. Plaintiffs in civil defamation suits were aided by a number of developments in the law. (1) The courts rejected the mitiori sensu rule, noting that "hypercriticism in actions of slander was carried much beyond the bounds of common sense in former times." Miller v. Parish, 8 Pick. 384, 386 (1829). Thus words would be held defamatory "without the aid of inuendoes" if they amounted to a "plain and intelligible" slander "to the most ordinary minds." Walker v. Winn, 8 Mass. 248, 255 (1811). For cases in which words were so construed, see Harding v. Brooks, 5 Pick. 244, 247 (1827); Chaddock v. Briggs, 13 Mass. 248

(1816); Fowle v. Robbins, 12 Mass. 498 (1815); Nye v. Otis, 8 Mass. 122 (1811). See also Bloss v. Tobey, 2 Pick. 320 (1824), where the court in holding a declaration for slander insufficient noted that it did so "with great regret, and not without much labor and research to avoid this result. . . ." Ibid., 324. But see Campbell v. Parker, SCP, 1-22 (demurrer sustained to declaration alleging defendant said, "Stop thief"). (2) The courts ruled that if a defendant pleaded truth as a defense and failed to prove the plea, the plea would then be taken as conclusive evidence that the defendant had published the defamatory words and had done so maliciously. See Alderman v. French, 1 Pick. 1 (1822); Jackson v. Stetson, 15 Mass. 48 (1818). But see Laws of 1826, ch. 107, §2, which overruled both those cases. The statute, however, was narrowly construed in Hix v. Drury, 5 Pick. 296 (1827). (3) Reversing an earlier rule, see Smith v. Nichols, BeCP, 1-02, rev'd on other grounds, BeSJC, 5-02, the Supreme Judicial Court held that evidence of general repute of the plaintiff's guilt of the crime charged in the defamation was inadmissible on trial. See Alderman v. French, 1 Pick. 1, 18 (1822). Contra, Dunham v. Pierce, SCP, 7-28. (4) The courts also rejected the old rule that a slander committed to contradict false and malicious slanders on the defendant was privileged, see Dickey v. Tomb, ESJC, 4-02, holding that such a defense was inappropriate "in a country where influence and usefulness depend upon reputation. . . ." Clark v. Binney, 2 Pick. 113, 118 (1824). See also Burges v. Story, ECP, 12-08, where a report of referees noted that in small towns "friendship among all the individuals is highly necessary to the happiness of the whole." (5) The courts held that a plea of truth would be insufficient if it failed to deny in precise terms each and every word alleged in a plaintiff's declaration. See Ball v. Cutter, MCP, 11-00.

In the late 1820s the lower courts began to evince a lessening concern for injuries to reputation, holding that bad words alone were not sufficient to justify criminal prosecution, see Commonwealth v. Henderson, DCP, 5-26; Commonwealth v. Grenough, Boston Police Ct., 1828, no. 1403; Commonwealth v. Burrows, Boston Police Ct., 1827, no. 254; and remanding persons complaining of defamation to their civil remedies. See Commonwealth v. Jennings, Boston Police Ct., 1828, no. 445; Commonwealth v. Campbell, Boston Police Ct., 1825, no. 1177; Commonwealth v. Thayer, Boston Police Ct., 1825, no. 397. Earlier such cases would have

been criminally prosecuted. See Miller v. Commonwealth, PGS, 11-92. Perhaps social attitudes toward the importance of reputation were beginning to change during the late 1820s.

62. Commonwealth v. Adams, SSJC, 2-99, in Francis Dana, Minute Books.

63. (Boston, 1801).

64. See ibid., 9-10.

65. See ibid., 28-31.

66. Ibid., 33.

67. See Perry v. Foster, HSJC, 9-98, reversing HCP, 1-98; Tower v. Grout, WCP, 6-04.

68. See March v. Jackson, ESJC, 4-02.

69. See Shute v. Barrett, 7 Pick. 82 (1828); Bodwell v. Osgood, 3 Pick. 379, 383-384 (1825).

70. 4 Mass. 163 (1808).

71. Ibid., 168-169. As in the colonial period, see Chapter 3, note 58, petitions to the General Court or even to one of its committees remained privileged, see Daggett v. Jepson, SCP, 7-87, although feigned petitions that were published but never presented to the legislature were not privileged. See Tyng v. Tyng, MCP Files, 11-95, appeal dism., MSJC, 10-97. See also Commonwealth v. Blanding, 3 Pick. 304, 314 (1825).

72. Commonwealth v. Clap, 4 Mass. 163, 169 (1808). But the publication of falsehoods remained libelous. See ibid., 169-170.

73. Ibid., 169-170. Parsons's opinion did not make clear the extent to which the privilege rested on the defendant's production of evidence that the libel was in fact true.

74. Dodds v. Henry, 9 Mass. 262, 264 (1812).

75. See Bodwell v. Osgood, 3 Pick. 379, 383-384 (1825).

76. See Shute v. Barrett, 7 Pick. 82, 86-87 (1828).

77. Another privilege introduced into the law during this period was the absolute privilege on the part of a legislator to make defamatory statements in the course of legislative business. See Coffin v. Coffin, 4 Mass. 1 (1808).

78. See Levy, Legacy of Suppression 202-204, 258-259, 299, 304.

79. See Chapter 3, notes 48-49, 59, and accompanying text.

80. See Clyde A. Duniway, The Development of Freedom of the Press in Massachusetts (Cambridge, Mass., 1906), 146, 156; Levy, Legacy of Suppression, 208-211.

81. 4 Mass. 163, 168-169 (1808).

82. 3 Pick. 304 (1825).

83. Ibid., 317. Meanwhile, both civil and

criminal suits for political libels had continued. See Pickering v. Smith, ESJC, 4-10;
Bigelow v. Spooner, WSJC, 9-06; Commonwealth v. Carleton, ESJC, 4-03; Pickering v.
Kneeland, ECP, 6-13, appeal dism., ESJC,
11-13.

84. See note 61 above.

85. See Laws of 1826, ch. 107. The defense was granted, however, in the form of a
qualified privilege that could be overcome by
proof of malice. See ibid.

86. See Commonwealth v. Gale, WCP, 3-
28 (nolle pros. entered since "the public
interest require[d]"); Commonwealth v. Gale,
WCP, 6-27 (nolle pros. entered).

87. Constitution of 1780, Part I, art. 29,
in Handlin and Handlin, *Popular Sources*,
447.

88. Benjamin F. Wright, ed., *The Federalist*, no. 81 (Cambridge, Mass., 1961), 506.

89. No one in Massachusetts, as far as I
have been able to discover, ever stated during
the 1780s or the 1790s that judges did or
should change the law, with one exception.
That exception was James Sullivan, who
wrote in 1779 that American judges would
adapt the common law "to our genius" by
adopting "from time to time . . . such rules as
may tend to the perfection of the practice."
Sullivan to Elbridge Gerry, Dec. 25, 1779, in
Sullivan Papers. Lawyers in the postrevolutionary period must also have been aware of
earlier statements, such as James Otis's reference in the Writs of Assistance case to the
superiority of principle over precedent. See L.
Kinvin Wroth and Hiller B. Zobel, eds., *Legal
Papers of John Adams* (Cambridge, Mass.,
1965), II, 144.

90. Edward S. Corwin, "The Progress of
Constitutional Theory between the Declaration of Independence and the Meeting of the
Philadelphia Convention," *American Historical Review*, XXX (1925), 511, 526.

91. Baron Montesquieu, *The Spirit of
Laws*, ed. J.V. Prichard (London, 1878), I,
170.

92. Blackstone, *Commentaries*, I, 69.

93. Benjamin Austin [Honestus], *Observations on the Pernicious Practice of the Law*
(Boston, 1794), 41.

94. *Independent Chronicle* (Boston), Sept.
4, 1777, p. 1, cols. 2-3.

95. "The People the Best Governors," in
Frederick Chase, *A History of Dartmouth
College* (Cambridge, Mass., 1891), II, 662.

96. Julian P. Boyd, *The Papers of Thomas
Jefferson* (Princeton, 1950-), VI, 315.

97. James M. Varnum, *The Case, Trevett
against Weeden* (Providence, 1787), 27.

98. Max Farrand, ed., *The Records of the
Federal Convention of 1787* (New Haven,
1911), II, 76 (remarks of Mr. L. Martin).
Accord, ibid., I, 97-98 (remarks of Mr. Gerry); II, 73 (remarks of Mr. Ghorum).

99. Wright, *Federalist*, no. 78, at 496.

100. A True Patriot to Mr. Collins, Apr.
18, 1781, in Austin Scott, ed., *Archives of the
State of New Jersey*, 2d ser., V (1917),
232-234.

101. Levy, *Legacy of Suppression*, 281.

102. Constitution of 1780, Part I, art. 15,
in Handlin and Handlin, *Popular Sources*,
445.

103. Jonathan Elliot, ed., *The Debates in
the Several State Conventions on the
Adoption of the Federal Constitution* (Washington, 1836), II, 109 (remarks of Mr.
Holmes).

104. See ibid., II, 109-114; William Cushing, Notes for Speech at Massachusetts Constitutional Convention, 1788, in Cushing Papers.

105. Haskell v. Frink, WCP, 6-86, appeal
dism., WSJC, 4-88, a suit against a justice of
peace for depriving a person convicted of a
crime before him of the right to appeal and
hence of a jury trial.

106. See Laws of 1777, ch. 33. See also
Day v. Gardner, SSJC, 2-80; Rice v. Wadsworth, SSJC, 2-79.

107. James Sullivan to Elbridge Gerry,
Dec. 25, 1779, in Sullivan Papers.

108. See Laws of 1785, ch. 66. See also
Weston v. Sampson, PGS, 10-89.

109. See Laws of 1778, ch. 49. See also
Hutchinson v. Commonwealth, SSJC, 2-94.

110. See Chapter 5, note 16 and accompanying text.

111. See Mountfort v. Hall, 1 Mass. 443
(1805); Bigelow v. Forbus, WCP, 3-85. In
both cases it was unsuccessfully argued that
the transfer of jurisdiction to the justices
violated the constitutional provision guaranteeing the right to trial by jury.

112. Commonwealth v. Green, 17 Mass.
515, 517 (1822).

113. Commonwealth v. White, CSJC,
1787, in Robert Treat Paine, Criminal Trials:
Minutes of the Attorney General, 1780 to
1789, in Paine Papers.

114. The procedural protections of the
federal Bill of Rights are, of course, well
known. The protections afforded by the Massachusetts Declaration of Rights are set out in
the Constitution of 1780, Part I, art. 12
(privilege against self-incrimination; right to
produce evidence, to confront witnesses, and
to assistance of counsel; right to jury trial),
art. 13 (right to jury of neighborhood), art.

14 (prohibition of unreasonable searches and seizures), art. 24 (prohibition of ex post facto laws), art. 25 (prohibition of bills of attainder), art. 26 (prohibition of excessive bail and fines or cruel or unusual punishments), in Handlin and Handlin, *Popular Sources*, 445, 447.

115. Commonwealth v. Foster, 1 Mass. 488, 493-494 (1805).

116. Edward Livingston, "Introductory Report to the Code of Procedure," in *The Complete Works of Edward Livingston on Criminal Jurisprudence* (New York, 1873), 387.

117. Ibid.

118. Commonwealth v. Green, 17 Mass. 515, 519 (1822).

119. Ibid., 517.

120. Isaac Parker, "A Sketch of the Character of the Late Chief Justice Parsons," 10 Mass. 521, 529 (1813).

121. See Commonwealth v. Proprietors of Newburyport Bridge, 9 Pick. 142 (1829); Commonwealth v. Inhabitants of North Brookfield, 8 Pick. 463 (1829); Commonwealth v. Gay, 5 Pick. 44 (1827); Commonwealth v. Maxwell, 2 Pick. 139 (1824); Commonwealth v. Perkins, 1 Pick. 388 (1823); Commonwealth v. Hall, 15 Mass. 240 (1818); Commonwealth v. Inhabitants of Stockbridge, 11 Mass. 279 (1814); Commonwealth v. Atwood, 11 Mass. 93 (1814); Commonwealth v. Houghton, 8 Mass. 107 (1811); Commonwealth v. Symonds, 2 Mass. 163 (1806); Commonwealth v. Mycall, 2 Mass. 136 (1806); Commonwealth v. Town of Northampton, 2 Mass. 116 (1806); Commonwealth v. M'Monagle, 1 Mass. 517 (1805); Commonwealth v. Smith, 1 Mass. 245 (1804); Commonwealth v. Stow, 1 Mass. 54, 55 (1804); Commonwealth v. Galloope, Cushing 35 (1781) (indictment defective for misnomer in Christian name, although not for misnomer in surname); Commonwealth v. Brown, NfSJC, 8-98 (indictment quashed for defect in caption); Hawks v. Gould, MSJC, 4-94 (defective qui tam complaint for disorderly conduct incapable of amendment); Commonwealth v. Williams, WSJC, 4-83 (indictment defective for misnomer in Christian name); Commonwealth v. Bartlett, ECP Files, 9-29 (indictment defective for failure to allege that defendant acted "unlawfully"); Commonwealth v. Tucker, BrCP, 6-24 (indictment defective for misnomer); Commonwealth v. Cotton, BrCP, 3-24 (indictment defective for not alleging kind and quantity of liquor sold); Commonwealth v. Humphrey, NfCP, 9-11 (indictment defective for not pursuing statute);

Commonwealth v. Pimbleton, HGS, 5-95 (indictment defective for misnomer); Commonwealth v. West Springfield, HGS, 5-95 (prosecution quashed for "a material Defect in the Presentment"). But see Commonwealth v. Parmenter, 5 Pick. 279 (1827); Commonwealth v. Arnold, 4 Pick. 251 (1826); Commonwealth v. Bolkom, 3 Pick. 281 (1825); Commonwealth v. Harrington, 3 Pick. 26 (1825); Commonwealth v. Inhabitants of Newbury, 2 Pick. 51 (1823); Commonwealth v. Carey, 2 Pick. 47 (1823); Commonwealth v. Holmes, 17 Mass. 336 (1821); Commonwealth v. Hoxey, 16 Mass. 385 (1820); Commonwealth v. Runnels, 10 Mass. 518 (1813); Commonwealth v. Lindsey, 10 Mass. 153 (1813); Brown v. Commonwealth, 8 Mass. 59 (1811); Commonwealth v. Gowen, 7 Mass. 378 (1811); Commonwealth v. Humphries, 7 Mass. 242 (1810); Commonwealth v. Messenger, 4 Mass. 462 (1808); Commonwealth v. Tibbets, 2 Mass. 536 (1807); Commonwealth v. Ward, 2 Mass. 397 (1807); Commonwealth v. Ross, 2 Mass. 373 (1807); Commonwealth v. Richards, 1 Mass. 337 (1805); Commonwealth v. Stevens, 1 Mass. 203 (1804); Commonwealth v. Bailey, 1 Mass. 62 (1804); Commonwealth v. Galloope, Cushing 35 (1781) (misnomer in surname immaterial); State v. Jones, Cushing 17 (1778) (no need to use word "rob" in indictment for robbery); Johonnot v. Commonwealth, LSJC, 7-96 (joinder of common law and statutory offenses not fatal when prosecution waived common law counts); Commonwealth v. Hadlock, LSJC, 7-90 (indictment for crime committed in place no longer within county at time of trial not defective); Whitney v. Commonwealth, WSJC, 4-86 (error in indictment as to disposition of fine held amendable); Government v. Taylor, SSC, 2-80 (indictment upheld); Commonwealth v. Ninth Massachusetts Tpke Corp., NfCP, 4-29 (indictment alleging several defects in road, only one of which indictable, sufficient, although unclear for which defect jury found defendant guilty); Commonwealth v. Robertson, WCP, 8-14 (addition of defendant immaterial). English law was at least as technical as that of Massachusetts until the technicalities began to be removed by statute beginning in the 1820s. See James F. Stephen, *A History of the Criminal Law of England* (London, 1883), I, 273-292.

122. Commonwealth v. Inhabitants of Stockbridge, 11 Mass. 279, 281 (1814).

123. Commonwealth v. Hall, 15 Mass. 240, 241 (1818).

124. Ibid., 240-241.

125. Commonwealth v. Inhabitants of Stockbridge, 11 Mass. 279, 281 (1814).

126. Constitution of 1780, Part III, art. 24, in Handlin and Handlin, *Popular Sources*, 445. Arrests were permitted without warrant "in cases of treason and felony, and . . . to preserve the peace and to prevent outrage." Commonwealth v. Foster, 1 Mass. 488, 494 (1805). Accord, Commonwealth v. Elwood, Boston Police Ct., 1824, no. 2152.

127. See Commonwealth v. Otis, 16 Mass. 198 (1819); Commonwealth v. Morey, 8 Mass. 78 (1811); Commonwealth v. Cheney, 6 Mass. 347 (1810); Commonwealth v. Ward, 4 Mass. 497 (1808); Commonwealth v. Foster, 1 Mass. 488 (1805).

128. See Vose v. Deane, 7 Mass. 280 (1811) (by implication); Commonwealth v. Elwood, Boston Police Ct., 1824, no. 2152. Courts became increasingly concerned that the criminal law not be used by private individuals as a substitute for their civil remedies, see Commonwealth v. Warren, 6 Mass. 72 (1809); Commonwealth v. Nokes, Boston Police Ct., 1825, no. 313; particularly in landlord-tenant cases, see Commonwealth v. Lowe, Boston Police Ct., 1827, no. 1388, cases of minor trespasses, see Commonwealth v. Brown, Boston Police Ct., 1826, no. 1030; Commonwealth v. Smith, Boston Police Ct., 1824, no. 884; cases of minor batteries, see Commonwealth v. Bartlett, Boston Police Ct., 1830, no. 1560, and cases of bad words. See Commonwealth v. Francis, Boston Police Ct., 1824, no. 1213. But see Commonwealth v. Willard, WSJC, 9-99; Commonwealth v. Chase, ECP, 6-06, in both of which a nolle prosequi was entered after the complainant received satisfaction.

129. See Commonwealth v. Hayward, 10 Mass. 34 (1813).

130. See In re Sperry, BeSJC, 10-97; Commonwealth v. Wilcox, SSJC, 8-92; Commonwealth v. Nubit, LSJC, 6-89; Dashwood v. Lovel, SSC, 2-79; Commonwealth v. Nash, ECP, 6-15; In re Nichols, BeGS, 4-81; Commonwealth v. Scudden, Boston Police Ct., 1825, no. 455; Commonwealth v. Billings, Boston Justice Ct., June 16, 1809. Cf. State v. Bristol, ESC, 11-79 (peace bond required upon representation of attorney general that defendant was dangerous). One who was committed for breach of a peace bond could be sued on the bond as well as indicted for the offense that constituted the breach. See Commonwealth v. Braynard, 6 Pick. 113 (1828).

131. Commonwealth v. Meriam, 7 Mass.

168 (1810). See also Laws of 1797, ch. 62. A final rule concerning the law of arrest permitted a citizen to assault an officer attempting to make an illegal arrest. See Commonwealth v. Kowse, Boston Police Ct., 1828, no. 1365. Cf. Commonwealth v. Roberts, Boston Police Ct., 1825, no. 408 (assault on officer justified if officer failed to identify himself).

132. Oystead v. Shed, 13 Mass. 520, 523 (1816).

133. Sandford v. Nichols, 13 Mass. 286, 289 (1816).

134. Daniel Davis, *A Practical Treatise upon the Authority and Duty of Justices of the Peace in Criminal Prosecutions* (Boston, 1824), 47. The unlawfulness of general warrants for searches was settled in England in Money v. Leach, 3 Burr. 1742, 1766-1768, 97 Eng. Rep. 1075, 1088 (K.B. 1765). However, general warrants to make arrests remained available, as did writs of assistance in smuggling cases. See Jacob W. Landynski, *Search and Seizure and the Supreme Court: A Study in Constitutional Interpretation* (Baltimore, 1966), 30.

135. See Sanford v. Nichols, 13 Mass. 286, 289 (1816); Application for Search Warrant, Boston Police Ct., 1827, no. 476; Davis, *Practical Treatise*, 45-47. See also Commonwealth v. Bridges, WSJC, 9-89 ("the facts found . . . did not warrant the defendants in breaking and entering the House"); Commonwealth v. Dinsmore, WSJC, 9-88, in Dana, Minute Books ("in case of Warrants to search for stolen goods . . . , the Doors of any person cannot be broken up").

136. Commonwealth v. Kennard, 8 Pick. 133, 136 (1829).

137. But not in civil cases. See Keith v. Woombell, 8 Pick. 211, 217 (1829).

138. Commonwealth v. Knapp, 9 Pick. 496, 507 (1830) (opinion of Putnam, J.). Accord, Commonwealth v. Chabbock, 1 Mass. 144 (1804). Confessions made voluntarily were admissible, however. Commonwealth v. Drake, 15 Mass. 161 (1818). English rules were similar to those of Massachusetts. See King v. Warickshall, 1 Leach 263, 168 Eng. Rep. 234 (Crown Cases, 1783).

139. See Ross's Case, 2 Pick. 165 (1824).

140. See Commonwealth v. Knapp, 9 Pick. 496, 498 (1830); Commonwealth v. Frost, WSJC, 4-84; Commonwealth v. Kerilly, SSJC, 2-84; Commonwealth v. Woodworth, HSJC, 4-82; Government v. McGregor, SSC, 8-80; State v. Gardner, CSC, 7-80; Government v. Green, MSC, 11-79. Although prerevolution-

ary court records do not indicate that the practice of appointing counsel existed during the colonial period, John Adams left a record of a case in which he received such an appointment. See John Adams, *Diary and Autobiography*, ed. L.H. Butterfield (Cambridge, Mass., 1961), I, 353. Modern writers agree that the practice existed at least in capital cases. See Edwin Powers, *Crime and Punishment in Early Massachusetts* (Boston, 1966), 438-439; Wroth and Zobel, *Legal Papers*, I, li-lii; II, 402. In England prior to 1836 a defendant was not permitted to retain counsel except in treason and misdemeanor cases; only in cases of treason, it appears, would counsel be appointed. See William M. Beaney, *The Right to Counsel in American Courts* (Ann Arbor, Mich., 1955), 8-9. In Massachusetts, of course, defendants could retain counsel in all criminal cases.

141. See Commonwealth v. Goddard, 13 Mass. 455 (1816); Commonwealth v. Cunningham, 13 Mass. 245 (1816); Commonwealth v. Dodge, LSJC, 6-04, in Dana, Minute Books; Commonwealth v. Ely, HGS, 2-88. But if the court in the former prosecution had lacked jurisdiction, see Commonwealth v. Fuller, WCP, 12-30, nolle pros. entered, WSJC, 4-31, if the jury had failed to agree on a verdict, see Commonwealth v. Purchase, 2 Pick. 521 (1824); Commonwealth v. Bowden, 9 Mass. 494 (1813); if the defendant had obtained an acquittal by fraud, see Commonwealth v. Sheldon, ESJC, 11-89 (dictum), in Dana, Minute Books, if the former prosecution had been terminated by a nolle prosequi, see Commonwealth v. Wheeler, 2 Mass. 172 (1806), or if the second prosecution were for a separate crime arising out of the same transaction as the first prosecution, see Commonwealth v. Andrews, 2 Mass. 409 (1807), then a plea of former jeopardy would be rejected. Since a conspiracy and its substantive offense were different crimes, see Commonwealth v. Davis, 9 Mass. 415 (1812); Commonwealth v. Warren, 6 Mass. 74 (1809); Commonwealth v. Judd, 2 Mass. 329, 337 (1807); a defendant could be prosecuted for both, although he could only be convicted of one, since the conspiracy was merged into the completed offense. See Commonwealth v. Kingsbury, 5 Mass. 106 (1809). Similarly, the institution of a qui tam action for a penalty was a bar to a subsequent indictment for the same offense, see Commonwealth v. Churchill, 5 Mass. 174 (1809), but other civil actions were not bars unless the injured party

was a government witness, see Commonwealth v. Elliott, 2 Mass. 372 (1807); Commonwealth v. Bull, BeCP, 6-20; or the defendant had been victorious in the civil suit. See Commonwealth v. Odiorne, MCP, 3-30. See also Commonwealth v. Willard, HSJC, 9-91, in Dana, Minute Books, in which the court held that an acquittal on one count of a two-count indictment was a bar to a subsequent retrial on appeal on the count of which defendant had been acquitted.

142. See Commonwealth v. Phillips, 16 Mass. 423 (1820); Commonwealth v. Andrews, 3 Mass. 126 (1807).

143. Commonwealth v. Keniston, 5 Pick. 420 (1827).

144. See Commonwealth v. Silsbee, 9 Mass. 417 (1812); Commonwealth v. Leach, 1 Mass. 59 (1804).

145. See Commonwealth v. Hayward, 10 Mass. 34 (1813); Commonwealth v. Barlow, 4 Mass. 439 (1808).

146. Commonwealth v. Green, 17 Mass. 515, 517 (1822). Immediately after the Revolution, the court could grant a new trial in a criminal case only if it received power to do so by way of a special legislative resolve. See Hall's Motion, WSJC, 4-81.

147. Commonwealth v. Battis, 1 Mass. 95, 96 (1804). Accord, Commonwealth v. Fortis, LSJC, 7-94; Commonwealth v. Frost, WSJC, 9-93.

148. See Commonwealth v. Hathaway, 13 Mass. 299 (1816); Commonwealth v. Braley, 1 Mass. 103 (1804). But they would be tried if a jury found that their insanity was feigned. See Commonwealth v. Moore, 9 Mass. 402 (1812).

149. 3 Mass. 126 (1807).

150. See Johnson v. Zerbst, 304 U.S. 458 (1938).

151. Commonwealth v. Andrews, 3 Mass. 126, 133 (1807).

152. See, e.g., Government v. Potamy, Suff. Files no. 148285 (Msex. 1777).

153. See Commonwealth v. Tarbell, Suff. Files no. 150465 (Msex. 1793).

154. See Commonwealth v. Waite, Suff. Files no. 150471 (Msex. 1793); Commonwealth v. Chadwick, Suff. Files no. 150460 (Msex. 1793); Commonwealth v. Baker, Suff. Files no. 150363 (Msex. 1792).

155. See, e.g., Commonwealth v. Lepear, Suff. Files no. 151077 (Msex. 1797).

156. See Davis, *Practical Treatise*, 106-107.

157. Caldwell v. Jennison, WSJC, 9-81 (ar-

gument of counsel), paraphrased in John D. Cushing, "The Cushing Court and the Abolition of Slavery in Massachusetts: More Notes on the 'Quock Walker Case,' " *American Journal of Legal History*, V (1961), 118, 123.

158. Caldwell v. Jennison, WSJC, 9-81 (argument of counsel), quoted in Cushing, "Cushing Court," 118, 125.

159. Return of Braintree, June 5, 1780, in Handlin and Handlin, *Popular Sources*, 769. See also "The Essex Result," ibid., 341; Return of Rochester, May 26, 1780, ibid., 707; Return of Petersham, 1780, ibid., 860.

160. "The Essex Result," in Handlin and Handlin, *Popular Sources*, 341.

161. *Boston Gazette*, May 11, 1778, p. 2, col. 1.

162. See ibid., p. 2, col. 1.

163. See Simon v. Osgood, ECP, 9-77. The suit was trespass by the slave for false imprisonment, to which the defendant pleaded in due form that the plaintiff was "his own proper negro slave. . . ." Parsons's demurrer to this plea was sustained.

164. See Kimball v. Kimball, ECP, 10-78.

165. Jones v. White, MSJC, 11-80.

166. Littleton v. Tutle, MSJC, 10-96, in Dana, Minute Books. See also Inhabitants of Lanesborough v. Inhabitants of Westfield, 16 Mass. 74, 75-76 (1819), which notes a decision of 1796 holding that "the issue of slaves, although born before the adoption of the constitution, were born free." Accord, Perkins v. Emerson, ESJC, 11-99, which determined the status of a female pauper who "in the American Revolution . . . claimed her freedom in common with other black persons. . . ." But see Inhabitants of Andover v. Inhabitants of Canton, 13 Mass. 547, 549 (1816), which spoke of a black who had "continued to be held in slavery until his death in 1780." Accord, Inhabitants of Boston v. Inhabitants of Falmouth, NfCP, 12-06, rev'd on other grounds, NfSJC, 3-08 (implying that blacks remained slaves until freed by the Constitution of 1780).

167. WSJC, 9-81 (argument of counsel), discussed in Cushing, "Cushing Court," 118, 125.

168. Cushing 50, 51 (1783).

169. See Adventurer v. Vanderhoaf, ECP, 7-82; Brom v. Ashley, BeCP, 8-81; Oiro v. Sacket, HCP, 8-80; Tarbet v. Howard, PCP, 10-79. Cf. Reed v. Ensign, BeCP, 2-83 (writ of case for inducing plaintiff's slave to run away); Sacket v. Dewey, HCP, 8-80 (identical writ); Williston v. Day, HCP, 11-82 (breach in 1782 of contract to convey slave to plaintiff).

170. See Tarbett v. Snell, PCP, 4-80.

171. See Commonwealth v. Sparks, BeSJC, 10-84.

172. White v. Johnson, SSJC, 2-86.

173. Abigail Adams to John Adams, March 1776, in Elizabeth C. Stanton et al., *The History of Woman Suffrage* (New York, 1881), I, 32.

174. See Sikes v. Johnson, 16 Mass. 389 (1820) (dictum). This was true even if she was operating a business as a feme sole. See Barber v. Vernon, SCP, 7-86. Thus a husband became liable for debts contracted by his wife before their marriage. See Glezen v. Richardson, MSJC, 10-00; Eveleth v. Huff, ECP, 4-90. A husband also became possessed of his wife's choses in action created before their marriage. See Vernon v. Fairservice, SCP, 10-81.

175. See Osgood v. Breed, 12 Mass. 525 (1815), discussing the power of a married woman to make a will. See also Catlin v. Ware, 9 Mass. 218 (1812); Fowler v. Shearer, 7 Mass. 14 (1810); Thacher v. Omans, SSJC, 8-90, in Dana, Minute Books; discussing techniques for barring a married woman's future claims to dower in lands conveyed by her husband during his lifetime. See also Hildreth v. Eliot, 8 Pick. 293 (1829); Keith v. Woombell, 8 Pick. 211 (1829); Gill's Case, SSJC, 2-91, in Dana, Minute Books; Magnor v. Waters, SCP, 7-04; for examples of antenuptial agreements giving married women control over their own property.

176. See Haines v. Corliss, 4 Mass. 659 (1808); Bass v. Bradford, SSJC, 2-90; Thomas v. Thomas, PCP, 4-22; Otis v. Otis, PCP, 8-18; Richardson v. Morton, SCP, 1-90, aff'd, SSJC, 2-91; Stearns v. Johnson, WCP, 12-76.

177. Martin v. Commonwealth, 1 Mass. 347, 362 (1805).

178. Ibid., 364. Accord, Commonwealth v. Neal, 10 Mass. 152 (1813); Commonwealth v. Trimmer, 1 Mass. 476 (1805). This rule did not apply, however, to "crimes forbidden by the law of nature, which are *mala in se,* and some where the wife may be presumed the principal agent." Commonwealth v. Neal, supra, at 152. See generally Sikes v. Johnson, 16 Mass. 389n3 (1820).

179. Administration would be turned over to any coadministrator, see Newell v. Marcy, 17 Mass. 341 (1821), or in one's absence to the wife's new husband. See Barber v. Bush, 7 Mass. 510 (1811); Lee v. Bond, MCP, 5-95.

180. Sikes v. Johnson, 16 Mass. 389 (1820).

181. See Howland v. Coffin, BrCP, 9-83.

182. See Barber v. Vernon, SCP, 7-86.

183. Commonwealth v. Cullins, 1 Mass. 116 (1804).

184. But see Petition of Foots, BeSJC, 10-98, where the court granted a petition by a married woman whose husband had abandoned her to sell her own realty for her support.

185. See Dean v. Richmond, 5 Pick. 461, 465-466 (1827) (dictum). But the husband had a right to property acquired before the separation. See ibid., 468-469.

186. See Abbot v. Bayley, 6 Pick. 89 (1827); Gregory v. Paul, 15 Mass. 31 (1818).

187. See Bittner v. Darne, SCP, 7-22, stating the plaintiff's practice of contracting as a feme sole and the acquiescence of her husband and her creditors in that practice.

188. See Russell v. Brooks, 7 Pick. 65. (1828).

189. Isaac Backus to Noah Alden, 1779, quoted in William G. McLoughlin, *Isaac Backus and the American Pietistic Tradition* (Boston, 1967), 143.

190. Constitution of 1780, Part I, art. 3, in Handlin and Handlin, *Popular Sources*, 443. The breakdown of the establishment is thoroughly traced in William G. McLaughlin, *New England Dissent, 1630-1833: The Baptists and the Separation of Church and State* (Cambridge, Mass., 1971), I, 591-693; II, 1065-1274.

191. Isaac Backus, *Policy as Well as Honesty Forbids the Use of Secular Force in Religious Affairs* (Boston, 1779), in William G. McLoughlin, ed., *Isaac Backus on Church, State, and Calvinism: Pamphlets, 1754-1789* (Cambridge, Mass., 1968), 383.

192. Phillips Payson, "Election Sermon," quoted in Isaac Backus, *Government and Liberty Described and Ecclesiastical Tyranny Exposed* (Boston, 1778), in McLoughlin, *Pamphlets* 353.

193. Constitution of 1780, Part I, art. 3, in Handlin and Handlin, *Popular Sources*, 442.

194. The Protestant orientation of the Commonwealth was illustrated in Bartlet v. King, 12 Mass. 537 (1815), where the court, in upholding a devise to the American Board of Commissioners for Foreign Missions, observed that "the propagation of the christian religion, whether among our own citizens or the people of any other nation, is an object of the highest concern, and cannot be opposed to any general rule of law, or principle of public policy." Ibid., 540. For an additional case upholding a devise for religious purposes, see Trustees of Phillips Academy v. King, 12 Mass. 546 (1815).

195. Barnes v. First Parish in Falmouth, 6 Mass. 401, 408 (1810) (dictum).

196. Burr v. First Parish in Sandwich, 9 Mass. 277, 290 (1812) (dictum).

197. Barnes v. First Parish in Falmouth, 6 Mass. 401, 406-407 (1810) (dictum).

198. Fuller v. Inhabitants of Princeton, Cushing 60 (1783). Accord, Goss v. Inhabitants of Bolton, Cushing 11, 13 (1778).

199. Montague v. First Parish in Dedham, 4 Mass. 269, 271 (1808) (dictum).

200. Thaxter v. Jones, 4 Mass. 570, 573 (1808) (dictum).

201. Barnes v. First Parish in Falmouth, 6 Mass. 401, 406, 411-412 (1810) (dictum).

202. Constitution of 1780, Part I, art. 3, in Handlin and Handlin, *Popular Sources*, 442-443. The provision was construed broadly enough to permit parishes to collect taxes to buy land and build a house on it as a parsonage. See Thompson v. White, Cushing 73 (1784).

203. BrCP, 3-82. See generally William G. McLoughlin, "The Balkom Case (1782) and the Pietistic Theory of Separation of Church and State," *William and Mary Quarterly*, 3d ser., XXIV (1967), 267.

204. No appeal was taken to the Supreme Judicial Court, since the case had been commenced before a justice of the peace.

205. Cutter v. Frost, 1784, discussed in McLoughlin, *New England Dissent*, I, 642-644; McLoughlin, *Pietistic Tradition*, 160-161. But see Cressman v. Inhabitants of Beverly, ESJC, 11-92, in Dana, Minute Books, which appears to have reached the opposite result.

206. But dissenters did make certain gains during the 1780s. One matter that became clear, for example, was that a dissenter would not be prosecuted for not attending the services of the established church provided he attended those of his own church. See State v. Lamb, HGS, 5-85 (Baptist who attended Baptist meetings prosecuted for missing church; nolle pros. entered on court advice). It also was settled by statute that a dissenting minister could perform valid marriages. See Laws of 1786, ch. 3. See also Commonwealth v. Spooner, 1 Pick. 235 (1822); Murray v. Farley, ESJC, 11-87.

207. See First Parish in Shapleigh v. Gilman, 13 Mass. 190, 192 (1816) (dictum); Kendall v. Inhabitants of Kingston, 5 Mass. 524, 531 (1809) (dictum); Montague v. First Parish in Dedham, 4 Mass. 269 (1808) (by implication).

208. See First Parish in Shapleigh v. Gilman, 13 Mass. 190 (1816); Minot v. Curtis, 7 Mass. 441 (1811); Thaxter v. Jones, 4 Mass. 570 (1808).

209. Goss v. Inhabitants of Bolton, Cushing 11, 14 (1778). Accord, Avery v. Inhabitants of Tyringham, 3 Mass. 160, 169 (1807); Hill v. Powers, Cushing 26 (1780).

210. Goss v. Inhabitants of Bolton, Cushing 11, 14 (1778).

211. Hill v. Powers, Cushing 26, 28 (1780).

212. Thompson v. Catholic Congregational Soc'y in Rehoboth, 5 Pick. 469, 479 (1827). Accord, Avery v. Inhabitants of Tyringham, 3 Mass. 160, 181-182 (1807).

213. Burr v. First Parish in Sandwich, 9 Mass. 277, 289 (1812). Accord, Fuller v. Inhabitants of Princeton, Cushing 60 (1783). On the procedure for calling such councils, see Thompson v. Catholic Congregational Soc'y in Rehoboth, 7 Pick. 160 (1828); Cochran v. Inhabitants of Camden, 15 Mass. 296 (1818).

214. See Sparrow v. Wood, 16 Mass. 457 (1820); Blanchard v. Guild, NfCP, 12-22. If a person was not a member of any other religious society, he was automatically a member of the first parish of the place in which he resided. See Oakes v. Hill, 10 Pick. 333, 345-346 (1830). In many places, parish boundaries were coincidental with those of a town. However, not all the inhabitants of the town were members of the parish, for the reasons already noted, and therefore the law required that town and parish business be kept strictly segregated. See Woodbury v. Inhabitants of Hamilton, 6 Pick. 101 (1827); Granger v. Parsons, 2 Pick. 391 (1824); Inhabitants of Milford v. Godfrey, 1 Pick. 91, 97-98 (1822); Dillingham v. Snow, 5 Mass. 547, 554-555 (1809); Dillingham v. Snow, 3 Mass. 276 (1807); Bigelow v. Goodenow, MSJC, 10-01. Whenever a new parish was formed, the already existing one, even though it had existed solely by legal implication, inherited all the town's religious property. See First Parish in Medford v. Pratt, 4 Pick. 222, 227 (1826); First Parish in Brunswick v. Dunning, 7 Mass. 445 (1811). But cf. Eager v. Inhabitants of Marlborough, 10 Mass. 430 (1813) (parish debts divided among original and newly formed parishes). The segregation of town and parish functions hurt dissenters by precluding the use of town institutions, in which they participated, to gain control of the parish, but helped them by preventing the levy of religious taxes under the guise of town taxes. See also First Parish in Sutton v. Cole, 3 Pick. 232, 242 (1825), holding that objections as to the qualifications of persons seeking to vote had to be taken at the parish meeting or were thereafter deemed waived.

215. See Jewett v. Burroughs, 15 Mass. 464, 469-470 (1819), where the court upheld the election of a Congregationalist minister which had been conducted in precisely this manner.

216. See Chapter 2, note 50 and accompanying text.

217. Constitution of 1780, Part I, art. 3, in Handlin and Handlin, *Popular Sources*, 443.

218. The case is reported in James Sullivan to ——, June 25, 1785, in Sullivan Papers.

219. Murray v. First Parish in Gloucester, Cushing 82, 86 (1786).

220. See Turner v. Second Precinct in Brookfield, 7 Mass. 60 (1810); Kendall v. Inhabitants of Kingston, 5 Mass. 524, 533 (1809); Washburn v. Fourth Parish of West Springfield, 1 Mass. 32 (1804).

221. See Sanger v. Third Parish in Roxbury, 8 Mass. 265 (1811).

222. See Montague v. First Parish in Dedham, 4 Mass. 269 (1808).

223. A minister was entitled to his tax exemption even if he had never been publicly installed, see Gridley v. Clark, 2 Pick. 403, 410 (1824), unless he was an itinerant. See Ruggles v. Kimball, 12 Mass. 337 (1815); Taylor v. Smith, HSJC, 9-97, in Dana, Minute Books.

224. 6 Mass. 401 (1810). Accord, Lovell v. Parish of Byfield, 7 Mass. 230 (1810); Turner v. Second Precinct in Brookfield, 7 Mass. 60 (1810).

225. See Paul Goodman, *The Democratic-Republicans of Massachusetts: Politics in a Young Republic* (Cambridge, Mass., 1964), 163-165; McLoughlin, *New England Dissent*, II, 1084-1100.

226. Laws of 1811, ch. 6.

227. 14 Mass. 340 (1817).

228. Ibid., 345. Adams v. Howe was the first Massachusetts case to give explicit recognition to the doctrine of judicial review, even though the doctrine was not applied in the case. It had, however, been applied in earlier cases. See Ellis v. Marshall, 2 Mass. 269, 276-277 (1807) (by implication); Goddard v. Goddard, SSJC, 2-89 (holding unconstitutional legislative resolve reinstating civil action on court docket and accordingly refusing to reinstate action). See also Merchant v. McNeil, SSJC, 2-93, in Dana, Minute Books (argument by counsel that legislative resolve granting new trial unconstitutional). In the colonial period, on the other hand, the doctrine had been rejected. See Wroth and Zobel, *Legal Papers*, II, 106; Little v. Thomas, PCP, 10-65 (rejecting plea by John Adams that private

bill pleaded by plaintiff unconstitutional); Little v. Jacobs, PCP, 4-65 (rejecting same plea). See generally William E. Nelson, "Changing Conceptions of Judicial Review: The Evolution of Constitutional Theory in the States, 1790-1860," *University of Pennsylvania Law Review*, CXX (1972), 1166.

229. Adams v. Howe, 14 Mass. 340, 349 (1817).

230. Ibid., 349-350.

231. See Laws of 1823, ch. 106.

232. See Adams v. Howe, 14 Mass. 340 (1817); Inglee v. Bosworth, 5 Pick. 498, 501 (1827).

233. See Holbrook v. Holbrook, 1 Pick. 248, 253-254 (1822). One who procured such a certificate could not even be taxed to pay debts incurred by the parish when he was a member. See Whittemore v. Smith, 17 Mass. 347 (1821).

234. See Gage v. Currier, 4 Pick. 399, 402-403 (1826). Once the certificate had been filed with the clerk of the town in which the person who obtained it resided, he did not have to obtain a new certificate if he moved to another town. See Sumner v. First Parish in Dorchester, 4 Pick. 361 (1826). On the means of obtaining such a certificate, see Oakes v. Hill, 8 Pick. 46 (1829).

235. See Gage v. Currier, 4 Pick. 399, 403 (1826).

236. See Turner v. Parish of Burlington, 16 Mass. 208 (1819); Morse v. Byfield Parish, ECP, 9-18.

237. See Chapter 3, text at notes 17-24.

238. See Laws of 1785, ch. 66.

239. In Middlesex, where records of confessions were filed, no confessions appear in the files after 1791. See William E. Nelson, "Emerging Notions of Modern Criminal Law in the Revolutionary Era: An Historical Perspective," *New York University Law Review*, XLII (1967), 450, 456n32. In Hampshire, where confessions were also recorded, only one case was recorded after 1790. See Commonwealth v. Russell, HCP, 3-18.

240. See Commonwealth v. Budd, BeSJC, 5-02; Commonwealth v. Hayden, NGS, 3-97; Commonwealth v. Crocker, BeGS, 1-94; Commonwealth v. Langworthy, BeGS, 9-93.

241. See, e.g., Commonwealth v. Willard, WSJC, 4-09; Commonwealth v. Winchell, BeSJC, 9-03.

242. See, e.g., Commonwealth v. Spear, Boston Police Ct., 1826, no. 815; Commonwealth v. Smith, Boston Police Ct., 1825, no. 1427.

243. See Commonwealth v. Howe, WSJC, 4-20; Commonwealth v. Holmes, WCP, 12-19.

See also Anonymous, Boston Police Ct., 1824, p. 1 (prosecution for mailing obscene pictures).

244. The actual rate for 1776-1785 was 23 cases per year.

245. See note 206 above.

246. See, e.g., Commonwealth v. Shepherd, HCP, 5-05; Commonwealth v. Cook, WGS, 3-02; Commonwealth v. Searle, Boston Justice Ct., July 19, 1814 (swimming on Sunday). In addition to the Sabbath cases, there were also occasional prosecutions for blasphemy, see, e.g., Commonwealth v. Rust, ESJC, 4-01; Commonwealth v. Walcutt, WSJC, 4-90; and profanity. See, e.g., Commonwealth v. Gould, FCP, 8-16; Commonwealth v. Powell, BeCP, 4-08; Commonwealth v. Dudley, BeCP, 4-06.

247. *Remarks on the Existing State of the Laws of Massachusetts Respecting Violations of the Sabbath* (Boston, 1816), 3.

248. In Middlesex alone, for instance, three divorces were granted in that year. See Lawrence v. Lawrence, MSJC, 10-93; Bemis v. Bemis, MSJC, 10-93; Blanchard v. Blanchard, MSJC, 4-93.

249. See note 241 above and accompanying text.

250. Hiley v. Farmer, MGS, 9-90.

251. See Hiley v. Farmer, MGS, 11-90.

252. See Brooks v. Frost, MGS, 11-95.

253. See, e.g., House v. Westgate, NGS, 3-01; Ramsdell v. Woods, MGS, 5-99.

254. See Goodman, *Democratic-Republicans*, 89.

255. Timothy Dwight, "A Discourse on Some Events of the Last Century," Jan. 7, 1801, quoted in Vernon Stauffer, *New England and the Bavarian Illuminati* (New York, 1918), 25.

256. See Stauffer, *Bavarian Illuminati*, 24.

257. William Cushing, Notes on Biennial Elections and Other Subjects under Debate in Massachusetts Ratifying Convention, Jan. 1788, in Cushing Papers.

258. See Stauffer, *Bavarian Illuminati*, 26.

259. Levy, *Legacy of Suppression*, 258-297.

260. See Goodman, *The Democratic-Republicans*, 86-96, 162-166.

261. Bigelow v. Spooner, WSJC, 9-06.

262. See March v. Jackson, ESJC, 4-02.

263. See Pickering v. Smith, ECP, 9-09.

264. Burgess v. Story, ECP, 12-08.

265. 7 Pick. 303 (1828).

266. Ibid., 324, 331.

267. Ibid., 308.

268. For the ancient practice, see Selectmen of Montgomery v. Mann, HGS, 5-87,

holding that a Quaker should be excused from serving in a town office since he could "not take the Oath by Law required to qualify him for sd. Office &c."

269. Commonwealth v. Smith, 9 Mass. 107, 110 (1812).

270. Laws of 1810, ch. 127; Laws of 1807, ch. 139, § 14.

271. Constitution of 1780, Part I, art. 3, in Handlin and Handlin, *Popular Sources*, 443.

272. Commonwealth v. Smith, 9 Mass. 107, 111 (1812).

273. Ross v. Lapham, 14 Mass. 275, 276 (1817).

274. Ibid., 277.

275. See Hunscom v. Hunscom, 15 Mass. 184 (1818). See also Caleb Cushing, *The Right of Universalists to Testify in a Court of Justice Vindicated* (Boston, 1828), 22-23.

276. See Commonwealth v. Knapp, 9 Pick. 496, 511-512 (1830); Commonwealth v. Green, 17 Mass. 515, 549 (1822). The old rule had been applied in many cases immediately following the Revolution. See Commonwealth v. Lawrens, MSJC, 4-93, in Dana, Minute Books; Newman v. Wright, MSJC, 4-92, ibid.; Commonwealth v. Manley, BrSJC, 10-88, ibid. Cf. Commonwealth v. Blood, MSJC, 4-90, ibid. (evidence of conviction of theft rejected when offered only to go to credibility of witness).

277. See Tucker v. Welsh, 17 Mass. 160 (1821).

278. Ibid., 166.

279. Brooks v. Barrett, 7 Pick. 94, 97-98 (1828).

280. Commonwealth v. Hutchinson, 10 Mass. 225 (1813).

281. Curtis v. Jackson, 13 Mass. 507, 513 (1816).

282. Clark v. Faunce, 4 Pick. 245, 246 (1826). For other cases on presumptions, see Newman v. Jenkins, 10 Pick. 515 (1830); Inhabitants of Attleborough v. Inhabitants of Middleborough, 10 Pick. 378 (1830); Tilson v. Thompson, 10 Pick. 359 (1830); Jenkins v. Hopkins, 9 Pick. 543 (1830); Davenport v. Mason, 15 Mass. 85 (1818).

283. See Chapter 2, note 138 and accompanying text.

284. See Geer v. Putnam, 10 Mass. 312 (1813).

285. See Commonwealth v. Knox, 6 Mass. 76 (1809).

286. See Pearce v. Atwood, 13 Mass. 324 (1816).

287. "The Spirit of Misrule," *Law Reporter*, VII (1844), 209.

288. See Commonwealth v. Edwards, HCP, 8-30; Commonwealth v. Spurr, NfCP, 4-25.

289. See Bolles v. Presbury, BrCP, 6-23 (common law action for damages by teacher whose class was disrupted). Cf. Luther v. Durfee, BrCP, 6-27 (action for damages brought by schoolmaster against students who had assaulted him); Commonwealth v. Avery, BeCP, 2-20 (prosecution for riot for disturbing school). See also Boynton v. Perley, ESJC, 10-20 (suit by parent against teacher who refused to instruct his children in reading and writing).

290. See Throop v. Stewart, SSJC, 11-24 (jury verdict giving damages to citizen interrupted by militia during sit-in on Boston Common to protest militia drill); Eaton v. Stevens, PCP, 4-17 (suit by militia officer for willful refusal of defendant "to shoulder his arms ... in a soldier like manner" and for "other acts of unmilitary conduct"); Curtis v. Alden, NfCP, 4-16 (suit by militia officer for penalty for "unmilitary conduct ... in a disorderly manner" by defendant).

291. Haskell v. Moody, ESJC, spring 1830.

292. See Roger Lane, *Policing the City: Boston, 1822-1885* (Cambridge, Mass., 1967).

293. Cushing, *Right of Universalists*, 26.

Chapter 7. Liberty and the Breakdown of Stability

1. Gamaliel Bradford, *State Prisons and the Penitentiary System Vindicated* (Boston, 1821), 5.

2. Gamaliel Bradford, *Description and Historical Sketch of the Massachusetts State Prison* (Boston, 1816), 15.

3. Bradford, *Penitentiary System Vindicated*, 12.

4. Thomas B. Chandler, *A Friendly Address to All Reasonable Americans on the Subject of Our Political Confusions* (New York, 1774), 5.

5. Charge to the Grand Jury, Quincy 218, 220 (1766).

6. Charge to the Grand Jury, Quincy 110 (1765).

7. John Adams, *Diary and Autobiography*, ed. L.H. Butterfield (Cambridge, Mass., 1961), I, 260.

8. Oliver Prescott, Town Clerk of Groton to Town of Boston, 1774, quoted in

Clifford K. Shipton, *Sibley's Harvard Graduates, 1746-1750* (Boston, 1962), XII, 570.

9. Adams, *Diary*, I, 264.

10. Charge to the Grand Jury, Quincy 218, 219 (1766).

11. Proclamation of the General Court, Jan. 23, 1776, in Oscar Handlin and Mary F. Handlin, eds., *The Popular Sources of Political Authority: Documents on the Massachusetts Constitution of 1780* (Cambridge, Mass., 1966), 68.

12. William Cushing, Draft of Grand Jury Charge, 1783, in Cushing Papers.

13. Commonwealth v. Russell, MSJC, 12-82; Commonwealth v. White, MGS, 9-85; Commonwealth v. Orr, MGS, 9-85; Commonwealth v. Frost, MGS, 9-81.

14. Commonwealth v. Richardson, MSJC, 10-84; Commonwealth v. Shattuck, MSJC, 4-82; Commonwealth v. Parker, MSJC, 4-81; Commonwealth v. Parker, MSJC, 4-81; Government v. Parker, MSC, 11-80.

15. Commonwealth v. Shattuck, MSJC, 4-82.

16. See Robert J. Taylor, *Western Massachusetts in the Revolution* (Providence, 1954), 111-113, 116-117, 120-121.

17. See ibid., 116-117.

18. See generally ibid., 128-167.

19. Quoted in Edwin Powers, *Crime and Punishment in Early Massachusetts* (Boston, 1966), 193.

20. Richards v. Inhabitants of Dover, NfGS, 9-98.

21. *Herald of Freedom* (Boston), Oct. 2, 1789, p. 1, cols. 1-2.

22. William Blackstone, *Commentaries on the Laws of England* (Oxford, 1765-1769), II, 2. See also Gray v. Blanchard, 8 Pick. 284, 288 (1829). The concern that the property of one individual not be put involuntarily to the use of another led the postrevolutionary courts to scrutinize carefully all eminent domain takings to insure that all takings were for public purposes. See Commonwealth v. Cambridge, 7 Mass. 158, 167 (1810).

23. See Scott v. Tuckerman, SSJC, 8-01, reversing SCP, 1-01.

24. See Quails v. Blood, MCP, 9-03, appeal dism., MSJC, 4-04.

25. See Blake v. Clark, SCP, 10-28; Smith v. Chace, DCP, 5-22. Cf. Commonwealth v. Barker, NGS, 10-99.

26. See Phelps v. Ely, HCP, 5-02, appeal dism., HSJC, 9-03; Hannum v. Ely, HCP, 5-02, appeal dism., HSJC, 9-03.

27. See Eddy v. Powell, BeCP, 6-23. Cf.

Briggs v. Briggs, PSJC, 6-01 (defendant corrupted plaintiff's well by throwing dead animal into it).

28. See Smith v. Dibble, BeCP, 1-04; Pratt v. Eddy, WCP, 9-02.

29. Cf. Shaw v. Cummiskey, 7 Pick. 76 (1828).

30. See Swan v. Coburn, SCP, 7-95.

31. See Shaw v. Cummiskey, 7 Pick. 76 (1828) (by implication); Taylor v. Greaves, SSJC, 11-22. See also Loring v. Bacon, 4 Mass. 575 (1808), where the owner of the second floor of a building was held to have a duty to the owner of the first floor to make repairs to prevent damage from rain leaking through the roof of the building down to the first floor.

32. See Badger v. Redding, SCP, 1-24.

33. See Hubbard v. Austin, SSJC, 8-93, reversing SCP, 4-93; May v. Parks, SCP, 1-27; Badger v. Boston Mill Corp., SCP, 10-11; Curwen v. West, ECP, 9-03, appeal dism., ESJC, 11-03. The owner of an ancient drain could use self-help to reopen it. See Minot v. Wheeler, MSJC, 4-96.

34. See Clark v. Nancrode, SSJC, 8-94; Brimmer v. Marshall, SCP, 7-89, aff'd, SSJC, 2-90.

35. See Brimmer v. Marshall, SSJC, 2-90 (argument of counsel), in Francis Dana, Minute Books.

36. James Sullivan, *The History of Land Titles in Massachusetts* (Boston, 1801), 193.

37. See March v. Darling, 8 Pick. 283 (1829); Sullivan, *Land Titles*, 193.

38. See Church v. Burghardt, 8 Pick. 327 (1829) (dictum); Boston Mill Corp. v. Bulfinch, 6 Mass. 229 (1810); Proprietors of Kennebeck Purchase v. Call, 1 Mass. 483, 487-488 (1805) (dictum). See also Coolidge v. Learned, 8 Pick. 504 (1829) (a case of prescription by the general public).

39. See Laws of 1807, ch. 74, which gave a trespasser the right to recover from a true owner the value of any improvements he had made on the land or to recover the land itself upon payment of its value. See Jones v. Carter, 12 Mass. 314 (1815). A trespasser could recover even if he claimed under a void title, as distinguished from no title at all. See Bacon v. Callender, 6 Mass. 303 (1810). The act did not apply, however, on behalf of a tenant holding pursuant to a contract of purchase from the true owner, see Knox v. Hook, 12 Mass. 329 (1815), or a trespasser who made improvements subsequent to the owner's commencement of an action to re-

cover the land. See Russell v. Blake, 2 Pick. 505 (1824).

40. M'Mechan v. Griffing, 3 Pick. 149, 156 (1825) (dictum); Davis v. Blunt, 6 Mass. 487 (1810); Farnsworth v. Childs, 4 Mass. 637, 639 (1808) (dictum); Norcross v. Widgery, 2 Mass. 506, 508 (1807) (dictum).

41. See Clap v. M'Neil, 4 Mass. 589 (1808).

42. See Berry v. Hayward, ECP, 6-15; Wood v. Church, PCP, 4-90; Commonwealth v. Monks, Boston Police Ct., 1827, no. 381; Commonwealth v. McDonald, Boston Police Ct., 1825, no. 410. See also Keay v. Goodwin, 16 Mass. 1 (1819), where a tenant in common holding a portion of the common land under an agreement with the other tenants was held to have sufficient possession to recover damages from another tenant who had removed the first tenant's chattels from the occupied portion.

43. To construct a dam it was necessary either to own the land on both sides of the stream or to have the consent of both owners. See Holmes v. Plymouth Cotton Manufactory, PCP, 4-19, aff'd, PSJC, 10-19.

44. See Cook v. Hull, 3 Pick. 269 (1825); Colburn v. Richards, 13 Mass. 420 (1816); Hodges v. Raymond, 9 Mass. 316 (1812); Phillips v. Emes, ESJC, 11-13; Minot v. Wheeler, MSJC, 10-98; Taft v. Sargeants, WSJC, 4-84; Dibbell v. Smith, BeCP, 4-00, rev'd, BeSJC, 5-02, rev'd, BeSJC, 9-03; Kennedy v. Bucklin, BrCP, 9-94; Rice v. Parker, WCP, 9-79; Sullivan, *Land Titles*, 273. Cf. Revere v. Leonard, NfSJC, 10-04 (plaintiff's right to flow rested on explicit grant from defendant).

45. See Leonard v. Revere, NfSJC, 10-04. Cf. Sumner v. Tileston, 7 Pick. 198 (1828); Hatch v. Dwight, 17 Mass. 289 (1821).

46. See Sumner v. Foster, 7 Pick. 32 (1828). The second owner could use a greater amount of water if some customary arrangement, see Bacon v. Lyon, WSJC, 4-23; Fales v. Fales, NfSJC, 2-19; Benson v. Morrison, PCP, 4-93, or contractual arrangement authorized him to do so. See Pearson v. Tenny (ESJC, 1802), in Nathan Dane, *A General Abridgment and Digest of American Law* (Boston, 1824), III, 14. Cf. Amesbury Wool & Cotton Mfg. Co. v. Winkley, ESJC, 4-25, for a case in which the plaintiff derived his water rights from a contract. A subsequent user could also take water away from a prior user for agricultural purposes, see Weston v. Alden, 8 Mass. 136 (1811), provided that he returned unused water to its natural channel. See Anthony v. Lapham, 5 Pick. 175 (1827). The Massachusetts doctrinal evolution is traced in detail in

Morton J. Horwitz, "The Transformation in the Conception of Property in American Law, 1780-1860," *University of Chicago Law Review*, XL (1973), 248, 262n40. English law likewise gave property rights in water to prior and natural users during the period here in question. See Liggins v. Inge, 7 Bing. 682, 693, 131 Eng. Rep. 263, 268 (C.P. 1831) (dictum); Bealey v. Shaw, 6 East 208, 102 Eng. Rep. 1266 (K.B. 1805); Robinson v. Lord Byron, 1 Bro. C.C. 588, 28 Eng. Rep. 1315 (Ch. 1785); Blackstone, *Commentaries*, II, 403; Horwitz, "Conception of Property," 262n39.

47. See Pope v. Nichols, ESJC, 6-85; Messinger v. Cheever, NfCP, 4-12; Burt v. Stone, BrCP, 9-92. Cf. Temple v. Sherman, WSJC, 9-99; Ward v. Proctor, HCP, 5-04, appeal dism., HSJC, 12-06, for cases in which water rushed out of upstream dams, in one case upon the dam's bursting, and downstream owners recovered damages for the flooding.

48. See Dench v. Jones, Cushing 73 (1784); Lumbard v. Allen, HdSJC, 5-21; Crane v. Leonard, SSJC, 8-93; Whitman v. Barker, PSJC, 5-06.

49. For cases in which defendants claimed such prescriptive rights, see Daniels v. Whiting, NfSJC, 2-16; Wall v. Green, WSJC, 4-07; Buckman v. Tufts, MSJC, 10-00; Capen v. Flixin, NfCP, 12-28; Hamilton v. Baker, HCP, 11-26; Goodale v. Ryther, FCP, 12-14; Batchelder v. Peabody, ECP, 10-00, rev'd by referees, ESJC, 11-01. Cf. Brown v. Tufts, WCP, 3-26 (owner of prescriptive right to water allowed to destroy dam of subsequent user).

50. See Avery v. Van Dusen, BeSJC, 9-27; Edmunds' Complaint, ECP, 3-29, rev'd on other grounds, ESJC, spring 1829; Parkhurst v. Parkhurst, WCP, 8-19, appeal dism., WSJC, 10-24; Wheelock v. Cole, HCP, 1-97.

51. See Complaint of Winslow, BrGS, 9-88.

52. Analogous results were achieved in cases that required adjoining landowners to maintain partition fences as they had been anciently maintained. See Binney v. Proprietors of Common Lands in Hull, 5 Pick. 503 (1827); Rust v. Low, 6 Mass. 90 (1809). Even in the absence of any prescriptive obligation, a landowner who was directed to do so by fence viewers had to maintain his fences in a location that was mutually beneficial to himself and to his neighbors. See Wolcott v. Ashley, HdCP, 8-28. A landowner could also obtain a prescriptive right to maintain gates across a highway bisecting his land. See Petition of Perkins, EGS, 4-85.

53. Spring v. Lowell, 1 Mass. 422, 430

(1805).

54. See Bates v. Sparrell, 10 Mass. 323 (1813).

55. Revere v. Gannett, 1 Pick. 169, 170 (1822).

56. Clap v. Draper, 4 Mass. 266, 268 (1808).

57. Storer v. Freeman, 6 Mass. 435, 438 (1810). Accord, Rust v. Boston Mill Corp., 6 Pick. 158 (1828); Doane v. Broad Street Ass'n, 6 Mass. 332 (1810); Commonwealth v. May, SSJC, 3-03, in *American Jurist*, III (1830), 190 note a; Thayer v. Hunt, NfSJC, 8-96; Eckely v. Scott, SCP, 4-97, rev'd on other grounds, SSJC, 2-98. See also Blackstone, *Commentaries*, I, 264. See generally Oscar Handlin and Mary F. Handlin, *Commonwealth: A Study of the Role of Government in the American Economy—Massachusetts, 1774–1861* (Cambridge, Mass., rev. ed., 1969), 207-208.

58. See Ingraham v. Wilkinson, 4 Pick. 268 (1826).

59. See Commonwealth v. Chapin, 5 Pick. 199 (1827); Bishop v. Hall, MSJC, 4-01. The owner of such a fishery could recover damages from one who prevented fish from coming upstream to it. See Strong v. Proprietors of Locks and Canals, HGS, 5-97. Conversely, he could not use his fishery in such a manner as to destroy the fishing rights of owners of upstream fisheries. See Commonwealth v. Chapin, supra, at 202-203; Commonwealth v. Ruggles, 10 Mass. 391 (1813). Cf. Lewis v. Leeds, SSJC, 8-94, on the duty of the owner of a dam not to obstruct the passage of fish upstream.

60. For a case of prescription by an individual, see Melvin v. Whiting, 10 Pick. 295 (1830). For cases of prescription by the inhabitants of a town, see Lufkin v. Haskell, ECP, 6-20, appeal dism., ESJC, 10-20; White v. Whittier, ECP, 3-05, rev'd by referees, ESJC, 11-05. See also Lufkin v. Haskell, ESJC, 11-25, upholding plaintiff's replication that the inhabitants did not possess any title in his land, as they claimed, and hence had no right to fish. For cases of prescription by town corporations, see Nickerson v. Brackett, 10 Mass. 212 (1813); Inhabitants of Randolph v. Inhabitants of Braintree, 4 Mass. 315, 318 (1808) (dictum). See also Handlin and Handlin, *Commonwealth*, 87.

61. See Coolidge v. Williams, 4 Mass. 140 (1808).

62. See Bailey v. Eaton, ECP, 9-85.

63. Frary v. Cooke, Cushing 19, 23 (1779).

64. See ibid.

65. See Commonwealth v. Chapin, 5 Pick. 199 (1827); Strong v. Proprietors of Locks & Canals, HGS, 5-97.

66. Compare Sullivan, *Land Titles*, 128, with Sargent v. Ballard, 9 Pick. 251 (1830); Hill v. Crosby, 2 Pick. 466 (1824); Strout v. Berry, 7 Mass. 385 (1811) (dictum). Easements acquired by 20 years' uninterrupted use were, technically speaking, easements arising by a presumption of a lost grant; easements arising by prescription, properly speaking, required 40 years' use, see Melvin v. Whiting, 10 Pick. 295 (1830); Kent v. Waite, 10 Pick. 138 (1830), during which time, however, there could be an interruption of up to 20 years. See Emerson v. Wiley, 10 Pick. 310 (1830); Sullivan, *Land Titles*, 128. Easements could also be created by grant, see Choate v. Burnham, 7 Pick. 274 (1828); White v. Crawford, 10 Mass. 183 (1813), and by necessity. See Grant v. Chase, 17 Mass. 443, 448 (1821) (dictum); Ware v. White, BrCP, 4-01. See generally Gayetty v. Bethune, 14 Mass. 49 (1817). If an easement were appurtenant to an estate of lesser duration than a fee simple, it would terminate upon the termination of that estate. See Hoffman v. Savage, 15 Mass. 130 (1818). The holder of an easement did not have title to the land over which the easement passed; title remained in the holder of the servient estate. See Miller v. Miller, 4 Pick. 244 (1826).

67. The law continued to recognize forms of easements that had existed during the colonial period, such as an easement to enter on a neighbor's land to repair one's own estate. See Hill v. Haskins, 8 Pick. 83 (1829). Compare Chapter 4, note 23.

68. See Story v. Odin, 12 Mass. 157 (1815); Lienow v. Ritchie, SSJC, 3-29; Orne v. Beckford, ESJC, 4-19; Rhoades v. Damblide, SSJC, 8-95; Dolbeaux v. Warre, SSJC, 2-94; Matchett v. Hooten, SSJC, 2-85; Baxter v. Adams, SCP, 7-94.

69. Compare Emerson v. Wiley, 10 Pick. 310 (1830), with Jones v. Percival, 5 Pick. 485 (1827).

70. See Reed v. Bowden, ESJC, 10-21; Druil v. Hopkins, SSJC, 2-86; Robinson v. Spear, SCP, 10-22; Richards v. Smith, NfCP, 4-12. See also Doane v. Badger, 12 Mass. 65 (1815), on the duty to repair such a well.

71. See Patch v. Johnson, WCP, 12-03, appeal dism., WSJC, 4-04 (upholding right to take manure left by cattle in neighboring pasture).

72. See Handlin and Handlin, *Commonwealth*, 70-71, 73-75.

73. See Gloucester By-Laws, EGS, 10-95;

Commonwealth v. Chadwick, EGS, 10-94 (prosecution for unlicensed slaughterhouse); Petition of Dodge, EGS, 8-91 (plea of license rejected in prosecution to abate slaughterhouse as nuisance). Cf. Fisk v. Richardson, ECP, 9-86 (suit for penalty for unlawful butchering in violation of state statute).

74. See Commonwealth v. Gardner, Boston Justice Ct., Feb. 21, 1814.

75. See Commonwealth v. Dockum, Boston Police Ct., 1830, no. 656.

76. See Order Granting Licenses, SGS, 9-17; Commonwealth v. Divol, BrGS, 12-85. See also Kimball v. Perley, ECP, 3-15 (suit for penalty for auctioning dry goods contrary to state statute); Fisk v. White, ECP, 9-86 (suit for penalty for manufacturing candles without license contrary to state statute).

77. See Cambridge By-Law, MGS, 11-03; License of Ward, EGS, 7-95.

78. See Commonwealth v. Williams, ECP, 9-29.

79. See Vandine, Petitioner, 6 Pick. 187 (1828), holding that such control by towns over the economy was not void as in restraint of trade and did not operate as a monopoly but constituted a reasonable use of municipal powers to preserve the health, safety, and well-being of a town's inhabitants. See also Commonwealth v. Dockum, Boston Police Ct., 1830, no. 656, where a city ordinance requiring the licensing of intelligence officers was upheld. See generally Handlin and Handlin, *Commonwealth*, 88-89. Most towns also regulated their town markets, see Charlestown By-Laws, MGS, 5-20; Boston By-Law, SGS, 4-17; Commonwealth v. Garfield, Boston Police Ct., 1826, no. 1819; Safford v. Archer, EGS, 4-94 (prosecution for penalty for market violation). Cf. Clarck v. Cushman, BrCP, 12-07 (suit for penalty for violating state statute regulating auctions), particularly for the purpose of preventing frauds on consumers. See Gloucester By-Law, EGS, 4-20 (regulating sizes of firewood); Marblehead By-Laws, EGS, 9-90 (regulating same); Newburyport By-Laws, EGS Files, 3-83 (regulating same); Commonwealth v. Brigham, Boston Justice Ct., Oct. 2, 1819 (prosecution for refusing to deliver weights and measures to selectmen).

80. See Petition of Robinson, HCC, 9-28 (granting petition by purchaser of ferry for license); Petition of Goodman, HGS, 3-27 (granting petition by owner of ferry to license his grantee); Petition of Nurse, WGS, 6-79 (granting petition by purchaser of inn for license). Cf. Burnham v. Manning, ESJC, 11-

08 (suit for breach of contract to rent inn with liquor license appurtenant thereto). See also Petition of Tewksbury, EGS, 4-84 (granting petition by ferry owner to have employees licensed); Petition of Hatch, PGS, 4-83 (granting petition by innkeeper for license in new house instead of old one).

81. See Petition of Cook, HCC, 4-29 (granting petition of executor of deceased holder of ferry license for license in own name); Petition of Basset, PGS, 8-14 (granting petition by son for liquor license held by deceased father). Cf. Petition of Bradley, MGS, 9-10 (granting petition for license by son whose father was then too old to run ferry).

82. See Petition of Clark, HGS, 3-25; Petition of Bradley, MGS, 9-24; Petition of Bradley, MGS, 9-10; Petition of Williams, SGS, 7-01.

83. See Petition of Norton, HGS, 3-25; Petition of Williams, HGS, 3-21, and HGS Files, 3-21; Petition of Armsby, WGS, 9-17; Petition of Wheeler, WGS, 9-17; Petition of Olds, BeGS, 8-08. Petitioners for licenses in newly built inns did not fare nearly as well; some of them succeeded in obtaining licenses if they could show that the public would be benefited by a new inn, see Petition of Moody, HGS, 4-28; Petition of Ammidown, WGS, 9-19; Petition of Jacobs, SCP, 4-08, but in the absence of such a showing, petitioners were unable to overcome the opposition of town selectmen. See Petition of Butler, WGS, 3-18. See also Petition of Merritt, EGS, 4-09 (petition for license denied since petitioner an alien). Sale of liquor without a license led to prosecution by the collector of excise in a suit for a statutory penalty. See Cone v. Ashley, BeSJC, 10-89.

84. See Grand Jury Remonstrance, HGS, 1-92 (holding that if owner of private bridge continued to charge excessive toll, county would build a parallel public bridge); Petition of French, BrGS, 12-21 (ferry license granted to petitioner upon original ferryman's failure to maintain adequate boats). Ferry rates continued to be set by the sessions courts. See Petition of Smith, DGS, 11-19; Tyngsborough Ferry, MGS, 1-09; Order re Fares of Ferriages, HGS, 9-98. Landowners also continued to hold their land subject to the right of the public to acquire an easement across it for a road. Although the public or, if the easement had been acquired for a turnpike, the turnpike corporation could make any use of their easement that was necessary for maintaining the road, see Tucker v. Tower, 9 Pick. 109 (1829), title to the soil remained in the

original owner, see Inhabitants of Millbury v.
Blackstone Canal Co., 8 Pick. 478 (1829),
who could continue to use the soil for any
purpose that did not interfere with the road.
See Perley v. Chandler, 6 Mass. 453 (1810);
Petition of Cook, MGS, 11-84. Cf. Adams v.
Emerson, 6 Pick. 57 (1827). When an easement was taken for a road or turnpike, compensation had, of course, to be given to the
owner. See Rust v. City of Boston, SCP, 7-28;
Petition of Peabody, EGS, 10-13; Richards v.
Inhabitants of Dover, NfCP, 9-98. Nothing
but monetary compensation could be given
when land was taken; its owner could not be
given other land in return. See Commonwealth v. Peters, 2 Mass. 125 (1806). A jury
appointed to assess damages could, however,
return a verdict that the owner was not
damaged by the taking of his land, see Commonwealth v. Justices of the Sessions for the
County of Middlesex, 9 Mass. 388 (1812), if,
for example, the jury found that the road
increased the value of the owner's remaining
land. See ibid.; Petition of Lovell, NfGS, 9-13;
Petition of Newhall, EGS, 10-06. In deciding
what land to take for a road, the courts of
sessions, which retained the power of determining the course of roads, were to act "in a
manner most conducive to public good and
least injurious to private property. . . ." Petition of Hill, MGS, 9-04. Accord, e.g., Order re
Road in Northampton, HGS, 3-17; Petition of
Sanderson, FGS, 11-12. Land could not be
taken for a road that would benefit a particular individual rather than the general public.
See Petition of Ames, NfGS, 4-30. Thus a
public highway could not come into existence
as a result of prescription or immemorial
usage, see Emerson v. Wiley, 7 Pick. 68
(1828); Hinckley v. Hastings, 2 Pick. 162
(1824), nor could a town way be so acquired.
See Commonwealth v. Low, 3 Pick. 408
(1826); Clap v. Barker, PCP, 4-89. A road that
had been so acquired could at most be a
private way or an easement. See Commonwealth v. Low, supra.

85. See Petition of Williams, HGS, 9-21,
where the holder of a license was unsuccessful
in preventing a prospective competitor from
also obtaining a license. But see Petition of
Coffin, HGS, 9-21 (opponent of license successful in preventing its grant).

86. See Smith v. Daggett, DCP, 11-19.

87. Chadwick v. Proprietors of Haverhill
Bridge, ECP, 4-96, aff'd on reference, ESJC,
11-98, reported in Dane, Abridgement, II,
686. English law similarly permitted an operator of a ferry to recover damages if a second

ferry was set up in competition with the first.
See Huzzey v. Field, 2 Cr. M. & R. 432, 150
Eng. Rep. 186 (Ex. 1835) (dictum); Blissett v.
Hart, Willes 508, 125 Eng. Rep. 1293 (C.P.
1744).

88. Petition of Marston, ECP, 4-95.

89. See Gilmore v. Wales, NfCP, 12-17;
appeal dism., NfSJC, 2-18.

90. See Pease v. Fisher, DCP, 11-09.

91. Clark v. Billings, Cushing 54 (1783).

92. Hayden v. Blake, SCP, 7-16. Accord,
Blunt v. Aken, ESJC, 11-06.

93. Mycall v. Jones, SSJC, 8-84.

94. See Swett v. Gale, ECP, 6-11, appeal
dism., ESJC, 11-11.

95. See Commonwealth v. Scarlet, Boston
Police Ct., 1824, no. 367.

96. Fowler v. Beebe, 9 Mass. 231, 234
(1812).

97. Cushing v. Vose, SCP, 10-85.

98. Prescott v. Tucker, ESJC, 4-21.

99. Goss v. Inhabitants of Bolton, Cushing
11, 13 (1778). Accord, Hill v. Powers, Cushing 26 (1780).

100. Carleton v. Joy, SSJC, 2-03 (suit for
damages against third party who induced servant to leave master). Accord, Richardson v.
Seward, SSJC, 2-02 (similar suit); Shearer v.
Lyman, HCP, 11-01, aff'd, HSJC, 5-02 (similar suit).

101. The true gist of most suits brought
by husbands who had lost the services of their
wives as a result of conduct of a defendant
was alienation of affections, seduction, or
rape. See Pierce v. Baker, BrSJC, 4-28; Cottle
v. Butler, BrSJC, 10-16; Bradstreet v. Foster,
ESJC, 11-11; Welsh v. Turner, SSJC, 2-02;
Curry v. Gay, SSJC, 8-77; Douglass v. Phelps,
HdCP, 11-21, appeal dism., HSJC, 5-22; Welsh
v. Newell, WCP, 8-00; Smith v. White, BrCP,
4-94. But a husband could recover damages
solely for loss of his wife's labor. See Cum-
stock v. Taft, WCP, 6-82, appeal dism., WSJC,
4-83 (defendant communicated smallpox to
plaintiff's wife).

102. See Day v. Everett, 7 Mass. 145
(1810); Benson v. Remington, 2 Mass. 113
(1806); Taft v. Grosvenor, WSJC, 10-82, in
Sargeant Papers, reversing Grosvenor v. Taft,
WCP, 6-82; Waters v. Webb, ESJC, 11-77;
George v. Pillsbury, ECP, 9-12; Brown v.
Baker, BeCP, 4-05; Robinson v. Alden, BrCP,
4-97; Grout v. Frizzle, WCP, 6-85. But cf.
Nightingale v. Withington, 15 Mass. 272
(1818). Many of the suits brought by fathers
against defendants who had deprived them of
the services of their daughters involved claims
of their daughters' becoming pregnant. See

Gile v. Moore, HdSJC, 5-26; Ferre v. Wallis, HCP, 11-08. But even in these cases loss of service was an important element of the father's claim. See Green v. Weston, BeCP, 2-28, aff'd, BeSJC, 5-28; Thing v. Coffin, ECP, 9-22; Harrington v. Coffin, BrCP, 9-17. A stepfather, however, had no right to the earnings of a stepchild, although he could recover on an implied assumpsit for support given to the child. See Freto v. Brown, 4 Mass. 675 (1808). Moreover, a father who expressly agreed to emancipate his son or whose agreement could be inferred from the son's conduct lost his right to his son's wages. See Whiting v. Howard, 3 Pick. 201 (1825); Jenney v. Alden, 12 Mass. 385 (1815). The parent of an emancipated child also was under no duty to support the child. See Angel v. McLellan, 16 Mass. 28 (1819).

103. See Holbrook v. Bullard, HdSJC, 4-31; Bardwell v. Train, HdCP, 3-22; Dickinson v. Edwards, HCP, 11-06; Luther v. Rounds, BrCP, 12-05; Garnet v. McFarland, PCP, 8-99; Ireson v. Burrell, ECP, 4-96; Curtin v. Florence, ECP, 10-94, appeal dism., ESJC, 11-94. A master could also sue the apprentice for breach of the indenture of apprenticeship and have the court order the apprentice to serve extra time in order to reimburse him. See Petition of Swift, PGS, 10-89.

104. See Stiles v. Stowell, WSJC, 4-00; Terry v. Farnum, BeCP, 6-25, rev'd on other grounds, BeSJC, 5-26; Terry v. Bradley, BeCP, 10-22; Powers v. Thayer, HCP, 8-15; Frost v. Whitwell, HCP, 8-05, rev'd on other grounds, HSJC, 9-05; Maxwell v. Johnson, ECP, 7-93. A master could also recover from a defendant to whom he had hired his apprentice any wages due under the contract of hiring. See Haskel v. Comstock, DCP, 11-19; Rowe v. Pool, ECP, 10-99.

105. Upon complaint, Boston municipal judges would either return apprentices to their masters, see Commonwealth v. Frothingham, Boston Police Ct., 1827, no. 1220; Commonwealth v. Flagner, Boston Justice Ct., Feb. 23, 1810, or sentence them to 20 days in jail. See Commonwealth v. Smith, Boston Justice Ct., Nov. 30, 1818; Commonwealth v. Starr, Boston Justice Ct., Nov. 22, 1806. The power of municipal courts was similarly used against fugitive seamen, see Commonwealth v. Williams, Boston Justice Ct., Dec. 11, 1818; Commonwealth v. Quasa, Boston Justice Ct., Sept. 24, 1807; Commonwealth v. Robinson, Boston Justice Ct.,

Feb. 9, 1807, and against other servants. See Commonwealth v. Lucy, Boston Police Ct., 1825, no. 1423.

106. See Cox v. Vincent, ECP, 7-93. Masters of vessels possessed similar power over their seamen, see, e.g., Jewett v. Morse, ESJC, 6-81; Simpson v. Hodges, ECP, 12-21, as did other owners of servants. See Watson v. Crosby, WCP, 7-94. A parent could not interfere with a master's punishment of a child who had been indentured as an apprentice, see Commonwealth v. Aiken, Boston Police Ct., 1827, no. 1173, but could bring an action to have the indenture set aside and to have his child discharged from the apprenticeship if the master had punished him cruelly. See O'Brien v. Roberts, MCP, 11-03; Railly v. Cassin, SCP, 1-02. A parent could also bring suit to have the indenture set aside if the master failed to provide proper food, clothing, or instruction for the apprentice, see Butler v. Hubbard, 5 Pick. 250 (1827); Kendall v. Andrews, SCP, 4-23; Bailey v. Aldridge, NCP, 10-10; Culver v. Benjamin, HCP, 1-02; cf. Selectmen of Boston v. Raynard, SCP, 4-08; if the master assigned the apprentice to a third person, see Davis v. Coburn, 8 Mass. 299 (1811); cf. Hall v. Gardner, 1 Mass. 172 (1804); if the master took the apprentice out of Massachusetts without the consent of the parent, see Coffin v. Bassett, 2 Pick. 357 (1824); Commonwealth v. Brown, Boston Police Ct., 1826, no. 1436 (stating rule but refusing to use criminal process to enforce it); or if the master otherwise breached the terms of the indenture. See Riley v. Greene, SCP, 1-15. In order to terminate his obligations under an indenture, a master could also sue to have it set aside. See Complaint of Gardner, NCP, 11-16; Petition of Cary, NCP, 3-04; Evonet v. Morris, SCP, 1-04.

107. See Slater v. Farnum, WCP, 3-29, appeal dism., WSJC, 4-29.

108. But see Utica Glass Co. v. Kupfer, BeSJC, 5-13 (suit for interference with contractual relations), reversing BeCP, 12-10 (writ abated on ground that New York corporation lacked standing to sue in Massachusetts).

109. See Commonwealth v. Holmes, Boston Police Ct., 1824, no. 885 (neither civil nor criminal remedy lay for attempt to induce employer to discharge employee).

110. See Commonwealth v. Isabella, Boston Police Ct., 1824, no. 689. Some 18 years later the leading case of Commonwealth v.

Hunt, 4 Metc. 111 (1842), held the criminal law inapplicable to labor combinations. See generally Leonard W. Levy, *The Law of the Commonwealth and Chief Justice Shaw* (Cambridge, Mass., 1957), 183-206.

111. Declaration and Resolves of the First Continental Congress, in Henry S. Commager, ed., *Documents of American History* (New York, 8th ed., 1968), 83.

112. Charles F. Adams, ed., *The Works of John Adams* (Boston, 1852), VI, 280.

113. Constitution of 1780, Part I, art. 1, in Handlin and Handlin, *Popular Sources*, 442. Indeed, the Founding Fathers even spoke of the "property, which every individual of the community has, in his *life, liberty* and *estate*...." "The Letters of 'A Republican Federalist,'" in Cecelia M. Kenyon, ed., *The Antifederalists* (Indianapolis, 1966), 122.

114. John Taylor, *Construction Construed and Constitutions Vindicated* (Richmond, 1820), 78. For further statements from the late eighteenth and early nineteenth centuries stressing the importance of property to the preservation of liberty, see Adams, *Works*, IX, 560; Nathaniel Chipman, *Sketches of the Principles of Government* (Burlington, Vt., 1793), 176; James Fenimore Cooper, *The American Democrat* (Cooperstown, N.Y., 1838), 135; Max Farrand, ed., *The Records of the Federal Convention of 1787* (New Haven, 1911), II, 204 (remarks of Mr. Madison); "Madison's Observations on Jefferson's Draft of a Constitution for Virginia," in Julian P. Boyd, ed., *The Papers of Thomas Jefferson* (Princeton, 1950-), VI, 310; "The Essex Result, 1778," in Handlin and Handlin, *Popular Sources*, 324; James Sullivan to Elbridge Gerry, July 30, 1789, Gerry II Papers (in MHS). See generally Richard Schlatter, *Private Property: The History of an Idea* (New Brunswick, N.J., 1951), `188-195, 199-200; Gordon S. Wood, *The Creation of the American Republic, 1776-1787* (Chapel Hill, N.C., 1969), 218-219, 404-405, 410-411, 503-504.

115. Petition of Vinal, MGS, 11-94. Hence it was urged that men "ought not to be deprived of the benefit they had a right to expect" from their property. Pelsue v. Middlesex Canal, MCP, 3-05.

116. See Billings v. Hayden, Cushing 24 (1780). See also Worthington v. Chapin, HSJC, 4-91, in Francis Dana, Minute Books; Plumb Island Case, ESJC, 11-90, ibid.

117. See Charles A. Beard, *Economic Origins of Jeffersonian Democracy* (New York,

1927), 304-318; Manning J. Dauer, *The Adams Federalists* (Baltimore, 1953), 56-57; Vernon L. Parrington, *Main Currents in American Thought: An Interpretation of American Literature from the Beginnings to 1920* (New York, 1927), I, 316-317.

118. Fisher Ames, *Works* (Boston, 1809), 125. See generally Parrington, *Main Currents*, II, 279-288. See also Samuel J. Konefsky, *John Marshall and Alexander Hamilton: Architects of the American Constitution* (New York, 1964), 121.

119. See Levy, *Shaw*, 29-33; Conrad Wright, *The Beginnings of Unitarianism in America* (Boston, 1955), 274-280.

120. For a case apparently growing out of a schism during the Great Awakening, see Wilson v. Fisher, SSC, 2-60. For another colonial dispute over ¬church property, see Emmerson v. Willis, MSC, 8-60, rev'd, WSC, 9-61. For two postrevolutionary cases involving schisms, see Hunt v. French, BrCP, 9-93; French v. Read, BrCP, 4-93.

121. 16 Mass. 488 (1820).

122. 10 Pick. 172 (1830).

123. See Levy, *Shaw*, 35.

124. See Humphrey v. Whitney, 3 Pick. 158 (1825), which adopted such an approach. But cf. Manning v. Fifth Parish in Gloucester, 6 Pick. 6 (1827), where the court held that its lack of a full equity jurisdiction precluded enforcement of the particular agreement. On the subject of equity, see William J. Curran, "The Struggle for Equity Jurisdiction in Massachusetts," *Boston University Law Review*, XXXI (1951), 269.

125. See Baker v. Fales, 16 Mass. 488, 496-497 (1820).

126. 13 Mass. 190 (1816).

127. Ibid., 190. Cf. Rector and Wardens of King's Chapel v. Pelham, 9 Mass. 501 (1813).

128. Baker v. Fales, 16 Mass. 488, 493 (1820). Accord, Stebbins v. Jennings, 10 Pick. 172, 186 (1830).

129. Baker v. Fales, 16 Mass. 488, 496 (1820).

130. Manning v. Fifth Parish in Gloucester, 6 Pick. 6, 19 (1827).

131. Cf. Episcopal Charitable Soc'y v. Episcopal Church in Dedham, 1 Pick. 372 (1823).

132. "The Exiled Churches of Massachusetts," *Congregational Quarterly*, V (1863), 216.

133. George E. Ellis, *A Half-Century of the Unitarian Controversy* (Boston, 1857), 31.

134. William W. Fenn, "The Unitarians,"

in John W. Platner et al., eds., *The Religious History of New England* (Cambridge, Mass., 1917), 111.

135. See George W. Cooke, *Unitarianism in America* (Boston, 1902), 121; Levy, *Shaw*, 38-42.

136. Daniel v. Wood, 1 Pick. 102, 104 (1822).

137. Howard v. First Parish in North Bridgewater, 7 Pick. 138, 139-140 (1828). Accord, Wentworth v. First Parish in Canton, 3 Pick. 344 (1825); Jackson v. First Parish in North Bridgewater, PCP, 8-27.

138. See Daniel v. Wood, 1 Pick. 102 (1822); Gay v. Baker, 17 Mass. 435 (1821).

139. Petition of Tucker, EGS, 10-19. For an example of a similar concern a decade earlier, see Committee Report, PGS, 4-04.

140. See Petition of Filley, HdGS, 9-29; Petition of Baker, HdGS, 9-29; Petition of Winslow, NGS, 10-22; Petition of Myrick, NGS, 10-18.

141. See Hale v. Wheelock, WCP, 12-25. Cf. Goff v. Fowler, 3 Pick. 300 (1825).

142. Others, however, did not. See, e.g., Petition of Homer, ECC, 7-30, one of the 14 cases in the July 1830 term in which the Essex County Commissioners granted licenses to persons who had not received the approbation of town selectmen.

143. See Petitions for Licenses, BrCC, 10-30.

144. Petition of Society for Suppression of Intemperance, DCC, 11-30.

145. See Licenses Granted, DCC, 11-32.

146. See Order re Licenses, BeGS, 9-29.

147. Petition of Hartshorn, MGS, 11-93.

148. Concord Gaol Limits, MGS, 3-96.

149. 4 Mass. 361 (1808).

150. Ibid., 365, 368.

151. See Order re Limits of Goal Yard, SGS, 10-08. See also Order re Gaol Limits, NfGS, 9-03.

152. 4 Mass. at 366.

153. Petition of Prisoners, SGS, 5-09. Accord, Petition re Prison Limits, NGS, 4-21; Petition re Gaol Limits, NGS, 3-18; Petition re Gaol Yard, NGS, 3-00.

154. See Order re Limits of Goal Yard, SGS, 10-08. See also Order re Gaol Limits, NfGS, 9-03. But see Order re Goal Yard in Newburyport, EGS, 4-09, where jail yard limits were drawn to include "the several Houses of Religious Worship" within them.

155. Petition of Prisoners, SGS, 5-09.

156. Laws of 1808, ch. 92, as amended, Laws of 1809, ch. 33.

157. See Locke v. Dane, 9 Mass. 360 (1812); Patterson v. Philbrook, 9 Mass. 151 (1812); Walter v. Bacon, 8 Mass. 468 (1812).

158. See Order re Prison Limits at Newburyport, EGS, 7-25; Order re Prison Limits in Newburyport, EGS, 7-23; Order re Jail Limits, HdGS, 8-20; Petition of Smith, EGS, 7-20; Petition of Chandler, SGS, 8-19; Order re Jail Limits, HdGS, 5-15.

159. See Report of Committee on Gaol Limits, BeGS, 2-12.

160. See Petition of Blossom, BeGS, 4-12.

161. See Committee Report re Goal Yard, PGS, 9-12.

162. See Report of Committee on Gaol Limits, BeGS, 4-10. Cf. Petition of Curtiss, BeGS, 8-10, in which a jail yard was extended to include private property on condition that the property owner execute a lease of it to the county.

163. See Report of Committee on Gaol Limits, BeGS, 8-11. Accord, Rules re Gaol Yard, NfGS, 4-13; Order re Limits to County Gaol Yard, HGS, 12-12.

164. Order re Gaol Limits, BeGS, 4-15.

165. See Order re Prison Grounds, BeGS, 9-20.

166. Report of Committee on Prison Limits, BeGS, 4-27.

167. 1 Pick. 418 (1823).

168. Ibid., 432.

169. See Handlin and Handlin, *Commonwealth*, 87-92.

170. See ibid., 157-160.

171. Bradley v. Larned, BeSJC, 10-96, in Dana, Minute Books.

172. Ellis v. Marshall, 2 Mass. 269, 273 (1807) (argument of counsel).

173. Ibid., 272 (argument of counsel).

174. This is the position taken by Handlin and Handlin, *Commonwealth*, 140-141. Since Merrick Dodd has found no evidence that eighteenth-century business corporations possessed like authority to levy assessments, see E. Merrick Dodd, *American Business Corporations until 1860* (Cambridge, Mass., 1954), 368-370; E. Merrick Dodd, "Book Review," *Harvard Law Review*, LXI (1948), 555, 558-560, he refuses to begin his analysis of the taxing authority of business corporations by reference to that of municipalities. It appears, however, that the eighteenth-century corporation that was most analogous to the business corporation, the proprietary of common lands, did have power to levy assessments on its members. See Wrentham Proprietors v. Metcalf, Quincy 36 (1763). Thus, apart from the fact that Dodd rests his argument on no more than a paucity of evidence of the sort

that historians often confront, the Handlins seem to have the better of the argument.

175. SCP, 1-00.
176. See generally Handlin and Handlin, *Commonwealth*, 139-151.
177. 2 Mass. 269 (1807).
178. Ibid., 274 (argument of counsel).
179. Ibid., 279.
180. Ibid., 276.
181. 6 Mass. 40 (1809).
182. See ibid. Accord, Chester Glass Co. v. Dewey, 16 Mass. 94, 102 (1819); Taunton & South Boston Tpke. Corp. v. Whiting, 10 Mass. 327, 333 (1813) (dictum); New Bedford & Bridgewater Tpke. Corp. v. Adams, 8 Mass. 138 (1811); Andover & Medford Tpke Corp. v. Hay, 7 Mass. 102 (1810) (by implication); Gilmore v. Pope, 5 Mass. 491 (1809); Worcester Tpke. Corp. v. Willard, 5 Mass. 80 (1809); Chapin v. Adams, WCP, 12-07. A shareholder was liable for assessments that he had promised to pay even if other shareholders had become insolvent and so were not compelled to pay theirs, see Salem Mill Dam Corp. v. Ropes, 9 Pick. 187, 196-197 (1829) (dictum), and even if an assessment for preliminary expenses was levied prior to incorporation. See Salem Mill Dam Corp. v. Ropes, 6 Pick. 23, 41-42 (1827).
183. Andover & Medford Tpke. Corp. v. Gould, 6 Mass. 40, 44 (1809). Accord, Salem Mill Dam Corp. v. Ropes, 6 Pick. 23, 37-38 (1827).
184. See Middlesex Tpke. Corp. v. Swan, 10 Mass. 384 (1813); Middlesex Tpke. Corp. v. Locke, 8 Mass. 268 (1811).
185. Tippets v. Walker, 4 Mass. 595, 597 (1808). Accord, Nichols v. Thomas, 4 Mass. 232 (1808).
186. Commonwealth v. Blue-Hill Tpke. Corp., 5 Mass. 420, 422 (1809).
187. Thus, as of 1810 a judgment creditor's sole remedy against a corporation was the levy of a common law writ of execution. But after the Massachusetts courts were granted equity jurisdiction, see generally Curran, "Equity Jurisdiction," 269, a creditor could also obtain equitable sequestration of the corporation's assets. See Jones v. Boston Mill Corp., 4 Pick. 507, 511-512 (1827).
188. See Laws of 1808, ch. 65, §6; Laws of 1807, ch. 31, §7. See generally, Handlin and Handlin, *Commonwealth*, 148-149.
189. See Spear v. Grant, 16 Mass. 9 (1819); Vose v. Grant, 15 Mass. 505 (1819).
190. Spear v. Grant, 16 Mass. 9, 14 (1819).
191. See Bond v. Appleton, 8 Mass. 472

(1812), construing a New Hampshire statute similar to the Massachusetts one. The court noted that in the absence of New Hampshire authority, it would construe the New Hampshire act "in the same manner [as] we should construe an act of our own legislature." Ibid., 475-476.
192. See Leland v. Marsh, BeCP, 2-18, aff'd, BeSJC, 9-20.
193. Marcy v. Clark, 17 Mass. 330, 335 (1821).
194. See Ripley v. Sampson, 10 Pick. 371 (1830); Child v. Coffin, 17 Mass. 64 (1820). However, assessments levied by the corporation did constitute a lien upon the shares. See Ripley v. Sampson, supra, at 373.
195. See Franklin Glass Co. v. White, 14 Mass. 286 (1817).
196. See Handlin and Handlin, *Commonwealth*, 148-149.
197. See Laws of 1826, ch. 137.
198. See Laws of 1829, ch. 53, §7.
199. Many other rules common in modern corporation law were also established in the first three decades of the nineteenth century. The courts decided cases dealing with such questions as the power of corporations, including corporations created under the law of other states, to sue and be sued in Massachusetts courts, see Portsmouth Livery Co. v. Watson, 10 Mass. 91 (1813) (foreign corporation could sue in Massachusetts); Utica Glass Co. v. Kupfer, BeSJC, 5-13, reversing BeCP, 12-10 (same holding); Taunton & South Boston Tpke. Corp. v. Whiting, 9 Mass. 321 (1812) (corporation had no residence for purposes of venue), and to enter into contracts with or without agents, see Proprietors of Canal Bridge v. Gordon, 1 Pick. 297, 304 (1823); White v. Westport Cotton Mfg. Co., 1 Pick. 215 (1822); Essex Tpke. Corp. v. Collins, 8 Mass. 292 (1811); Middlesex Tpke. Corp. v. Tufts, 8 Mass. 266 (1811); Tucker v. Bass, 5 Mass. 164 (1809). They also decided cases dealing with the transferability and heritability of corporate shares, see Hussey v. Manufacturers & Mechanics' Bank, 10 Pick. 415 (1830); Sargent v. Essex Marine Ry., 9 Pick. 202 (1829); Sargent v. Franklin Ins. Co., 8 Pick. 90 (1829); Nesmith v. Washington Bank, 6 Pick. 324 (1828); Merchants Bank v. Cook, 4 Pick. 405 (1826); Jarvis v. Rogers, 13 Mass. 105 (1816); Quiner v. Marblehead Social Ins. Co., 10 Mass. 476 (1813); Russell's Appeal, SSJC, 2-98, in Dana, Minute Books, the power of state and municipal governments to tax corporate assets, see Amesbury Woollen & Cotton Mfg. Co. v. Inhabitants of

Amesbury, 17 Mass. 461 (1821); Amesbury Nail Factory Co. v. Weed, 17 Mass. 53 (1820); Portland Bank v. Apthorp, 12 Mass. 252 (1815); Salem Iron Factory v. Inhabitants of Danvers, 10 Mass. 514 (1813); Thompson v. Massachusetts Bank, SSJC, 2-93, the power to tax corporate stock owned by individuals, see Little v. Greenleaf, 7 Mass. 236 (1810); and the rights and remedies of shareholders for misconduct of corporate officers. See Little v. Obrien, 9 Mass. 423 (1812); Commonwealth v. Union Fire & Marine Ins. Co., 5 Mass. 230 (1809); Gray v. Portland Bank, 3 Mass. 364 (1807). See Handlin and Handlin, *Commonwealth*, 158-160.

200. *Herald of Freedom* (Boston), Oct. 2, 1789, p. 1, cols. 1-2.

201. *Independent Chronicle* (Boston), Mar. 4, 1805, p. 2, col. 1.

202. *Herald of Freedom* (Boston), Oct. 2, 1789, p. 1, col. 2.

203. Ibid., Oct. 2, 1789, p. 1, col. 1.

204. Willard Phillips, *Manual of Political Economy* (Boston, 1828), 210, quoted in Handlin and Handlin, *Commonwealth*, 225.

205. Boston Hat Manufactory v. Messinger, 2 Pick. 223, 232 (1824).

206. Livermore v. Newburyport Marine Ins. Co., 1 Mass. 264, 276 (1804).

207. Wyman v. Hallowell & Augusta Bank, 14 Mass. 58, 61 (1817).

208. See Paul v. Frazier, 3 Mass. 71 (1807), holding that no action lay in contract against a man who had seduced a woman and gotten her pregnant unless he had made an express promise of marriage. But see Symmes v. Frazier, 6 Mass. 344 (1810), where an individual was held to contractual liability beyond the express terms of his promise. With the abandonment of relationship as a basis for contractual liability, the new doctrinal basis became consideration. Thus the colonial rules precluding inquiry into issues of consideration in cases of written and sealed contracts, see Chapter 4, notes 129-130, 137, and accompanying text, were substantially modified near the turn of the century. See Chapter 5, notes 196-212 and accompanying text. Courts also began to inquire into the lawfulness of particular considerations, see Coolidge v. Inglee, 13 Mass. 26 (1816), and to rule that moral obligation was not a sufficient consideration except in cases where a valuable consideration had once existed. See Mills v. Wyman, 3 Pick. 207 (1825). The courts also used the requirement of consideration as a basis for excusing promissors from their liability to pay subscriptions to charitable institutions, see Phillips Limerick Academy v. Davis, 11 Mass.

113 (1814), unless the institution had spent money in reliance on the promise, see Amherst Academy v. Cowls, 6 Pick. 427 (1828); Bridgewater Academy v. Gilbert, 2 Pick. 579 (1824); Farmington Academy v. Allen, 14 Mass. 172 (1817), or others had entered into subscriptions in reliance on the promise, see Church and Congregation in the Second Precinct in Pembroke v. Stetson, 5 Pick. 506 (1827), or the subscription was in the form of money paid to the institution followed by a loan from the institution to the subscriber and a promise by the subscriber to repay the loan. See Fisher v. Ellis, 3 Pick. 322 (1825). Although the doctrine of consideration can provide courts with a mechanism for policing the fairness of an exchange, it was not used for that purpose in early nineteenth-century Massachusetts. Instead, as the above cases suggest, it was used primarily to limit the liability of individuals upon moral obligations—a fact that accounts, perhaps, for the doctrine's rise to prominence during the period.

209. See Sanches v. Davenport, 6 Mass. 258 (1810).

210. See Reynolds v. Toppan, 15 Mass. 370 (1819); Hussey v. Allen, 6 Mass. 163 (1809).

211. Sumner v. Williams, 8 Mass. 162, 178 (1811). In general, one could be held as a party to a contract only if he had manifested an intention to adhere to it. See Flagg v. Upham, 10 Pick. 147 (1830); Holbrook v. Bullard, 10 Pick. 68 (1830); Mayhew v. Prince, 11 Mass. 54 (1814); Felton v. Dickinson, 10 Mass. 287 (1813); Mann v. Chandler, 9 Mass. 335 (1812); Forster v. Fuller, 6 Mass. 58 (1809); Tippets v. Walker, 4 Mass. 595, 597 (1808).

212. Padelford v. Boardman, 4 Mass. 548, 551 (1808).

213. For cases in which the courts explicitly remarked on the absence of precedent, see Shed v. Brett, 1 Pick. 401, 404 (1823); Whitney v. Dutch, 14 Mass. 457, 460 (1817); Skinner v. Somes, 14 Mass. 107, 108 (1817); Amory v. Gilman, 2 Mass. 1, 10 (1806); Porter v. Bussey, 1 Mass. 436, 440 (1805).

214. Boston Hat Manufactory v. Messinger, 2 Pick. 223, 231-232 (1824).

215. Upham v. Smith, 7 Mass. 265, 266 (1811).

216. Appleton v. Crowninshield, 3 Mass. 443, 471 (1807).

217. Taylor v. Lowell, 3 Mass. 331, 338 (1807).

218. Appleton v. Crowninshield, 3 Mass.

443, 471 (1807). For cases in which the courts construed contracts in accordance with this principle, see Bird v. Richardson, 8 Pick. 252 (1829); Mayo v. Maine Fire & Marine Ins. Co., 12 Mass. 259 (1815); Trustees of Phillips Limerick Academy v. Davis, 11 Mass. 113 (1814); Higginson v. Pomeroy, 11 Mass. 104 (1814); Fowle v. Bigelow, 10 Mass. 379 (1813); Ellis v. Wild, 6 Mass. 321 (1810); Pollock v. Babcock, 6 Mass. 234 (1810); Pearce v. Phillips, 4 Mass. 672 (1808); Cleveland v. Fettyplace, 3 Mass. 392 (1807); Holbrook v. Brown, 2 Mass. 280 (1807); Blunt v. Melcher, 2 Mass. 228 (1806); Tucker v. Bass, NfSJC, 3-09.

219. See Wightman v. Coates, 15 Mass. 1, 5 (1818). Parties were deemed to have contracted in accordance with the facts that they knew or ought to have known rather than with the actual facts. See Green v. Merchants' Ins. Co., 10 Pick. 402 (1830); Pomeroy v. Fifth Massachusetts Tpke. Corp., 10 Pick. 35 (1830); Dorr v. New England Marine Ins. Co., 4 Mass. 221 (1808) (dictum). See also Pearson v. Lord, 6 Mass. 81 (1809), on the effect of mutual mistake in the absence of a court of equity. A party's mere knowledge of a fact would not, however, be binding on him in the absence of evidence of his assent to its inclusion in the contract. See Wiggin v. Boardman, 14 Mass. 12, 14 (1817); Parker v. Jones, 13 Mass. 173 (1816).

220. See Loring v. Gurney, 5 Pick. 15 (1827); Chickering v. Fowler, 4 Pick. 371, 372-373 (1826); Clark v. VanNorthwick, 1 Pick. 343 (1823); Lincoln & Kennebeck Bank v. Hammatt, 9 Mass. 159 (1812); Lincoln & Kennebeck Bank v. Page, 9 Mass. 155 (1812); Tyler v. Binney, 7 Mass. 479, 481 (1811); Lowry v. Russell, 8 Pick. 360 (1829). Cf. Hayden v. Middlesex Tpke. Corp., 10 Mass. 397 (1813), implying that a corporation would be liable in assumpsit on the basis of conduct of its agents sanctioned by longstanding acquiescence on the part of the corporation's members.

221. Stevens v. Reeves, 9 Pick. 198, 202 (1829).

222. See Blanchard v. Hilliard, 11 Mass. 85, 88 (1814).

223. Homer v. Dorr, 10 Mass. 26, 29 (1813). Accord, Blanchard v. Hilliard, 11 Mass. 85, 88 (1814). In some cases parties expressly incorporated usage into their agreements, as in the case of a contractor who promised to construct a turnpike "agreeable to the common method of making turnpike roads in the United States. . . ." Gould v. Robinson, HCP, 5-05. Cf. Fowler v. Bott, 6

Mass. 63, 68 (1809), holding that when parties wrote their contract in words that had acquired a particular meaning as a result of past judicial construction, they would be presumed to have agreed to abide by that construction. Accord, Locke v. Swan, 13 Mass. 76, 79 (1816). The extent to which parole evidence was admissible to vary or explain a writing was not yet established. See Russell v. Clark, SSJC, 3-04, in Dana, Minute Books; Sewall v. Stone, YSJC, 6-90, ibid.

224. 11 Mass. 6 (1814).

225. 13 Mass. 68 (1816).

226. On the trade patterns of colonial New England merchants, see generally Richard Pares, *Yankees and Creoles: The Trade between North America and the West Indies before the American Revolution* (London, 1956), 48, 65-71, 95-96, 103-105.

227. Kettell v. Wiggin, 13 Mass. 68, 73 (1816).

228. Quoted in Chapter 4, text at note 115.

229. Cf. Whipple v. Dow, 2 Mass. 415, 419 (1807). In the absence of an express contract, plaintiffs continued, of course, to recover in quantum meruit and quantum valebant upon a theory of implied contract. See Gwinneth v. Thompson, 9 Pick. 31 (1829); Hall v. Marston, 17 Mass. 575 (1822); Mason v. Waite, 17 Mass. 560 (1822); Trustees of Farmington Academy v. Allen, 14 Mass. 172 (1817); Jackson v. Mayo, 11 Mass. 147 (1814) (dictum); Goodridge v. Lord, 10 Mass. 483 (1813); Brigham v. Eveleth, 9 Mass. 538 (1813); Goodwin v. Gilbert, 9 Mass. 510 (1813); Sproat v. Porter, 9 Mass. 300 (1812); Lawrence v. Dalton, CSJC, 5-04, in Dana, Minute Books; Inhabitants of Hatfield v. Cook, HSJC, 4-93, ibid.; Worthington Tpke. Corp. v. Clapp, HCP, 3-28, appeal dism., HSJC, 9-28; Atkins v. Greenwood, HdCP, 3-26. But see Greene, v. First Parish in Malden, 10 Pick. 500 (1830); Inhabitants of Roxbury v. Worcester Tpke Corp., 2 Pick. 41 (1823); Miller v. Inhabitants of Somerset, 14 Mass. 396 (1817).

230. Whiting v. Sullivan, 7 Mass. 107, 109 (1810). But cf. Gates v. Caldwell, 7 Mass. 68, 70 (1810) (dictum).

231. See Barney v. Coffin, 3 Pick. 115, 116 (1825) (dictum); Stark v. Parker, 2 Pick. 267 (1824); Faxon v. Mansfield, 2 Mass. 147 (1806). However, if the plaintiff was prevented from completing his work by an act of God, he could recover in quantum meruit for the value of the work performed. See Peabody v. Wood, ESJC, 6-97, in Dana, Minute Books.

232. See Taft v. Inhabitants of Montague, 14 Mass. 282 (1817). However, if a plaintiff did not intentionally quit work and performed the task so that it was of some value to the defendant, although it was not perfect, he could recover in quantum meruit for the value of the work performed, which would be determined by deducting from the contract price the cost of repairing the imperfections. See Hayward v. Leonard, 7 Pick. 181 (1828).

233. See Gilbert v. Williams, 8 Mass. 476 (1812). Cf. Johnson v. Johnson, 11 Mass. 359, 361 (1814) (dictum); Chapman v. Durant, 10 Mass. 47 (1813), both ruling that receipt of a promissory note in consideration of a debt due by a simple contract discharged the contract. See also Aspinwall v. Bartlet, 8 Mass. 483 (1812), holding that the contract of the onwer of a vessel to sell her and delivery pursuant to the contract terminated the liability of the original owner to the seamen for wages.

234. See Moses v. Stevens, 2 Pick. 332 (1824); Thurston v. Percival, 1 Pick. 415 (1823).

235. See Hill v. Green, 4 Pick. 114 (1826); Seymour v. Bennet, 14 Mass. 266 (1817) (dictum).

236. See Willington v. Inhabitants of West Boylston, 4 Pick. 101 (1826).

237. See Cornwall v. Gould, 4 Pick. 444, 448 (1827); Gibbs v. Bryant, 1 Pick. 118 (1822); Emerson v. Providence Hat Mfg. Co., 12 Mass. 237, 244 (1815).

238. See Emerson v. Brigham, 10 Mass. 197 (1813). Accord, Conner v. Henderson, 15 Mass. 319 (1818) (by implication). On the colonial rule, see Chapter 4, note 117 and accompanying text. The case of Allen v. Bruce, WSJC, 4-87, in which a jury found that a defendant had innocently sold a plaintiff a counterfeit settlement certificate and the court permitted recovery, apparently on a theory of breach of an implied warranty, suggests that something like the warranty of merchantability was still implied in the 1780s. Everett v. Gray, 1 Mass. 101 (1804), suggests the opposite rule for the turn of the century. See also Hastings v. Lovering, 2 Pick. 214 (1824), implying a warranty that goods would conform to their description in the contract, and Bradford v. Manly, 13 Mass. 139 (1816), holding that an action could be maintained on a warranty implied from a sale of goods by sample since "a sale by sample . . . [was] tant-amount to an express warranty. . . ." Ibid., 145. Accord, Williams v. Spafford, 8 Pick. 250 (1829).

239. See Stark v. Parker, 2 Pick. 267

(1824); Davis v. Boardman, 12 Mass. 80 (1815); Stiles v. Campbell, 11 Mass. 321 (1814).

240. Minot v. Durant, 7 Mass. 436, 438 (1811).

241. Phillips v. Stevens, 16 Mass. 238, 241 (1819). For other cases in which the courts held liable a "defendant [who] intended to make himself liable in some form," see Moies v. Bird, 11 Mass. 436, 440 (1814); Afridson v. Ladd, 12 Mass. 177 (1815); Baker v. Mair, 12 Mass. 121 (1815); Richardson v. Maine Fire & Marine Ins. Co., 6 Mass. 102, 116 (1809); Sargent v. Appleton, 6 Mass. 85 (1809); Bond v. Farnum, 5 Mass. 170 (1809).

242. Woodward v. Cowing, 13 Mass. 216, 217 (1816).

243. Harris v. Clap, 1 Mass. 308, 313 (1805). Accord, Allen v. Ayres, 3 Pick. 298, 299 (1825).

244. See Peck v. Cochran, 7 Pick. 34 (1828); Chazournes v. Edwards, 3 Pick. 5 (1825); Higginson v. Gray, 8 Mass. 385, 397 (1812); Lee v. Gray, 7 Mass. 349 (1811); Upham v. Smith, 7 Mass. 265 (1811); Murray v. Hatch, 6 Mass. 465 (1810); Bill v. Mason, 6 Mass. 313 (1810); Richardson v. Maine Fire & Marine Ins. Co., 6 Mass. 102, 121-122 (1809); Jones v. Fales, 4 Mass. 245, 251 (1808); Stocker v. Harris, 3 Mass. 409, 419 (1807); Rice v. Stearns, 3 Mass. 225 (1807); Toppan v. Atkinson, 2 Mass. 365, 370 (1807); Badger v. Shuttleworth, SCP Files, 7-17 (husband not liable when wife made commercial contract without his authorization). Cf. Brewer v. Knapp, 1 Pick. 332 (1823) (refusing to treat covenant in a lease as one running with the land and so binding the defendant after the expiration of the term). Thus a shipper could not recover damages from a common carrier that had clearly manifested an intention to limit its liability to less than what customary principles would impose. See Phillips v. Earle, 8 Pick. 182, 184-185 (1829) (dictum).

245. Gardiner v. Corson, 15 Mass. 500, 503 (1819). Accord, Powers v. Ware, 2 Pick. 451, 456 (1824); Couch v. Ingersoll, 2 Pick. 292, 300-301 (1824); Tileston v. Newell, 13 Mass. 406, 410 (1816). Compare Chapter 4, notes 92-95 and accompanying text.

246. Dana v. King, 2 Pick. 155, 156 (1824).

247. Willington v. Inhabitants of West Boylston, 4 Pick. 101, 103 (1826). See also Dana v. King, 2 Pick. 155 (1824).

248. Johnson v. Reed, 9 Mass. 78, 83 (1812).

249. Maneely v. M'Gee, 6 Mass. 143, 146 (1809). One rule arising out of the nature of the transaction that continued to be applied

was the rule that rendered the contract of an
infant voidable, although not void, at the
infant's election. See Oliver v. Houdlet, 13
Mass. 237 (1816) (dictum). One exception to
the rule was that an infant could not avoid a
contract for necessaries. See Williams v.
O'Brien, SCP, 10-18; Goss v. Wiburt, SCP,
7-08; Butts v. Gifford, BrCP, 6-08; Hart v.
Goodson, BrCP, 9-06. A contract for goods
needed by an infant in his occupation also
was not voidable, see Childs v. Morton, NfCP,
1-03, although a contract for goods furnished
in learning a new profession was voidable. See
Fisk v. Dix, WCP, 6-05, appeal dism., WSJC,
9-06. The fact that a plaintiff had relied to his
detriment on an infant's affirmation that he
was of full age was immaterial and would not
bar the infant from avoiding the contract. See
Martin v. Mayo, 10 Mass. 137, 139-140
(1813); Smith v. Mayo, 9 Mass. 62, 64 (1812)
(dictum); Jones v. Brown, SCP, 4-19.

250. See Borden v. Borden, 5 Mass. 67
(1809).

251. See Penniman v. Hartshorn, 13 Mass.
87 (1816). Morton J. Horwitz, "The Historical Foundations of Modern Contract Law,"
Harvard Law Review LXXXVII (1974), 917,
920-922, 929-931, maintains that actions for
breaches of executory contracts, including the
recovery of mere expectation damages, first
succeeded throughout England and America
around the turn of the century. For an early
Massachusetts case on expectation damages
for breach of a contract that may not, however, have been purely executory, see Wheeler
v. Fisher, ESJC, 11-90, in Dana, Minute
Books, where the issue was whether "the rule
to assess damages should be the value of the
securities at the time they were to have been
delivered . . . or the present day." See also
Sampson v. Williams, NCP, 10-84, a suit "to
make Good all Damages" resulting from a
seller's failure to perform a contract to deliver
bricks, for which, however, the buyer had
paid earnest money.

252. One ethical standard that did not die
out was the rule that a promise given in return
for an illegal consideration was void. See
Randal v. Jones, YSJC, 6-90, in Dana, Minute
Books (note given in return for nonprosecution of offense); Bigelow v. Brigham, WSJC,
9-88, ibid. (note given by debtor in return for
sheriff's waiver of levy of execution). Cf.
Russell v. DeGrand, 15 Mass. 35 (1818) (insurance on voyage to " 'ports interdicted by
the laws of the United States' " void). See
also Commonwealth v. Pease, 16 Mass. 91
(1819) (indictment on charge of compound-
ing a felony for receiving a note in return for

nonprosecution of larceny charge). A party in
pari delictu could not recover any of the
consideration paid on an illegal contract. See
Gates v. Winslow, 1 Mass. 63 (1804). But see
Mason v. Waite, 17 Mass. 560 (1822). For
other illustrations of ethical standards over-
coming the expressly manifested intentions of
the parties, see Stocker v. Merrimack Maine &
Fire Ins. Co., 6 Mass. 220, 226 (1810) (holding that insured cannot conceal material facts
from insurer); Bliss v. Thompson, 4 Mass.
488, 492 (1808) ("good morals" held to
require "that every man in his contracts
should act with common honesty, without
overreaching his neighbors by false allegations
or fraudulent concealments").

253. 7 Mass. 112 (1810).

254. Ibid., 121-122.

255. See Handlin and Handlin, *Commonwealth*, 225-226. For Massachusetts cases on
usury, see Butterfield v. Kidder, 8 Pick. 512
(1829); Brigham v. Marean, 7 Pick. 40 (1828);
Knights v. Putnam, 3 Pick. 171 (1825); Train
v. Collins, 2 Pick. 145 (1824); Frye v. Barker,
2 Pick. 65 (1823); Bartlett v. Williams, 1 Pick.
288 (1823); Frye v. Barker, 1 Pick. 267
(1822); Hartford Bank v. Barry, 17 Mass. 94
(1821); Darling v. Homer, 16 Mass. 287
(1820); Fox v. Whitney, 16 Mass. 118 (1819);
Simpson v. Warren, 15 Mass. 460 (1819);
Bridge v. Hubbard, 15 Mass. 96 (1818); Green
v. Kemp, 13 Mass. 515 (1816); Flint v. Sheldon, 13 Mass. 443 (1816); Boardman v. Roe,
13 Mass. 104 (1816); Baxter v. Wales, 12
Mass. 375 (1815); Thacher v. Gammon, 12
Mass. 274 (1815); Hills v. Eliot, 12 Mass. 26
(1815); Johnson v. Johnson, 11 Mass. 359
(1814); Jones v. Whitney, 11 Mass. 74 (1814);
Northampton Bank v. Allen, 10 Mass. 284
(1813); Chadbourn v. Watts, 10 Mass. 121
(1813); Wheaton v. Tisdale, 9 Mass. 326
(1812); Maine Bank v. Butts, 9 Mass. 49
(1812); Bearce v. Barstow, 9 Mass. 45 (1812);
Cutler v. Johnson, 8 Mass. 266 (1811),
Cutler v. How, 8 Mass. 257 (1811); Thompson v. Woodbridge, 8 Mass. 256 (1811);
Thompson v. Thompson, 8 Mass. 135 (1811);
Gardner v. Flagg, 8 Mass. 101 (1811); Portland Bank v. Storer, 7 Mass. 433 (1811);
Thomes v. Cleaves, 7 Mass. 361 (1811); Putnam v. Churchill, 4 Mass. 516 (1808); Churchill v. Suter, 4 Mass. 156 (1808); Newman v.
Parkhurst, MSJC, 4-92, in Dana, Minute
Books. One who took usury was even subject
to indictment. See Commonwealth v. Frost, 5
Mass. 53 (1809).

256. *Independent Chronicle* (Boston), Mar.
4, 1805, p. 2, col. 1.

257. *Monthly Anthology and Boston Re-*

view, IX (1810), 194, quoted in Handlin and Handlin, *Commonwealth*, 226.

258. Armory v. Gilman, 2 Mass. 1, 3 (1806) (argument of counsel).

259. Ibid., 11. Accord, Mason v. Waite, 17 Mass. 560, 563 (1822); Stetson v. Massachusetts Mutual Fire Ins. Co., 4 Mass. 330, 336-337 (1808); Barrell v. Cabot, ESJC, 11-89, in Dana, Minute Books. One way in which restrictions on wagering were narrowed in the postrevolutionary period was by expanding the concept of insurable interest so as to give individuals the right to insure against the occurrence or nonoccurrence of innumerable events. See Strong v. Manufacturers' Ins. Co., 10 Pick. 40 (1830); Wiggin v. Mercantile Ins. Co., 7 Pick. 271 (1828); Lord v. Dall, 12 Pick. 115 (1815); Oliver v. Greene, 3 Mass. 133 (1807); Sullivan v. Massachusetts Mutual Fire Ins. Co., 2 Mass. 318 (1807). Cf. Merry v. Prince, 2 Mass. 176 (1806) (holding policy of reassurance a valid contract). In taking out insurance a person did not have to state the nature of his insurable interest unless he was asked. See Bixby v. Franklin Ins. Co., 8 Pick. 86 (1829). No one, however, could collect from an insurance company more than the true value of whatever was insured, even if he had taken out more than one policy. See Gardner v. Bedford Ins. Co., 17 Mass. 613 (1822); Lee v. Massachusetts Fire & Marine Ins. Co., 6 Mass. 208 (1810).

260. The breakdown in the late eighteenth and early nineteenth century, in both England and America, of fair price and equal exchange is thoroughly traced in Horwitz, "Historical Foundations" 936-946.

Chapter 8. Economic Growth and the Law

1. See Albert B. Hart, ed., *Commonwealth History of Massachusetts* (New York, 1929), III, 353-354, 361-363; Samuel E. Morison, *The Maritime History of Massachusetts, 1783-1860* (Boston, 1921), 29-32, 38.

2. Ezra Stiles, *The United States Elevated to Glory and Honor* (New Haven, 1783).

3. Noah Webster, *A Collection of Essays and Fugitive Writings on Moral, Historical, Political and Literary Subjects* (Boston, 1790), 36. See generally Oscar Handlin and Mary F. Handlin, *Commonwealth: A Study of the Role of Government in the American Economy—Massachusetts, 1774-1861* (Cambridge, Mass., rev. ed., 1969), 51-52; Edward C. Kirkland, *A History of American Economic Life* (New York, 4th ed., 1969), 76-79, 131-133.

4. John P. Kennedy, "Address of the Friends of Domestic Industry, New York, 1831," in *Political and Official Papers* (New York, 1872), 110.

5. John P. Kennedy, "An Address Delivered Before the American Institute, New York, 1833," in *Occasional Addresses and the Letters of Mr. Ambrose on the Rebellion* (New York, 1872), 51.

6. See Hart, *Commonwealth History*, III, 359-361, 527-529; Morison, *Maritime History*, 32.

7. See Hart, *Commonwealth History*, III, 529-539; Morison, *Maritime History*, 41-95.

8. See Petition of Ashley, HdGS, 8-19; Petition of Waters, WGS, 9-10; Petition of Hide, BeGS, 9-97.

9. Petition of Ashley, HdGS, 8-19.

10. Petition of Lyman, HdGS, 8-21. See also Petition of Tucker, BrGS, 9-06, where a road was sought since "business very much increases . . . and we are in hopes still will increase."

11. Petition of Waters, WGS, 9-10. Accord, Petition of Wadsworth, WGS, 9-19; Petition of Batcheller, WGS, 6-10.

12. Petition of Chamberlain, BeGS, 12-08. Cf. Petition of Farncer, MGS, 11-93 (petition to alter road "to save at least a mile").

13. Petition of Ring, BeGS, 2-19.

14. See Kirkland, *Economic Life* 134-136; Frederic J. Wood, *The Turnpikes of New England* (Boston, 1919), 55-211. Along with improved roads came better wagons and carriages. See Archer B. Hulbert, *The Paths of Inland Commerce* (New Haven, 1920), 57; Hugh McCausland, *The English Carriage* (London, 1948), 13-25; Wood, *Turnpikes*, 45-50.

15. See Wood, *Turnpikes*, 53. Indeed, it became possible to travel from Salem to Boston in a single hour. See Hart, *Commonwealth History*, IV, 420.

16. See Hart, *Commonwealth History*, IV, 420-423.

17. An important by-product of improved transportation was the modern tort doctrine of negligence. The development of the modern doctrine has been brilliantly analyzed by Morton J. Horwitz, "Damage Judgments, Legal Liability and Economic Development before the Civil War" (unpublished paper in possession of Professor Horwitz, Harvard Law School). The Massachusetts evidence serves to confirm Horwitz's conclusions and to add some supporting details to them. According to Horwitz, negligence in the eighteenth century did not imply a theory of fault liability; it referred simply to the long-established right

of a citizen to sue an officer who failed to perform a duty imposed by law. See Horwitz, "Damage Judgments," 44-48. See also Patten v. Halsted, 1 Coxe 277, 279-280 (N.J. 1795).

In the 1790s, however, this old conception began slowly and imperceptibly to break down, as the commercial prosperity and improved transportation network of the 1790s led to frequent collisions either between ships moving at sea or between carriages in motion on land. There had been only one case in Massachusetts involving such a collision during the 30 years prior to 1790. See Waterman v. Gillings, PCP, 7-70 (ship collision case). This case was probably the source of the entry under the heading of "Case for carelessly managing a vessel" in Theophilus Parsons, Precedents, no. 61. But after 1790 such cases became rather frequent. See Fales v. Dearborn, 1 Pick. 345 (1823); Reed v. Read, SSJC, 11-23; Merrill v. Corliss, ESJC, 4-08; Burnham v. Paine, ESJC, 11-02; Thorndike v. Lee, ESJC, 4-02; Peirce v. Sternes, ESJC, 6-98; Danforth v. Bailey, SSJC, 2-98; Smith v. Cotton, BaSJC, 5-93; Dunn v. Barnard, NfCP, 9-23; Pond v. Richards, NfCP, 9-17, appeal dism., NfSJC, 2-18; Wilbore v. Pickins, BrCP, 3-16; Morgan v. Woodward, SCP, 4-11. The doctrinal significance of these cases lay in the fact that the old concept of strict liability was of no use in analyzing collision cases, for inquiry into the issue of causation inevitably led to inquiry into the issue of fault. The difficulty was that collisions occurred as a result of acts of all parties involved in them; determination of the question of cause in fact did not assist in the resolution of questions of legal cause and legal liability. A court trying a collision case had to determine not only who caused the accident, but who was at fault, and the making of the latter determination gradually shifted the emphasis of negligence from causation to carelessness. Since the determination of causation and hence of fault was one that was made by the jury in its rendition of a general verdict, records showing in detail the steps by which the shift occurred have not been preserved. Indeed, the individual steps may have been imperceptible even to contemporaries. By the 1810s, however, the shift had clearly taken place, as juries in collision cases began frequently to return verdicts finding defendants not guilty, see, e.g., Clark v. Farnum, HCP, 8-28; Burnap v. Batcheller, WCP, 12-26; Dunn v. Barnard, NfCP, 9-23; Wilbore v. Pickins, BrCP, 3-16; Morgan v. Woodward, SCP, 4-11, even in cases where the defendants had admit-

ted that a collision had occurred. See Barber v. Backus, BeCP, 2-24, where a defendant was found not guilty on a plea that the collision had resulted from the plaintiff's own negligence—an admission, in effect, that the collision had occurred. Such verdicts can only be understood as finding that although a defendant's acts may have contributed to a collision, his acts were blameless and that blame and fault lay with the plaintiff rather than with the defendant, for it seems unlikely that such cases would ever have gone to trial if in fact the collisions had not taken place.

Once the shift had occurred, the courts quickly accorded recognition to the new conception of negligence as a matter of law. First, they upheld the validity of defensive pleas of contributory negligence by the plaintiff on the ground that "unless the plaintiff . . . [could] show that he used ordinary care . . . it . . . [was] by no means certain that he himself was not the cause of his own injury." Smith v. Smith, 2 Pick. 621, 623 (1824). See also Thompson v. Inhabitants of Bridgewater, 7 Pick. 188, 189-190 (1828) (holding that "want of ordinary care" by a plaintiff barred recovery even when there was proof of the defendant's negligence); Wood v. Inhabitants of Waterville, 5 Mass. 294, 299 (1809) (recovery denied to a plaintiff for an injury "arising from his own default"). In the early Massachusetts cases the plaintiff apparently had the burden of pleading and proving his own absence of contributory negligence. See Wesson v. Inhabitants of Needham, WCP, 12-18; Bostwick v. Tenth Massachusetts Tpke. Corp., BeCP, 4-16, rev'd on other grounds, BeSJC, 9-18. That doctrine made considerable sense when freedom from contributory negligence was seen merely as an element of the plaintiff's proof of causation. Ultimately, in the 1833 case of Sproul v. Hemmingway, 14 Pick. 1 (1833), the Supreme Judicial Court held that even a nonnegligent plaintiff could not recover for damages sustained in a collision without proving negligence on the part of the defendant—a holding that marked the birth of the modern tort action of negligence.

The new conception of negligence soon expanded beyond collision cases as the courts began to extend the doctrine to cover other matters even before it had been fully adumbrated. Personal injury actions that, unlike the standard collision case, did not involve joint actors but merely a passive plaintiff injured by allegedly negligent conduct on the part of a defendant became frequent. Plaintiffs recovered damages, for example, for injuries caused by defects in roads, see Lord v. Fifth Massachusetts Tpke. Corp., 16 Mass. 106 (1819), HSJC, 9-19 (containing interesting analysis of requisite standard of care; arising from defendant's failure to keep turnpike free of ice); Adams v. Clarke, NfCP, 12-27 (dismissing suit alleging failure to clear snow off road for failure to allege that defendant had been duly appointed a surveyor of highways or that he had had notice of the snow and for failure to state a cause of action); Winslow v. Inhabitants of Shelburne, FCP, 8-26 (defect in road); Wesson v. Inhabitants of Needham, WCP, 12-18 (defect in road), for negligence in driving a wagon, see Barker v. Wilber, NCP, 10-05; Haskell v. Twish, SCP, 10-96, or navigating a ship, see Leach v. Myrick, ESJC, 11-06; Pierce v. Fish, BrCP, 6-26, appeal dism., BrSJC, 4-27; Proprietors of New Bedford Bridge v. Griffith, BrCP, 6-15, appeal dism., BrSJC, 3-16, into a stationary object, and for negligence in firing a gun, see Osgood v. Kendall, ECP, 7-99, or frightening the plaintiff's horse. See Lisle v. Whitney, NfCP, 9-07. The old standard of strict liability was also superseded by a standard of fault in fire-spreading cases, where in the vast majority of the suits tried between 1790 and 1810 juries returned verdicts for defendants. Like the not guilty verdicts in collision cases, these verdicts cannot be understood as findings that a fire did not spread but rather as findings that the spread was not the result of fault on the part of the defendant. For cases in which jury verdicts were returned for defendants, see Merrill v. Snow, BeSJC, 5-03; Baxter v. Thompson, PSJC, 5-96; Burnham v. Libbey, YSJC, 6-95; Haskins v. Williams, BrCP, 6-09; Jones v. Whitney, WCP, 6-07, aff'd, WSJC, 9-09; Sprague v. Rider, PCP, 10-88. For cases in which jury verdicts were returned for plaintiffs, see Billings v. Seeger, HSJC, 9-14; Tripp v. Howland, BrCP, 4-01. Concepts of fault liability were also extended to situations in which one entrepreneur injured another. See Boynton v. Rees, 9 Pick. 528 (1830). Efforts were even made near the turn of the century to import the modern concept of negligence as a standard of fault liability into matters where defendants have always been held to strict liability; thus one defendant in an action of trespass for breaking the plaintiff's close sought to limit his liability to the actual damages done by pleading that he had entered the close negligently and not intentionally. See Nicholls v. Dean, BrCP, 4-97. But his effort came to naught when the jury found his "trespass . . .

voluntary." Nicholls v. Dean, BrSJC, 10-97. Standards of tort liability, in short, were in flux at the turn of the century, although by 1810 the contours of modern negligence had begun to emerge.

18. See Hart, *Commonwealth History*, IV, 409-416.

19. See Handlin and Handlin, *Commonwealth*, 42-46; Oscar Handlin and Mary F. Handlin, "Revolutionary Economic Policy in Massachusetts," *William and Mary Quarterly*, 3d ser., IV (1947), 3, 24-26.

20. Theophilus Parsons, Memorandum Book. That this assumption continued to be held by many men in the early nineteenth century, see Charles Warren, *Bankruptcy in United States History* (Cambridge, Mass., 1935), 15-16; George P. Bauer, "The Movement against Imprisonment for Debt in the United States" (Ph.D. diss., Harvard University, 1935), 151-153.

21. The confusion of debtors in the 1780s can be seen in the Petition of the Middlesex County Convention, Oct. 3, 1786, in *Worcester Magazine*, II, 358. The convention condemned "the taking of men's bodies, and confining them in jail, for debt, when they have property sufficient to answer the demands of their creditors," but saw nothing wrong with such imprisonment when a debtor had no property. It seems strange to us, given our orientation toward economic analysis, that a group of men might propose abolition of imprisonment for debt for a man who might prefer to go to jail while his land remained productive in the hands of his family but not propose abolition for totally landless men who had no resource but their own labor to keep themselves and their families alive. That the Middlesex proposal was something of an aberration, inconsistent with the general trend of legal development, in that it did not first seek exemption of the landless from imprisonment, see notes 40-47 below and accompanying text. The explanation for the Middlesex proposal, of course, is that the convention was unable to break away totally from the colonial ideal that all men ought to be forced to pay their debts even if totally impoverished. Such indecisiveness and confusion, however, are not unusual in transitional periods like the 1780s.

22. Laws of 1781, ch. 36.

23. See Laws of 1782, ch. 10. Creditors not wishing to accept such tender could obtain a continuance of their actions until the expiration of the statute. See ibid.

24. See Laws of 1786, ch. 45, as amended,

Laws of 1787, chs. 6, 20, 53. A creditor could decline such a tender if he preferred to wait until the expiration of the act for payment in specie.

25. See Laws of 1784, ch. 57.

26. See Laws of 1783, ch. 62.

27. See Laws of 1780, ch. 47, establishing forms for the writ of audita querela. On the purpose and scope of that writ, see generally William Blackstone, *Commentaries on the Laws of England* (Oxford, 1765-1769), III, 405-406. For examples of the writ in Massachusetts, see Brackett v. Winslow, 17 Mass. 153 (1821); Little v. Newburyport Bank, 14 Mass. 443 (1817); Lovejoy v. Webber, 10 Mass. 101 (1813); Blood v. Wooley, MSJC, 10-86; Blood's Habeas Corpus, MSJC, 4-86.

28. Laws of 1783, ch. 57.

29. Laws of 1787, ch. 29.

30. Including such items as hay in a barn, see Campbell v. Johnson, 11 Mass. 184 (1814), money, see Knowlton v. Bartlett, 1 Pick. 271 (1822), a stagecoach that had completed its route but still contained passengers, see Potter v. Hall, 3 Pick. 368 (1825), freight in the hold of a ship, see Naylor v. Dennie, 8 Pick. 198 (1829), and shares of stock. See Plymouth Bank v. Bank of Norfolk, 10 Pick. 454, 459 (1830) (dictum). Possession of a chattel as a pledge barred a creditor from seizing other property from which to collect his debt. See Cleverly v. Brackett, 8 Mass. 150 (1811). Conversely, a creditor in possession of his debtor's property without having a lien thereon could not proceed against it without first attaching it. See Allen v. Megguire, 15 Mass. 490 (1819). Goods seized upon mesne process were to be maintained at the cost of their owner, not of his creditor. See Sewall v. Mattoon, 9 Mass. 534 (1813).

31. See Laws of 1805, ch. 100; Gibson, v. Jenney, 15 Mass. 205 (1818).

32. See Williams v. Chester, HSJC, 4-87. Cloth that had been taken to a tailor to be cut into clothing was also exempt. See Bardwell v. Dwight, HCP, 8-24.

33. See Laws of 1805, ch. 100. Tools of trade did not, however, include implements of husbandry, see Daily v. May, 5 Mass. 313 (1809), nor "complicated machinery or expensive utensils ... now used in manufactures...." Buckingham v. Billings, 13 Mass. 82, 86 (1816). Accord, Danforth v. Woodward, 10 Pick. 423, 427 (1830). The purpose of the exemption was "to secure to *handicraftsmen* the means by which they are accustomed to obtain satisfaction in their respective occupations." Howard v. Williams, 2 Pick.

80, 83 (1824). The exemption conferred by the statute was broad enough to extend to tools used by employees of a debtor provided that the debtor's business operation was a small one. See ibid., 83.

34. Execution could be levied on a reversion or a remainder, see Williams v. Amory, 14 Mass. 20 (1817), on land held in tenancy by the courtesy, see Roberts v. Whiting, 16 Mass. 186 (1819), on a mortgagor's equity of redemption, see Start v. Sherwin, 1 Pick. 521 (1823) (by implication); White v. Bond, 16 Mass. 400 (1820), on land subject to a prior attachment, see Byrne v. Crowninshield, 1 Pick. 263 (1822), and on land other than that on which a creditor had agreed with his debtor to make his levy. See Hammatt v. Bassett, 2 Pick. 564 (1824). Execution could not be levied, however, on a widow's right to have dower assigned, see Gooch v. Atkins, 14 Mass. 378 (1817), on a mortgagee's interest prior to his entry for condition broken, see Eaton v. Whiting, 3 Pick. 484 (1826), or on land not described by metes and bounds. See Tate v. Anderson, 9 Mass. 92 (1812). Execution by metes and bounds could not be made on a joint tenancy or on a tenancy in common. See Baldwin v. Whiting, 13 Mass. 57 (1816); Bartlet v. Harlow, 12 Mass. 348 (1815). Levy of execution constituted full satisfaction of a judgment, see McLellan v. Whitney, 15 Mass. 137 (1818), and gave the creditor seisin of the land. See Porter v. Millet, 9 Mass. 101 (1812); Willington v. Gale, 7 Mass. 138 (1810); Langdon v. Potter, 3 Mass. 215 (1807). But a levy on land in which the judgment debtor had no property interest, see Bott v. Burnell, 9 Mass. 96 (1812); Baldwin v. Dench, MSJC, 10-96, or on land that previously had been conveyed for a good and valuable consideration by an unregistered conveyance known to the creditor, see Priest v. Rice, 1 Pick. 164 (1822); Prescott v. Heard, 10 Mass. 60 (1813), did not give title to the creditor. In such a case, however, the creditor could bring a new writ of debt on his judgment, Greene v. Hatch, 12 Mass. 195 (1815), or with court leave, a scire facias. See Kendrick v. Wentworth, 14 Mass. 57 (1817). Where only a portion of a debtor's land was taken on execution, provision for access had to be given both to the debtor, see Russell v. Jackson, 2 Pick. 574 (1824); Pernham v. Weed, 2 Mass. 203 (1806), and to the creditor. See Tailor v. Wild, SSJC, 2-94.

35. For cases on the appraisers, see Nye v. Drake, 9 Pick. 35 (1829); Moffitt v. Jaquins, 2 Pick. 331 (1824); Barrett v. Porter, 14 Mass.

143 (1817); Eddy v. Knap, 2 Mass. 154 (1806).

36. Of course, the creditor could still elect whether to seize the body or the estate of his debtor on mesne process. See Brinley v. Allen, 3 Mass. 561 (1801).

37. An auction had to be held within four days of a seizure. See Caldwell v. Eaton, 5 Mass. 399 (1809). But even the auctioneer could buy at it if he made his purchase without any fraudulent intent and otherwise conducted a fair auction. See Libbey v. Marshall, CSJC, 7-92, in Francis Dana, Minute Books.

38. As in the prerevolutionary period, many of the cases in which questions as to the propriety of a levy arose involved claims of competing creditors. See Plymouth Bank v. Bank of Norfolk, 10 Pick. 454 (1830); Tuxworth v. Moore, 9 Pick. 347 (1830); Merrill v. Sawyer, 8 Pick. 397 (1829); Carter v. Gregory, 8 Pick. 165 (1829); White v. Bagley, 7 Pick. 288 (1828); Lord v. Baldwin, 6 Pick. 348 (1828); Sawyer v. Merrill, 6 Pick. 478 (1828); M'Gregor v. Brown, 5 Pick. 170 (1827); Bagley v. White, 4 Pick. 395 (1826); Bayley v. French, 2 Pick. 586 (1824); Cutting v. Rockwood, 2 Pick. 443 (1824); Gordon v. Jenney, 16 Mass. 465 (1820); Denny v. Hamilton, 16 Mass. 402 (1820); Gates v. Gates, 15 Mass. 310 (1818); Buffington v. Gerrish, 15 Mass. 156 (1818); Atkins v. Bean, 14 Mass. 404 (1817); Gale v. Ward, 14 Mass. 352 (1817); Bridge v. Wyman, 14 Mass. 190 (1817); Vinton v. Bradford, 13 Mass. 114 (1816); Northampton Bank v. Whiting, 12 Mass. 104 (1815); Brown v. Maine Bank, 11 Mass. 153 (1814); Pierce v. Jackson, 6 Mass. 242 (1810); Green v. Parker, MSJC, 10-93; Stover v. Randall, CSJC, 6-88; Reed v. Upton, ECP Files, 3-30.

39. See Laws of 1732, ch. 6. See also Morgan v. Inhabitants of Westfield, HSJC, 9-89, in Dana, Minute Books; Bartlett v. Claflin, Cushing 56 (1783).

40. See Laws of 1787, ch. 29; Heard v. Baldwin, MSJC, 10-91; Wheelock v. Hemenway, WCP, 8-90. But see Hannum v. Giguet, HCP, 2-89, which failed to apply the 1787 act in holding that a prisoner whom a creditor agreed to support committed an escape when he left the prison after taking the poor prisoner's oath. The oath that the debtor was required to take could be administered outside the prison, and the prisoner did not commit an escape by taking himself to the place appointed by the justices of the peace administering the oath. See Commonwealth v.

Alden, 14 Mass. 388 (1817). Proceedings under the 1787 act could not be negatived by showing that some of the required documents were signed by a justice of the peace in blank and subsequently filled out and used. See Haskell v. Haven, 3 Pick. 404 (1826).

41. See Willington v. Stearns, 1 Pick. 497 (1823). This was true even if the creditor claimed that the debtor's oath had been fraudulent, unless the creditor could show that the debtor had been convicted of perjury for taking the oath.

42. See Washburn v. Hathaway, PSJC, 5-90.

43. See Dyer v. Hunnewell, 12 Mass. 278 (1815).

44. See Laws of 1821, ch. 22; Richards v. Crane, 7 Pick. 216 (1828); Blood v. Austin, 3 Pick. 259 (1825). The purpose of the 1821 act was to save towns from their liability under the poor law to support paupers imprisoned in jails within their borders.

45. See Brooks v. Hoyt, 6 Pick. 468 (1828); Nye v. Smith, 11 Mass. 188 (1814). They likewise permitted recovery only of nominal damages if a jailer or other officer in some other manner failed to perform his duty. See Rich v. Bell, 16 Mass. 294 (1820); Shackford v. Goodwin, 13 Mass. 187 (1816); Weld v. Bartlett, 10 Mass. 470 (1813); Burrell v. Lithgow, 2 Mass. 526 (1807). But cf. Whiting v. Putnam, 17 Mass. 175 (1821). The courts also aided indigent debtors by permitting process servers, see Walker v. Haskell, 11 Mass. 177 (1814), and jailers, see Bridge v. M'Lane, 2 Mass. 520 (1807), to give parole evidence of consent by creditors that the full rigor of the law not be used against their debtors.

46. Weld v. Bartlett, 10 Mass. 470, 473 (1813).

47. See Brooks v. Hoyt, 6 Pick. 468 (1828).

48. See Montgomery v. Partridge, PSJC, 5-90. But a prisoner who did not give bond had to be kept in close confinement. See DeGrand v. Hunnewell, 11 Mass. 160 (1814).

49. Order re Limits of Prison Yard, WGS, 9-83.

50. Trull v. Wilson, 9 Mass. 154 (1812).

51. See Clap v. Cofran, 10 Mass. 372 (1813); Jacobs v. Tolman, 8 Mass. 161 (1811); Freeman v. Davis, 7 Mass. 200 (1810); Bartlett v. Willis, 3 Mass. 86 (1807).

52. Compare M'Lellan v. Dalton, 10 Mass. 190 (1813), with Partridge v. Emerson, 9 Mass. 122 (1812).

53. See Laws of 1811, ch. 85; Spear v.

Alden, 11 Mass. 444 (1814).

54. Buckingham v. Billings, 13 Mass. 82, 87 (1816).

55. But see Cargill v. Taylor, 10 Mass. 206 (1813).

56. See Laws of 1855, ch. 444.

57. As was true in cases dealing with executions, many mortgage cases involved a clash between competing creditors rather than between debtor and creditor. See Adams v. Wheeler, 10 Pick. 199 (1830); Hedge v. Holmes, 10 Pick. 380 (1830); Wade v. Howard, 6 Pick. 492 (1828); Reed v. Bigelow, 5 Pick. 281 (1827); Saunders v. Frost, 5 Pick. 259 (1827); Barker v. Parker, 4 Pick. 505 (1827); Cushing v. Hurd, 4 Pick. 253 (1826); Spear v. Hubbard, 4 Pick. 143 (1826); Clark v. Austin, 2 Pick. 528 (1824); Bigelow v. Willson, 1 Pick. 485 (1823); Kelly v. Beers, 12 Mass. 387 (1815); Portland Bank v. Stubbs, 6 Mass. 422 (1810).

58. See Boston Bank v. Reed, 8 Pick. 459 (1829); Wilder v. Houghton, 1 Pick. 87 (1822).

59. See Wood v. Felton, 9 Pick. 171 (1829).

60. Such a bill was the only remedy that a mortgagor out of possession had to recover his land from the mortgagee. See Parsons v. Welles, 17 Mass. 419, 425 (1821).

61. See Tirrell v. Merrill, 17 Mass. 117 (1821).

62. See Laws of 1821, ch. 85, §1. See also Battle v. Griffin, 4 Pick. 6 (1826); Willard v. Fiske, 2 Pick. 540 (1824). Minor, unintentional errors in the accounting would not render the mortgagee's account void. See Whitwood v. Kellogg, 6 Pick. 420 (1828). Debtors also benefited from rules requiring a creditor to give his debtor notice of any entry into the mortgaged premises for the purpose of foreclosure, see Skinner v. Brewer, 4 Pick. 468 (1827); Thayer v. Smith, 17 Mass. 429 (1821); Pomeroy v. Winship, 12 Mass. 514, 517 (1815), and permitting a debtor to redeem his land by paying only the money due on his mortgage without paying any additional debts that he may have owed the creditor. See Loring v. Cooke, 3 Pick. 48 (1825).

63. See Laws of 1783, chs. 24, 32, 36; Drinkwater v. Drinkwater, 4 Mass. 354, 357 (1808); Wyman v. Brigden, 4 Mass. 150, 153 (1808); Prescott v. Tarbell, 1 Mass. 205 (1804); Henshaw v. Blood, 1 Mass. 35 (1804); Prince v. Prince, ESJC, 11-92. See also Brigden v. Cheever, 10 Mass. 450 (1813); Bigelow v. Jones, 4 Mass. 512 (1808).

64. Laws of 1788, ch. 16.

65. See Hancock v. Fisk, WCP, 12-92; Gay v. Chickering, WCP, 8-92.

66. Capen v. Fosdick, SSJC, 8-93.

67. Undated Fragment, Sargeant Papers, which appears to be connected with the Capen case.

68. See Laws of 1794, ch. 65.

69. See generally Luther S. Cushing, Appendix, in Asahel Stearns, Lectures on Law (in HLS).

70. See Goffe v. Preston, WCP, 8-25 (action of slander).

71. See Stearns, Lectures, 69.

72. See Union Tpke. Co. v. New-England Marine Ins. Co., 2 Mass. 37 (1806).

73. See Pollard v. Ross, 5 Mass. 319 (1809); Wilder v. Bailey, 3 Mass. 289 (1807). Cf. Brooks v. Cook, 8 Mass. 246 (1811); Barnes v. Treat, 7 Mass. 271 (1811); Chealy v. Brewer, 7 Mass. 259 (1811); Penniman v. Ruggles, 6 Mass. 166 (1809).

74. Land was not liable to the trustee process, see Gore v. Clisby, 8 Pick. 555 (1829); Bissell v. Strong, 9 Pick. 562 (1830), unless the alleged trustee had received rents and profits or proceeds from a sale of the land. See ibid., 564 (dictum); Hazen v. Emerson, 9 Pick. 144 (1829); Russel v. Lewis, 15 Mass. 127 (1818). When both real estate and personal estate were transferred to a trustee to be held for payment to preferred creditors of the principal debtor, the preference was required to be paid out of the real estate so that the personal estate could be attached pursuant to the trustee process. See Webb v. Peele, 7 Pick. 247 (1828).

75. Physical attachment of the property in the hands of the trustee was not required, nor was it necessary that the property be capable of such attachment. See Burlingame v. Bell, 16 Mass. 318, 319-320 (1820); Clark v. Brown, 14 Mass. 271 (1817). But if the trustee had conveyed the property to another or reconveyed it to the principal debtor, he was not liable. See Andrews v. Ludlow, 5 Pick. 28, 30-31 (1827); Gordon v. Webb, 13 Mass. 215 (1816); Thomas v. Goodwin, 12 Mass. 140 (1815).

76. See Curtis v. Norris, 8 Pick. 280 (1829); New England Marine Ins. Co. v. Chandler, 16 Mass. 275 (1820); Shuttelsworth v. Noyes, 8 Mass. 229 (1811); Sebor v. Armstrong, 4 Mass. 206 (1808); Coburn v. Ansart, 3 Mass. 319 (1807). But negotiable instruments and choses in action assigned by the debtor to the trustee, on which the trustee had not yet made collection, were not attach-

able under the trustee process. Mayhew v. Scott, 10 Pick. 54 (1830); Gore v. Clisby, 8 Pick. 555 (1829); Lupton v. Cutter, 8 Pick. 298 (1829); Andrews v. Ludlow, 5 Pick. 28 (1827); Dickinson v. Strong, 4 Pick. 57 (1826); Perry v. Coates, 9 Mass. 537 (1813); Eunson v. Healy, 2 Mass. 32 (1806).

77. See Hawes v. Langton, 8 Pick. 67, 69 (1829); Whitman v. Hunt, 4 Mass. 272 (1808); Barker v. Taber, 4 Mass. 81 (1808); Comstock v. Farnum, 2 Mass. 96 (1806). Out-of-court statements, such as letters, were not admissible against the trustee, see Stackpole v. Newman, 4 Mass. 85 (1808), unless the trustee verified their contents. See Willard v. Sturtevant, 7 Pick. 193 (1828). Failure on the part of a trustee to answer interrogatories was taken as an admission of liability. See Patterson v. Buckminster, 14 Mass. 144 (1817). If the trustee answered falsely, the plaintiff in the trustee process had no remedy but to bring a special statutory action for false swearing, see Whitman v. Hunt, 4 Mass. 272 (1808), except that a creditor of the trustee, particularly the principal debtor, could be examined if the trustee sought to deny that he owed a debt to him. See Groves v. Brown, 11 Mass. 334 (1814); Andrews v. Herring, 5 Mass. 210 (1809). An assignee of the contract right originally due to the principal debtor could also be admitted to give evidence of the assignment. See Ammidown v. Wheelock, 8 Pick. 470 (1829), construing Laws of 1817, ch. 148. But see Wood v. Partridge, 11 Mass. 488, 491-492 (1814); Foster v. Sinkler, 4 Mass. 450 (1808).

78. See Harris v. Aiken, 3 Pick. 1 (1825); Brigden v. Gill, 16 Mass. 522 (1820); White v. Jenkins, 16 Mass. 62 (1819). Thus contractual obligations payable only on a contingency or otherwise unmatured were not subject to attachment. See Williams v. Reed, 5 Pick. 480 (1827); Williams v. Marston, 3 Pick. 65 (1825); Willard v. Sheafe, 4 Mass. 235 (1808); Wrigley v. Geyer, 4 Mass. 102 (1808); Frothingham v. Haley, 3 Mass. 68 (1807); Wentworth v. Whittemore, 1 Mass. 471 (1805).

79. See Kidd v. Shepherd, 4 Mass. 238 (1808). Thus an attachment pursuant to the trustee process gave a trustee sufficient ground for obtaining a continuance in a suit previously brought by his principal debtor. See Winthrop v. Carlton, 8 Mass. 456 (1812).

80. See Foster v. Jones, 15 Mass. 185 (1818); Perkins v. Parker, 1 Mass. 117 (1804). Liability was not terminated, however, if the principal debtor could prove that the trustee action had been brought collusively to defeat

his rights. See Cooke v. Sage, HCP, 11-97, appeal dism., HSJC, 4-98. Compare Gridley v. Harraden, Cushing 30 (1780), which produced similar results through use of the writ of audita querela.

81. See Howell v. Freeman, 3 Mass. 121 (1807); Sharp v. Clark, 2 Mass. 91, 95-96 (1806).

82. Commonwealth v. Nokes, Boston Police Ct., 1828, no. 647.

83. The common law permitted such preferences. See Prince v. Bradford, SSJC, 3-04, in Dana, Minute Books; Wallingford v. Clark, YSJC, 6-93, ibid. The policy of the law, as Judge Sedgwick observed, was "to give a preference to the most cautious and vigilant creditor." Grosvenor v. Gold, 9 Mass. 209 (1812). At common law a debtor could even make a gift of property to another, and that gift could not subsequently be challenged by a creditor, provided that the debtor at the time of the gift retained enough property to pay his then existing debts. See Bennett v. Bedford Bank, 11 Mass. 421 (1814); Parker v. Proctor, 9 Mass. 390 (1812).

84. Payson v. Payson, 1 Mass. 283, 292 (1805) (opinion of Sedgwick, J.).

85. See 2 Stat. 19 (1800).

86. See Warren, *Bankruptcy*, 10-18. The act had the desired effect. See Foster v. Lowell, 4 Mass. 308 (1808); Locke v. Winning, 3 Mass. 325 (1807); Theophilus Parsons, Notes of Jury Instructions, Nov. 10, 1806, in Taft Papers (in MHS).

87. See Jenkins v. Stanley, 10 Mass. 226 (1813); Payson v. Payson, 1 Mass. 283 (1805). Cf. Champion v. Noyes, 2 Mass. 481, 487-488 (1807); Selfridge v. Lithgow, 2 Mass. 374 (1807). Nothing arising under a commission of bankruptcy except a discharge would so protect the debtor. See Whitney v. Crafts, 10 Mass. 23 (1813); Lummus v. Fairfield, 5 Mass. 248 (1809). Moreover, a debtor could waive a discharge by promising thereafter to pay his debt in full. See Maxim v. Morse, 8 Mass. 127 (1811).

88. See 2 Stat. 248 (1803).

89. See Russell v. Woodward, 10 Pick. 408, 414 (1830); Borden v. Sumner, 4 Pick. 265 (1826); Harris v. Sumner, 2 Pick. 129 (1824); Hastings v. Baldwin, 17 Mass. 552 (1822); Stevens v. Bell, 6 Mass. 339 (1810); Widgery v. Haskell, 5 Mass. 144 (1809); Hatch v. Smith, 5 Mass. 42, 49-50 (1809). See also Ward v. Lewis, 4 Pick. 518 (1827); Harrison v. Trustees of Phillips Academy, 12 Mass. 456 (1815). Such a composition could be modified only if all the original parties to it agreed

to the modification. Andrews v. Etheridge, 9 Mass. 383 (1812). A creditor who failed to become a party to a composition within the period specified therein could not subsequently do so absent modification. See Phenix Bank v. Sullivan, 9 Pick. 410 (1830).

90. See Eaton v. Lincoln, 13 Mass. 424 (1816).

91. See White v. Dingley, 4 Mass. 433 (1808), holding, however, that a debtor so discharged could not bring an action for malicious prosecution against a creditor who sued him but could merely plead his discharge as a defense to the creditor's suit.

92. See Marston v. Coburn, 17 Mass. 454 (1821).

93. Speech of Henry Clay, 1824, quoted in Warren, *Bankruptcy*, 38.

94. Ibid.

95. Speech of Daniel Webster, Detroit, 1837, quoted ibid., 55.

96. Ibid.

97. Joseph Story to John McLean, May 10, 1837, ibid., 56.

98. Cotton Mather, *Fair Dealing between Debtor and Creditor* (Boston, 1716), 13. See generally Chapter 3, notes 112-115 and accompanying text.

99. On the bankruptcy acts of 1841, 1867, and 1898, see generally Warren, *Bankruptcy*, 49-159.

100. The development of a market economy in the early nineteenth century also led to new rules of law permitting creditors to obtain a secured interest in the personal property of their debtors, usually in the form of a chattel mortgage, see Adams v. Wheeler, 10 Pick. 199 (1830); Woodruff v. Halsey, 8 Pick. 333 (1829); Ward v. Sumner, 5 Pick. 59 (1827); Homes v. Crane, 2 Pick. 607 (1824), a conditional sale, see Reed v. Upton, 10 Pick. 522 (1830); Ayer v. Bartlett, 6 Pick. 71 (1827), or a contract of sale or return. See Meldrum v. Snow, 9 Pick. 441 (1830); Patten v. Clark, 5 Pick. 5 (1827). But see Shumway v. Rutter, 7 Pick. 56 (1828). The courts indicated that even mortgages of land were security transactions rather than sales of property when they permitted a widow with an equity of redemption to have dower in a tract of land against all but the mortgagee. See Snow v. Stevens, 15 Mass. 278 (1818). Massachusetts debtor-creditor law is generally discussed in Peter J. Coleman, *Debtors and Creditors in America: Insolvency, Imprisonment for Debt, and Bankruptcy, 1607-1900* (Madison, 1974), 37-52.

101. 13 Mass. 68 (1816). The case is discussed in Chapter 7, notes 225-228 and accompanying text.

102. Putnam v. Sullivan, 4 Mass. 45, 55 (1808).

103. Rice v. Austin, 17 Mass. 197, 206 (1821). Accord, Shed v. Brett, 1 Pick. 401, 410 (1823).

104. Stocker v. Harris, 3 Mass. 409, 413 (1807).

105. Oliver v. Newburyport Ins. Co., 3 Mass. 37, 58 (1807). For other cases in which the courts explicitly referred to the needs of the commercial community, see Prescott v. Trueman, 4 Mass. 627, 631 (1808); Padelford v. Boardman, 4 Mass. 548, 554 (1808); Brooks v. Dorr, 2 Mass. 39, 44 (1806). Cf. Symmes v. Frazier, 6 Mass. 344, 346 (1810); Erick v. Johnson, 6 Mass. 193, 196 (1810).

106. Oliver v. Newburyport Ins. Co., 3 Mass. 37, 56 (1807). Accord, Shed v. Brett, 1 Pick. 401, 404 (1823); Manly v. 9 Mass. United Marine & Fire Ins. Co., 9 Mass. 85, 88 (1812); Richardson v. Maine Fire & Marine Ins. Co., 6 Mass. 102, 120 (1809); Martin v. Salem Marine Ins. Co., 6 Mass. 420, 428 (1807).

107. Dumas v. Jones, 4 Mass. 647, 651 (1808).

108. Lee v. Boardman, 3 Mass. 238, 247-248 (1807).

109. 6 Mass. 277 (1810).

110. Ibid., 281-282.

111. 8 Mass. 536 (1812).

112. Ibid., 540-541.

113. Hemmenway v. Eaton, 13 Mass. 107, 111 (1816). Accord, Brown v. Gilman, 13 Mass. 158, 161 (1816).

114. Wilson v. Clements, 3 Mass. 1, 11 (1807). For other illustrations of explicit adherence to precedent in contract cases, see Chesterfield Mfg. Co. v. Dehon, 5 Pick. 7, 9 (1827); Whitney v. Bigelow, 4 Pick. 110, 112 (1826); Copp v. M'Dugall, 9 Mass. 1, 7 (1812); Shaw v. Grifith, 7 Mass. 494 (1811); Thurston v. M'Kown, 6 Mass. 428, 430 (1810); Denny v. Lincoln, 5 Mass. 385, 387 (1809); Gold v. Eddy, 1 Mass. 1, 3 (1804).

115. Brooks v. Dorr, 2 Mass. 39, 48 (1806).

116. Baxter v. New England Marine Ins. Co., 6 Mass. 277, 299 (1810). Accord, Oliver v. Newburyport Ins. Co., 3 Mass. 37, 65 (1807).

117. See Chapter 4, notes 132-133 and accompanying text.

118. Fuller v. Wheelock, 10 Pick. 135, 138 (1830) (dictum).

119. Nathan Dane, *A General Abridge-*

ment and Digest of American Law (Boston, 1824), III, 427.

120. See ibid., 427-428.

121. See ibid., 417.

122. See Fisher v. Willard, 13 Mass. 379 (1816); Dane, *Abridgement*, III, 412. An agent, however, could not testify if in fact he had a substantial interest in the outcome of the suit. See Marland v. Jefferson, 2 Pick. 240 (1824); New-York Slate Co. v. Osgood, 11 Mass. 60 (1814); Marquand v. Knap, ESJC, 6-92, in Dana, Minute Books. Nor could a party to a negotiable instrument ever give testimony to impeach its validity, since the "circulation of negotiable paper . . . [was] extremely useful to trade, as it multiplie[d] commercial credit, and the notes pass[ed] from man to man as cash." Churchill v. Suter, 4 Mass. 156, 161 (1808). Accord, Packard v. Richardson, 17 Mass. 122 (1821); Inhabitants of Worcester v. Eaton, 11 Mass. 368, 375 (1814) (dictum); Widgery v. Munroe, 6 Mass. 449 (1810); Parker v. Lovejoy, 3 Mass. 565 (1795); Warren v. Merry, 3 Mass. 27 (1807). If, however, a party failed to make timely objection to the testimony of an interested witness, his testimony was then received, see Donelson v. Taylor, 8 Pick. 390 (1829), and he was subject to full cross-examination. See Webster v. Lee, 5 Mass. 334 (1809).

123. Zephaniah Swift, *A Digest of the Law of Evidence in Civil and Criminal Cases* (Hartford, 1810), 74-75.

124. Dane, *Abridgement*, III, 412.

125. Laws of 1857, ch. 305.

126. 4 Mass. 330 (1808).

127. 13 Mass. 68 (1816).

128. Stetson v. Massachusetts Mutual Fire Ins. Co., 4 Mass. 330, 338 (1808).

129. Ibid., 338. When an addition to a building increased the risk—a question of fact to be resolved by the jury—the insurer was discharged from the policy. See Curry v. Commonwealth Ins. Co., 10 Pick. 535, 542 (1830).

130. 4 Pick. 471 (1827).

131. 13 Mass. 68 (1816).

132. Thorndike v. Bordman, 4 Pick. 471, 472 (1827).

133. Ibid., 489.

134. Ibid., 474.

135. For other cases on the law of deviation, see Hobart v. Norton, 8 Pick. 159 (1829); Hale v. Mercantile Marine Ins. Co., 6 Pick. 172 (1828); Houston v. New England Ins. Co., 5 Pick. 89 (1827); Chase v. Eagle Ins. Co., 5 Pick. 51 (1827); Ward v. Wood, 13 Mass. 539 (1816); Wiggin v. Amory, 13 Mass.

118 (1816); Breed v. Eaton, 10 Mass. 21 (1813); Clark v. United Fire & Marine Ins. Co., 7 Mass. 365 (1811).

136. Montague v. Gay, 17 Mass. 439, 440 (1821).

137. Connor v. Shepherd, 15 Mass. 464 (1818).

138. See Commonwealth v. Charlestown, 1 Pick. 180 (1822).

139. This and the following paragraph are based on Morton J. Horwitz, "The Transformation in the Conception of Property in American Law, 1780-1860," *University of Chicago Law Review*, XL (1973), 248-290.

140. See Laws of 1713, ch. 15.

141. Laws of 1795, ch. 74.

142. See Stowell v. Flagg, 11 Mass. 364 (1814). Accord, Johnson v. Kittredge, ESJC, 10-20. As late as 1813, however, the Supreme Judicial Court had reserved decision on the question whether the statutory remedy was exclusive, see Staple v. Spring, 10 Mass. 72, 74-75 (1813), and even in later years lawyers continued to argue that the statute "should have been regarded as only giving an additional remedy." Johnson v. Kittredge, 17 Mass. 76, 79n5 (1820). See also Boston & Roxbury Mill Corp. v. Gardner, 2 Pick. 33 (1823). Cf. Stevens v. Middlesex Canal, 12 Mass. 466 (1815), holding that a statutory remedy for damages incurred as the result of the construction of a canal excluded common law remedies.

143. Stowell v. Flagg, 11 Mass. 364, 366 (1814).

144. See Horwitz, "Conception of Property," 272. On the emergence of equity in Massachusetts, see William J. Curran, "The Struggle for Equity Jurisdiction in Massachusetts," *Boston University Law Review*, XXXI (1951), 269.

145. Wolcott Woolen Mfg. Co. v. Upham, 5 Pick. 292, 294 (1827). In 1830, however, the legislature enacted a statutory provision for lump-sum damages. See Laws of 1829, ch. 122.

146. 5 Pick. 182 (1827).

147. The decision in the Avery case had been anticipated in Lowell v. Spring, 6 Mass. 398 (1810), where the court assumed that a defendant did not have to pay for flooding in the absence of actual damages. Apparently this had been the Massachusetts rule since the colonial period. See Mandell v. Gay, BrSC, 10-64, in Robert Treat Paine, Minutes, vol. 1. See also Chapter 4, note 30 and accompanying text. Similarly, in the postrevolutionary eminent domain cases involving construction

of highways, the rule was that a landowner whose land was taken for a road could not recover damages if the benefits he gained from the road outweighed his injuries. See Chapter 7, note 84.

148. See Chapter 4, notes 26-30 and accompanying text; Chapter 7, notes 43-52 and accompanying text.

149. Cushing 57 (1783).

150. See Minot v. Wheeler, 1798, reported in James Sullivan, *The History of Land Titles in Massachusetts* (Boston, 1801), 273. See generally ibid., 273-274.

151. See Hamilton v. Baker, HCP, 11-26; Sullivan, *Land Titles*, 273-274. As to the reduction elsewhere, see Thurston v. Hancock, 12 Mass. 220, 225 (1815).

152. Another arguably prodevelopmental property case was Thurston v. Hancock, 12 Mass. 220 (1815). Unfortunately, the opinion contains no clear prodevelopmental language, nor would the economic effect of the case have been to promote development. However, there seems to be no other way to explain the court's sharp departure from English law in the case, see Chapter 1, notes 28-31 and accompanying text, except as a product of a desire to promote development. Horwitz, "Damage Judgments," 72, views Thurston as a prodevelopmental decision.

153. 4 Pick. 425 (1827).

154. Boston Glass Manufactory v. Binney, SCP, 10-25.

155. Such an action would not have been appropriate upon the facts of the case. See Chapter 7, notes 108-109 and accompanying text.

156. 4 Pick. at 428.

157. Charles River Bridge v. Warren Bridge, 7 Pick. 344 (1829), aff'd, 11 Pet. (36. U.S.) 420 (1837). The following discussion of the case is based on Morton J. Horwitz, "Competition and Economic Development before the Civil War," 32-47 (unpublished paper in the possession of Professor Horwitz, Harvard Law School).

158. 7 Pick. at 532.

159. The statistics are gathered in Horwitz, "Competition and Economic Development," 32-33.

160. 7 Pick. at 456-459, 462.

161. See Horwitz, "Competition and Economic Development," 44.

162. 11 Pet. at 552-553.

163. 7 Pick. at 503.

164. 11 Pet. at 608.

165. See Joseph Story, "Value and Importance of Legal Studies: A Discourse Pro-

nounced at the Inauguration of the Author as Dane Professor of Law in Harvard University, Aug. 25, 1829," in William W. Story, ed., *The Miscellaneous Writings of Joseph Story* (Boston, 2d ed., 1852), 511-512.

166. John Taylor, *Construction Construed and Constitutions Vindicated* (Richmond, 1820), 78.

167. See Nathaniel Chipman, *Sketches of the Principles of Government* (Burlington, Vt., 1793), 176; Thomas Cooper, *Propositions Respecting the Foundation of Civil Government* (London, 1787), 26-27, 35-36.

168. Nathaniel Chipman, *Principles of Government: A Treatise on Free Institutions* (Burlington, Vt., 1833), 71. But see ibid., 85-86.

169. Thomas Cooper, *Lectures on the Elements of Political Economy* (Columbia, S.C., 1826), 56.

170. Ibid., 57. See generally Richard Schlatter, *Private Property: The History of an Idea* (London, 1951), 199-201.

Chapter 9. Toward a Modern American Jurisprudence

1. Cogswell v. Essex Mill Corp., 6 Pick. 94, 96 (1828) (argument of counsel).

2. Gay v. Whiting, NfCP, 12-10.

3. Bridge v. Eggleston, 14 Mass. 245, 250 (1817).

4. Wait v. M'Neil, 7 Mass. 261, 262 (1811) (argument of counsel).

5. Quoted in Richard E. Ellis, *The Jeffersonian Crisis: Courts and Politics in the Young Republic* (New York, 1971), 190.

6. Lemuel Shaw, "A Sketch of the Life and Character of the Hon. Isaac Parker," 9 Pick. 566, 569-570 (1830).

7. Preface, 1 Mass. at vii-viii (2d ed., 1839). Accord, Shaw, "Parker," 9 Pick. 566, 569-571 (1830). See also notes by James Kent in his copy of *Massachusetts Reports*, vol. I, in Julius Goebel, ed., *The Law Practice of Alexander Hamilton: Documents and Commentary* (New York, 1969), II, 525.

8. Answer of House of Representatives to Governor's Speech, Jan. 18, 1804, in *Columbian Centinel* (Boston), Jan. 21, 1804, p. 1, col. 2. Accord, Shaw, "Parker," 9 Pick. 566, 571 (1830).

9. See Laws of 1803, ch. 154.

10. Sessions also supervised the use of those buildings, including the county jails and jail yards. See, e.g., House of Correction Rules, MGS, 5-97.

11. See Rules on Accounts, MGS, 3-95.

12. The actual "laying of County Taxes on the Inhabitants of the Counties by the respective Courts of General Sessions of the Peace for the several Counties" was thought, however, to be "repugnant to the twenty-third Article of the Declaration of Rights of the Constitution," Representation re County Tax, HGS, 11-80, and accordingly sessions itself did not vote the tax as in the colonial period; instead, the General Court voted the tax and sessions then collected it. See, e.g., Order re County Tax, MGS, 9-83.

13. See Chapter 7, notes 72-88 and accompanying text.

14. Petition of Dickinson, HCC, 9-29. Accord, Petition of Kellogg, HGS, 9-25; Petition of Goddard, WGS, 9-01; Petition of Hill, MGS, 5-81. Sessions also possessed similar regulatory power over town ways, see Petition of Parker, MGS Files, 11-80; Petition of Mellen, MGS Files, 5-77, but Common Pleas also possessed that power in turnpike cases. See Stone v. Stoughton Tpke., NfCP, 4-24. Finally, sessions continued to appoint juries and receive jury verdicts determining road damages. See, e.g., Petition of Francis, MCC, 9-28; Cambridge v. Craige, MGS Files, 1-13; Petition of Wood, MGS Files, 9-94.

15. Bylaws, for example, regulated the playing of sports, see Gloucester By-Laws, EGS, 10-95; Pittsfield By-Laws, BeGS, 9-91; Marblehead By-Laws, EGS, 9-90, prohibited the throwing of stones and snowballs, see Charlestown By-Laws, MGS, 5-20; Gloucester By-Laws, EGS, 10-95; Marblehead By-Laws, EGS, 9-90; established rules for driving on and other use of town roads, see Charlestown By-Laws, MGS, 5-20; Gloucester By-Laws, EGS, 10-95, regulated smoking and other fire hazards, see Charlestown By-Laws, MGS, 5-20; Gloucester By-Laws, EGS, 10-95; Marblehead By-Laws, EGS, 9-90; Beverly By-Laws, EGS Files, 7-87, prohibited rudeness and lewdness on the part of youth, see Newbury By-Laws, ECP, 9-06, and, in some towns, made parents liable for their children's breaches of the laws. See Gloucester By-Laws, EGS, 7-24; Newbury By-Laws, ECP, 9-06; Haverhill By-Laws, ECP, 12-04; Newbury Port By-Law, EGS, 10-94. Usually the bylaws did not specify the precise scope of parental liability, although they probably intended only to make parents liable to pay fines. See Pittsfield By-Laws, BeGS, 9-91. Another function of bylaws was the regulation of the local economy. See generally Chapter 7, notes 73-79 and accompanying text.

16. See Laws of 1807, ch. 11, as amended, Laws of 1807, ch. 57.

17. See Laws of 1809, ch. 17.

18. See Laws of 1818, ch. 120; Laws of 1815, ch. 10; Laws of 1813, ch. 197, Laws of 1811, ch. 81.

19. See Laws of 1827, ch. 77.

20. On the political background of the legislation overhauling the appellate system, see Ellis, *Jeffersonian Crisis*, 184-206.

21. See Laws of 1803, ch. 154, as amended, Laws of 1811, ch. 33, § 4; Laws of 1817, ch. 185; Laws of 1820, ch. 79, § 4.

22. See Hemmenway v. Hickes, 4 Pick. 497 (1827).

23. See Laws of 1804, ch. 105, §5.

24. Ibid.

25. Motions were made on such grounds in five cases between the Revolution and the 1804 legislation. See Carto v. Geyer, SSJC, 2-03; Waters v. Gowen, MSJC, 10-02; Downs v. Lloyd, SSJC, 8-91, in Francis Dana, Minute Books; Worthington v. Spencer, HSJC, 9-89, ibid.; Day v. Richards, NfCP, 4-99. There were two instances during the same period of bills of exceptions on similar grounds. See Sumner v. Wesson, WSJC, 4-92; Brown v. Austin, MCP Files, 5-99.

26. Coffin v. Alexander, 2 Mass. 36, 37 (1806).

27. See Storer v. White, 7 Mass. 448 (1811); Middlesex Canal Corp. v. M'Gregore, 3 Mass. 124 (1807); Inhabitants of Ware v. Inhabitants of Wilbraham, HSJC, 9-26; Spaulding v. Marcy, MSJC, 3-21; Long v. Colburn, SCP, 6-30; Newhall v. Ames, MCP Files, 3-30; Westford v. Osgood, MCP Files, 9-28; Sanger v. Ballard, SCP, 7-28; Prescott v. Bennett, MCP Files, 5-28; Waitt v. Shattuck, SCP, 4-28; Clark v. Doyle, MCP Files, 3-27; Adams v. Leland, MCP Files, 12-26, appeal dism., MSJC, 4-28; Inhabitants of Boxford v. City of Boston, ECP, 9-26; Drury v. Baxter, SCP, 4-25; Baker v. Pierce, NfCP, 9-22; Woster v. Tucker, WCP, 3-20; Curtis v. Linfield, NfCP, 4-19; Long v. Colburn, SCP Files, 6-13; Howe v. Hussey, SCP Files, 1-12; Stetson v. Linfield, NfCP, 12-09; Trefether v. Curtis, SCP, 4-06.

28. See Aylwin v. Ulmer, 12 Mass. 24 (1815); Withington v. Eveleth, MSJC, 10-28; Whitcomb v. Williams, MSJC, 4-27; Stearns v. Spaulding, MSJC, 4-27; Inhabitants of Wilmington v. Inhabitants of Burlington, MSJC, 4-27; Inhabitants of Ware v. Inhabitants of Wilbraham, HSJC, 9-26; Inhabitants of Groton v. Inhabitants of Acton, MSJC, 3-19; Adams v. Johnson, HdCP, 11-30; Sweet v. Bacon, NfCP, 4-29; Knowles v. Hastings, MCP Files, 3-27; Stevens v. Harrington, NfCP, 4-25; Knowlton v. Walbridge, HdCP, 3-24; Parker

v. Kittridge, MCP Files, 3-24; Bates v. Winslow, MCP Files, 9-23; Bosworth v. Phelps, HdCP, 8-21; Brown v. Smith, WCP, 12-19; Holmes v. Norcross, MCP Files, 3-19; Jones v. Homes, MCP Files, 3-15; Willis v. Wingate, ECP, 9-13; Gibbs v. Hutton, SCP Files, 3-13; Beal v. Dunlap, SCP Files, 7-12; Newell v. Russell, SCP Files, 1-12; Chamberlain v. Freeman, SCP, 4-11; Lewis v. Oneil, SCP Files, 10-10; Searle v. Godfrey, SCP, 10-08; Newburyport Marine Ins. Co. v. Lunt, ECP, 9-07; Fay v. Boyd, MCP Files, 12-06; Sawyer v. Malone, MCP, 6-05. Objections to instructions had to be made with sufficient time for the trial judge to write a report of them for the full court, see Commonwealth v. Child, 10 Pick. 252 (1830); Wait v. Maxwell, 5 Pick. 217 (1827); Train v. Collins, 2 Pick. 144, 153-154 (1824), but there was apparently no requirement that the objection be raised before the instruction was given. See Inhabitants of Buckland v. Inhabitants of Charlemont, 3 Pick. 173, 175 (1825). Similarly, a new trial would not be granted if an error in an instruction or in the admission of evidence was harmless or otherwise not prejudicial. See Prince v. Shephard, 9 Pick. 176, 183 (1829); Remington v. Congdon, 2 Pick. 310, 315-316 (1824). But cf. Sargent v. Roberts, 1 Pick. 337 (1823).

29. See Laws of 1803, ch. 133, as amended, Laws of 1805, ch. 80.

30. 4 Mass. 1 (1808). Accord, Inhabitants of Buckland v. Inhabitants of Charlemont, 3 Pick. 173, 175 (1825) (argument of counsel); Page v. Pattee, 6 Mass. 459 (1810). But instructions on some issues, such as damages, remained rudimentary, with a judge required to say no more than that the jury ought not to give either excessive or insufficient damages. See Coffin v. Coffin, supra, at 5-6. A verdict would, of course, be set aside if damages were excessive, see Fletcher v. Howe, MCP, 3-29, or insufficient. See Taunton Mfg. Co. v. Smith, 9 Pick. 11 (1829); Wallack v. Clemens, SSJC, 2-85. See also Silvester v. Kidd, HSJC, 4-93; Gilson v. Shattuck, MSJC, 10-91; How v. Barns, MSJC, 10-88; Haggins v. Farns, ESJC, 6-85; Palmer v. Wolcott, SCP Files, 3-13; Rust v. Stanwood, ECP, 6-07; Hawes v. Baldwin, SCP, 4-04, all of which denied motions for new trials on the ground of excessive damages. See also Wait v. Boston & Roxbury Mill Corp., NfCP, 12-21 (motion for new trial on ground of quotient verdict overruled).

31. 4 Mass. at 25.

32. Page v. Pattee, 6 Mass. 459, 460 (1810).

33. See Haggins v. Farns, ESJC, 6-85; Lane v. Allen, SCP, 10-04; Patterson v. Hildreth,

MCP, 9-04; Miller v. Porter, PCP, 8-99. No such motions were made, nor would they have been granted if they had been made during the prerevolutionary period. See Chapter 2, notes 145-148 and accompanying text.

34. See Lane v. Allen, SCP, 10-04.

35. See Butterfield v. Mason, MCP Files, 3-20; Clark v. Eaton, MCP Files, 9-14; Foster v. Wheeler, MCP Files, 6-13; Belknap v. Pratt, SCP Files, 7-12; Wyman v. Rogers, SCP Files, 4-12; Lewis v. Oneil, SCP Files, 10-10; Lane v. Burroughs, SCP Files, 10-06; Brooks v. Clap, SCP, 4-06.

36. Turner v. Ulmer, MCP Files, 6-12. Accord, Commonwealth v. Worcester, 3 Pick. 462, 473 (1826); Smith v. Newburyport Marine Ins. Co., 4 Mass. 668, 670 (1808). See also Lewis v. Gamage, 1 Pick. 347, 349 (1823); Ellis v. Page, 1 Pick. 43, 49-50 (1822); Allen v. Phillips, SCP, 4-04.

37. See Goulding v. Skinner, 1 Pick. 162 (1822); Sweet v. Bacon, NfCP, 4-29. See also Ellery v. Merchants' Ins. Co., 3 Pick. 46, 48 (1825). In criminal cases the jury did not fully lose its power to decide law as well as fact. Thus in Commonwealth v. Knapp, 10 Pick. 477, 496 (1830), the court instructed the jury that in deciding the general issue of guilty or not guilty, the jury "must necessarily . . . decide such questions of law as well as of fact, as are involved in this general question. . . ." The court, however, further charged that its instructions on the law "may safely guide the consciences of the jury, unless they *know* them to be wrong." Ibid., 496.

38. 16 Mass. 488 (1820).

39. BrCP, 4-93.

40. See Chapter 7, note 123 and accompanying text.

41. See Chapter 5, note 211 and accompanying text.

42. See the cases cited in notes 33-35 above.

43. Samuel Howe, Lectures on the Practice of the Courts, 357nn158-159 (in HLS).

44. See Chapter 2, notes 145-146 and accompanying text. See also Leavitt v. Inhabitants of Charlemont, HSJC, 5-86, the only case between the Revolution and the turn of the century in which a verdict was set aside on evidentiary grounds.

45. Hammond v. Wadhams, 5 Mass. 353, 355 (1809). Accord, Wait v. M'Neil, 7 Mass. 261 (1811); Wood v. Jarvis, SCP, 1-26; Howe, Lectures, 351.

46. Baker v. Briggs, 8 Pick. 122, 126 (1829).

47. Gardner v. Mitchell, 6 Pick. 114, 115 (1828).

48. Howe, Lectures, 360.

49. See Baxter v. New England Marine Ins. Co., 7 Mass. 275 (1811), upholding the constitutionality of such a presumption on a claim that it deprived a litigant of his right to trial by jury.

50. See Ropps v. Barker, 4 Pick. 239, 242 (1826) (upholding instruction that jury in civil case must find the facts "beyond a reasonable doubt"); Adams v. Johnson, HdCP, 11-30 (upholding challenge to instruction concerning jury's right to draw inferences from the facts).

51. See Emory v. Woodward, FCP, 4-25 (suit dismissed for failure of plaintiff to offer proof of want of probable cause in action for malicious prosecution). Cf. Shaw v. Wilson, BrCP, 6-10 (overruling motion for new trial on ground plaintiff failed to offer evidence on material point in issue).

52. James Sullivan, The History of Land Titles in Massachusetts (Boston, 1801), 342-343, 345.

53. Ex parte Dunbar, 14 Mass. 393, 394 (1817).

54. Suffolk Bank v. Worcester Bank, 5 Pick. 106, 108 (1827).

55. Bickford v. Page, 2 Mass. 455, 462 (1807).

56. Potter v. Hall, 3 Pick. 368, 373 (1825). See also Soule v. Soule, 5 Mass. 61, 67 (1809), where Judge Parker indicated his awareness of the abiding nature of change in seeking "to guard against the precedent in this case being extended too far. . . ."

57. Horace Binney, An Eulogium upon the Hon. William Tilghman (Philadelphia, 1827), 15.

58. Joseph Story, "Value and Importance of Legal Studies: A Discourse Pronounced at the Inauguration of the Author as Dane Professor of Law in Harvard University, Aug. 25,

1829," in William W. Story, ed., The Miscellaneous Writings of Joseph Story (Boston, 2d ed., 1852), 526.

59. Ibid., 508.

60. Henry D. Sedgwick, "Review of William Sampson's 'An Anniversary Discourse Delivered before the Historical Society of New York, on Saturday, Dec. 6, 1823; Showing the Origin, Progress, Antiquities, Curiosities, and Nature of the Common Law,' " North American Review, XIX (1824), 429.

61. "Written and Unwritten Systems of Law," American Jurist, V (1831), 29. Accord, H. D. Gilpin, "Review of Edward Livingston's System of Penal Law," North American Review, XLIII (1836), 298-299; David Hoffman, A Course of Law Study: Respectfully Addressed to the Students of Law in the United States (Baltimore, 1817), viii-ix, xix-xx; William Sampson, An Anniversary Discourse, Delivered Before the Historical Society of New York, on Saturday, December 6, 1823; Showing the Origin, Progress, Antiquities, Curiosities, and Nature of the Common Law (New York, 1824), 57; Joseph Story, "Review of David Hoffman's 'Course of Law Study,' " North American Review, VI (1817), 45, 49; Henry Wheaton, A Discourse Intended to Have Been Delivered before the New-York Law Institute on Its Anniversary Celebration (New York, 1834), 30.

62. Portico, III (1817), 193.

63. Henry D. Sedgwick, The English Practice: A Statement, Showing Some of the Evils and Absurdities of the Practice of the English Common Law (New York, 1822), 12.

64. James Kent, Commentaries on American Law (New York, 1826), I, 47.

65. The following paragraph is based on David M. Ellis, Landlords and Farmers in the Hudson-Mohawk Region, 1790-1850 (Ithaca, N.Y., 1946).

Index

Abatement: for technical insufficiencies in writs, 20, 75–77, 77–78, 206n29; renewal of suit after, 20, 206n29; for failure to allege county in which suit arose, 188n34; resolution of fact issues upon, 190n77; for improper joinder, 209n67. *See also* Civil procedure, law of; Pleading

Accessories, 100

Accord and satisfaction, 73. *See also* Discharge, of contracts; Modification, of contracts

Account, writ of, 80, 201n77, 204n136

Acquittal, by fraud on part of defendant, 227n141

Adams, John, 18, 19, 73, 103, 227n140, 230n228; on power of jury, 3, 21, 28; on protection of property, 118, 120, 127

Adams v. Howe, 108–109

Ad damnum, 78

Additions, 76, 77–78, 197n1, 210n88. *See also* Pleading

Administrators, *see* Executors and administrators

Admiralty, 31, 97, 189n39

Adulterated goods, 38, 40. *See also* Fraud

Adultery, 37, 110

Adverse possession, 49. *See also* Limitation of actions; Possession; Prescription and prescriptive rights; Property, law of

Affirmations, in lieu of oaths, 113. *See also* Evidence

Agency, law of. *See* Agents

Agents: joinder of, 75; contracts by, 137, 138; testimony by, 156; to pay debts, 200n73; of corporations, 241n199, 243n220

Alienation of affections, 237n101

Amendment, of writs and documents, 77–78

Ames, Fisher, 127

Ancient lights, 123. *See also* Customary rights; Property, law of

Andover and Medford Turnpike Corporation v. Gould, 134

Animals, damage by, 198n21

Antenuptial agreements, 228n175. *See also* Husband and wife

Antirent movement, in New York, 173

Appeal, 15, 16, 70, 84, 167, 224n105. *See also* Civil procedure, law of; Jurisdiction; Trial de novo; Writs, of error

Appointment of officials, 14, 93

Appraisal of debtor's property, 41. *See also* Debtor and creditor, law of

Apprentices: as property, 51, 161; duty of master to educate and support, 52, 187–188n24, 238n106; corporal punishment of, 125; rights and remedies of master, 125; religious duties of, 190n50; in England, 197n11, 200n50. *See also* Children; Indentured servants; Laborers; Servants; Slaves and Slavery

Appropriation of public funds, 14, 15, 166

Arbitration, 23, 57, 61, 73. *See also* References

Arrest, 17–18, 92, 98–99; immunity of soldiers and sailors from, 14; by creditors agreeing to composition, 153; witness at General Court protected from, 187n10; forcible resistance to, 226n131. *See also* Warrants

Arrest of judgment, 26–27, 28

Assault, 37, 79; plea of justification in, 23, 73; as defense to unlawful arrest, 226n131

Assignments: for benefit of creditors, 152; of contract rights, 252n77. *See also* Contract; Debtor and creditor, law of

Assumpsit, writ of, 54–61, 72, 79–80; evidence of performance in, 23, 73–74;